ĀZĀDĪ

Funded by the Government of Canada
Financé par la gouvernement du Canada

Demeter Press
140 Holland Street West
P. O. Box 13022
Bradford, ON L3Z 2Y5
Tel: (905) 775-9089
Email: info@demeterpress.org
Website: www.demeterpress.org

Demeter Press logo based on the sculpture "Demeter" by Maria-Luise Bodirsky
<www.keramik-atelier.bodirsky.de>

Front cover design: Kara Springer.

Printed and Bound in Canada

Library and Archives Canada Cataloguing in Publication

Atluri, Tara, 1979-, author
        Āzādī : sexual politics and postcolonial worlds / Tara Atluri.

Includes bibliographical references.
ISBN 978-1-926452-99-9 (paperback)

        1. Sex crimes--Political aspects--India. 2. Women--Crimes against--India. I. Title.

HV6569.I4A86 2016   364.15'320954   C2016-900128-8

ĀZĀDĪ

SEXUAL POLITICS AND POSTCOLONIAL WORLDS

TARA ATLURI

DEMETER PRESS

TABLE OF CONTENTS

ACKNOWLEDGEMENTS

I would like to thank all those who were part of *Oecumene: Citizenship After Orientalism* at the Open University in the UK between 2012-2014 where I was a postdoctoral researcher funded by the Social Sciences and Humanities Research Council (SSHRC) of Canada. The collegial support I received was remarkable. In particular, I wish to thank Engin Isin for supervising my postdoctoral studies.

I have been challenged and inspired by countless students and scholars transnationally. I hope to continue to have meaningful intellectual relationships, beyond borders. I am also grateful for the impressive research, writing, and philosophical critique of so many intellectuals throughout the world, some of whose ideas I attempt to engage with in this book.

I wish to extend my gratitude to all those at Demeter Press for publishing this manuscript and for their impressive editorial critique and attention to detail.

A special thank you to artist Kara Springer who designed the cover of this text and whose creativity and skills are boundless.

Vijaya and Satya Atluri have offered me infinite wisdom, compassion, and generosity. There are few words with which to fully express my gratitude for their support. Thank you to friends and family, to those whose humour, brilliance, humility, and resilience are truly remarkable. Courtesies and platitudes cannot fully capture the joys of human relationships.

Finally, I wish to sincerely thank all of the inspiring people whom I met and spoke with in the Indian subcontinent between 2012-2014 about sexual politics and postcolonial worlds.

Āzādī.

INTRODUCTION[1]

Every generation must discover its mission, fulfil it or betray it, out of relative opacity. (Fanon 132)

IN DECEMBER OF 2013, I stood in the streets of India. One year after the gang rape and murder of a young woman led to massive protests throughout the Indian subcontinent, I was again in the same place. In Delhi,[3] India, capital city of a country as impure as any nation, as impure as any person, as impure as all the cacophonies of routes and roots that bring people to a place, that birth a place out of the variant and untranslatable histories of its people. Days before the anniversary of the Delhi gang rape case of 2012, the Supreme Court of India made the decision to uphold Section 377[4] of the Indian Penal Code, recriminalizing same-sex desire and queer people after the 2009 decision by the Delhi high court to read down these colonial laws.[5] Again, as with the Delhi gang rape protests of 2012, which I bore witness to, I came at just the right or wrong time, depending on how one tells the story. While the 2012 Delhi gang rape protests were comparatively much larger than those that followed the 2013 Supreme Court decision regarding Section 377 of the Indian Penal Code, there was a common refrain heard and felt in the streets. Against so much of the cynicism and defeat that this moment gestured to regarding ideas of gendered and sexual freedom, I clung to this one word like the chorus of an old song, or the refrain of some prayer recited across time and space: Āzādī.

The Āzādī of sexual politics in India is as timeless as ideas of dissent and desire are. Āzādi is loosely translated into "freedom." It is a word that has become popular in Hindi, Urdu, Farsi, and many other

1

languages. It is the name of a hip rock band in Pakistan, a square in Tehran where protests are staged, and a protest chant that has in the last decade gained a great deal of international media coverage over Internet wires through YouTube videos broadcasting images of defiant Arab youth "springing" forward in revolt, often also cheering Āzādī. I stood in the streets in 2012 and 2013 and with many of the people of Delhi, with many of the people of India, and I cried out: Āzādī, unsure then as I am still unsure now of what this fully means. Was this just a trendy phrase trying to attach itself to the panorama of images that followed the Arab Spring, perhaps trying to catch some revolutionary fire and media coverage from the remnants of global spectacle that have surrounded people in the Middle East and North Africa over the last few years? Was this just an exotic chant that echoed of revolutionary fervour against the usual candlelight vigils and rainbow flags that often appear at feminist and queer protests the world over? Was this just a word, flawed in its translation across time and borders, as flawed as any word is in fully translating bodily and emotive desire?

JYOTI: THE 2012 DELHI GANG RAPE CASE

On December 16, 2012 in the capital city of the Indian subcontinent, a woman was gang-raped, tortured, and inflicted with such bodily harm that she died two weeks later.[6] Jyoti and her friend Awindra saw a film after which they attempted to travel home by public transportation. They caught an off duty bus that had been hijacked by a group of men and were unaware of the gruesome events that would follow.[7] The group of men on the bus proceeded to gang-rape Jyoti, by using a metal rod to commit crimes of extreme bodily violence. The use of the rod and the nature of the crimes can only be called torture. Awindra was also severely beaten by the attackers. Jyoti's injuries were so severe that her internal organs were damaged during the assault. She was taken to a Delhi hospital and then flown to Singapore to receive medical treatment in a final attempt to save her life. She died less than two weeks after this incident. The case caused massive public protests in Delhi and throughout the Indian subcontinent. The public outcry that this case garnered led to attempts to change national laws pertaining to gender-based violence and sexual assault; increased global media attention; the formation of new social movements in the Indian subcontinent regarding gender justice; a resurgence in existing sexual political movements in India; similar mobilizations throughout Asia and Pakistan; and a transnational public discourse regarding gender in contemporary India ("Delhi Gang Rape 2012").

Jyoti's parents spoke about this case to local and global media and demanded harsher penalties for those who were charged (Roychowdhury 282). Her family released her name to the press, suggesting that they wanted the world to know her name and for her to be remembered as a hero, whose spirit would give strength to survivors of gender-based violence. Awindra later released his own name to the press (Losh). Roychowdhury discusses the making of the case into an international media spectacle that constructed Jyoti as a symbol of a "modern Indian woman" and her assailants as migrant men whose violence was used to construct those from rural India as "backwards" in comparison to the imagined "progress" of urban elites. Roychowdhury further discusses how this construction positioned the impoverished migrant displaced in the city as an adversary of the urban Indian woman, in need of salvation from brown male barbarism. The author states, however, that while Jyoti was represented by the global media as "highly individuated and 'westernized'" (Roychowdhury 283) as with many of her assailants who were represented in the media as migrants to the city, her family members were also migrants from a rural village. Roychowdhury states that "Pandey's family was part of the Kurmi community, a lower caste group with agricultural origins; her attackers, it turns out, also belonged to lower caste groups" (Roychowdhury284). The author further states that despite narratives that attempted to construct Jyoti as a symbol of urban wealth, her father worked at a Delhi airport as a luggage handler, earning the same level of income as some of the attackers (Roychowdhury 282-284).

This book discusses the 2012 Delhi gang rape protests in conjunction with the 2013 decision to criminalize same-sex desire to consider how the Indian woman as an imagined consummate victim of violence was positioned in opposition to the imagined brown patriarch. Roychowdhury writes of how Awindra's assault, which involved a gruesome beating and his body being stripped naked and left by the side of the road, was often downplayed in the press. The author suggests that Awindra disappeared from narratives regarding the case, "because brown men are not typically viewed as allies of brown women" (Roychowdhury, 283). In considering sexual politics in contemporary India as involving a unity of interests between feminists and queers who are discussed as political figures rather than victimized corpses, this book looks to tragic and shocking events of gender-based and sexual violence, both through acts of bodily harm and the epistemic violence of legality, as moments that inspire events of the political (Badiou Being and Event). As Roychowdhury states in regards to the 2012 Delhi gang rape case:

> The brown woman who needs saving today is no longer a passive repository of white men's graces. She rises above the victimization rhetoric that has consumed international feminist legal politics and deprived women of agency and cultural and historical specificity. The media's Pandey represents a female subject who is relatively empowered in comparison to her predecessor: she exerts herself, struggling to survive while demanding rights and justice. (Roychowdhury 285)

Six men were arrested and accused of committing the heinous crimes that took place on December 16, 2012 and led to the murder of Jyoti and the vicious assault of her companion. One of the accused committed suicide in prison while awaiting trial. The other five were tried and convicted. One of those convicted was given a lesser sentence as he was tried as a minor while the other four assailants were sentenced to death. At the time of writing, the use of the death penalty is still being debated by the Supreme Court of India. Journalists report that the implementation of the death penalty has been "stayed till further orders" and debates continue regarding what a meaningful enactment of justice might entail in this deeply tragic case ("Nirbhaya Gang-Rape Case"). The Delhi gang rape case raised questions regarding the use of the death penalty in the Indian subcontinent, the sentencing of those deemed to be "young offenders," and the (im)possibilities of legal grievance to offer any semblance of justice for unspeakable forms of grief. The case received attention from political figures in Delhi and national politicians as well as transnational media coverage. It garnered outcry from multiple factions of feminist, queer, and leftist activists and intellectuals in Delhi and transnationally (Lodia). As I discuss drawing on interviews, this case as with the 2013 decision to uphold Section 377 of the Indian Penal Code, criminalizing same-sex desire and queer people, also led to massive public protests involving a broad range of the Indian population. While the violent disciplining of bodies, sexualities, and desires in contemporary India was clearly expressed in 2012 and 2013, the demonstrations that followed gesture to the vitality of postcolonial sexual politics ("Section 377: `The Way Forward'").

"WE EXIST … FOR ALL THOSE WHO WOULD RATHER NOT SEE US": THE NALSA RULING AND SEXUAL POLITICS IN THE INDIAN SUBCONTINENT

At the time of writing, one year after the tragic gang rape case of 2012 and mass mobilizations regarding gendered violence in India, only months after the decision to uphold Section 377 by the Supreme Court of India, another landmark legal decision was made that moved towards the countenance of Hijras, often referred to as transgender persons in English secular discourse, as full citizens, as human beings with entitlements to dignity. One day after Ambedkar Day, the birth date of Indian revolutionary anti caste leader B. R. Ambedkar, the Supreme Court of India delivered the National Legal Services Authority (NALSA) judgment recognizing the constitutional rights of India's transgendered people of which there are almost two million counted in many official statistics and ledgers. The judgment recognized Hijras' right to declare themselves to be neither man nor woman and to be legally acknowledged by the state as a "third sex" ("India Court Recognises Transgender People As Third Gender"). The translation of figures such as Hijras into a language of "third sex" gestures to a larger landscape of sexual and gender-based politics in which the language of sexual politics in countries in the Global South, such as in India, is perhaps increasingly informed by globalized knowledge regarding sex and sexuality, which cannot be divorced from cultures of transnational neoliberal branding and neocolonial forms of governance. I discuss the complex philosophical and epistemic apprehension of sexual politics in India through secular English language grammar. Translating diverse forms of desire into secular English language categories has strategic political value, but may implicitly equate sexual and gendered freedom with colonial ideas of "progress." Such ideas of temporal advancement are foretold in ways that bind understandings of sexual politics to economically wealthy Western nations and to countries in the Global South that are imagined to be "following" in their footsteps. This rhetoric reproduces imperialist thinking in subtle ideological ways while also imprisoning sexual politics in a system and language of Western-led aid and development.[8]

Yet writing these words in Delhi, where the NALSA victory gave a great deal of hope to many people I speak with, particularly in light of the 2013 decision to uphold Section 377 of the Indian Penal Code, I sense that the tactical language of transnational terminologies perhaps cannot be discounted. One Hijra in Delhi who states that she was deeply hurt and worried by the 2013 Supreme Court verdict expresses a great deal of joy regarding the 2014 NALSA verdict:

> I am so happy. It is not about the word Hijra or whatever word they are using for us. They are using some word and it's there in the newspapers, radio, in the court so whatever they are saying, we exist for all these people in the society who before this would have rather not seen us. (Atluri Personal interviews)[9]

The law in this instance speaks to Alan Badiou's assertion that law is fundamentally a matter of existence [10] (Badiou Ethics). Badiou suggests that the law does not simply legislate lives but constructs them through making certain lives and bodies intelligible and livable (Badiou Ethics). In this regard, the NALSA ruling offered a countenance of Hijras as Indian citizens in a country with a long and ongoing nationalist ethos in which the inclusion of those often seen to be sexual minorities within the socio-legal fabric of the nation state has symbolic and practical value. Following this decision, Laxmi Narayan Tripathi, a prominent transgender rights activist, stated that for the first time she "feels proud to be Indian" ("India Court Recognises Transgender People As Third Gender"). In remapping the Indian citizen as queer, a different genealogy is opened up, one that places sexual politics firmly in the pre-colonial, colonial, and postcolonial history of India rather than in the time of market-driven and Western-led images of queer culture.

Writing in Delhi, after this victory was declared, it was strange to bear witness to this political moment and all that it offers in regards to considering the contradictory mappings of both the sexual and the political in the Indian subcontinent. I will discuss this judgment throughout this work in regards to law, social movements, sexualities, and this word and perhaps never fully translated and yet passionately resilient idea that echoes across borders, bodies, and time—Āzādī. What is of interest lies in how the 2014 NALSA judgment seemed to offer hope for those believing and acting in the name of something called justice or perhaps, as heard in the steady hum of voices in the streets, something called Āzādī.

SHAADI.COM, TAJ MAHAL SHOPPING MALLS, AND "MARITAL RAPE": GLOBALIZATION AND SEXUAL POLITICS

The respect of Hijras as Hijras—not to the extent that they suit the biopolitical wills of an "India shining,"[11] or correspond to Western categories of gender and sexuality—speaks to the haunting of revolutionary thinking and action that informs contemporary sexual politics in India ("India Shining"). Yet as I watched news unfold and writing emerge in Delhi, it was perhaps striking to see who relates to the political and how. Many feminists, queers, activists, academics, students and those who would be counted as part of what might be termed "the left" were elated. However, what could the victories of Hijras mean for increasingly neoliberal consumer-driven Hindu middle classes, often as invested in transnational capital as in the unconscious and conscious maintenance of colonial moralities concerning gender and sex? There was a deep divide in speaking with people about this legal victory in Delhi, among those for whom politics is vocation, education, passion, and personal investment and for those who seem unaffected by the political. Far from being endemic to India's middle class, perhaps the divided reactions to a political victory and particularly its affective resonance in regards to who cares and who could care less speaks to a wider global culture of neoliberal capitalism.

While the rise of "lifestyles" that mimic those of Western cities and suburbs have been used to brand India as a neoliberal success story, perhaps consumerism has obscured the political landscape through its prioritization of individualized lives. Two great testaments to the supposed progress of our times, the rise of neoliberal consumerism and identity-based politics, may have produced a moment in which a landmark Supreme Court victory was something that urban businessmen in office clothes and young workers buried in MacBooks have little time or need to see as their victory, as the workings of their constitution. Similarly, while identity politics is often used to create "safe spaces" for women, queers, Hijras, Dalits, migrants, and others, it may also allow the fear of the general population against so-called minorities to continue. Identity politics, much like the discourse of privatized consumerism, can also create a language in which politics itself is like private property, where feminist or queer rights are one person's topic of interest but not another's, where academics can declare that they do not "do" Dalit rights or that Hijras are not their concern. I want to suggest that this language of privatization binds one to an ethic of fear,[12] one in which many say and do nothing for fear of being incorrect and for not having mastered a language of feminist and political expertise. This understanding of politics as profession and bodies as private property is perhaps implicitly tied to colonial and capitalist ideologies.[13]

In 2014, when I left India, the Supreme Court of India was deliberating a verdict regarding a curative petition filed by India's queer, feminist, and activist community regarding Section 377 of the Indian Penal Code.[14] This legal plea has been made possible owing to the tireless work of courageous voices in the region. As we wait to see what fate has in store for the ghost of Lord McCauley, whose repressive colonial laws appear again to haunt an "India shining," another recent legal decision has sanctioned "marital rape." Despite recommendations made by the Justice Verma Committee, a judiciary review board that was assembled following the Delhi gang rape case of 2012, the word rape has no legal or political countenance within a marriage in contemporary India.[15] In a 2015 statement, India's Ministry of Home affairs said that "the concept of marital rape, as understood internationally, cannot be suitably applied in the Indian context" (Rana). While justifications of gender-based violence within a marriage are legally sanctioned based on a rhetoric of "Indian values," many laws and collective moralities pertaining to gender and sexuality are expressive of lingering colonial values. As I will discuss throughout this work, one can read the Delhi gang rape case of 2012, the Supreme Court's 2013 decision to uphold Section 377 of the Indian Penal Code, and other related struggles regarding gender and sexuality in tandem, as archives of colonialism's returned repression and as testaments to illusory images of gendered/sexual freedom as consumer "progress." Neoliberal images and narratives of betterment at the level of increased middle-class consumerism and images of a new "sexy" urban India seem not to alter gendered colonial moralities that strip women and queer people of any basic countenance as citizens and as people. In fact, as I will discuss throughout this work, one can ask how anxieties generated regarding the imagined threat to Indian culture brought about by neoliberal capital and globalization might be managed through a preservation of a timeless concoction of "culture" as sexual moralism, ironically most aggressively enforced during colonial rule.[16] As I comment on throughout this text, drawing on interviews done in India, while the "India shining" moment of global capitalism has, as Chowdhury suggests, given way to images of a "New Indian citizen" and a "New Indian woman" through illusions of freedom in the form of middle-class conspicuous consumption and aesthetics, gendered and sexual bodies in the Indian subcontinent continue to be violently marked by colonial history (Chowdhury).

The "New Indian woman" that Chowdhury writes of—as one of mall chic fashion and Western-imported foods, of laptops, girly drinks, gym memberships, and Hinglish text messages—is not only used to make the majority of the nation that still struggles against malnutrition and dehydration invisible, it obscures the legal and material constraints that prevent the actualization of meaningful forms of bodily, psychic, social, and political freedom (Chowdhury). As with the Delhi gang rape case of 2012, the recent decision to uphold "marital rape" as legally and culturally sanctioned in India speaks to the wretched paradoxes of an "India shining," one shadowed by the ghosts of colonial rule. A woman can attend a foreign English language movie such as *Life of Pi* in a shopping mall, and never return home, tortured and gang-raped to death on a bus in an "India shining." A woman can surf Shaadi. com or other Internet dating sites, register for wedding presents at a Western multinational store in a "Taj Mahal" of shopping malls, and honeymoon in Europe. However, if raped by a man named as her husband through laws that reflect the ghostly ethos of colonial discourse, lingering mythologies of Hindu nationalism, and selective readings of religion and culture, she was never raped. In a sickening script haunted by all of the violence and perversion of colonial and patriarchal moralities, she was "loved."

BLEACHED OUT MORALITIES:
CRIMINAL QUEERS AND FAIR AND LOVELIES

One should perhaps consider the larger political context that produces what Puar terms homonationalism, a discourse through which sexual politics coincide with fiscal aims of warring Western powers. While Puar discusses the United States, her assertions are important transnationally (Puar). Homonationalism aligns idealized white, secular gay male subjects in America with the life of the nation in a post-AIDS crises moment and a global "war on terror," in which the death of America is associated with imagined "terrorists" through an Islamophobic rhetoric. Puar's concept of homonationalism cannot be applied uncritically to contemporary India where same-sex desire is now criminalized. Rather, as I develop throughout this text drawing on ethnographic research done in India and theoretical texts, the queer body and the Muslim body as well as many others who fall outside of nationalist constructions of an idealized "Hindustan" are associated with the death of the nation (Puar and Rai). Queers continue to be criminal to India in ways that upper middle-class, white, secular gay men are not within America owing to a radically different history and genealogy of Hindu nationalism that maps deviance onto both queer and Muslim bodies. As I also suggest throughout this work, upper-caste, upper-class women and queers are increasingly used to support capitalist aims through the multinational branding of cities against the bodies of migrants and the poor. There is a push and pull between the regulatory powers of colonial laws, religious moralities, and the will to brand an "India shining" in which sexual freedom is sold through advertising spectacle and mall chic, while the streets and courthouses are haunted by puritanical repression (Das Purkayastha).

Das Purkayasha states that "heterosexism in India again cannot be explained simply on religious moral grounds. Cultures of nationalism play a crucial role in the disempowerment of the queer in India" (Das Purkayastha 121). The author goes on to discuss how queerness in India is associated with Westernization and seen to be foreign to politically constituted constructions of India as "Hindu," middle class, upper caste, patriarchal, sexphobic, and heterosexual. While Das Purkayasha argues that queerness in India is represented by conservative elites as "foreign" and therefore antithetical to the nation, one can consider that within a moment of neoliberal capitalist globalization, foreign multinational capital is welcomed into the subcontinent. While Das Purkayastha states that the contemporary postcolonial state is "ever cautious to guard its borders and repress all manifestations of foreignness" (Das Purkayasha 121) that are associated with threats of "impure" sex, Western multinational companies and products are often wholeheartedly embraced by nationalist leaders. I discuss this further in the second section of this book in relation to the image of Hindu nationalist leader Narendra Modi as the ideal "new Hindu man" who is arguably both an ardent Hindu nationalist and an ardent capitalist.

The scripting of queerness as "foreign" produces an idealized Gay image increasingly sold to middle-class Indian consumers, an image that associates sexuality with whiteness, Western secularism, Western queer history, and wealth. The paradoxical marketing of sexuality as "freedom to buy" for women in urban India who are afforded no meaningful freedom from sexual violence is one that also besets the lives of queer people, who are at once aggressively marketed to by transnational businesses while also facing legal criminalization and violence in the public sphere. Capitalist secular patriarchies still sell women an image of "freedom" that is deeply conservative and revolves around the construction of the female body as a consumer whose desires, aesthetics, and embodiment are deftly manipulated by marketers to sell women products that would make them desirable to the idealized male gaze. Similarly, the assumed "freedom" offered to queer people through transnational "Legalize Gay" branding often amounts to a very reductive understanding of desire and an ageist, racist, and classist image of idealized sexual "freedom." For example, in contemporary India the skin bleach Fair and Lovely, often sold to middle-class Hindu women to lighten their skin, launched an advertising campaign following the 2009 decision to read down Section 377 of the Indian Penal Code by the Delhi High court that contained homoerotic images of a "fair and lovely" man who became desirable to the male gaze by bleaching his skin (Fair and Lovely for Men).

The paradoxes of homonationalism in the Indian context lie in the conjoined ability for the state to legally support continued anxieties regarding imagined sexual deviance marked onto the skin of criminal queers, and to profit from the anxious skins of those desiring a globalized "body beautiful" image of whiteness. With contemporary neoliberal branding increasingly prevalent in urban India, sexual desire is expressed as capitalist desire in ways that resonate with colonial histories of aesthetics and with contemporary homonationalist images of white gay male culture. White-wigged magistrates criminalize queers and deem "marital rape" to be "fair" in India while skin bleach is sold to middle-class Indian women and men. Queerness and female sexual agency are constructed as foreign to the nation while images of whiteness and wealth are sold en mass as a sign of supposed progress.

OF DR. SIRAS AND JYOTI:
THE TORTURE OF DESIRING BODIES

While some saw the 2012 Delhi gang rape protests as being unconnected to the 2013 protests that emerged following the Supreme Court decision to continue the criminalization of diverse enactments of sexualities, these moments of protest and the discursive terrain that informs normative understandings of gender and sexuality unite feminist and queer politics. Singh discusses the relationship between private and public desire and the criminalization of same-sex desire challenged by the 2009 decision made by the Delhi high court to read down Section 377 of the Indian Penal Code. Singh writes, "The Delhi High Court in the Naz case offered a formulation of privacy that linked privacy to persons and not places" (Singh1). Singh suggests that the extension of the right to private enactments of diverse sexual desire in public is one that is especially important in the Indian context where "norms of gender and sexuality within the home and outside shape one's experience of the public and the private, the spatial and the zonal take on a special significance in matters of individual agency" (1). Singh discusses the 2010 case of Professor Shrinivas Ramchander Siras, a lecturer at Aligarh Muslim University, who was videotaped having consensual same-sex relations with a man in his home. The videos were subsequently circulated and Dr. Siras was suspended from his position, despite the 2009 Delhi high court decision to read down Section 377 of the Indian Penal Code, India's colonial sodomy law (Singh). A public debate and legal case ensued. Dr. Siras died of mysterious circumstances in 2010 with his death being termed a suicide. The Siras case much like the 2012 Delhi gang rape case both involve a complete inability to afford any dignity to those whose bodies and desires exist outside of spaces of martial homes and the sanctified heteronormative Hindu middle-class marriages that they are imagined to house. Both the material body of the unmarried woman on the street and the body of the queer man are constructed as being deviant and warranting spectacle, physical violence, and harassment. The body of an unmarried woman is afforded no space as a sexual agent who is entitled to pleasure, just as the sexual desires of queer people are either made invisible or into public spectacles of ridicule, contempt, and rage, to the point of death.

A recent widely publicized case in India offers an example of the need to unite feminist and queer struggles. In this case, a medical doctor in Delhi was arrested on charges of abetment of suicide after his wife killed herself. Journalists reported that the woman "had committed suicide alleging harassment by claiming that her husband lied to her about his sexual orientation" ("Doctor Commits Suicide"). In framing this case in a way that pathologized the queer man as supposedly torturing his wife, same-sex desire was constructed as an enemy to women's lives. This case offers evidence of how queer men can be used as scapegoats within a wider political climate in which same-sex desire is criminalized by the state in ways that overlook the legalized and commonplace abuse of women in the marital home by heteronormative patriarchal men. The construction of this case is reflective of a divisive rhetoric being espoused by mainstream media and the state that pits feminists against queers, while the implicit and explicit violence of heteronormative middle-class men is an unquestioned truth that does not often make for headlines or legal convictions.

In the aforementioned case, the woman who committed suicide is imagined as needing to fulfil the role of an idealized, heteronormative wife to the point that her husband's supposed queer desire caused her to take her own life ("Doctor Commits Suicide"). Within this narrative of a woman who desires marriage and a middle-class Hindu family above even the desire to live itself, any queer female sexuality or enactment of female sexual agency outside of the biopolitical[17] scripts of the nation-state are made invisible. The "good" victim is constructed as a "good" wife, while women and queers are constructed in both symbolic and legal terms as "guilty." Those who stray from happy, heteronormative homes are constituted as justified targets for violence. Women on buses are marked for death just as many queer people, particularly since the 2013 decision to uphold the criminalization of same-sex desire, are subject to routine harassment, blackmail, and abuse. A broader sexual political movement that involves both feminists and queers continues to be enacted on the streets of Delhi, beginning with the 2012 Delhi gang rape protests and continuing with the protests that followed the 2013 decision to criminalize same-sex desire. A right to public space, desire, and sexual agency unites contemporary feminist and queer politics in urban India in ways that offer a freedom from the narrow appraisal of bodies and lives through colonial laws and trite familial scripts.

SEXUAL POLITICS IN POSTCOLONIAL WORLDS:
SECURITIZATION, DESIRE, AND THREAT

While this book discusses political struggles that are worlds apart in terms of geography, historical genealogies of politics, and means of dissent, I suggest that sexual politics in India cannot be separated from questions of global governance. As Amar points out, constructions of sexuality, morality, and gender were central to the Arab Spring protests that took place in Egypt. Amar cites a young female protester, Yousra Aboustait, who said of her experiences in Tahir Square, "Women feel like they can be around and involved without any fear of being bothered or abused. It is like they have finally been given the way to be an equal, effective and important part of society with no constraints or barriers" (Amar1). Although there were reports of sexual violence that occurred against women in Tahir Square, Aboustait suggests that the moments of protest opened up liminal spaces in which the barriers of gender were loosened to give way to mass political participation. Amar further discusses the importance of sexuality in the securitization of the state in Egypt through which the military arrested, detained, and disciplined the bodies of protestors. He writes that the Egyptian military:

> detained women protestors and administered "virginity tests," hymen inspections that are of course forms of molestation or rape in themselves, insisting that only pious single young women could speak as legitimate voices of the people, and that the army would exclude from politics the working class "whores" whose public presence was an attack on national honour. (Amar 3)

14

While the 2012 Delhi gang rape protests and the 2013 protests that followed the Supreme Court of India's decision to criminalize same-sex desire are part of a very different history and set of political circumstances, Amar understands sexual politics as being central to state securitization and nationalism. Amar's reading of sexuality as being inseparable from national politics resonates with contemporary cultures of protest in Delhi. Discussing the state securitization that followed the Arab Spring protests, Amar suggests that the "human security governance regime" is

> explicitly aimed to protect, rescue, and secure certain idealized forms of humanity identified with a particular family of sexuality, morality, and class of subjects, and grounded in certain militarized territories and strategic infrastructures. (Amar 6)

Amar's insights are important to consider in analyzing the often-contradictory mappings of sexuality within the moments of protest that I discuss in this book. His understanding of the state protection of certain visions of humanity can perhaps help to explain how the 2012 Delhi gang rape case could be narrated by political leaders as a crime against "India's daughter," while protestors at Jantar Mantar were water cannoned with brute force, and the Indian state ruled against the criminalization of "marital rape" despite judicial appeals.

The exclusionary construction of a human subject through sexual- and class-based norms can also cause one to question how and why the same state that grieved for "India's daughter" could also pathologize impoverished migrant men as the likely assailants in cases of sexual violence, criminalize same-sex desire, and legally uphold "marital rape." Conservative commentators and politicians throughout India often used the Delhi gang rape case to justify a protectionist rhetoric concerning female safety, thereby curtailing queer and female desire, mobility, and the right to pleasure (Phadke, Ranade, and Khan).

I draw on Amar's definition of sexual politics to offer a reading of the political as a sexualized regime of power that is always historically and discursively constituted by politics, in the broadest sense of the term. Amar's definition of sexual politics builds on the writing of Michel Foucault and Hazel Carby. He argues that these authors have "reconceptualised sexuality not as a set of orientations or minority identities, nor as a category of personal rights or reproductive health issues, but as a contradictory set of humanization dynamics and hypervisibilization processes" (Amar16). Drawing on their insights Amar offers a definition of sexual politics as politics. He writes,

> I conceive of sexual politics in terms of security-sector strug-
> gles to discipline dangers and desires that mark the controlled
> boundary of the human. These uses of sexuality render overly
> visible certain race, class, and gendered bodies as sources of
> danger and desire, while rendering invisible the political nature
> of hierarchy and the identity of powerful agents. (Amar 16-17)

I utilize Amar's definition and the insights of scholars who offer critical perspectives pertaining to sexualities and political struggle in India to discuss sexual politics in relation to the disciplinary will to mark certain bodies as sources of risk and desire. In discussing the 2012 Delhi gang rape protests in conjunction with the 2013 Supreme Court of India decision to uphold Section 377 of the Indian Penal Code, India's sodomy law, I suggest that the narrative of the "woman in danger" is a convenient trope often supported by mainstream conservative political elites to discipline female desire at the same moment that queer desire is marked as a supposed threat to national culture and made criminal. The repressive imprisonment of sexualities in India by colonial law and moralities is made visible in moments of state-sanctioned sexual violence, just as the urgency of uniting feminist and queer struggles is heard in the streets: Āzādī.

HAUNTED STREETS AND REVOLUTIONARY SPIRIT:
A SPIRITED SEXUAL POLITICS

There was an eeriness to the 2012 Delhi gang rape case, one that perhaps resonated with people throughout the Indian subcontinent in poignant ways, leading to unprecedented political action. There is also something chilling about the recent decision to legally sanction "marital rape," and the return of the repressed ghosts of Lord MacCaulay and his colonial compatriots who criminalized same-sex desire using colonial sodomy laws. Bearing witness to these moments in 2013 and 2014, I grasped to find some meaning to the mood that hangs like Delhi's winter fog over the muffled desires of a postcolonial nation. Avery Gordan's exemplary writings on haunting are invaluable in writing about contemporary sexual politics in India in relation to ghostly matters of colonial rule, moralities, and desires that haunt moments of sexual violence and movements for social justice. Gordan suggests that the idea of haunting makes one aware of social and political violence that often remains invisible to the everyday, with the ghosts of history appearing in the cracks of national fantasies of progress. Gordan states that:

> What's distinctive about haunting is that it is an animated state in which a repressed or unresolved social violence is making itself known, sometimes very directly, sometimes more obliquely. (17)

While neoliberal Lords with less regal colonial names like "Bill," erecting testaments to imperialism through Google statues seem a world away from colonial ghosts, I suggest that the gendered body in India is a haunted body. The unresolved social violence of the sexual was expressed in chilling cases such as the 2012 Delhi gang rape case and the decision to uphold colonial sodomy laws in 2013 despite the Delhi high court's reading down of Section 377 of the Indian Penal Code in 2009. Unresolved and ongoing social violence was also apparent in the forceful legal sanction of rape against women as "wives," seen as neither citizens nor human beings. Throughout this work, I discuss sexual politics in India as moments of both colonial and anticolonial haunting, ones in which the un-homeliness of the gendered and sexed body, of bodies marked as "woman" or "sexual other" through colonial categorizations are made homeless to the nation. In these moments, the gendered body in India is a haunted body, one that is marked by the violence of colonial laws and moralities that exist outside of timescales that can be seen. This body might also be haunted by past histories of political revolt that open up in the resilient cries and will of protestors crying out against time and borders, with a breathless and haunted: Āzādī. Gordan further suggests that what makes haunting distinct from trauma is that it gestures to that which "must be done":

> haunting was precisely the domain of turmoil and trouble, that moment (of however long duration) when things are not in their assigned places, when the cracks and rigging are exposed, when

the people who are meant to be invisible show up without any sign of leaving, when disturbed feelings cannot be put away, when something else, something different from before, seems like it must be done. (19)

Drawing on interviews and conversations with passionate activists, feminists, queers, young people, working people, protestors and many others whom I encountered in India, this work suggests that if the violence of colonial desire haunts postcolonial sexual politics, the spirit of anticolonial resistance also breathes and whispers across time and space.

ĀZĀDĪ

The Āzādī of sexual politics in contemporary India matters. It matters not simply to women, to queers, to Hijras, to activists, or to academics. The Āzādī of freeing oneself, one's thinking, and contemporary India from the colonial baggage of history is a freedom that gestures to the often forgotten histories of the political that are the histories of many of the people of India and that affect all people. The Āzādī of the Hijras of India, with a religious and cultural lineage that resonates across Hindu and Muslim mythologies, and well predates colonial rule perhaps represents the lasting presence of figures such as Ambedkar whose life informed the etching of principles of bodily dignity and integrity in the Indian constitution. The Āzādī of sexual politics and postcolonial worlds created by many in India expresses a lingering haunting of that which "must be done," of histories and postcolonial futures that dance in the streets outside of cramped visions of white-wigged colonial ghosts. Lord Macaulay—who once penned Section 377 of the Indian Penal Code, India's sodomy bill, in a tight-lipped repressive and fearful bourgeois grammar of Victorian morality—is chased through the streets of an "India shining" by the ghosts of Mughal courtesans and Hijras, whose laughter still hangs in the air.

MOTHER INDIA'S "OTHER WOMEN":
BEYOND A RHETORIC OF COLONIAL MORALISM

There is no proper or perfect way to read these moments of protest and the refrains that propel them forward. I only knew in the streets in December 2013 as I knew in the streets in December 2012 that this word, Āzādī, seemed to give life and momentum to political action. The refrain of Āzādī generated a spirit of rebellion rather than a silent resignation to what were tragic examples of the inability for words like "democracy" and "citizenship" to allow gendered bodies meaningful freedom from violence and all the forms it takes, whether through the chilling indifference of court rulings or the brutal force of bodily torture. What is interesting in considering the term Āzādī, is how it unites contemporary feminist and queer movements, as the refrain could be heard at the 2012 Delhi gang rape protests and the 2013 protests regarding Section 377. This book reads these struggles in tandem, departing from mainstream media coverage, which apprehends these moments as discrete and separate, often constructing feminist politics through a discourse of female victimization separate from questions of sexual desire. The 2012 Delhi gang rape case and the 2013 decision to criminalize same-sex desire are connected at the level of ideology and in relation to constructions of normative masculinity, femininity, and sexualities in the Indian subcontinent. These moments are both part of what particularly younger feminists and queers refer to as a social movement that is politicizing gender and sexuality, particularly in urban cities such as Delhi. Following the Delhi gang rape case and decision to uphold Section 377, those whom I spoke with in India emphasized that contemporary feminism and queer politics in India are reflective of a broader political movement and moment within the Indian subcontinent.

Writing in regards to relationship between female sexuality and Section 377, Diyuti Aliwada discusses a commercial venture called Azaad Bazaar that was started by two women in 2009. Azaad Bazaar created a series of queer-friendly products that could be worn or displayed to give visibility to queer people in India and to also offer visual signs of solidarity within public spaces. What is interesting about Aliwada's analysis regarding the relationship between Section 377 of the Indian Penal Code, colonial legality, and female sexuality lies in the emphasis that she places on the reclaiming of public space as an integral part of both queer and feminist struggles, as well as the connections she draws between patriarchal ideas of male ownership over the bodies of all women as central to both feminist and queer politics. Moving away from an argument that solely centres privatized "rights," which often presuppose a neoliberal subject and a struggle only for recognition by the state, Aliwada's arguments trouble the foundations of colonial law and the erasure of all forms of non-traditional female desire from the law, from the public imaginary, and from public spaces. What is crucial in regards to Aliwada's writings in considering both the Delhi gang rape case of 2012 and the 2013 Supreme Court's decision to criminalize diverse enactments of sexuality is the privatization and control of female sexuality as a form of capital that can be bought and sold by men. Aliwada draws on Foucault to discuss how Section 377 of the Indian Penal Code, like much of the personal law that came to govern Indian sexualities can be traced back to colonial rule. The author discusses Section 377 in relation to the enforcement of rigid Victorian moralities of sexual repression and disciplinary power. As Aliwada states,

> Penal laws were imposed as a means of repression. The existence of Section 377 in the Indian Penal code can be located within this discourse on repression. Sexuality came to be associated with reproduction, which was a service to be exploited. (240)

Aliwada draws on Foucault who writes that with the advent of Victorian bourgeoisie repression, sex became associated with the future, not a personal future or a politicized future, but the future of the nation and the idealized citizens it could and should reproduce (241). In this formation of Victorian penal codes, Aliwada suggests that two actors emerged as legal sexual subjects:

> Power with regards to sexuality was in the hands of two people namely the man to whom the woman is attached (father, husband, brother, head of community) who controlled the sexual activity of the wife and the transgressors who by transgressing was upsetting the law (which is heteronormative) and in doing that anticipate freedom. (241)

Within this reading, the threat to Victorian codes of sexual morality that derive from colonialism lies in the body of the woman who transgresses puritanical sexual norms. As Aliwada states, "A woman does not have control over her sexuality or expression. Single women, lesbian women and trans women questioning this often fall in the latter category" (241). In this regard, one can ask how the Āzādī of December 2012 and the

Āzādī that followed the 2013 Supreme Court ruling concerning Section 377 of the Indian Penal Code might gesture to a wider discourse of sexual freedom in which sex is divorced from ownership by elite men within heteronormative patriarchal familial structures.

While there was an effort to turn the 2012 Delhi gang rape case into a biopolitical moment where migrant men were attacking "good Hindu girls," thereby jeopardizing the reproduction of idealized citizens, one can also read these protests as a public articulation against the policing of women's bodies as "citizens," outside of their countenance as the property of men. The efforts to turn the Delhi gang rape protests into a moment of outrage against impoverished migrant men attacking "India's daughter" colonizes the energies of many feminist and queer protestors who saw this moment as part of a wider revolt against colonial sexual norms, the quarantining of desire to the marital home, violence within public space, and the lingering anxiety that surrounds supposedly unruly female sexualities. In conducting interviews for over two years in the Indian subcontinent, many young people I spoke with moved away from the language of protectionism, fear of migrant men, and sexual repression to a language of freedom—Āzādī. The body of the single woman on the Delhi street—in the darkness of the night, and with a man who was not her husband—provoked a grotesque form of disciplinary power in the form of gang rape, torture, and murder. Such spectacles cannot be divorced from the Indian state's use of colonial laws to discipline desire, enforce sexual repression, and "cleanse" the public sphere of all expressions of non-familial and non-reproductive desire.

I want to suggest that what both political events gesture to in the streets of Delhi and in the energies and efforts of feminists, queers, and activists is a broader questioning of discourses of "citizenship" and public space. What is interesting about the nature of both moments, as moments that many suggest are tied to a broader movement, is that both the Āzādī of December 2012 and the Queer Āzādī of December 2013 involve public acts of protest. These political events involve occupying visible public spaces transnationally with protests termed global "days of outrage" being held throughout the world to protest the criminalization of queer desire in India. Aliwada discusses the relationship between the privatization of female sexuality in India through Victorian colonial laws and ideologies of sexual repression, and the erasure of women as citizens entitled to occupy public space.

If as Aliwada states drawing on Foucault, "sex became placed on the agenda of the future," (Foucault qtd. in McCance 110) the female body had to be repressed, regulated, disciplined, and controlled as a private body whose "unruly" desire would potentially threaten the blood, purity, and lives of idealized citizens of "Hindustan" if she strayed from ideals of female sexual respectability. Women's bodies are not counted as citizens with rights to the city or the nation but only valued for their privatized roles as breeders of the Hindu middle class. Drawing on David Harvey, Aliwada writes,

> The public dominant domain constructs, legislates and oversees aspects of citizenship, decision-making, economic exchange and governance. The private realm was primarily for family and reproduction, assigned to an inner, hidden space. (Aliwada 235)

In counting women's value through colonial laws, as lying only in their familial and reproductive roles, women are therefore not entitled to full access to the public domain and are denied full countenance as citizens (Aliwada 235). In this regard, the Āzādī of December 2012 and December 2013 can perhaps be read as articulations of gendered and sexual citizenship struggles in which the woman's body acts not as an object of colonial laws, bourgeois Victorian sexual anxieties, or as property exchanged between men but rather as an agent of social and political change.

AT THE BARRICADES:
INDIA GATE AND GATEWAYS TO POSTCOLONIAL SOCIAL MOVEMENTS

Aliwada suggests that the very act of taking over public space as a means of protest among queer communities in Mumbai, and specifically among those aligned with both queer and feminist struggle, is an expression of changing consciousness. The author states that

> Taking over the public space has been a "mark" of conscious-
> ness rising among people, signifying taking over of the space of economic, cultural, political and legal exchange, marking a conscientisation of people and space, since space is socially produced. (235)

Following the decision made regarding Section 377 by the Supreme Court of India this December of 2013, my email inbox was lit up with only this line, "I guess I know where we'll be meeting AGAIN this year. See you soon." In December of 2012, I stood at Jantar Mantar in Delhi, India, protesting the gang rape and murder of a woman. One year after the Delhi gang rape protests of 2012, a crowd assembled to protest against the Supreme Court's 2013 decision to uphold Section 377 of the Indian Penal Code, India's colonial sodomy law. The occupying of this space of state power, one imbued with colonial history, speaks to a politicization of these moments outside of individual questions of gendered agency to a broader questioning of state power. Furthermore, public space is acutely important in times when, globally, people often only assemble within the privatized spaces of domestic homes or commercial businesses. Naomi Klein discusses the dissolution of spaces of freedom that haunt the imagined rhetoric of neoliberal progress. As Klein states, "What haunts me is not exactly the absence of literal space so much as a deep craving for metaphorical space: release, escape, some kind of open-ended freedom" (64). The creation of political spaces free from the haunting ethos of colonial sexual moralities was heard and felt in the streets of India through the collective cry of Āzādī.

In a recent article that looked at five the big protests fights at Jantar Mantar, it is interesting to note that protests regarding the Supreme Court's 2013 decision to uphold Section 377 and the Delhi gang rape protests of 2012 are listed alongside other political protests that are not explicitly tied to gender and sexuality. The author also makes reference to activist Anna Hazare's protests against state corruption, protests regarding separate statehood for Telangana, and protests demanding justice for Nido Tania, a young man from the Northeast of India who was murdered in an attack that reflects the ongoing problem of racist violence endured by people from the Northeast within Delhi and throughout India (Arvind). One can perhaps read all of these struggles as being united through the broader questions they pose regarding who counts as a citizen of India and how they are counted. The bodies of imagined minorities, ranging from linguistic to racial to gendered and to sexual subalterns, all make their appearance in the space of Jantar Mantar, as did an anti-corruption movement lead by activist Anna Hazare which posed questions regarding whose interests the Indian state in an "India shining" moment protects and invests in. Rather than simply being about the private rights of gendered and sexual expression, the Āzādī of December 2012 and December 2013 can perhaps be seen as articulating a broader desire for freedom from orientalist and colonial constructions of the citizen that fail to represent much of the subcontinent. As one writer states, recounting the Delhi gang rape protests of 2012,

> What started as a spontaneous protest from students, citizens and activists began to slowly result in mass protests at Jantar Mantar and India Gate. The vivid images of students trying to break barricades at Raisina Hill remain etched in our minds. (*India Today*)

The image of students trying to break police barricades is a far cry from the usual commemorative sadness of candlelit vigils that often colour protests related to feminism and gender violence transnationally. In the act of trying to break the barricades, Āzādī was not only articulated in word but in an embodied defiance against state power and the state's ability to keep people from occupying public space, whether through an inability and unwillingness to create safe cities for women or through the creation of barricades of disciplinary power. The writer further says of the protests regarding Section 377 held one year later,

> Besides the LGBT community, angry activists and citizens vented their dismay and anger against the apex court's order setting aside the Delhi High Court's decision to decriminalise gay sex, at the Capital's favourite protest site. (India Today)

As I will attempt to discuss throughout this text, drawing on the inspirational and deeply humbling words, narratives, stories, and ideas of activists, feminists, queers, and many others who took the time to speak with me in India, it is by claiming ownership to the "Capital's favourite protest site" as a space of politics, as a public space owned by people outside of colonial law that the "citizens" of the streets not only enact citizenship but challenge its colonial and occidentalist foundations. As one activist suggests, the language of political defiance and liberation perhaps broke with the usual tone of pity that often frames discussions concerning violence against women and queers. She states,

...you saw a lot of new language. There wasn't just the language of othering, the rhetoric which suggests that these are other people who need our sympathy but it affects all of us. It affects all of our human rights and all of our constitutional rights. (Atluri Personal interviews)

Hannah Arendt once wrote that pity is an enemy of politics as it often amounts to the glorification of the suffering of others:

Parasitic on the existence of misfortune, pity can be enjoyed for its own sake, and this will almost automatically lead to a glorification of its cause, which is the suffering of others. (Arendt qtd. in Bowring 67)

Arendt counters the idea of pity with that of solidarity:

Solidarity ... can, by means of worldly principles and ideals (such as respect, honor and human dignity), unite the strong and the weak in a dispassionate "community of interest." (Arendt qtd. in Bowring 68)

"Āzādī" is an inspiring refrain for all those who sacrifice their time, safety, community, and familial reputation, labour power, and really in many ways their lives to meet in the streets. Protestors wrench the spaces of Indian streets, squares, and national landmarks from histories of Victorian repression and translate them into sites of opening, spaces where one can pose meaningful questions regarding human dignity, respect, desire, and freedom.

NIDRA POYE VADINI NIDRA LEPPOCHU KANI; NIDRA POYINNATU NATINCHE VADINI NIDRA LEPALEM

Diasporic South Asian immigrants from Canada are often inundated with both cautionary right- and left-wing warnings as to if and how one should participate in and write about political struggles in the Indian subcontinent. Firstly, it should be noted that following the Delhi gang rape and murder case of 2012, conservative voices from the South Asian diaspora and the wider Canadian public narrated tales of shock and outrage, some of which were haunted by a colonial tone of judgment towards the assumed misogyny of India as compared to the imagined peace of Canada. As Dordi and Walton-Roberts discuss, the incident was used by many conservative voices as a justification for border security against migrants from India. A corresponding rhetoric of ahistorical nationalism was espoused that celebrated Canada as a feminist and queer utopia with no reference made to the inordinate amount of ongoing violence experienced by Aboriginal women and Two Spirited people, a testament to Canada's white-settler colonial project.[18] While countries in the Global South and the people in them are often constructed within a racist imaginary as being "backward," white-settler colonialism often functions through processes of denial regarding both racism and gendered violence. There is a Telugu proverb that comes to mind in comparing the mass mobilizations of those throughout India following the 2012 Delhi gang rape case as compared to the obscene silence on the part of much of the mainstream Canadian public regarding the countless numbers of "missing" and murdered Aboriginal women in Canada—

Nidrapoyevadininidraleppochukani; Nidrapoyinnatunatinchevadininidralepale—You can wake up someone who is sleeping; It is impossible to wake up a person who is pretending to be asleep. (Atluri Personal interviews)

Dordi and Walton-Roberts go on to discuss the Slutwalk protests, which began in Toronto following misogynistic comments made by a Toronto police officer that are perhaps reflective of Canada's own rape culture, which like most places in the world, functions according to specific historical norms and racist, classist hierarchies. As the authors further write,

And to freshen one's memory, wasn't it a Canadian police officer who declared that if women would like to prevent rapes, they should "avoid dressing like sluts"? The point is that every society has its own form of rape culture. But to generalize that to an entire national population is nothing but foolishness. (Dordi and Walton-Roberts)

Furthermore, the authors' write of the more nuanced and complex ways gender-based and sexual violence is made sense of within South Asian diasporic communities in places such as Canada. They make reference to key cases of gendered and sexual violence and murder in Canada, often justified by diasporic South Asian Canadians in the name of antiquated ideas of communal honour. Conservative members of South Asian Diasporas espouse a similar rhetoric of justifiable sexism and violence, in the name of something called "our culture" and something else called "tradition."

What Hordi and Walton-Robarts highlight is the very selective imaginings of "East" and "West" that are often mobilized by diasporic South Asian communities as well as within mainstream conservative Canadian narratives to justify an ahistorical amnesia regarding the Canada's colonial, white-settler ethos and its implicit and explicit misogyny. As the authors state,

> when South Asian-Canadian women are intimidated, assaulted, raped, or even killed, there is a very uncomfortable debate about whether these events represent the "west's" or the "east's" version of rape culture. (Dordi and Walton Roberts)

There are several issues at play in the binary, reductive, and orientalist divisions of "East" versus "West" in relation to the shifting positionality of diasporic South Asian women's bodies.[19] By imagining violence against South Asian Canadian women to be a problem of Indian culture, the body of the migrant woman is not granted full countenance as someone who is part of Canada or other Western nations. At an ideological level, the wider Western public and state can forego any responsibility regarding violence against women by turning the diasporic migrant body into a representative of the East in ways that allow Canada to be imagined as a feminist utopia. This mapping of "the East" as inherently "backwards" also has implications for border security, with the perceived barbarism of non-Christian and "Eastern" cultures being used as a justification to stop migrants from South Asia and other countries in the Global South from crossing borders (Butler). This reductive East versus West justification of misogyny also allows elite male community representatives of South Asian diasporas to selectively imagine a "back home" divorced of any political histories or mention of ongoing sexual political struggles in ways that hearken back to originary orientalist writings of passive,

submissive Eastern women (Said). Finally, reductive and simplistic us-
ages of loaded and often empty words such as "culture," "community,"
and "tradition" can be easily used to place the body of the South Asian
woman at the impossible impasse between conservative patriarchal families and a white-settler state. The often-glorified rhetoric of Canadian
multiculturalism supports the erasure of the bodily integrity and libidinal desires of the migrant woman based on a multicultural rhetoric of
respect for "culture," which often amounts to a respect for the interests
of patriarchal male elites. One should, however, make note of the creative
activism of many South Asian feminists and queers within diasporas.
For example, the group Masala Militia—a transnational collective of
South Asian feminists, women, transgender, and queer people—began
with the work of Toronto-based South Asian activists. The group now
includes transnational participation, produces online zines and other
resources, participates in conferences and panels, and offers a space for
South Asians to exist between white-settler nationalism and patriarchal
ideas of "community"[20] (Irani).

The overarching point made by Dordi and Walton Robarts as well
as many other South Asian Canadian feminists and others writers and
critics is that cultures of rape, sexism, and gender-based violence exist
globally and are often structured and supported by systemic issues of
classism and racism. Furthermore, spectacles of violence in India and
other countries in the Global South can be used to overshadow and
minimize violence against women of colour in North America. One can
consider the brutal gang beating and murder of Reena Virk, a young
South Asian Canadian woman who was killed by a group of teenagers
under a bridge in Victoria, British Columbia. As discussed by many
writers in *Reena Virk: Perspectives on a Canadian Murder*, the case was an
example of the racialized sexism and abuse that women of colour face in
white-settler colonies in which whiteness is heralded as a feminine ideal
that connotes inclusion into social life as a microcosm for inclusion into
the nation-state as a citizen. One can consider that the male attacker
in the case of the murder of Reena Virk had a history of previously
attacking Aboriginal people in Canada, and the racist comments that
were made by several of Virk's attackers. At one point during the brutal
assault, one of the accused is reported to have stamped a cigarette butt
into Virk's forehead in the place where a bindi—a religious and cultural
symbol often worn by Indian Hindu women—is adorned (Bhattacharya

and Rajiva). Spectacles of extreme suffering in the Global South such as the 2012 Delhi gang rape can be used to herald "the West" as a space of enlightened gendered norms apart from any nuanced understanding of how violence is structured through class, race, religion, and colonial history across borders.

When South Asian diasporic subjects are only encouraged to discuss the political traumas of an imagined home, particularly within the post-September 11 period, the trope of the native informant discussed by Gayatri Spivak and other postcolonial feminists often emerges. The native informant role is one in which racialized Others, migrants, and other constructed minorities are often called on to tell saleable narratives of both exotic spectacle and titillating violence that position the spectator and audience as beyond political implication or responsibility (Spivak 6). As Usamah Ansari points out, the Muslim, Arab, or brown diasporic woman within an ongoing global "war on terror" is often positioned as one who knows enough to speak on behalf of others in the Global South while also knowing enough to act as an enlightened critic, who inevitably judges countries such as Canada to be a safe haven of gendered freedoms (Ansari). Ansari discusses the film *Return to Kandahar*, made by Afghani Canadian Nelofar Pazira. In the film, Pazira who is searching for a childhood female friend in a crowd of women wearing Burqas poses a question to herself before the camera, asking herself whether she should tear off the Burqas of Afghani women. Ansari suggests that this is an implicitly violent gesture that articulates her position as both a supposed liberator of and an aggressor against Afghani women in ways that are reminiscent of the neocolonial imperatives of Western soldiers in the "war against terror."[21] Similarly, as Chowdhury discusses in relation to films like *Fire*, the diasporic South Asian female subject is also often constructed as one who can speak on behalf of and in solidarity with her oppressed "sisters in the South" with little to no attention to overarching issues of class and global economic power. Chowdhury suggests that this native informant position affords diasporic female artists and writers the economic capital and authorial voice to advance a neoliberal form of feminism that discounts their implication in ongoing histories of (neo)colonial and global capitalist exploitation facing women in the Global South who are assumed to be sexually repressed by "tradition" (Chowdhury). This tale of the diasporic female subject as colonial explorer and "liberator" of "her sisters" is often told with little reference to the contexts of war, occupation, transnational labour exploitation, and economic impoverishment produced in the Global South by Western powers. The parable of gender-centric analysis pays no attention to global economic realities that continue cycles of colonial impoverishment in countries such as India to support the wealth of Western nations.

Frantz Fanon once wrote, "You are rich because you are white, you are white because you are rich" (Fanon *The Wretched of the Earth* xx). In this regard, one can ask how the lucrative capital that diasporic subjects can attain from narrating popular tales of "brown barbarism" for Western audiences who remain as unimplicated spectators is a means of securing access to Western capital and colonial respectability. As a diasporic South Asian, I am cognizant of all the glaring privileges that structure my writing of this work, the way it is written, and who will perhaps read it. I am also aware of the lure of telling tales of the "barbaric east" to serve larger global economic interests and the racist colonial amnesia of white-settler states. I am also aware of the nuanced ways in which gendered violence occurs across, because of, and beyond borders. As Yasmin Jiwani, Sheila Bhatacharya, Mythili Rajiva and many other South Asian Canadian feminists discuss, the body of the brown woman who challenges dominant norms of both imagined "pure" diasporic communities and imagined "liberated" Western nations is often a body out of place. The diasporic racialized subject who does not wave a Western flag in praise of a global "war on terror" or of the ongoing seizure of Native land, but who also refuses to sing the praises of the imagined "pure" and pastoral traditions of a community is often left between a rock and a hard place, sometimes the hardest of places. The murder of Reena Virk is a haunting reminder of the body of a brown woman who was made both all too visible and simultaneously invisible within the racist imaginaries of a white-colonial public. Racialized female bodies exist in relation to a lingering white-settler panorama of images, haunted by colonial history. Colonized women in white-settler nations are forcibly removed from supposedly peaceful nations as evinced by the rising numbers of missing and murdered Aboriginal women in Canada(Bhattacharya and Rajiva, and Jiwani). A woman like Reena Virk was also often represented as sources of shame for South Asian disaporic communities who constructed her as unable to live up to orientalist ideas of Indian femininity(Bhattacharya and

Rajiva). There are many cases of racialized, migrant, Aboriginal, and Two Spirited women and queer people who fall through the cracks of narrow lines between "East" and "West," nation and community, often in the most chilling ways (Razack; Bannerji).

There are also many stories of activists, feminists, queers, writers, artists, intellectuals, and everyday people who enter into these moments as sites of struggle, as chances for nuanced critiques, creative expression, and as moments to articulate an imagi/nation beyond the narrow understandings of women, sexuality, and desire that often support dominant nationalisms, often sealed in the blood of women. In writing this book, I offer no authentic narrative of India, Indian, or Indian sexuality. I offer no perfect feminist mantra or maxim. I offer no nostalgic tale of a back home, orientalist "Om Shanti Om," or colonial *Jungle Book* tale of brown male barbarism. In writing this book, I offer only what I often think all acts of thought and attempts at creative intervention can offer us—Questions. As Frantz Fanon once called out for from the pages of his groundbreaking and thoughtful text *Black Skin, White Masks*, "Oh my body, make of me always a man who questions" (206). I offer this text as a lingering question regarding the limits and meanings of freedom—Āzādī.

TIME AFTER TIME: RETURNED REPRESSIONS OF COLONIAL (AND ANTI-COLONIAL) DESIRE

At protests following the 2012 Delhi gang rape case and the subsequent 2013 Supreme Court decision to uphold Section 377, India's colonial sodomy law, I saw many of the same faces. I saw many young queers who were not afraid to be counted as part of the feminist movement and many young feminists who welcomed their countenance within queer movements, outside of how they might have identified sexually or articulated and embodied sexual and romantic desire. As one activist who works for a Delhi-based NGO states in discussing the relationship between the 2012 Delhi gang rape protests and those that followed the 2013 decision to criminalize same-sex desire,

> The scale of the protests changed dramatically. But then you had a similar commonality. Similar communist, leftist groups and feminist queer groups who were part of both. And of

course, I'm not saying all queer groups were part of this and all women's groups were part of that. But yes a lot of young people were present to protest for both issues. And a lot of them were saying, I don't care if my orientation is gay, lesbian, bisexual, trans or straight. The fact that this is a human rights issue did come across very strongly in the protests and the writings since this decision. So, I think this was a very good thing. I am very happy about that. (Atluri Personal interviews)

At the Section 377 protests in December of 2013, a another young activist tells me there is a growing willingness for people to "offer support to one another, and to see all these things as connected … after the gang rape case and then this with 377, people realize they need to not just care if they are a woman, or if they are gay. I think it's more about all of us and what it means to be part of this country" (Atluri Personal interviews). The protests regarding Section 377 and the Delhi gang rape case of 2012 are also united in this common refrain, Āzādī, which could be heard at protests, one that perhaps reflects a deeper common desire for freedom. This freedom could be freedom from police powers that assaulted crowds with water cannons during the 2012 Delhi gang rape protests. This freedom could also mean freedom from gendered, sexual, and moral policing. This freedom could involve the basic freedom to occupy city space, to feel entitled to walk, to live, to love in the streets of the city and the streets of the nation. This freedom could mean freedom from gendered and sexual categorization. This freedom could also mean the very liberty that comes with the act of protest, where the internalized stigma that can come from being associated with both feminism and queer rights is broken with a shrill chorus of Āzādī.

This book is written over years of protest, writing, research, thinking, philosophical questioning, and the impossible work of translation. The translations of the passionate demands and desires of Hindi and other Indian language-speaking protestors, feminists, queers, activists, and many others throughout India are as incomplete as my ability to fully express awe and gratitude for their hospitality in often speaking in English with me, when possible. The translations of desire for freedom, joy, pleasure, and political countenance into discussions regarding the passage of law and rights are as incomplete as the enduring struggles of those united in the name of this dream or another, who stand in this city or the next, in this country or beyond that border, where two people can still miraculously find each other in a moment of protest and cry out in unison, Āzādī.

****

In December of 2012, I stood in the streets of India. I stood in the streets of India with people who represent every facet of the nation. I stood on the pavements of great cities of great histories, pavements that are erected over earth, pavements walked on by religious gurus, the business elite, and one-legged beggars slithering like snakes on the concrete, the sound of the one coin clinking in their cup offering a small city symphony. These streets, the streets of the urban city were ones that I walked as a child-From rural village to bus stop to train station, to the towering skyscrapers of the city that would carry us as diasporic migrants across country and continent. These streets that I stood on, watching from childhood to adolescence to adulthood, watching across borders through Internet screens as a whole continent changed. Watching, in the streets, feet on ground, as girls with flowers in braided hair ran to catch the last bus to the all-night call centre shift, their flowers falling into the rush of traffic.

In December of 2012, I stood on the cool concrete floor of a growing urban jungle and with so many of the people of the Indian subcontinent I cried out for justice and for something called Āzādī. Many of the people of India have been crying out for justice for much longer than I have been alive, for much longer than any of us have been alive. On December 16, 2012, a brutal gang rape and murder occurred that expressed such bodily and emotive violence; it is beyond verbal and written translation. There are no words, no metaphors, no quotes or references to express the loss of a person's life. In these instances, one can recall the words of a character from Toni Morrison's novel *Beloved*, "This is not a story to pass on" (Morrison 274-275). Perhaps the story to pass on lies in the tremendous courage of those in India who politicized this moment in remarkable ways. [22]

In his text *Violence: Six Sideways Reflection*, Slavoj Žižek suggests that one must move away from the liberal humanitarian blackmail that often dilutes the political in favour of panics regarding violence. He discusses the cries that often abound within liberal media that "a woman is raped every 60 seconds" (Žižek 2) or similar statistics regarding starving children in the Global South. Žižek suggests that such pleas for humanitarian aid obscure the more objective forms of systemic violence that would lead one to question political structures that enable violence. Žižek critiques the lure of humanitarian blackmail, which can prevent intellectual reflection by appealing to emotional and reactionary gestures. This work counters dominant media and mainstream neoliberal writings that have apprehended these moments and others through a discourse of pity, one that might draw strength from a long history of colonial discourse. From colonial history to the contemporary global "war on terror," the image of the barbaric brown man has surfaced again and again, with missionary pleas to save brown women being used to mask and justify imperialism (Spivak "Can the Subaltern Speak?"). My work counters this narrative, which equates misogyny with cultural inferiority. I am interested in looking at moments such as the Delhi gang rape of 2012 and the Supreme Court of India's criminalization of diverse enactments of sexual desire in 2013 as giving rise to events of politics.

Standing in the city streets of an urban India of towering shopping malls, booming call centres, smoke churning factories, and sparkling skyscrapers blinding out the sun and stars, all I could hear against the shrieking police sirens, the wail of water cannons, and the endless rush of traffic was one repeating refrain: Āzādī. In Delhi, in Kolkata, in Bangalore, in Hyderabad, in Mumbai, in Chennai, I heard this refrain of Āzādī. In cities throughout the expanse of an Indian subcontinent where there is an old adage which states that "Every two miles the water doth change, and every four the dialect," I heard this refrain over and over again: Āzādī.

PERFECT PEOPLE MAKE GRAVES: THE NEED FOR IMPURE FEMINISMS

A spectre of endless critique haunts contemporary feminist and leftist movements, a spectre of endless critique. Increasingly, many movements that call themselves feminist, queer, leftist, or anti-racist cannot seem to escape the open-air prison of list servs, language policing, and endless debate that often replaces solidarity and affective sentiments towards politics. Some writers and activists pointed out that the 2012 Delhi gang rape case simply wasn't radical enough for the left, as Jyoti was an aspiring urban student making her death unimportant compared to preferred "perfect" victims, such as tribal people, Adivasis, and slum dwellers. The history of subaltern studies in India has largely been one that champions the poorest of the poor. I want to suggest that the policing of what counts as political, of who counts as an "activist" is often born out of narrow ideas of bodies and acts that increasingly do little to describe contemporary sexual politics in India and growing political movements transnationally. Slavoj Žižek suggests that within times of neoliberal Western secular capitalism, increasingly the ultimate right lies in the right not to be harassed. An ethos of fear increasingly defines both conservatives and those affiliated with sexual politics and the left wing. While gated communities allow the privileged few to claim their right to remain at a fearful distance from the poor and working class, feminists are often taught to live in fear of both anti feminist sentiment in the streets and of using the "wrong" terminology, which can be read as an epistemic form of violence. This overarching rhetoric of the petrified can prevent the unlikely event of politics that happens in the streets through the meeting and mobilization of strangers—people who may be estranged from happy bourgeois homes and from self-righteous scripts of the intellectually informed left wing. Feminist wills to political and linguistic "purity" can mimic the construction of imagined pure spaces of elite membership in which those without the proper identification card or feminist passwords are excluded.[23] The fixation on leftist nomenclatures within feminist and Marxist struggles cannot contain the kernel of the visceral real that people express in instinctive and passionate moments in the streets. If, as Badiou suggests, politics is an exercise of public judgment, one can see how new actions transnationally function as political without an immediate manifesto or a clear moniker or institution under which they are organized. Drawing on a history of the French resistance, Badiou suggests that political acts are not ordered, bureaucratized acts of rationality. He writes of the spontaneous eruption of the political, not as choice, but as necessity, "… resistance, proceeding by logic, is not an opinion. Rather it is a logical rupture with dominant and circulating opinions" (Metapolitics 5). While contemporary feminist and leftist organizations transnationally often organize under certain nomenclatures or fixed identity and "community"-based positions, Badiou sees the politics of resistance as beginning with a set of contingent circumstances that lead to moments of political possibility. As Badiou argues,

When all is said and done, all resistance is a rupture in thought, through the declaration of what the situation is, and the foundation of a practical possibility opened up through this declaration. (Metapolitics 8)

One could see this moment of rupture in the streets of Delhi in 2012 and in the wave of protests that spread throughout the subcontinent of India. Despite the statistical betterment of India at the level of economic growth and flows of transnational capital, the on the ground experiences of gender-based violence and state inefficiency produced a logical outrage.

There was a fearless spirit to the actions that took place throughout India in December of 2012. It was a breath of fresh air for someone like me who has watched political movements, particularly in North America and Europe, dissolve into endless Internet threads debating the use of the right English language words. The real politic of many leftist and particularly feminist movements has, transnationally, often been diluted by the mainstreaming of politics through academia, social work, and NGO structures that muzzle the cries of people in the streets, in bureaucratic paper work. This spirit of fearless, often spontaneous action does not begin or end with this one moment or with the Indian subcontinent. From Slutwalk to Occupy movements, to anti-austerity protests, to riots in London and Paris by racialized and migrant youth, the language that people are using to enact politics perhaps cannot be contained by fixed nomenclatures. One can for example, consider The Umbrella Revolution protests that occurred in Hong Kong in 2014, which demanded that the city elections be fully democratic. The movement was named in the real time and material struggle of the streets through the photo of a protestor holding an umbrella, amid thick clouds of tear gas that were reminiscent of the haze of the water cannons used by Delhi police. The umbrella became emblematic of protestor's willingness to risk, unwavering in their desires for political change. The photo of a protestor holding an umbrella reached audiences globally through the Internet and transnational media coverage of the protests. As one journalist reports, "Without a word, it explains how this quizzical yet ubiquitous object has become the symbol of what is being called the greatest political challenge to China in a quarter century" (Nogel).

Badiou suggests that "every philosophy is conditioned by a real politics" (Metapolitics 16). Just as many contemporary social movements globally emerge through political action, this book attempts to philosophically approach sexual politics in contemporary India through the political struggles that emerged in 2012 and 2013. Analyzing contemporary protests concerning gender and sexuality in India through Badiou's understanding of political philosophy, one can ask how these protests condition a new philosophical approach to understanding both the postcolonial moment in India and sexual politics in the Indian subcontinent. The real politic of the street produces a philosophical approach to the sexual postcolonial body politic that reflects a glaring gap between formalized legal right and the bloody mess of bodies. The real politic of contemporary struggles for Āzādī in India also produces a philosophical approach that centres the importance of technology and globalization as a means through which India is both further tied to neo-colonial, multinational capitalist projects while also providing the means through which local protest causes global interest.

This is a book about sexual politics as politics. Yes, it is a book that falls apart again and again only to be reassembled by the real politic of the Indian streets. In what follows, I do not offer a full stop on questions of gender, sexuality, and political movements in India; rather, I offer open-ended philosophical ideas, thoughts, and questions that are forever in transit and in translation. These are transitory ideas that move from screaming, sweaty, enraged, passionate, and hopeful bodies in the streets of the Indian subcontinent to words on a screen, to words on a page. This book is an impossible attempt to translate desire into text, emotion into word, to turn the unspeakable bone-chilling violence of just another day in India into an archive of the constant chorus heard in the streets, with the everyday in contemporary India being defined by the inspiring miracle of the political event: Āzādī.

ROAD MAPS FOR THE EXILED READER:
WHERE WE MIGHT BE GOING FROM HERE

The first theoretical section of this text is a philosophical precursor to the second half of the book, which includes interviews done with people in the Indian subcontinent. The theoretical reading of sexual politics through the lens of philosophy is further elucidated and challenged by the narratives of those whom I was deeply inspired by and who generously afforded me the chance to speak with them in India. Chapter One offers a theoretical discussion regarding the Internet in India. This chapter further comments on the role that technology and media play in sexual politics in the Indian subcontinent. Chapter Two discusses sexual politics in contemporary India in relation to social movement history. I offer a genealogy of sexual politics that moves away from Eurocentric understandings of political temporality. In Chapter Three, I discuss the limits and possibilities of law and question how the law turns grief into grievance in cases pertaining to gender-based violence. I also discuss the relationship between sexuality, the law, and colonial history. In Chapter Four, I consider space. I write of the relationship between gender, sexuality, and space within contemporary India and transnationally. The second half of this book draws on interviews in the Indian subcontinent, participation in protests, and reflections regarding the sexual political struggles that were evident throughout India between 2012 to 2014. Chapter One of the second section of this text involves interviews done at the one-year anniversary protest of the 2012 Delhi gang rape case and considers the politicization of often taken for granted ideas of "love." Chapter Two discusses the relationship between citizenship and sexual politics, while Chapter Three discusses neoliberal capitalism, labour, and sexual politics in urban India. Subsequently in Chapter Four I question the conflicting meanings of desire within a nation pushed and pulled by competing discourses of market-based "freedom," colonial history, religious nationalisms, and divergent understandings of sex. Chapter Five draws on interviews done in India to discuss masculinity. The conclusion, much like the entirety of the text, does not offer a definite final statement regarding sexual politics in a subcontinent of ancient and often paradoxical histories, rapidly changing urban economies, haunting colonial laws, and a political culture that is beyond textual translation. I conclude as I begin, with the passionate cries heard in the streets: Āzādī.

WHO HAS THE LAST LAUGH? "THE REBEL FACE OF HOPE"

There is a photo that comes to mind: a haunting image sent over Internet lines, seen through the screens of computers, gracing the glossy pages of newspapers with translated text in German, French,

Hebrew, Greek, Italian, Arabic, Cantonese, Mandarin, Vietnamese, Urdu, Hindi, English, endless languages that cannot capture the look of defiance in the eyes of the young woman photographed. Standing in the streets of Delhi, with the faint blur of riot cops and barricades in the background, she stares courageously into the camera. In her hands she holds a sign that reads: "You can get raped, but you can't protest rape—World's largest democracy."There is a look in her eyes that I have no words for, a look of rage, a look of defiance, a look of something that might be called Āzādī. The words, a simply ironic quip that pointed to the glaring gaps between legality and the embodied and phenomeno-logical experiences of being a person in the Indian subcontinent. The knowing winks and nudges, the sly civility,[24] the same old jokes that many in India have been told and have been telling themselves since the days of colonial rule. Fingers flicker through images on screens, in newspapers, across borders and through windows of social media sites. There she is again, another photo of a new-fangled Bollywood heroine of the day. The sign is gone now and she is screaming defiantly, screaming with crowds of people standing face to face with masked riot police. I cannot hear the words that she is screaming. I cannot hear the endless stream of traffic and horns; I cannot hear the sound of water cannons being fired, leaving wet ground and skin in a nation where so many die of dehydration. I cannot hear her voice, yet I recall the chorus of protestors heard throughout the Indian subcontinent: Āzādī. Inspired by their cries and the resilient look in her eyes I see what Agha Shahid Ali once called "the rebel face of hope" (Ali 59).[25] Āzādī.

ENDNOTES

[1]The author would like to thank all those who met with her in the In-dian subcontinent for in-depth interviews as well as all of those whom I spoke with on the street, at protests, meetings, panel discussions, and other public events in Delhi and throughout the Indian subcontinent. Note, names have been changed or omitted due to the sensitive nature of gendered violence and sexual politics. Efforts have been made to protect the anonymity of those whom I spoke with in India while conducting fieldwork for this book. Further gratitude is extended to all of those who were part of *Oecumene: Citizenship After Orientalism* at the Open University, where I acted as a postdoctoral researcher while

conducting research and writing this book. Chapter four of the first section of this text, "Cars, Colonies, and Crime Scenes: Space, Gender, and Violence" was informed by the useful and intelligent comments offered by those who participated in the Third Oecumene symposium where I presented a draft of this chapter. In particular, the comments provided by discussants Melissa Butcher and Rahul Rao informed the writing of the final draft of this chapter. The scholarly critique that I was offered as part of Oecumene was remarkable, and without the support of colleagues who were part of this project, the research and writing of this book would not have been possible. In particular, I wish to thank Dr. Engin Isin, whose academic supervision and intellectual critique informed the research and writing of this manuscript. Finally, I wish to acknowledge the Social Sciences and Humanities Research Council of Canada, the funding body that contributed to my postdoctoral research in both the United Kingdom and the Indian subcontinent.

[2] While Fanon's writings often focused on anti-racist, postcolonial nationalist struggles without explicit attention to gender and sexuality, and in ways that some argue are patriarchal and heteronormative, one can ask how contemporary postcolonial political protests in the Global South involve feminist and queer enactments of the political, as evinced in the 2012 Delhi gang rape protests (Fanon The Wretched of the Earth).

[3] I use both the terms "New Delhi" and "Delhi" throughout this book, as they were often used interchangeably by many whom I spoke with in the Indian subcontinent. However, the distinction between these terms should be noted. "Delhi" refers to the

> city and national capital territory, north-central India. The city of Delhi actually consists of two components: Old Delhi, in the north, the historic city; and New Delhi, in the south, since 1947 the capital of India, built in the first part of the 20th century as the capital of British India. One of the country's largest urban agglomerations, Delhi sits astride (but primarily on the west bank of) the Yamuna River, a tributary of the Ganges (Ganga) River, about 100 miles (160 km) south of the Himalayas. The national capital territory embraces Old and New Delhi and the surrounding metropolitan region, as well as adjacent rural areas. ("Delhi")

[4] Section 377 refers to Section 377 of the Indian Penal Code, a colonial sodomy law dating back to the 1860s in the Indian subcontinent. I refer

to Section 377 of the Indian Penal Code as "Section 377 of the Indian Penal Code" and "Section 377" as it was often referred to by protesters, activists, and many people whom I spoke with in conducting fieldwork in India.

[5]In 2009, the Delhi high court in India overturned Section 377 of the Indian penal code, a colonial law that criminalizes same-sex desire. This happened after a petition was filed by the Naz Foundation in India and after a campaign by the activist group Voices Against 377 in India.

[6]Shah discusses the Delhi gang rape case in relation to the obsessive agency on the part of those who engage in crimes against humanity. Shah draws parallels between the obscene and incomprehensible brutalities enacted against Jyoti's body and those of Nazi soldiers. Shah draws on the work of Elaine Scarry and her understanding of the body in pain and the role it plays regarding the forming of subjectivity. Shah's work also gestures to the writings of Slavoj Žižek who discusses the obscene underbelly of the official scripts of law and order. One can consider that the 2012 Delhi gang rape happened at a time when the Indian subcontinent was branding itself a neoliberal success story, an "India shining" with technological progress and a growing urban middle class. The obscene underbelly perhaps lies in the lived material violence enacted against the bodies of women and queers. One can also consider laws that are discussed throughout this work that make "marital rape" legal. The obscene underbelly of the official law that allows men as husbands to rape women as wives is perhaps expressed in these extreme spectacles of street-based assaults, while normative abuse and rape is hidden from public view in Hindu middle-class family homes, and is supported by law (Shah; Žižek Violence).

[7]As this incident occurred on a hijacked bus it cannot be said to be representative of everyday experiences of transport in the city of Delhi or governance regarding public transportation in the city.

[8]As I discuss throughout this book, the idea of sexual "progress" informs contemporary global politics and the use of the body of the imagined victimized queer/feminist subject in the Global South to support neo-colonialism. For example, as discussed in later chapters of this work, David Cameron's 2012 "Gay conditionality" proposal suggested that British aid to countries in the Global South should be dependent on their institution of secular English language categorizations of LGBTQ rights. This proposal indicates that a language of gendered and sexual

universalism can potentially be used to strip formally colonized peoples, arguably first impoverished because of colonial rule, of financial aid from the former Empire (Rao).

[9]Unless otherwise noted, names have been changed or omitted throughout the text because of the sensitive and often contentious nature of sexual politics in India and transnationally. Efforts have been made to protect the anonymity of those I spoke with and who are cited in this text. To reduce redundancy, most in-text citations to these interviewees have been removed.

[10]I draw on concepts from Badiou's philosophy regarding this work to discuss sexual politics in India through the idea of the political event. This book however, cannot give full justice to Badiou's political ideas in their entirety (Badiou Being and Event; Metapolitics; Ethics).

[11]"India Shining" was a marketing slogan referring to the overall feeling of economic optimism in India in 2004. The slogan was popularized by the then-ruling Bharatiya Janata Party (BJP) for the 2004 Indian general elections" ("India Shining"). The phrase is often used by authors and political commentators to discuss the rhetoric of neoliberal growth in India, a narrative of supposed economic "progress" that often overlooks much of the country's poor and other systemically marginalized people (Chowdhury).

[12]While not discounting the explicit and implicit violence of Hinduism and Hindu nationalism used to police women's bodies, dehumanize Dalits, and push Muslims, other religious minorities, and migrants to the symbolic and material borders of the Indian subcontinent, one can consider creative revisionist texts that suggest that there is an ethic of fearlessness to be found in some narratives and goddesses within Hindu mythologies. The goddess "Kali" for example has often be used creatively as a symbol of contemporary feminism and strength in India and transnationally. Similarly, the comic book *Priya's Shakti* was created by an artist who participated in the 2012 Delhi gang rape protests. The comic uses the aesthetics of Hinduism in a revisionary feminist manner to tell the story of a survivor of gendered violence, through the form of the comic book, often used to tell Hindu stories to children in India. The author of the comic suggests that he understands Hinduism as fundamentally being tied to a desire to overcome fear (Devenini, Srivastava, and Goldman; Thacker).

[13]Slavoj Žižek writes of a contemporary moment of fear. Žižek discusses

how increasingly within times and spaces of secular capitalist individualism, now existent throughout the world, political passions often only
erupt through a rhetoric of fear. One can consider how this "right to not
be harassed" unites both right and left wing sentiments, with political
outrage emerging from right-wing commentators who fear migrants
and racialized others, just as left-wing politics, and specifically feminist and queer politics, can remain affectively tied to the fear of sexist,
heteronormative violence. Throughout this book, I attempt to discuss
contemporary feminist and queer politics in India through the refrain
"Āzādī," as a symbol of the ethos of freedom that defined protests in
India in 2012 and 2013. I discuss how the desire to claim public space,
pleasure, and political solidarity were central to these moments of protest
(Phadke, Ranade, and Khan). While the gendered and sexual violence
that women and queer people experience within India can be used to
promote a conservative rhetoric of protectionism and a justifiable level
of apprehension in many, the cries of Azadi are perhaps reflective of
desires for freedom from the anxieties, aggressions, and fears projected
onto female, queer, and Hijra bodies (Žižek "Liberal Multiculturalism").
[14]Authors discuss the decision to strike down the initial petitions
against the Supreme Court of India's decision to uphold Section 377
of the Indian penal code and further state that the curative petition is
the next method for appealing the state's decision ("Section 377: The
Way Forward").
[15]At the time of writing, the Indian government has made marital rape
officially legal, despite recommendations from the Verma Committee
following the Delhi gang rape case of 2012.
[16]One can consider Partha Chatterjee's exemplary essay, "Woman, Nationalism, and the Colonial Question" in regards to how and why one
sees the returned enforcement of sexist, homophobic law and colonial
moralism at the level of desire in a time of increased transnational and
corporate globalization within an "India shining." Chatterjee suggests that
Indian nationalists managed the imagined threat of cultural alienation
brought about by British colonial rule by supporting "Westernization"
in the public sphere of business and by enforcing strict ideas of "culture"
in the private sphere. Chatterjee further notes that this idealization of
the "purity" of the Indian home had specific implications for the figure
of the idealized Hindu, middle-class "Indian woman." Within the
nationalist period, the Indian woman became prized as a homemaker,

wife, and keeper of timeless orientalist ideas of "culture" against the bodies of "Other" women, namely the poor, sex workers, and religious minorities. In this defensive and anxious effort to preserve "culture" as an opposition to the realities of colonial rule and capitalist expansion, the body of the middle class woman became fetishized as timeless object of "tradition." One can ask how within a time of globalization, in which India opens its doors to English language transnational corporate capital, again the body of the "Indian woman" is overinvested in as a mythic object whose domestic servitude and imagined "purity" can be preserved to guard against the realities of what Alan Badiou terms the "worldless space of global capitalism" (Chatterjee; Žižek "On Alain Badiou and Logiques des mondes").

[17]Foucault discusses biopolitics as "an anatomo-politics of the human body" and as "a biopolitics, of the population," (Foucault 139) which refers to state regulations over citizens, often in service of supporting the reproduction of certain populations. In the media narratives that followed the recent suicide of a woman in Delhi owing to her husband's supposed queer desire, the body of the wife becomes an object that is grieved over, while the queer male body is constructed as a threat to the reproduction of an ideal Hindu population. The woman's life as wife and mother is useful for the nation-state as her body could potentially reproduce new middle- and upper-class Hindu citizens. Conversely, women who stray from roles of wife and mother and queer men are constructed as either invisible to many nationalist aims or as potentially threatening normative gendered and sexual roles that are supposedly sacred to the imagined sanctity of the heteronormative Hindu middle-class family.

[18]The authors state that,

> One could see the vitriol that people had penned. Some asked for a complete trade ban on India, while others wondered why the Canadian government were allowing "such people"[Indians] into the country. It was disconcerting to see such self-proclaimed saintliness from North American readers, who have seemingly forgotten the level of police indifference to the disappearance of aboriginal women from downtown Vancouver. (Dordi and Walton-Roberts)

[19]The terms "east" and "west" have been contested by scholars such as Edward Said whose writings have been foundational in demonstrating that the imagined regions and corresponding ideologies of a succinct

"east" and "eastern" culture came into being as an assertion of colonial power. As Said and many other influential scholars point out, the east is a creation of the west that served to solidify western superiority by constructing an essentialist and unchanging Orient that was imagined in relation to the colonizing Occident. I am aware of the historical and philosophical baggage that terms such as east and west have and use them with caution, as a heuristic device that gestures to the continued use of these highly suspect terms. I use these terms to reflect a contemporary political reality in which Orientalism continues to exist. This is a reflective of neo-orientalist invocations of "east" and "west" within popular and political discourse and is in no way a statement of support for such reductive and troubling binaries. In the interests of style I have not used scare quotes around every use of "east" and "west" in this text (Said *Orientalism*).

[20]There are several examples of feminist, queer, anti racist and political organizations involving diasporic South Asians. An exhaustive list and detailed discussion of diasporic South Asian activism is beyond the scope of this text.

[21]Ansari writes,

> At one point, Pazira asks herself, "Should I go and pull her burqa off?" Given how the invasion of Afghanistan was cloaked in supposedly feminist desires to liberate Afghani women, it is not surprising that this question implies a "benevolent" or "modernizing" intervention. (Ansari 48)

Ansari discusses how Pazira asks herself this question as an Afghani subject, in the presence of a Western audience. He further writes,

> Although this may support contemporary debates around authority over voice and representation, it also produces the native informant: the classic anthropological sidekick who tells her faithful audience about the novel idiosyncrasies of her "traditional" society while inviting various interventionist discourses (Ansari 48).

[22]Following the Delhi gang rape and protests that followed, many have documented the routine forms of sexual harassment, abuse, threats of death and physical violence that women in New Delhi experience daily. More than this, many have also written of the colossal indifference of the Delhi police force and Indian state who often not only offer little to no meaningful redress for these crimes but often make light of these

abuses and participate in misogynistic ideology that blames women and queer people for the violence that they experience. Furthermore, some have pointed to a larger problem of state and police corruption and how crimes against everyday people within India are ignored or dismissed, with only the very upper-caste elite body being protected by the Indian state. Some have written of the inefficiency of bureaucratic complaint procedures used by the police, suggesting that complaints regarding sexual harassment, assault, and bodily violence are often ignored, forgotten, and not investigated unless one is of the most elite, upper-caste faction of the society(Nagam "Dismiss the Delhi Police Commissioner"; Biswas "Do India's Political Parties Condone Corruption?").

[23]As Žižek states in "Against Human Rights,"

> Liberal attitudes towards the other are characterized both by respect for otherness, openness to it, and an obsessive fear of harassment. In short, the other is welcomed insofar as its presence is not intrusive, insofar as it is not really the other. Tolerance thus coincides with its opposite. My duty to be tolerant towards the other effectively means that I should not get too close to him or her, not intrude into his space—in short, that I should respect his intolerance towards my over-proximity. This is increasingly emerging as the central human right of advanced capitalist society: the right not to be 'harassed', that is, to be kept at a safe distance from others. (Žižek "Against Human Rights")

[24]For a more in-depth discussion regarding the concept of sly civility, India, and colonialism see: Homi Bhabha, *The Location of Culture*. London: Taylor and Francis, 1994.

[25]Agha Shahid Ali, "Homage to Faiz Ahmed Faiz." This poem was written in memory of the poet Faiz Ahmed Faiz. It commemorates Faiz's writing and his resilient commitment to political struggle and justice. Ali writes,

> When you permitted my hands to turn to
> stone, as must happen to a translator's
>
> hands, I thought of you writing Zindan-Nama
> on prison-walls, on cigarette-packages,
>
> on torn envelopes. Your lines were measured so carefully
> to become in our veins the blood of prisoners.

In the free verse of another language I imprisoned each line—but
I touched my own exile.
This hush, while your ghazals lay in my palms,

was accurate, as is this hush which falls at news of your death
over Pakistan
and India and over all of us no

longer there to whom you spoke in Urdu.
Twenty days before your death you finally

wrote, this time from Lahore, that after the sack
of Beirut you had no address. . .I
had gone from poem to poem, and found
you once terribly alone, speaking

to yourself: "Bolt your doors, Sad heart! Put out
the candles, break all cups of wine. No one,

now no one will ever return." But you
still waited, Faiz, for that God, that Woman,

that Friend, that Revolution, to come at
last. And because you waited, I

listen as you pass with some song,
A memory of musk, the rebel face of hope. (Ali 58-59)

WORKS CITED

"AIMS Doctor Commits Suicide, Blames 'Gay' Husband, Also a Doc-
    tor." ndtv.com. New Delhi Television Limited, 20 April 2015. Web.
    10 June 2015.
Ali, Agha Shahid. *The Veiled Suite: The Collected Poems*. New Delhi:
    Penguin, India. 2010. Print.
Amar, Paul. *The Security Archipelago: Human-Security States, Sexuality
    Politics, and the End of Neoliberalism*. Durham: Duke University Press,
    2013. Print.

Ansari, Usamah. "'Should I Go and Pull Her Burqa Off?': Feminist Compulsions, Insider Consent, and a Return to Kandahar." *Critical Studies in Media Communication* 25.1 (2008): 48-67. Print.

Arendt, Hannah. *On Revolution.* New York: Penguin, 1965. Print.

Arvind, Ayesha. "Welcome to Protest Central: How Jantar Mantar Became Delhi's Hotbed of Social Unrest." *The Daily Mail*, 18 Feb. 2014. Web. 28 May 2015.

Atluri, Tara. Personal interviews. 2014-2015.

Badiou, Alain. *Being and Event.* London: Continuum, 2005. Print.

Badiou, Alain. *Ethics: An Essay on the Understanding of Evil.* Trans. Peter Hallward. London: Verso, 2012. Print.

Badiou, Alain. *Metapolitics.* London: Verso, 2005. Print.

Bhabha, Homi. T*he Location of Culture.* London: Taylor and Francis, 1994. Print.

Benjamin, W. "On the Concept of History." Trans. H. Zohn. *Walter Benjamin: Selected Writings.* Volume 4: 1938-1940. Eds. H. Eiland and M.W. Hennings. Cambridge: Harvard University Press, 2003. 389-411. Print.

Biswas, Southik. "Do India's Political Parties Condone Corruption?" British Broadcasting Corporation, 24 Jan. 2013. Web. 30 July 2013.

Butler, Judith. Sexual Politics, Torture, and Secular Time." *The British Journal of Sociology* 59. (2008): 1-23. Print.

Chatterjee, Partha. "Colonialism, Nationalism, and Colonialized Women: The Contest in India."*American Ethnologist*16.4(1989):622-633.Print.

"Delhi." *Encyclopedia Britannica*, 2015. Web. 9 July 2015.

"Delhi Gang Rape 2012." Wikipedia, 2013. Web. 29 July 2013.

Devineni, Ram. "Interview with Ram Devinenion Priya's Shakti." British Broadcasting Corporation, 25 Dec. 2014. Web. 17 June 2015.

Devineni, Ram, Lina Srivastava, and Dan Goldman. *Priya's Shakti. Online Comic Book.* Rattapallax, 2014. Web. 18 June 2015.

Dordi, Huzan and Margaret Walton-Roberts. "The Delhi Gang Rape and the South Asian Diaspora: Apathy or Empathy?" Centre for International Governance Innovation, 7 Feb. 2013. Web. 11 Nov. 2015.

"Fair and Lovely for Men." YouTube. 2 April 2007.Web.10 June 2015.

Fanon, Frantz. *Black Skin, White Masks.* Trans. Richard Philcox. London: Grove Press, 2008. Print.

Fanon, Frantz. *The Wretched of the Earth.* Trans. Constance Farrington. London: Penguin Books, 1969. Print.

Foucault, Michel. *The History of Sexuality: An Introduction.* Trans. R. Hurley. London: Penguin Books, 1990. Print.

"India Court Recognises Transgender People As Third Gender." British Broadcasting Corporation, 15 April 2014. Web. 10 June 2015.

"India Shining." Wikipedia, 2015. Web. 23 Nov. 2015.

Irani, Nish. "From Zines to Online Community: Masala Militia's One Year Anniversary." *Shameless Magazine,* 23 May 2014. Web. 18 June 2015.

Klein, Naomi. *No Logo.* Toronto: Vintage Canada, 2009. Print.

Lodia, Sharmila. "From 'Living Corpse' to India's Daughter: Exploring the Social, Political and Legal Landscape of the 2012 Delhi Gang Rape." *Women's Studies International Forum* 50 (2015): 89–101. Print.

McCance, Dawne. *Posts: Re-Addressing the Ethical.* Albany: State University of New York Press, 1996. Print.

Morrison, Toni. *Beloved.* New York: Plume, 1988. Print.

Nagam, Aditiya. "Dismiss the Delhi Police Commissioner." *Kafila,* 21 April 2013. Web. 30 July 2013.

Narrain, Arvind. "Violation of Bodily Integrity: The Delhi Gang Rape among Others." *Economic and Political Weekly,* 2013. Web. 30 July 2013.

"Nirbhaya Gang-rape Case: Supreme Court Stays Hanging of 2 Convicts." *The Times of India,* 14 July 2014. Web. 25 Sept. 2015.

Nogel, Randolph. "Humble Umbrella Symbolises Hong Kong Protests." Aljazeera, 1 Oct. 2014. Web. 20 June 2015.

Oecumene: Citizenship after Orientalism Website. The Open University, 2015. Web. 15. June 2015.

Phadke, Ranade, and Khan. "Why Loiter? Radical Possibilities for Gendered Dissent." *Dissent and Cultural Resistance in Asian Cities.* Eds. Melissa Butcher and Selvaraj Velayutham. London: Routledge, 2009. 185-203. Print.

Rana, Preetika. "Modi Government's Reasons Why Marital Rape Is Not a Crime." *The Wall Street Journal,* 30 April 2015. Web. 12 Sept. 2015.

Rao, Rahul. "On 'Gay Conditionality', Imperial Power and Queer Liberation: Rahul Rao." *Kafila,* 1 Jan. 2012. Web. 17 June 2015.

Roychowdhury, Poulami. "The Delhi Gang Rape": The Making of International Causes." *Feminist Studies* 39.1 (2013): 282-292. Print.

Said, Edward. *Orientalism.* New York: Vintage Books, 1979. Print.

"Section 377: 'The Way Forward.'" *The Hindu,* 1 Feb. 2013. Web. 7 Sept. 2014.

Singh, Pawan. "Subjects of Privacy: Law, Sexuality and Violence in India." George Snow Scholarship Fund, 2014. Web. 10 June 2014.

Spivak, Gayatri Chakravorty. *A Critique of Postcolonial Reason*. Boston: Presidents and Fellows of Harvard College, 1999. Print.

Spivak, Gayatri Chaktravorty. "Can the Subaltern Speak?" *The Postcolonial Studies Reader*. Eds. Bill Ashcroft, Gareth Griffiths, and Helen Tiffen. London: Routledge, 1995. 28-37. Print.

Thacker, Purvi. "Meet Priya, a Comic Superhero Fighting the Social Stigma of Rape in India." *Vice Magazine*, 9 Feb. 2015. Web. 17 June 2015.

Žižek, Slavoj. "A Leftist Plea for Eurocentrism." *Critical Inquiry* 25.4 (Summer 1998): 988-1009. Print.

Žižek, Slavoj." Against Human Rights." Libcom, 9 Oct. 2006. Web. 27 July 2015.

Žižek, Slavoj. "Liberal Multiculturalism Masks an Old Barbarism with a Human Face." *The Guardian*, Oct. 2010. Web. 16 June 2015.

Žižek, Slavoj. "On Alan Badiou and Logiques des mondes." lacan.com. N.p., 2007. Web. 31 July 2013.

Žižek, Slavoj. *Violence: Six Sideways Reflections*. London: Profile Books, 2009. Print.

I.
IN THEORY

I.

CAN THE SUBALTERN TWEET?

TECHNOLOGY AND SEXUAL-TEXTUAL POLITICS

LINDSAY LOHAN AND OTHER TRAGEDIES:
CELEBRITY, SPECTACLE, AND ACTIVISM IN THE AGE OF
THE INTERNET

LINDSAY LOHAN. It seems strange to begin a chapter regarding the relationship between mass media and gendered politics in India with such a name. Lindsay Lohan's tweeted fantasies regarding missionary feminist work, however, shed a glaring light on the paradoxes of transnational activism in a time of globalization, celebrity cultures of late capitalism, and cyberspace. Lohan, like many Western celebrities, sought to "save India," perhaps as a way of trying to save herself from addiction, perhaps as a way to gain favourable press, or perhaps as a means of engaging in some sort of altruistic politics. Yet, the reason Lohan's bourgeois charity work sparks interest lies in the controversies that were caused regarding her declarations of activism on the Internet. Lohan became embroiled in a media scandal when she used her twitter account to declare that she had "saved" several children from a garment factory in India, while critics in the Indian subcontinent pointed out that she was not even there at the time. Lohan, who was involved in a BBC Three program regarding child trafficking, tweeted the following message which was subsequently removed from her account, "Over *40 children saved* so far ... Within one day's work ... This is what life is about ... Doing THIS is a life worth living!!!" (Nelson). Whether or not Lohan was in fact in India seems less important than what this moment can offer in thinking about politics in the Global South within the technologically driven time of globalization.

Lindsay Lohan@lindsaylohan
"Over *40 children saved* so far …Within one day's work …
This is what life is about … Doing THIS is a life worth living!!!"

Lindsay Lohan@lindsaylohan
Tunisia we are with you #jesuisbardohttps://instagram.com/p/0i-fidppc3m/

Narendra Modi PM@Narendramodi_PM
PM salutes the unparalleled accomplishments of the girl child,on
National Girl Child Day http://nm4.in/1z1Cbw2 via @narendramodi
PM greets girl children and young women on New Year's Day
http://nm4.in/1vwVVj9 via @narendramodi

Queer Azaadi@queer_azaadi
india first pride walk. 'Friendship walk' #yaariyanOn 2nd July
1999 at kolkatta.#lgbtqteen…https://instagram.com/p/0XWv-oEaV3/

@IndiasDaughter equates rape with escalating TEROR of #Gan-
gRapes here. They're different See http://www.hystericalfemi-
nisms.com/138/ @ZulaQi

Communication Cell@bjpsamvad May 2
#KashmiriPandits to protest against forced exile at #**JantarMantar**
at 10 am on 3rd May, 2015.

AL Jazeera Arabic@AJArabi 8 Aug 2012
نامهيهج دافحأ نحن نامهيهجاي كمحري هللا # ليهاعلا ةماطل ليهاحلا ةحابذ ةبيتع انح
اليعتيب #Egypt#Kuwait#ksa#Qatar#Oman#UAE#bahrain

How spectacular fantasies regarding politics in the Global South can be engaged in online both by those making declarations of participation and those watching spectacles stretch beyond Lohan. There was for example, a mass outpouring of attention that was generated by the Arab Spring protests in Egypt in 2010 (Bady). Again, the Internet allowed for an imagined participation, with people throughout the world participating in a voyeuristic form of politics that gestured to the desire to engage in revolution as entertainment. As authors also point out, overemphasizing the role that the Internet plays in social movements in the Global South also serves to construct Western Internet companies as creating moments of revolution. Such a celebratory reading of Internet-based mediums pays little attention to the work of activists in the Global South and to histories of political revolt that foreground contemporary politics in non-Western contexts. Morozov argues that "revolutionary claims for social media now circulating throughout the west are only a manifestation of western guilt for wasting so much time on social media" (Morozov qtd. in Cook 4). The Lohan controversy, while somewhat ridiculous, is perhaps part of a larger defining discourse of our time, one in which information, spectacle, and action are conflated. Rather than praising the Lindsay Lohans of the world for their bourgeois missionary tales of salvation or berating them for the lack of truth in their statements, perhaps we should ask how these moments offer inroads into considering the relationship between politics as action, politics as speech, and politics as spectacle.

The Internet plays a role in both politically mobilizing bodies to participate in protests and simultaneously informing the performances of gendered bodies online within contemporary feminist and queer movements in India. While many have written about about the use of Internet technology in the Arab Spring and political movements transnationally, little attention has been given to the gendered significance of technology. Cyberspace can allow young feminists and queers the tools of not only organizing political protests but staging gendered dissent through the creation of online counter-publics that allow for a reimagining of gender outside of material bodies and all the histories of nationalism and violence that haunt the lived spaces of an Indian city. Arjun Appadurai discusses his concept of *mediascapes*, which he suggests offers scripts through which realities can be formed and reformed. Appadurai argues that mediascapes are "image-centred, narrative-based accounts of strips of reality" (Appadurai 295). Apparduai further writes of the use of the mediascape to construct a narrative script of one's life as well as the lives of others who might live in distant locales (Appadurai). Mediascapes come to structure global politics, with political protests being staged as events that take on a narrative dimension. The scripting of stories such as the 2012 Delhi gang rape as a saleable narrative that one can enter into at a distance bridges the geographical, linguistic, and cultural distance between places and people. Again, the Arab Spring is perhaps the most obvious and spectacular example of how a place such as Egypt, which might be unfamiliar to those outside of the Middle East, can be narrativized for Western spectators, with the Arab Spring protests taking on global significance. The beauty of these translations lies in how the discrete political turmoil of nations becomes matters of global importance in ways that might put pressure on national leaders, opening governmental regimes to forms of global "public judgment" in Badiou's sense of the political discussed in the introductory chapter (Badiou *Metapolitics*). However, the trouble with this scripting of the political as a saleable story lies in the overarching global capitalist machinery that turns tragedy into commodity. Furthermore, stories end.

The danger of a globalized media that turns ongoing anticolonial and postcolonial struggles regarding sexual politics into fantastical stories is the temporal dimension of these narratives. When narrated through the frames of a rapid-fire global media the case of the Delhi gang rape and subsequent protests can be told as a story that begins in December of 2012 and ends within a span of months. The world's cameras can turn to a different tragedy, leaving ongoing questions of gender justice within India behind. One can perhaps ask how the rapid ways in which news stories are narrated and disseminated through Internet-based mediums might support Slavoj Žižek's writings on the sos panics of objective violence that are turned into grandiose, and temporally limited spectacles on the world stage. Žižek discusses a 2006 issue of *Time Magazine* that featured a story regarding the ongoing political strife and violence in the Democratic Republic of the Congo. The story recounted how approximately four million people died there as part of a decade of political violence. Žižek writes that "None of the usual humanitarian uproar followed, just a couple of reader's letters—as if some kind of filtering mechanism blocked this news from achieving its full impact in our symbolic space" (Žižek *Violence* 3). He goes on to write that; "To put it cynically, *Time* picked the wrong victim in the struggle for hegemony in suffering. It should have stuck to the list of usual suspects: Muslim women and their plight or the families of 9/11 victims and how they have coped with their losses" (Žižek *Violence* 3). Žižek discusses this as an example of how humanitarian panics are overdetermined by political considerations. In this regard, it could be asked how the spectacle of the 2012 Delhi gang rape case emerged through a pre-existing structure of global political coordinates. While Western capitalist interests in India are growing the residues of colonial discourses in which India is imagined as "savage" in gendered and sexual terms informs the will to focus on certain political narratives. The seemingly humanitarian concern for "women in India" often focuses on gender-based violence as symptomatic of cultural failing, rather than questioning how violence is enabled in a neoliberal India in which the coveting of foreign finance is privileged by state actors while working people's ability to move freely in public space is threatened. The same Western spectators who may express shock and horror regarding cases such as the Delhi gang rape case may also benefit from the violence of outsourced neoliberal economies such as call centres and Western multinational corporate sweatshops. The Western spectator may not feel implicated within a global economic order in which deaths in impoverished places correspond to the privileged lives of those in affluent Western nations. A further question can be posed regarding how the Internet and technologically driven cultures of spectacle not only change how news is reported but how news itself is made and unmade. The spectacles of Indian female suffering and the spectacles of revolt that defined the 2012 Delhi gang rape case and appeared on Internet screens worldwide can function as saleable neoliberal spectacle. One can ask how the images that circulated during and after the Arab Spring protests of 2010 set the stage for the glorification of images of young people in the Global South engaged in protest. One can further ask how images of Indian women as consummate victims, often found throughout colonial history, now appear in media spectacles of women in the Indian subcontinent as perpetual children "born into brothels."[1] Such Orientalist imagery could also explain the high levels of attention that cases of extreme gender-based violence in India garner globally in times of image-driven narratives powered by online media.

When Žižek suggests that "there is something inherently mystifying" (Žižek *Violence* 3) in forms of imagined direct contact with violence, one can ask how contemporary cultures of the Internet, in which the visual spectacle of suffering and revolt can be selectively and rapidly disseminated, might act as a medium through which such processes of mystification become the norm. He writes that "the overpowering horror of violent acts and empathy with the victims inexorably function as a lure which prevents us from thinking" (Žižek *Violence* 3). This inability to think about one's implication in the global structures of capitalism, which produce commonplace death among poor women in poor places, can within a time of rapid speech and ideas lead in the most obscene and banal ways to the twitter missionary fantasies of the Lindsay Lohans of the world. Furthermore, through the mass dissemination of certain narratives and images through Internet-based mediums, online media might prevent the public from questioning why certain cases of violence garner more attention and empathy than others.

MEMORABLE TWEETS AND FORGOTTEN RELIGIOUS RIOTS: THE BRANDING OF NARENDRA MODI AND THE BJP THROUGH TECHNOLOGY

While this chapter discusses the use of Internet technology within grassroots resistance movements in contemporary India, with a focus on political struggles pertaining to gender and sexuality, the Internet also allows conservative political leaders to use the high-speed nature of the technological moment to brand themselves as gentile figures, creating historical amnesia among many. Joyojeet Pal discusses the use of Internet-based technologies in the election campaign of right-wing Hindu nationalist Narendra Modi. Pal argues that one of the means through which Modi is able to gain a wide following in contemporary India is through his careful and strategic use of social media, including Twitter, Facebook, Pinterest, YouTube, and other Internet-based mediums. Like much of Modi's campaign, his online persona and use of social media are reflective of his paradoxical discourse of Hindu conservatism and simultaneous support of neoliberal capitalism. I discuss these paradoxes in greater detail in the final chapter of this book, regarding new Hindu masculinities in India and Modi's shocking election victory to the position of prime minister. Although Modi and the Hindu right-wing party The Bharatiya Janata Party (BJP) rose to national power, it is important to point out that at the time of writing, the Aam Aadmi Party (AAP) party, led by Arvind Kerjiwel, won the state elections in Delhi through a platform based on "anti-corruption." Election coverage also documented how the Delhi gang rape protests and the promises made by the party regarding proposed programs to support feminist movements also informed the AAP victory (Saxena). Following the elections, the Internet continued to function as a space of political fantasy. As Journalists reported, "The landslide victory of AAP in Delhi on Tuesday sent netizens into a frenzy as they flooded social networking sites with messages congratulating Arvind Kejriwal and his party" ("Internet Goes into Frenzy"). While celebratory messages can be rapidly posted online to connote political change, just as Lindsay Lohan purported to end child poverty over Twitter, what this election will mean for Delhi in the long term is perhaps beyond the high-speed temporalities of e-motions. What is of interest is questioning how the relationship between politics and Internet-based technology unfolds within a country in which the majority of the population is under the age of thirty-five. With cities being particularly populated by younger generations, the Internet can be used to simultaneously create and erase political history. Modi has faced a great deal of backlash from the international community because of his role in the Gujarat riots and his long history of attacks on religious freedom and the persecution of various minorities. However within a time of rapid speed media in which today's tweet is forgotten within minutes and hours—he has been able to construct a new, gentle political image. As Pal writes of Modi's online persona,

> The gentle tenor of his twitter banalities on global events, carefully crafted and global public thank you notes, and consistent reinforcement of national development themes suggest no shadow of a man who was once rejected by the international community and was banned from entering the U.S. for gross violations of religious freedom. (Pal 378)

Just as Lindsay Lohan used her twitter account to create a political fiction regarding her presence in India, so too can Modi become a fictionalized online celebrity who uses Internet-based technologies to create a highly stylized identity. The textual renderings of words on screens can be divorced from material bodies. The bodies of Western celebrities such as Lindsay Lohan, tweeting from North America or Europe, are far removed from the children in the Global South that they purport to "save," just as the bodies of Hindu fundamentalists now creating new friendly Internet personas are far removed from the bloody corpses of Muslims and other oppressed people in the subcontinent that they enact violence against. Pal further suggests that the Internet generation in India, often understanding politics only through contemporary high-speed media, apprehend Modi through only social media, allowing for a one-dimensional portrayal divorced from histories of oppressive conservatism. As Pal states,

> The younger demographic of Twitter users in India are from a generation that has grown up with little memory of the riots of 2002—the enduring memory of Modi for them will be the political maverick who talks directly to the people. (Pal 387)

Lindsay Lohan fans can forget her delusional missionary tweets as quickly as they can be removed from her twitter account. Similarly, those who support the "new" online Modi are invited into a world of political amnesia, with carefully crafted slogans and slick images appearing much faster than the scars of religious violence will ever heal.

"GENDERSCAPES": FROM "PURITY" TO GRINDR

Although political leaders and celebrities use the Internet to produce stylized fictions to support their brand image, it is important to pay attention to how people use Internet-based technologies to performatively enact gender and sexuality in subversive ways. For example, it is important to consider the role of the Internet in sexual politics in contemporary urban India. Janina Geist draws on Apparduai's writings coupled with ethnographic research done in India to document uses of technology by queer communities in Delhi. Geist uses the term *gender-scapes* to, "comprehend the imagined worlds of various heterogeneous queer spaces and to assert the allocation of gender/sexuality forms in fields of assymetrical power" (Geist 85).

Geist suggests that queer counter-publics in urban Indian cities should be thought of in relation to a wider public sphere of heteronormativity, homophobia, and gender-based violence that often disciplines queer bodies explicitly through brute force and implicitly through ideological silencing.

From her detailed ethnography with queer communities in Delhi, Geist argues that Internet sites such as Facebook and other online dating sites are crucial in offering a space for the articulation of queer desire, non-traditional femininities and masculinities, and queer politics. Geist writes that "Since the 1990s, mobile phones, audio visual media, and cyberspace emerged as new spaces enabling an explosion of sexual desires in Delhi by facilitating easier direct communication" (Geist 85). Geist also suggests that queer spaces— particularly in the context of India where the political and societal landscape often shifts and changes rapidly because of changes brought about by national politics, globalization, and urbanization—should be read as transitory. She states that queer space is always contested space that has to be negotiated and is often violently policed by heteronormativity at the level of both law and social norms (Geist).

The decision made by the Supreme Court of India in 2013 to uphold Section 377 offers evidence of the shifting political landscape that make queer spaces unstable. As I will develop in greater detail, it is important to move away from a usual Western-centric analysis of globalization, which suggests that transnational flows of media begin in the West and then spread to the Global South. Sean Chabot and Jan Willem Duyvendak state that within literatures on globalization and transnational flows of culture there is an "assumption that today's turbulent world basically emanates from developments in Europe, the U.S. and other Western democracies" (Chabot and Duyvendak 297). They go on to suggest that while authors differ in their writings regarding the effects of globalization, there seems to be a unified understanding of the temporal origins of transnational flows of media, labour, and ideologies pertaining to social movements that are thought to originate in the West and then spread to the Global South. As I will discuss in relation to both feminist and the queer movements in India, the flow of ideas, cybercultures, and forms of political dissent cannot be read as moving from the West to the rest, as is often thought. The massive amount of Internet users in India coupled with the size of the Indian population and the large youth demographic, with the majority of the Indian population being under the age of thirty-five, can cause sexual and gender-based struggles to begin in the subcontinent and then spread to the West. One could clearly see this in the Delhi gang rape protests of 2012 that began in Delhi and garnered global attention, generating debates regarding gender justice, protests of solidarity, and media coverage throughout the world. Losh notes that Twitter users throughout the world used online mediums to engage in gender-based politics and to memorialize Jyoti.[2] Similarly, protests in Delhi against the criminalization of same-sex desire in 2013 gave way to subsequent global days of rage, with the Internet being the medium through which protestors in the West and Europe garnered information about the issue and subsequently organized protests of solidarity using social media. Owing to a wired Indian media, an increasingly urban country, and a large population of Internet-savvy young people, local-ized political struggles in India spread to Europe and the West. Much like the example of the Arab Spring, which had people in Europe and North America glued to Twitter and online media, the sexual politics of India are not globalized appropriations of Western struggles but are themselves global.

Increasingly, due to the proliferation of the IT sector in Indian cities and the many Indians who are being recruited by IT firms throughout the world, a certain segment of urban India is at the centre of cybercul-ture. While feminists and queer theorists often discuss cyberfeminism and queer online cultures from a Eurocentric perspective, one can ask how Internet-based feminism and queer politics in India are not novel Western ideas but are part of the technologically driven, youth-oriented culture of contemporary urban India. Chabot and Duyvendak discuss the culturally chauvinist and essentialist discourse that often informs writings regarding globalization, which suggest that ideologies and tools of "freedom" and political dissent originate in the West and are then outsourced to countries in the Global South, such as India. They instead suggest that a reciprocal flow of ideas exists between coun-tries transnationally through transnational labour, technologies, and transnational mobility (Chabot and Duyvendak). I want to suggest that this transnational flow is deeply relevant to cyberfeminism and online queer life worlds and protest cultures in India, where there is no clear origin where ideas about protest tools and Internet-based feminisms begin. Uses of the Internet in political struggles pertaining to gender and sexuality in India are diverse in their referencing of traditions of gender, sexuality, and political dissent that predate feminism, queer movements, and leftist struggles in much of North America and Europe. Simultaneously, the increasingly mobile Desi population, the influx of many IT labourers to the Indian subcontinent from throughout Asia, the Middle East, and other parts of the Global South as well as the spread of global media online should be seen as informing cyberpolitics in urban India.

Geist discusses the use of cyberspace by queers in Delhi as serving two interrelated functions: the expression of non-normative gendered and sexual performatives online and the creation of networks that lead to public meetings of queers in city space. As Geist suggests, "Queer online spaces can be mapped as a vast, heterogeneous conglomeration of cyber sites which impacts into social offline worlds of actors" (Geist 86). It is important to ask how the December 2013 protests against Section 377 were enabled through the existence of queer cybercultures, which provide psychic and social support for the vitality of queer lives and facilitate meetings, panel discussions, and public protests. The gap between the spectral and the material in uses of the Internet can obviously be critiqued. However, it is precisely because of this gap between the material body in the streets and its scripting within mainstream mediascapes through reductive narratives of gender and sexuality that that the Internet acts as a site of radical desire and dissent. Outside of the heteronormative, transphobic, and often sexist discourses within mainstream news media, cultures of mainstream Bollywood film and television, queer cyber counter-publics emerge online to challenge the discursive construction of the gendered body as one held in place through trite, colonial narratives. Consider for example, a recent online video for a clothing company in India titled "The Visit" which received millions of views online and depicts a lesbian couple who are preparing to meet one of the woman's parents. While this advertising campaign is a means of selling products that are undoubtedly implicated in neo-liberal ideas of "freedom," as the freedom to buy, this overt depiction of queer desire happens in the context of statewide criminalization through the enforcement of Section 377 of the Indian Penal Code. Cyber-lifeworlds can offer images of desire that are violently policed in the material world (Inani). Geist also discusses uses of social media and dating sites by queers in Delhi who often use the Internet to post photos in drag or to defy masculine-feminine binaries in other aestheticized ways. The author subsequently discusses how the Internet allows for articulations of sexual desire that would often have no place for articulation within the real time of the Indian city or the familial home. The use of genderscapes as fantasy spaces to creatively refashion gender and sexual identity and desire in India cannot be divorced from a broader politicized queer movement. It is precisely through the freedom and support that many queer people in India gain from cyberspace that offers potential for a politicization of sexuality in the public sphere. As with the Azaad Bazaar example discussed in the introductory chapter of this book, the Internet allows for public shows of support for groups of people who live in isolated and disparate contexts throughout the Indian subcontinent. Geist states that within the context of an India steeped in heteronormative thinking and compulsory heterosexuality, "Cyberspace ... provides an incentive for LGBTQs to create spaces exclusively for themselves" (Geist 89). Geist discusses online spaces as those of solidarity that are particularly important in sprawling cities such as Delhi,

> LGBTQ social circles are highly fragmented. Since social meetings happened mostly in private houses, access to such publically less visible spaces is highly restricted depending e.g on friendship ties, empathy, class, age, and gender expression. (Geist 89)

The glaring point of critique that can be made in Geist's analysis of Internet usage among queers in India is that of class. Middle-class urban queers often access queer cybercounter-publics, while lower income and rural people can be implicitly barred from full inclusion into the genderscapes of urban India. However, Geist also suggests that lower-income queers—in cities such as Delhi where pirated technologies are increasingly made financially accessible—are also able to access some aspects of queer Internet counter-publics. The use of social media, blogs, online news articles, YouTube videos, and queer listservs are integral to both organizing public protests throughout India and in garnering international support (Geist). The gap between the virtual and the real within queer cultures and politics is necessarily blurred at the level of both reimagining femininity and masculinity online and reimagining the entitlements of citizens.

FROM GAYSIA TO ĀZĀDĪ: DECENTRING "THE WEST" ONLINE

Just as the refrain "Āzādī" heard in contemporary sexual political struggles in India cannot be divorced from globalized political cultures within a time of technology that crosses borders, I also want to suggest that the Internet worlds of queer and feminist India cannot be read as mimicking or deriving from Western space or time. While Eurocentric neoliberal discourse constructs India as "lagging behind" the "Legalize Gay" branding of the West, cybercultures of sexual politics in the region gesture to a much more complex mapping of both temporality and geography[3] (Butler). Much of the queer cyberworld in contemporary India is tied to a pan-Asian queer community, with ideas, images, and information being disseminated from countries such as Thailand, Singapore, and China. One can also consider that the refrain of "Āzādī" and Queer Āzādī campaigns speak to a lineage that moves outside of Eurocentric and Western-centred temporality and geography. Given the great deal of Internet-based production and usage within cities throughout Asia, is interesting to question how sexual movements throughout Asia might be informed by dialogues that rupture a Western-centric understanding of sexual politics. Queer and feminist movements in Asia might affect each other, speak in languages, and make reference to political histories outside of the purview of western temporalities[4] (Callan). For example, following the Delhi gang rape case of 2012, protests regarding gender-based violence were held in several Asian countries. Feminists and activists in places such as Cambodia, where high rates of gang rape occur, used this moment to garner inspiration from Delhi-based feminists often through online cyberfeminist networks. Asian feminists used the global media coverage garnered by the Delhi gang rape protests to also gain media attention regarding similar patterns of group violence against women in their countries of residence. Similarly, the relatively open queer cultures that exist in Thailand and Singapore can be accessed online by queer Indians, and many queer activists in the region draw on examples from other parts of Asia and the Global South to garner inspiration for political protest and legal and constitutional accountability.

The rise of online leftist, feminist, queer, and activist countercultures globally has led to the creation of new forms of organizing and the creation of transnational networks. The daily political gestures that happen in the performative utterances of queers online can also bleed into the streets, where social networks are used to mobilize queers and allies to stage public forms of protest. Cultures of cyberspace allow for a vitality of emerging movements regarding sexual politics in India. Cyberspace can also enable certain lives and desires to be actualized both in the genderscapes of online imaginaries and in the real time of queer and feminist meetings and encounters that begin online. Worlds of social media that cross borders and encompass transnational networks can and do permeate social spaces in the material worlds of the urban polis. Geist suggests that "The concept of 'genderscapes' provides...an understanding of how gender categories are grounded by and at the same time fluid in everyday life" (Geist 85). The fluidity of online space can translate into the creation of spaces of protest that support gender transgressions in public spaces in the real time of the Indian polis. These online genderscapes can be used to not only unsettle the surety of gender and sexual identity but to challenge state structure.

The remarks made by political leaders, judges, and others, who represent the face of power in India, regarding both queers and women in 2012 and 2013 gestures to very different imaginings of gender and sexuality in the subcontinent. The majority of people in India are under the age of thirty-five and have increasingly been raised in cities with access to Internet-based mediums, which present a whole host of images of women and queers. However, due to political decisions such as the criminalizing of diverse sexualities using Section 377 and religious conservatism, these lives and desires are often erased within the mainstream public imaginary, which might correspond to the privatization of queer and feminist communities online. The ironies of the disjuncture between digital citizens and state power are also expressed in examples of political movements such as Slutwalk 2010, which began when a Toronto police officer publically stated that rape could be prevented if women did not "not dress like sluts" (Teekah, Scholz, Friedman and O'Reilly). The Internet was used to generate a global protest movement, termed Slutwalk, against gender-based violence. As with the 2012 Delhi gang rape protests and those following the 2013 decision by the Supreme Court of India to criminalize same-sex desire, the gap between the sensibilities of this generation of feminists and queers and those in positions of state power also expresses a corresponding gap that lies between state ideology and public sensibility. The Internet can offer women and queers images, discourses, and communities of support, struggle, and survival. However, it seems to not touch the wider spheres of state and political power, often governed by those who do not reflect the interests of the majority.

GOOGLE "JUSTICE"? E-GOVERNANCE AND SEXUAL POLITICS

As I will discuss in the second section of this work, drawing on interviews done following the Delhi gang rape protests of 2012 and the protests concerning Section 377 in 2013, the Internet has provided a source of vitality for both feminist and queer activism, communities, and lives particularly among urban middle classes. However, there is a disjuncture that emerges between the uses of the Internet to create solidarity among young people, feminists, queers, and left-wing activists who are engaged in struggles regarding sexual politics and the uses of the Internet by the state, the law, and governance, which often seem a world away from these cyber-lifeworlds. As one young woman whom I spoke with and who was involved in the 2012 Delhi gang rape protests states, "The Internet, the media and all the tweeting made me feel better about the whole case and it helped spread the word about things. But when it comes to what they decide about police and laws, it's not like it's decided on Facebook" (Atluri Personal interview). Researchers suggest that India is in fact heavily promoting what is termed "e-governance" through the creation of governmental websites and modes of governance that utilize Internet technologies. However, Haque notes that within India, the realities of poverty make the use of models of e-governance different than those that exist in European and North American countries. India's massive divisions in class between the rich and poor threaten to create Internet-based political cultures that will further erase, obscure, and make a large segment of the population invisible. Haque goes on to discuss e-governance in relation to the startling gap between the rich and poor within India:

India is one of the poorest countries in the world with severe problems of poverty, inequality, illiteracy, and external dependence, which represent major impediments to the effectiveness of e-governance in ensuring equal public access to state institutions, empowering ordinary citizens to exercise their basic rights and obliging political and administrative officials to be responsive and accountable. (Haque 232)

While young urban largely middle-class and Internet-savvy feminists and queers have access to the Internet in the forms of social media and blogs, larger processes of state governance are often informed by colonial history. Colonial history haunts contemporary India through lingering caste- and class-based divides between the rich and the poor, growing urbanization that has magnified poverty in rural areas, and in rulings such as the Supreme Court of India's decision regarding Section 377 of the Indian Penal Code. Norris suggests that in evaluating the use of e-governance, the key issue lies in how it might affect "the nature of the relationship between political institutions, bureaucracies and citizens, and whether it facilitates a relationship of accountability and participation" (Norris qtd. in Haque 237).

While many discuss the importance of the Internet in the life worlds of queer people in urban India, these online counter-publics do not seem to effect decisions at the level of law. Norris, Haque, and others discuss the use of e-governance by all major political parties in India as a means of branding themselves as saleable celebrities to win votes. However there is little evidence to suggest that the Internet makes these parties more accountable to their constituency or less economically and politically corrupt. In this regard, I want to suggest that two broad issues (among others) arise in relation to cyberspace, politics, and sexuality-gender in contemporary India. The first is the stark reality of poverty documented by many researchers. Haque concludes that,

> One needs to understand that after two decades of e-commerce, e-governance, and the e-citizen, India remains one of the poorest countries in the world with a 44.3% adult literacy rate, 25% of people living below the poverty line, $100 billion external debt and a 128th ranking in the recent Human Development Index. (247)

Women remain the poorest of the poor in India. Issues such as gender violence, female unemployment, and women's lack of access to basic healthcare can be thought of in relation to a broader problem of poverty in the country, which often overshadows changing gendered

ideologies and the rise of cyberfeminism largely among the urban
middle class. The other issue of relevance to Internet and sexual politics
is the legal system of the country, in which laws regarding sexuality,
desire, and gender-based violence derive from colonial rule. While the
imaginative ways that young feminist, queers, and urban people often
draw on the Internet to create politicized lifeworlds may allow for a
changing consciousness and habitus[5] among individual Internet users,
the broader economic realities of India make gender and sexual equality
in the age of the Internet an often privatized performance enacted by
the privileged few (Bourdieu). Internet "democracy" does not often
affect uses of colonial law and neoliberal models of financial growth. I
want to suggest, however, drawing on the example of the Delhi gang
rape case of 2012, that the use of the Internet as a tool to support public
protests and to shame the state might serve to increasingly bring often
silently accepted gender-based oppressions in India into the public
realm. While the protests of December 2012 following the gang rape
and murder of Jyoti and the protests following the 2013 Supreme Court
decision regarding Section 377 may not touch broader issues of severe
poverty, they do point to the use of online media to challenge the state.
Yet as I discuss in relation to the lack of spectacle surrounding some
deaths, namely those of rural farmers, what emerges in the common
sense rhetoric of Internet temporality are brutal realities regarding those
whose lives and deaths are counted as grievable spectacles and those
who become murderously invisible.

DIGITAL DIVIDES AND DIGITAL DEATHS:
URBANIZATION AND THE UNGRIEVABLE, UNTWEETABLE LIFE

Following the anniversary of the Delhi gang rape protests, I watched
as farmers from rural India marched through Delhi to demand that the
government confront an ongoing agricultural crisis, which has arguably
resulted in the largest case of mass suicide in human history, with
Indian farmers committing suicide en mass because of the failed green
revolution and an inability to sustain themselves in a globalized and
increasingly urban country. Yet, these protests in many ways remained
more fictional than Lindsay Lohan's ambitious tweets. The panorama
of Internet-based lives produce a situation of deep political paradox
in which the very coordinates of global capitalism that structure the

digital divide give global vitality to certain moments of protest while also scripting the deaths of others by virtue of a virtual silence. The digital divide, which increasingly separates urban from rural India, is also a divide that not only structures who lives and who dies but whose lives and deaths matter in the national and global imaginary. There was an old refrain throughout the Indian subcontinent in which it was once said that "India lives in her villages." To this, author and activist Arundhati Roy responded, "India doesn't live in her villages. India dies in her villages" (Roy). In their report *Every Thirty Minutes*, the Center for Human Rights and Global Justice at New York University Law School reports that a farmer in India commits suicide every thirty minutes owing to the failed green revolution and a swift move from rural subsistence-based economies to urban industrialization (CHRGJ "Every Thirty Minutes"). The obscene spectacles of gender-based violence that defined the 2012 Delhi gang rape case can be thought of in relation to these less spectacular and yet more consistently macabre deaths. Vandana Shiva has made connections between the Delhi gang rape case and wider processes of neoliberal globalization. Shiva states,

> While we intensify our struggle for justice for women, we need to also ask why rape cases have increased 240 percent since the 1990's when the new economic policies were introduced. Could there be a connection between the growth of violent, undemocratically imposed, unfair economic policies and the intensification and brutality of crimes against women?

The spectacle of gender-based violence can promote a titillating humanitarian gaze that allows apolitical audiences to feel an Orientalist pity towards the long-suffering Indian woman while feeling no implication in wider systems of neoliberal capitalism that produce displaced and disposable bodies within the Indian subcontinent.[6]

ENJOY TRAGEDY!
VIEWING PUBLICS, VIOLENCE, AND THE GLOBAL SOUTH

Slavoj Žižek has discussed the true fear of cyberspace as lying not in the usual paranoia that one is being spied on but in the fear that one is not being watched at all (*The Plague of Fantasies* 127). In a time in which celebrity, identity, and subjectivity are blurred, it is as though an online existence is needed to exist. The bodily, emotive, and economic violence done to those who are working in exploitative conditions in the Indian subcontinent is less important within a time of mass spectacle than the translatable tale told by a celebrity in less than 140 characters over Twitter. However, as evinced by the Arab Spring protests and the protests following the Delhi gang rape and murder, the translation of bodily violence into globalized media narrative also serves to turn local politics into global spectacle in ways that might pressure national governments to take feminism and sexual politics seriously. Whether or not Lindsay Lohan was in India to "save the children," or whether or not Internet spectators could find Jantar Mantar or Tahir Square on a map seems less important than considering the paradoxes and possibilities of political change in the Global South in a time when what was once distant, foreign, and out of reach becomes a spectacular political presence that crosses borders and reverberates globally through Internet wires. Had the world's eyes not been on India in December 2012, the murder of Jyoti and subsequent protests may not have caused such a strong reaction from the Indian state and there may not have been as much pressure on national leaders to change rape law and address sexual- and gender-based violence. However, the temporal dimensions of media narratives of tragedy not only fail to capture the magnitude of loss and problems of governance within the Indian subcontinent it might also lull spectators into understanding politics in ways that are similar to fictionalized media. The ongoing systemic failure of the Indian state to offer meaningful forms of justice in cases of gender-based violence is as quickly forgotten as yesterday's twitter controversy or last week's celebrity scandal.

Just as Lohan's efforts to "save the children" are contained within a temporal framework that finishes as quickly as a pop song, the Delhi gang rape case risks becoming a media-saturated event that garners an immediate and unsustained reaction that does little to address broader systemic problems regarding gender-based violence and governance in the subcontinent. The "story" of gender-based violence, misogyny, and state failure, one as old and complex as the subcontinent itself, can be told as one that begins in December of 2012 and ends with minor changes in law. Yet, I want to suggest that how the media functions within India and globally might be, in fact, more complex and give way to new forms of sexual politics precisely because of the Internet.

BOLLYWOOD OR BUST:
INDIA IN THE WORLD, THE WORLD IN INDIA

Drawing on the work of Apparduai, I believe that the idea of the imagination is central to discussing the role that media plays in structuring global spectacles of politics. Appadurai suggests that the imagination should be seen as "a social practice," and he highlights the relationship between the image, the imagined, and the imaginary. The inculcation of the Indian subcontinent into the time and grammars of Internet-based technologies creates a space in which political characters are created through the limited characters of online mediums such as Twitter. While Narendra Modi and Lindsay Lohan use imagination as a social practice through performing fictionalized political personas online— quite separate from material realities of affluent Western privilege and conservative political violence—the Internet is also used by activists to challenge orientalist images of India and the Indian woman in the global imaginary. It is in this connection between images, imaginations of viewers, and the imaginary of various life worlds that the complexities of media narratives such as the Delhi gang rape case reveal themselves. The beauty of Appadurai's thought is that images and imaginaries are not written of as the monopoly of one set of producers or users. Within an Internet-driven era in which narratives can be and are told through a variety of mediums, the Indian public, protestors, and activists, defying the authoritative voice of corporate media, also produce their own images and draw on their own imaginative tools. For example, the image of protest for those within India and those interested in gender justice in India is used to reimagine gender and sexuality within the region.[7] In the case of the Delhi gang rape protests, the transnational political imagination allowed viewers and Internet users to feel that they had participated politically by consuming and distributing narratives of protest online. One also saw how individual agency in the form of Internet-based mediums used by protestors in India engendered the possibility of a global movement for gender justice. Yet the image of gender-based violence in India is troubled by histories of colonialism that haunt sexual politics. The image of the politically naïve and patriarchally dominated brown woman has been one that has historically served imperialist interests and continues to inform mainstream Western-feminist discourse and international development rhetoric. Similarly, images of brutalized Muslim women have been a defining feature of the global "war on terror" with an imagined victimized Muslim woman being conjured up to generate fantasies of white missionary salvation and politically righteous intervention that mask economic and oil interests (Spivak; Ansari; Puar). The play of images that globalization generates cannot be divorced from a history of imperialist image production.

WOULD RUDYARD KIPLING TWEET THIS?
WHITE MEN's BURDENS AND BROAD BANDS

The spectacle of bodies on screens has become a common feature of global political life. The iterative power of images used throughout colonial history to fuel racist discourse cannot be divorced from contemporary global spectacles of brown bodies. Image production within advertising, science, news media, and political propaganda was always a component of the production and dissemination of colonial discourse[8] (McClintock 207-231). The image of the brown body that pops up through Internet screens cannot be divorced from those that have surfaced and resurfaced historically. In his groundbreaking text *Orientalism,* Said draws on the writing of French poet Flaubert and his relationship with Kuchuk Hanem, an Egyptian courtesan to discuss the pattern between the imagined East and West as a relationship of patriarchal domination. Said suggests that Flaubert had authorial power over Hanem whom he spoke on behalf of, often constructing her in derogatory ways in Orientalist travel narratives. Said suggests that the relationship between Flaubert and Hanem is a microcosm for a broader colonial relationship between occident and Orient. He writes that the relationship "stands for the pattern of relative strength between East and West, and the discourse about the Orient that it enabled" (Said 6). While Said was writing about imperialist writers and contexts of colonial domination, the overarching point regarding gendered and colonial representation still has resonance in regards to contemporary narratives of the imagined "Orient" and "Oriental woman." However, this Orientalist dynamic of the weak, silent, passive Eastern woman is increasingly challenged by images and stories of revolt and protest such as narratives regarding the 2012 Delhi gang rape case. Internet-based technologies can be used to subvert Orientalist narratives and highlight the tremendous political will of many feminists within postcolonial nations such as India. While the "typical" Oriental woman is scripted as being dominated by men and is stripped of sexual desire within essentialist narratives of culture and religion, the terms through which these representations of people in the Global South are made possible has changed a great deal within the digital age. The spectacle of the Arab Spring protests points to the creation of counter-discourses of Orientalist image production. The images of people, many of them young women, protesting in the streets of Egypt challenges the history of Orientalist representations of "the east" as politically immature and passive. Consider for example the many images and narratives disseminated online of young women in Egypt who were represented as being leaders within the Arab Spring protests (Newsom and Lengel). The rise of the Internet-based commons and online tools of political dissent are not evidence of ostensible Western progress but instead are part of a larger genealogy of anticolonial resistance.

Following the Arab Spring, Hardt and Negri referred to Egyptian protestors as "the new pioneers," drawing on a language of Eurocentric conceptions of the figure of "the citizen" (Hardt and Negri). While the construction of those who were part of the Arab Spring demonstrations as inspirational political actors can be read as an expression of solidarity, the use of terms such as "pioneers" evoked colonial metaphors to describe those in non Western contexts as being part of white setter genealogies. Many scholarly and news narratives regarding the "awakening" of Arabs eluded to those in the imagined Orient as emerging from a political slumber that does a deep injustice to ongoing histories of revolt that pre-date European colonialism and struggles against the ongoing violence of imperial power. Rather than seeing the young protestors in the so-called Orient as having "awakened" supposedly "unenlightened" political cultures, the haunting residues of empire continue to be felt and fought against with the Internet acting as a new tool of dissent. In the 2012 Delhi gang rape protests, the Internet was also used to express dissent against colonial laws and moralities. The Internet became one of the means to organize protests to challenge the haunting truth of gendered and sexual power that often disciplines bodies in public spaces, to the point of death. If as Gordan suggests, haunting is also an affective state that gestures towards a futurity, a "something to be done" (Gordan "Some Thoughts on *Haunting* and *Futurity*") then protestors globally can be seen as using the tools of cyberspace to occupy the commons. In these acts of defiance, postcolonial political actors gesture towards a future sexual politics not contained by gendered colonial ideology, law, and moralities.

The mass circulation of photos of tortured Arab prisoners at the Abu Ghraib prison in Iraq and other productions of gender-based images of violence against feminized brown bodies in the Global South plays a role in both gender-based violence and contemporary Orientalism. While such imagery purports to document violence, it can lend itself to a fetishistic gaze that garners its force from colonial ideology (Atluri, "Is Torture Part of Your Social Network?"). Imagining women in India to be brutalized by Indian men because of assumed cultural inferiority gives force to old colonial scripts that leave spectators feeling unimplicated and redeemed in the assumed superiority of mainstream Western capitalist life worlds. In *Society of the Spectacle*, Guy Debord comments that "The spectacle is not a collection of images; rather it is a social relationship between people that is mediated by images" (Debord 4). The social relationships that are formed through spectacles of protest in the Global South are complex and contentious issues that Debord, writing in 1960s Europe, could not predict. Today, the social of social media cuts across borders, language, and radically different material spaces and life worlds. The danger within a time of mass-produced and mass-circulated spectacle lies in how images of protest, and specifically protests concerning gender-based violence in India, can mediate relations between North and South in ways that reassert colonial ideologies.

While Internet-based media tools such as Twitter disseminate colonial tales of bourgeois missionary salvation, as in the case of the aforementioned Lindsay Lohan, social media is also increasingly employed by those within the Global South as a means of not only organizing protest but of authorizing narratives of dissent (Thörn). An Internet-savvy population within Delhi and throughout India is capable of using mass media as a tool of dissent to express alternative genealogies of the Indian subcontinent within the political imaginary. This re-signification of India in the global imaginary has particular implications for sexual politics. Barn writes that

What has been striking about the Indian protests is that while they were led by both young men and women, who were educated, urban and middle class, they reached out and connected with others from a diverse range of backgrounds throughout Indian society. It is evident that India as a country is witnessing a significant technological revolution. It is estimated that the number of broadband connections in India is more than twice the size of the British general population. And there are 65 million Facebook users and an estimated 35 million Twitter accounts (Barn).

Barn also points to the generational gap previously discussed in this chapter between the Indian public and those in political power. The nature of contemporary mass media and its ability to be used by a politically astute public challenges a fetishistic colonial gaze through narratives of resistance that counter discourses of pity. The problem of "protest porn", which glorifies the suffering and assumed barbarism of patriarchal culture in India, is actively interrupted by political uses of new digital media technologies by many within the Indian subcontinent.

"BECAUSE IT HAPPENED OVERSEAS": POSTCOLONIAL HISTORY AND HIGH-SPEED (DIS)CONNECTION

In *Location of Culture*, Homi K. Bhabha quotes Salman's Rushdie's *The Satanic Verses*. Bhabha writes,

The Western metropole must confront its postcolonial history, told by its native narrative internal to its national identity; and the reason for this is made clear in the stammering, drunken words of Mr. "Whisky" Sisodia from *The Satanic Verses:* "The trouble with the Engenglish is that their hiss hiss history happened overseas, so they dodo don't know what it means." (9)

I want to consider Bhabha's reading of Rushdie and Sisodia's words in reference to contemporary globalization and the geographical mappings of colony and metropole. The ability for Europe to narrate a linear story of temporal progress, civility, and rationality is possible because the darker side of histories of colonial violence happened elsewhere.

Contemporary globalization offers the ability for voices to enter from overseas through Internet wires. These unauthorized narratives articulated through globalized media trouble the ability for those in the so called "centre" to continue to deny their relationship to their former colonies. During campaigns to repeal section 377 of the Indian Penal Code, India's sodomy bill, many activists and allies within and from the Indian subcontinent pointed out that laws policing sexuality were a British import. Those writing in regards to the 2014 NASLA ruling to count Hijras as "third sex" citizens of India also make reference to the criminalization of Hijras as a ghostly remnant of British colonial law (Pandey). Similarly, following the Delhi gang rape case, journalists, activists and commentators challenged dominant discourses of Western superiority and Third World barbarism by suggesting that India's problems of poverty and poor governance, which also exacerbate gender-based violence, can be attributed to histories of colonialism. Many also suggest that the Orientalist fantasies tourists have of India, as a spiritual paradise of yoga tours and ethereal wisdoms, should be placed alongside stories such as the Delhi gang rape, which reveal the daily traumatic realities that define lives and deaths within formerly colonized countries (Atluri Personal interviews). One can consider the tourist branding of India through "Incredible India" campaigns that utilize Internet-based technologies to spread images and narratives of an India that is resplendent with new age wisdoms and beautiful exotic landscapes. This attempt to sell the nation to tourists often draws on Orientalist evocations of timeless beauty and spirituality at the same moment that growing protests against sexual violence and the criminalization of same sex desire occur in the Indian subcontinent (*Incredible India*).

It is important to question how an "India shining" rhetoric that has been celebrated within mainstream neoliberal capitalist discourse obscures the material and epistemic violence of globalization. Contemporary urban India is often praised as "progressing" in capitalist terms due to the rise of a multinational division of labour such as a boom in the IT sector. This supposed advancement now leads many in the Indian subcontinent to serve as cheap surplus labour for Western call centres and foreign businesses in ways that could be termed neocolonial exploitation. Journalists report the suicide of workers in China who labour to make iPads. Aside from pitiable shock stories, these narratives reflect a larger ideological gap between the assumed freedom of technology and the confined bodies of workers who are physically and psychically alienated to the point of death. Similarly, cases such as the 2012 Delhi gang rape and the 2013 criminalization of same-sex desire in India point to the material violence enacted against the body, which challenges narratives that equate globalization with betterment. The apparent freedom that exists within online worlds of labour meets the gross violence enacted onto bodies of caged workers and raped women within the material spaces of Asian cities (Bilton).

In using the Internet to elucidate the increased and persistent violence experienced by those in the Indian subcontinent, everyday people employ the tools that structure their oppression to articulate dissent. Bhabha and others have written lyrically and concisely regarding how the English language, a form of epistemic colonial violence, was adopted by Indians in subversive ways to support anticolonial and postcolonial political struggles. While the English language was an originary colonial wound, its words were used by Indian writers and scholars to repair some of the mistaken and misguided lies of Europe's forked tongue. With the rise of the IT generation, the tools of oppression that are employed by major multinationals to exploit IT-based labourers in the Global South are now being used by urban Indians in subversive ways.

CAN THE SUBALTERN TWEET?
CYBERFEMINIST TEXTUALITY-SEXUALITY

While contemporary consumer capitalism can lead to reductive biopolitical scriptings of gender, sex, and sexuality, new social movements use technology in radical ways to defy postfeminist consumerism, neoliberal technological labour exploitation, and nationalist branding.[10] Bhabha suggests that the relationship between textuality and sexuality is one that bares consideration. He writes,

> there is no knowledge—political or otherwise—outside representation ... the dynamics of writing and textuality require us to rethink the logics of causality and determinacy through which we recognize the 'political' as a form of calculation and strategic action dedicated to social transformation. (Bhabha 33)

The ability of text and image to cross borders can turn the discrete and localized pain done to a gendered body in the Global South into a transnational narrative that effects change. While the bodily and psychic violence of the 2012 Delhi gang rape case is beyond translation, the textual utterance of dissent forms a historical moment of political action in which the unauthorized online play of signification performed by an Internet-savvy public becomes part of postcolonial genealogies of protest. Those who use technology as a political tool, stage a mimicry of neocolonial capitalist grammars that makes a mockery of teleological narratives of western "progress." Cyberfeminists and queers in contemporary India employ technological tools to hold up a mirror to the scandals of the Indian state, the violent laws regarding sexual desire that originated with colonial rule, and the complicity of multinational corporations that do not offer bodily justice to workers. The unspeakable bodily violence and death of the gendered body in postcolonial space can be considered in relation to strategic uses of technology to articulate the gap between the textual and the sexual, as a space that sheds light on the breathtaking gaps between skin and screen, openings that necessitate political vitality.

WHEN THE WORLD HAS BEEN TURNED ON ITS HEAD:
HATE CRIMES IN A WORLD OF "LIKE" BUTTONS

In *The Society of Spectacle* Guy Debord suggests that "In a world that has really been turned on its head, truth is a moment of falsehood" (14). We can return to Lindsay Lohan. In a world in which speech, celebrity, politics, and action are conflated there is perhaps a truth to the falsity of utterance as action. In a time in which spectacles of political action in the Global South seem to cause as much if not more resonance in their retelling over Internet screens, the writing and image production of gender-based politics in India cannot be separated from the politics of the street. The moment of discursive utterance that happens through uses of media on the part of protestors, that happens through globalized media narratives of the Delhi gang rape case, and the politicization of Jyoti's death form part of the falsity of Internet-based mediascapes. The falsity of the narrativization and image production of moments that occur in real time on the streets India are a reflection not of a world that was really turned on its head in December 2012 or 2013 but a world that has been turned on its head since the colonial encounter. The falsity of the image and word also speaks to the "worldless space of global capitalism" (Žižek *Violence* 79) in which the truth of secular Western capitalist rationalities that cut across all cultures and life worlds can only be told as a lie, in the grammars of English-language speakers whose words are haunted by the colonial imposition of language . The falsity of the political voice of our time speaks a truth that is not its own, that is not a human voice but one of lines dancing across screens. One irony of an age of technologically powered narratives lies in how bodily and emotive violence against the "wretched of the earth," those who are among the poorest of the poor, is translated into a falsely authorized text by those who are privileged enough to live to tell and tweet "the story," in a saleable Internet-based grammar (Fanon *The Wretched of the Earth*).

The mobility of words across borders speaks to the ironies of bodies held captive. As these keys make words appear on a screen, workers in China commit suicide in iPad factories. Their deathly labour powers cyberfeminism—more dead people to be commemorated in candlelit vigils, to spark transnational protests that they will never witness, their names appearing in narratives not of their own telling. As Bhabha writes, "Between the banal act of freedom and its historic denial rises silence" (21). It is the falsity of these words, typed on keyboards and appearing across glowing pieces of plastic that gesture to the "banal act of freedom" within a wired world. False celebrity shamelessness meets the truly unspeakable and inaudible absent body in postcolonial space, a life lost to violence. The truth of bodily, psychic, epistemic, and ontological violence can never be spoken in text, yet is translated in ways that still somehow resonate with people across borders, often through unauthorized image and text. In a world turned on its head in which a "citizen" of the Indian subcontinent with "rights" and "freedoms" is tortured, gang raped, and dies in a foreign hospital, it is only in the always-false word and image, which can never capture the material desires, deaths, and visceral *jouissance* of protesting bodies, that the true scandal of the state is told.

Translations of psychic and bodily harm are narrated in the fictional grammars that have been offered to a late-capitalist Internet generation, forked tongues of text, tweet, and sound bite. Poor English translations, poor one-dimensional e-motions for affective and embodied sexual politics that persevere from screen to street: #jyotisinghpandey #we-wantjustice #neveragain #TheekHai?[11]

ENDNOTES

[1]Kotiswaran discusses the "sex panic" often narrated by the global media and filmmakers regarding sex work in India. The author discusses Sonagachi, the red-light district in West Bengal, in which the film "Born into Brothels" was made as being a site of global anxieties concerning the labour of sex workers in the Indian subcontinent. As the author writes,

> In the throes of a global sex panic, governments today are actively rethinking laws regulating sex work. While the normative status of sex work continues to be deeply contested, both feminists and governments display an unwavering faith in the power of the criminal law to at once repress sex markets and liberate sex workers. While much has been written about the politics of criminalization, far less is known about its economic implications. Based on a legal ethnography of Sonagachi, Kolkata's oldest and largest red-light area, I demonstrate how highly internally differentiated groups of stakeholders, including sex workers, are variously endowed by a plural rule network consisting of formal legal rules, informal social norms and market structures and routinely enter into bargains in the shadow of the criminal law whose outcomes cannot be determined a priori. I problematize the simplistic narrative of criminalization by examining the economic impact of criminalizing customers on Sonagachi's sex industry. (Kotiswaran 1)

[2]Losh offers an interesting discussion regarding the relationship between legality, the disclosure of the names of those subject to gender-based violence, and the use of Twitter to reveal the names of those who experience sexual assault, rape, and other gender-based crimes as a means of politicizing the lives and deaths of women and queer people. As Losh states,

> After the father of the victim came forward to name his daughter publicly, Jyoti Singh Pandey, so that she could be mourned and memorialized, some news outlets wary of prosecution still avoided publishing her legal proper name in full. In contrast

81

there was little hesitation on the part of many Twitter users who embraced the #jyotisinghpandey hashtag in their postings. (Losh 10)

[3]While Butler is discussing the specific use of sexual politics as an excuse to police Europe's borders from low-income migrants from the Global South—specificially Muslim migrants who are imagined to be "backwards" through a Eurocentric understanding of queerness and desire, tied to homonationalist aesthetics of neoliberal secular gay branding—the theoretical point the author makes regarding sexual politics is of relevance to contemporary India. As Butler states,

the way in which debates within sexual politics are framed are already imbued with the problem of time, of progress in particular, and in certain notions of what it means to unfold a future of freedom in time. That there is no one time, that the question of what time this is, already divides us, has to do with which histories have turned out to be formative, how they intersect—or fail to intersect with other histories—and so with a question of the how temporality is organized along spatial lines. (1)

Butler further discusses how mappings of time and space imagine Europe and the West to be the origin and site of sexual radicalism. In discussing the 2012 Delhi gang rape protests and 2013 protests following the decision to criminalize same-sex desire, this book challenges such a reading examining how these protests acted as a precursor to sexual political struggles transnationally but specifically in Asia.

[4]Callan discusses the high levels of gang rape in Cambodia and suggests that the attention that was garnered from the 2012 Delhi gang rape protests offered a means for creating public dialogue and protest regarding rape culture, misogyny, and sexual politics in Cambodia and other Asian countries. As the author states,

Gang rape hit the headlines last year after the brutal attack of a woman on a bus in India's capital, Delhi. But new research suggests that gang rape is a wider problem across Asia—with some of the highest recorded levels of violence against women in the world to be found within the Asia-Pacific region. ("It's a Man's World")

[5]Habitus is a concept taken from Pierre Bourdieu and is often used to discuss how sociality is embodied. One's habits, behaviours, and em-

bodiment is formed by the wider milieu they inhabit (Maton 48-65).
[6]As Vandana Shiva further remarks, "We need to change the ruling paradigm that reduces society to economy, the economy to the market, and is imposed on us in the name of "growth." Shiva further ties this obsession with market-based growth as the index of civilizational "progress" to gender-based violence within India. She writes, "Ending violence against women needs to also include moving beyond the violent economy to nonviolent, sustainable, peaceful, economies that give respect to women and the Earth" (Shiva).
[7]Apparduai suggests that one must within a time of mediascapes take the media seriously, not simply as a distorted mirror of a political reality or a distraction from the real politic, but as part and parcel of politics itself. He suggests that the image is,

> No longer mere fantasy (opium for the masses whose real work is elsewhere), no longer simply escape (from a world defined principally by more concrete purposes and structures), no longer elite pastime (thus not relevant to the lives of ordinary people) and no longer here contemplation (irrelevant for new forms of desire and subjectivity), the imagination has become an organized field of social practices, a form of work (in the sense of both labour and culturally organized practice), and a form of negotiation between sites of agency (individuals) and globally defined fields of possibility. (Appadurai 327)

[8]McClintock discusses the use of advertising as a tool of empire. Advertising spread images of racial and colonial domination throughout Europe and reached illiterate masses with racist and Eurocentric imagery. The globalized image was simultaneously used to sell European goods to those in the colonies and the metropole and to produce a panorama of whiteness that would come to imbed itself into the psyches of spectators. The globalization of images in advertising at the height of imperial rule also allowed divisions between the public sphere of colonial governance and the private sphere of the home to be crossed, through the sale of domestic goods. As the author states,

> By trafficking promiscuously across the threshold of private and public, advertising began to subvert one of the fundamental distinctions of commodity capital....From the outset, moreover, Victorian advertising took explicit shape around the reinvention of racial difference. Commodity kitsch made possible, as never

before, the mass marketing of empire as an organized system of images and attitudes. (McClintock 209)

[9]Barn writes,

Significantly, virtual protests through hash tags such as #theekhai (Hindi for "all is well") sought to humiliate and punish the lack of sensitivity and inactivity of ageing politicians. It is instructive to note that whilst two-thirds of the Indian population is under the age of 35, the average age of an Indian politician is 65. In the wake of the Mumbai terror attacks, the growing urban, young and middle class elite have demonstrated that they are agitated and feel under-protected. And they demand change.

[10]The uses of Internet-based media by urban Indians as a means of collective protest and dissent seriously, as a form of strategic postcolonial resistance should be taken seriously. Bhabha writes,

Political positions are not simply identifiable as progressive or reactionary, bourgeois or radical, prior to the act of critique engage, or outside the terms and conditions of their discursive address. It is in this sense that the historical moment of political action must be thought of as part of the history of the form of its writing. (Bhabha 33)

[11]When addressing crowds in Delhi following the 2012 Delhi gang rape case, then Prime Minister Man Mohan Singh used the Hindi phrase "Theek Hai" meaning, "all is well" to try to soothe the public. His comments provoked outrage and mockery with the tag "#TheekHai?" being used ironically on Twitter and other Internet-based mediums to mock the political leader's efforts to minimize the unrest that followed this case. As one journalist reported, "The Twitterverse promptly went into overdrive with strong comments under the hashtag #TheekHai about the PM's ability to lead the nation at a crucial time like this." ("Delhi Gang Rape"). "#TheekHai?," along with several other phrases, was also used over Internet-based mediums to mobilize protestors to attend demonstrations concerning gender-based violence in the city and to draw attention to feminist and queer issues (Atluri Personal interviews).

WORKS CITED

Appardurai, Arun. "Disjuncture and Difference in the Global Cultural

Economy." *Colonial Discourse and Post-Colonial Theory: A Reader.* Eds. Patrick Williams and Laura Chrisman. New York: Columbia University Press, 1994. 324-340. Print.

Atluri, Tara. Personal interviews. September 2012-September 2014.

Atluri, Tara. "Is Torture Part of Your Social Network?" *Žižek and Media Studies: A Reader.* Eds. Matthew Flisfeder and Louis-Paul Willis. London: Palgrave Macmillan, 2014. 241-257. Print.

Badiou, Alain. *Metapolitics.* London: Verso, 2005. Print.

Bady, Aaron. "Spectators to Revolution: Western Audiences and the Arab Spring's Rhetorical Consistency." *Cinema Journal* 52.1 (2012): 137-142. Print.

Barn, Ravinder. "Social media and protest: The Indian Spring?" *The Huffington Post*, 1 Sept. 2013. Web. 10 June 2015.

Bhabha, Homi. *The Location of Culture.* London: Routledge, 1994. Print.

Bilton, Richard. "Apple 'failing to protect Chinese factory workers.'" British Broadcasting Corporation, 18 Dec. 2014. Web. 19 June 2015.

Butler, Judith. "Sexual Politics, Torture, and Secular Time." *The British Journal of Sociology* 59.1 (2008): 1-23. Print.

Callan, Aellen. "It's a Man's World." *Al Jazeera Media Network*, 8 March 2013. Web. 18 June 2015.

Chabot, Sean, and Jan Willem Duyvendak. "Globalization and Transnational Diffusion between Social Movements: Reconceptualizing the Dissemination of the Gandhian Repertoire and the "Coming Out" Routine." *Theory and Society* 31.6 (2002): 697-740. Print.

Center for Human Rights and Global Justice (CHRGJ). *Every Thirty Minutes: Farmer Suicides, Human Rights, and the Agrarian Crisis in India.* New York: NYU School of Law, 2011. Print.

Cook, Jordan. "Social Media, American Interests, and the Arab Spring." *Dalhousie Journal of Interdisciplinary Management* 9 (Spring 2013): n.pag. Web. 4 Aug. 2015.

"Delhi Gang-Rape: Indian PM Manmohan Singh's 'Theek Hai' Gaffe Sets Twitter on Fire." *Emirates News*, 24 Dec. 2012. Web. 11 June 2015.

Debord, Guy. *The Society of the Spectacle.* Trans. Donald Nicholson-Smith. New York: Zone Books, 1995. Print.

Fanon, Frantz. *The Wretched of the Earth.* Trans. Constance Farrington. London: Penguin Books, 1969. Print.

Geist, J. "Queer Urban Spaces in New Delhi: Negotiating Femininity, Masculinity and Thirdness from a Kothi Perspective." *Verorten—Ver-*

handeln—Verkörpern. Interdisziplinäre Analysen zu Raum und Geschlecht. Eds. SilkeFörschler, RebekkaHabermas, Nikola Roßbach. Bielefeld: Transcript 2014. 85-116. Print.

Gordon, Avery F. "Some Thoughts on *Haunting* and *Futurity.*" *Borderlands* 10 (2) (2011): 1–20. Print.

Hardt, Michael and Antonio Negri. "Arabs Are Democracy's New Pioneers." *The Guardian,* 24 Feb. 2011. Web. 14 June 2015.

Haque, M. Shamsul. "E-governance in India: Its Impacts on Relations among Citizens, Politicians and Public Servants." *International Review of Administrative Sciences* 68.2 (2002): 231-250. Print.

Inani, Rohit. "India's First Lesbian Ad Goes Viral." *Time Inc.,* 11 June 2015. Web. 20 Oct. 2015.

Incredible India. N.p., 2015. Web. 26 Nov. 2015.

"Internet Goes into Frenzy at AAP win in Delhi." *DNA India,* 10 Feb. 2015. Web. 21 Nov. 2015.

Kotiswaran, Praba. "Born Unto Brothels—Towards a Legal Ethnography of Songachi's Sex Industry." *Social Sciences Research Network,* 18 May 2011. 1-82. Web. 15 Oct. 2015.

Losh, Elizabeth. "Hashtag Feminism and Twitter Activism in India." *Social Epistemology Review and Reply Collective* 3.12 (2014): 10-22. Print.

Maton, Karl. "Habitus." *Pierre Bourdieu: Key Concepts.* Ed. Michael James Grenfall. New York: Routledge, 2014. 48-65. Print.

Nelson, Dean. "Lindsay Lohan Attacked over Claims She Helped to Rescue 40 Indian Children." *The Telegraph,* 11 Dec. 2009. Web. 10 June 2015.

Newsom, Victoria A., and Lara Lengel. "Arab Women, Social Media, and the Arab Spring: Applying the Framework of Digital Reflexivity to Analyze Gender and Online Activism." *Journal of International Women's Studies* 13.5 (2012): 31-45. Print.

Pal, Joyojeet. "Banalities Turned Viral: Narendra Modi and the Political Tweet." *Television and New Media* 16.4 (2015): 378-387. Print.

Pandey, Geeta. "India Court Recognises Transgender People as Third Gender." *British Broadcasting Corporation,* 15 April 2014. Web. 4 Aug. 2015.

Puar, Jasbir K. *Terrorist Assemblages: Homonationalism in Queer Times.* Durham: Duke University Press, 2007. Print.

Roy, Arundhati. "The Greater Common Good." Friends of River Narmada. N.p., 1999. Web. 19 June 2015.

Said, Edward. *Orientalism*. London: Routledge, 1979. Print.

Saxena, Anmol. "It is AAP All the Way in Delhi." Al Jazeera Media Network, 10 Feb. 2015. Web. 2 July 2015.

Shiva, Vandana. "Vandana Shiva: Our Violent Economy is Hurting Women." *Yes Magazine*, 18 Jan. 2013. Web. 10 June 2015.

Spivak, Gayatri Chaktravorty. "Can the Subaltern Speak?" *The Postcolonial Studies Reader*. Eds. Bill Ashcroft, Gareth Griffiths, and Helen Tiffen. London: Routledge, 1995. 28-37. Print.

Teekah, Alyssa, Erika Jane Scholz, May Friedman, and Andrea O'Reilly, eds. *This Is What a Feminist Slut Looks Like: Perspectives on the Slutwalk Movement*. Toronto: Demeter Press, 2015. Print.

Thörn, Håkan. "Social Movements, the Media and the Emergence of a Global Public Sphere From Anti-Apartheid to Global Justice." *Current Sociology* 55.6 (2007): 896-918. Print.

Žižek, Slavoj. *The Plague of Fantasies*. London: Verso, 1997. Print.

Žižek, Slavoj. *Violence: Six Sideways Reflections*. London: Picador, 2008. Print.

2.

SEX IN THE CITY JAIL

TRANS/NATIONAL MOVEMENTS FOR GENDER JUSTICE

"*YOU KNOW, I haven't been able to watch* Life of Pi *since it happened,*" *he mutters, making reference to the night in the capital city of the Indian subcontinent when two people were returning from seeing the film* Life of Pi, *the night that led to unspeakable and incomprehensible violence. His dark eyes stare into the night carrying a look of ghostly haunting, an image of grief beyond literal translation. On a street corner in the East end of London, a young British Desi boy talks about the case of a gang-raped and murdered woman that happened oceans, miles, airplanes, economies, histories, languages, faiths, and borders away. How does a young man who was born in rural England, and has lived and worked in London as an artist for years know enough and feel enough about this case to speak about it with any understanding or conviction? Or, does he? Or is anyone in a place to judge who has an affective reaction to the political? How does a story, an event, a staging of events generate an emotive response? The young man is queer and he tells me that he sincerely believed that "things were changing in India" when he saw that Section 377 of the Indian Penal Code was read down by the Delhi high court in 2009. A few months later I leave London again for Delhi. I arrive days after the global media has reported that the Supreme Court of India has ruled to uphold Section 377 of the Indian Penal Code, criminalizing same sex desire and queer people despite the judgment by the Delhi High Court to read down Section 377 in 2009. We talk a bit more, and he tells me that he is interested to see what will happen with queer politics in India. When I ask him if he is British, he still answers in the same 1970's multicultural way. After hundreds of years of colonialism and years of diasporic Indian communities that have been in England long enough to make curry a national dish he mutters, "Well, yes, I'm British, but…." And we continue to speak of India on a street corner in the hip disaffected area of the city—an Indian and Bangladeshi neighbourhood where off-licence operators and families outside the East London Mosque and Indian community centres have also heard the news of the Delhi gang rape case and the protests that followed in December of 2012. "Makes you glad to be in this country. People shouldn't complain," says an old man with sunken eyes behind the counter of the twenty-four hour off licence, a convenience store where exhausted ex-colonials sell Bombay Sapphire gin over the counter in the centre of a former empire full of stolen Indian jewels now housed in ornate London museums. "You reckon things like that don't happen to girls all the time here? You just don't hear about it," his wife quips. Dressed in a full salwar suit, she never looks up from filling the fridge with cheap beer, wine, and Bombay Sapphire spirits.*

TIME AFTER TIME: HAUNTING TEMPORALITIES

I want to suggest that gender and sexual politics in contemporary India are as much formed, reformed, questioned, and struggled within these diasporic moments as they are on the streets of India. This chapter suggests that it is impossible to understand cases such as the 2012 Delhi gang rape and murder and other related movements such as the 2013 upholding of Section 377 of the Indian Penal Code without considering the uneven effects that globalization has had in relation to sexual politics, particularly among young urban Indians in cities such as Delhi. The fetishization of "authentic" experience or an "authentic" postcolonial Indian subject threatens to support Orientalist and colonial discourses that are framed by narrow binaries of East-West. However, along with rising forms of transnational media that can help to make political events in Delhi the topic of conversation on the streets of London, Toronto, Montréal, New York, Hong Kong, and globally, ideas of gender and sexuality, subjectivity, and politics also cross borders. Sexual politics in India have been influenced by and have influenced the world since the days of colonial rule and the many precolonial invasions that make the history of the subcontinent as impure as history itself.

What also emerges in examining both the Delhi gang rape protests of 2012 and the protests regarding Section 377 in 2013 is a skewed sense of temporality and geography regarding social movements and how they act on, inspire, and inform one another. Chabot and Duyvendak discuss literature on social movement theory that has largely suggested that because of globalization, protest movements are thought to originate in the West and spread to countries in the Global South. The authors cite the work of major social movement theorists who "assume that innovative protest methods or routines originate in the West and spread outwards—initially within the world system's core and eventually (after becoming 'modular') to its periphery"(Chabot and Duyvendak 701).The social movement literature tends to take for granted, firstly, that social movements originate in Europe and North America, and secondly, that the West is therefore necessarily the centre of political turbulence that the rest of the world inevitably follows. The Delhi gang rape protests of 2012 as well as the protests regarding Section 377, India's sodomy bill, are reflective of how social movements dealing with localized issues of gender and sexuality in India do not mimic movements in the West. Rather, these moments and movements are both specific to India and subsequently influence the rest of Asia and the rest of the world through flows of media and Internet-based technologies.The landscape of sexual politics in India is also ever-changing and vital in regards to political possibility. As discussed, after writing much of this work, months after the ruling regarding Section 377, the Supreme Court of India made a historic ruling regarding Hijras and transgender persons. The NASLA ruling granted rights and protections to Hijras outside of binary gender frameworks. While this decision was informed by international legis-lation and global transgender rights movements, it also addressed the needs, countenance, and perhaps implicitly, the historical role that Hijras play and have always played in the Indian subcontinent. To write about the contemporary sexual political moment in India is in many ways to race against the multiple temporalities—skewed senses of time as fast as broadband connections lighting up screens declaring some people to be newly emancipated by law and others newly criminalized, and those as slow as age-old prose and the steady hands that once etched images of desire onto temple walls.

While this book touches on the significance of the NASLA deci-sion regarding sexual politics in India, as the judgment was issued after much of this work was written, the discussion regarding Hijra and transgender politics in India lies beyond the scope of this work. However, the victory of the Hijra community is deeply important as it offers inroads into thinking about sexual political struggles in India that are distinctive to the nation and tied to mythologies that belie

Western conceptions of feminist and queer politics and histories. As I have discussed in the previous chapter, the Arab Spring protests of 2010—while often referred to as an "awakening" of the Middle East that draws on Orientalist evocations of Arabs as being "awakened" from an imagined political slumber—still spoke to a moment in which the centrality of the West as the imagined cite of political radicalism was challenged. Chabor and Duyvendak discuss the importance of challenging Eurocentric social movement theory and draw on Gandhian principles as informing civil rights struggles in America (709-711). I draw on the insights of these writers and others, to decentre European and North American history as the originary sites from where political dissent is imagined to begin.

BUS:[1] THE GHOST OF ROSA PARKS

Imagining Europe and the West as the origins of political radicalism obscures how traditions of radical thought beginning in the Global South have historically inspired and informed struggles in the West. Chabot and Duyvendak, for example, discuss the relationship between Gandhian philosophy and the African-American civil rights movement. They state that,

> The Gandhian repertoire underwent constant modifications, from the moment of its invention in South Africa to its widespread application during the Indian nationalist movement, and eventually, its adoption by the American civil rights movement. (Chabot and Duyvendak 709)

The authors go on to specifically make reference to the Montgomery Bus Boycotts as being informed by Gandhi's philosophy of *satyagraha*. It is perhaps important to note that Gandhi's politics have been rightly and necessarily critiqued by several authors who point to the ways in which Gandhi implicitly supported the caste system and other religious nationalist sentiments (Roy qtd. in Burke). However, for my purposes what is of interest is the use of Indian political struggles as a historical reference point that informs struggles globally. Chabot and Duyvendak use *diffusion*, a popular term often used by social movement theorists, in discussing how the basic principles of satyagraha—those of truth, self-sacrifice, and non-violence—were translated into the bus boycotts. The reinvention of Gandhian satyagraha continued throughout the history of the civil rights movement as activists often drew on Gandhi's philosophy to inform their organizing strategies and actions such as sit-ins and freedom rides. In this regard, rather than seeing the Delhi gang rape protests of 2012 and the centrality of the right to public space and public transportation as a result of the "Westernization" of young urban Indians, the phenomenon is better understood as a cyclical nature of protest movements, in which political struggles in India continue to resonate both implicitly and explicitly with anti-oppression struggles transnationally (Chabot and Duyvendak 710-711). The symbolic bus boycotts by civil rights activists in America, and in the symbol of the "bus" as one of extreme gendered violence experienced in public spaces in Delhi cuts across linear notions of progressive politics and discrete geographies of dissent.

Chabot and Duyvendak draw on the work of McAdam who discusses *initiator* and *spin off* social movements. Initiator movements emerge because of radical shifts in the balance of power within a society and give way to remarkable cycles of protest, while spin off movements gain inspiration both locally and transnationally from these initiating protests (Chabot and Duyvendak 704). While the authors use these concepts to discuss social movements transnationally and histori-cally, they also trouble Western-centric views of social movements implicitly informed by Orientalist mappings of both geography and temporality. The authors critique those who see initial movements as only beginning in North America and Europe. Secondly, they critique the assumption within social movement theory that the diffusion of protest movements spreads from the imagined centre to the periphery. They also critique an understanding of social movements informed by and informing only those who are within the same geographical and temporal milieu (Chabot and Duyvendak 704-705). The use of the Internet within protest movements globally challenges the idea that protests are locally contained and temporally connected in "real time." The inspiring images, ideologies, and theories of radical dissent proliferating through online mediums, from places as distant as Egypt to New Delhi to New York to London, gesture to the skewed temporalities of social movements within a wired world. The ability for African-American civil rights movements to be informed by anti-colonial politics in the Indian subcontinent also disrupts narratives of teleological Western temporal "progress." I want to suggest that the linear mappings of both space and time within mainstream Western social movement theory fails to do justice to revolutionary thought and action within the Global South and draws too straight a line in the traffic of thought and bodies.

The symbol of "the bus" in Delhi, which led to nationwide protests, carries traces and hauntings of other buses, of other bodies, of other histories of violence that cannot fully be verified as the truth of memory but exists in the psychic life of nations. The bus conjures up others spaces and place of dissent: the bus ridden by Rosa Parks, and the buses boycotted by African-American students who much like the protesters in Delhi in 2012 expressed the desire for a sense of freedom, an Āzādī, beyond history's violent marking of skin. Across oceans, languages, and all the markings of bodies and nations that divide humanity from itself these moments can be assembled in what Walter Benjamin once referred to as "messianic time," an idea that troubles a reliance on secular-capitalist visions of the world and their inability to allow the past and present to rest side by side. Khanna discusses Benjamin's critique of secular capitalist temporalities,

> Walter Benjamin's notion of "homogeneous, empty time" ... is structured by the existence of the calendar and clock, and which prevents us from experiencing a messianic sense of absolute simultaneity between past, present, and future events. (Khanna "Post-Palliative: Coloniality's Affective Dissonance")

The "empty time" of Western teleological narratives of progress—also reliant on a geographical marking of originary nations of supposed Western civility and their assumed colonized mimics—does not allow satyagraha to sit on a bus with Rosa Parks and with women, Hijras, and queer people in India. While many Western feminist commentators and journalists suggest that the 2012 Delhi gang rape protests are examples of India's imagined "feminist awakening" these readings are already structured by concepts of "homogeneous empty time" that divorce present and future feminisms from colonial history transnationally. As I discuss in greater detail throughout this book, listening to and for the "Āzādī" of contemporary sexual political revolts in India involves listening to that which haunts and that which gestures to what is to come regarding not only gender justice but anticolonial revolt.

In *The Year of Dreaming Dangerously* Slavoj Žižek discusses two French words that cannot be fully translated into English: *futur* and *avenir*. *Futur* refers to "the future," while *avenir* can loosely be translated into that which is to come, but is not fully known or guaranteed to arrive (134). Žižek suggests that political movements such as Occupy, the Arab Spring, and anti-austerity movements throughout Europe are signs from the future, not *futur* as the uninterrupted time of secular capitalism but as *avenir*, signs of what is to come, but is not yet known (*The Year of Dreaming Dangerously*). An interesting question to ask is how the 2012 Delhi gang rape protests might be reflective of an avenir, a sign of an unpredictable future. Reading alongside Benjamin's idea of messianic time allows one to consider how *avenir*, what may come, cannot be separated from the time of the supposed past. In the future buses of Delhi, the buses of *avenir*, perhaps Mahatma Gandhi, Rosa Parks, and Jyoti can share space and share in the lingering dreams of something called Āzādī.

FROM STONEWALL TO TEMPLE WALLS: CLOCKING DESIRES

While theorists attempt to trouble the Western-centric and implicitly colonial ideology informing social movement theory by discussing the initiating force of Gandhism, these same theorists often locate originary movements for queer rights within the West. Chabot and Duyvendak for example discuss the wave of "coming out" protests that originated among LGBTQ groups in America as being foundational to queer rights. Chabot and Duyvendak state,

> In June 1969 the police raided Stonewall Inn, a popular bar among homosexuals. While harassment by the authorities was quite common, the reaction to it was not: for the first time, gays and lesbians actually fought back and, in the aftermath of the riot, they created the New York Gay Liberation Front (GLF) to give substance to their disaffection. (Chabot and Duyvendak 213)

The authors argue that the Stonewall uprisings of 1969 resulted in similar protests throughout Europe and North America and were "pioneering" movements for sexual justice (Chabot and Duyvendak 711-714). They further discuss how it was the police raids of the Stonewall Inn that led to "coming out" as a defiant political protest among queers in North America. From interviews and research done following the 2013 decision to reinstitute Section 377 of the Indian Penal Code, there seems to be a truth to this as many young queer urban activists in India discuss the use of similar "coming out" strategies during the 2009 political campaigns, which led to the historic Delhi high court decision to read down Section 377. Activists also suggest that "coming out" publically served as a radical revolt in 2013 by queers who asserted their sexualities defiantly despite the decision by the Supreme Court to uphold Section 377. Sexual politics in contemporary India cannot be divorced from this history: uses of strategies by queers and feminists in the subcontinent that make reference to Western history are often tactical to gain global media attention and transnational solidarity. However, this logic of the "pioneering" West, which the postcolonial world comes to mimic, is deeply ahistorical and ideologically informed by Orientalism. These understandings of history fail to see how contemporary sexual politics in India are haunted by the lingering ethos of anti-colonial revolt, a queer affront to Victorian puritanical norms and embodiment. Sugata Ray discusses the construction of an effeminate male body as a privileged aesthetic signifier used as an embodied symbol of anti-colonial resistance. Ray states,

> Internalizing colonial accusations of the "effeminacy" of the native male body, nineteenth-century Indian ideologues and reformers attempted to redeem the national body through a range of phallocentric body cultures. ("Darcy Grimaldo Grigsby and Sugata Ray in Conversation in Berlin")

In examining art history as being central to anti-colonialism, Ray goes on to say,

> Anti-colonial art history...deliberately appropriated colonizing discourses of the effeminate native body to epistemologically challenge the hegemonic hyper-masculinity advocated by both the regulatory mechanisms of the British Empire and a larger

nationalist body culture in colonial India. The ingenious invention of a discursive intimacy between yoga and an aesthetics of demasculinization led to the strategic resignification of the male body in early Indian sculpture as both a sign and the site of an imagined national life. ("Darcy Grimaldo Grigsby and Sugata Ray in Conversation in Berlin")

Symbols of anti-colonial, revisionist, sacrificial masculinity rupture divisions between the public and the private, between body and world, and between thought and embodied action. The trouble with the "No Going Back" refrain heard by those protesting the criminalization of same-sex desire in India in 2013 lies in how this charting of time fails to see how in order to not "go back" to a colonial past, one must perhaps "go back" to a wider anti-colonial imaginary. An anti-colonial discourse of sexual politics might conceive of queer liberation as being foundational not to an imagined pure pre-colonial past, but might read the body and its gestures as always carrying hauntings that elude clear maps of space, time, and all the confounding histories of desire that both bodies and nations contain.

PREMATURE EMANCIPATION:
CHALLENGING THE PATERNALISTIC GAZE OF ORIENTALISM

The universal "coming out" story, often narrated by English-speaking middle classes or by English translators throughout Asi, should be analyzed in terms of how it relates to a broader framework of Orientalism that imagines the East to be sexually repressed. Writing in reference to the "outing" of non-normative sexualities in Japan by Western researchers, McClelland discusses the gendered colonial authority that enables affluent European male writers to speak on behalf of feminized "Eastern" bodies. This epistemic violence solidifies histories of colonial authority, with Western writers claiming the right to categorize, discipline, and author the lives of "Oriental" others. This will to name and speak for the other also allows Orientalist writers to solidify their own identities as powerful European men whose bodies and voices become normative and idealized through abject and inferior others. McLelland reviews the work of queer theorists who often write about Japan's "new" queer culture, one that is imagined to mimic histories, ideologies, and cultures of sexuality in the West. He suggests that much of this research is already informed by several author's Orientalist perceptions of Japanese societies as sexually repressive, intolerant, and in need of benevolent Western translation in order for proper "gay" subjects to find articulation, agency, and rights. There is an implicit understanding that desire does not exist or is "improperly" articulated if it is not translated in grammars of Western English secular-capitalist norms (McClelland 105-122).

Within Orientalist travel writings, the perversity of the imagined East and its assumed repression, while seemingly contradictory, express an overarching inability to understand grammars of desire outside of Eurocentric histories. The Hijra body is an example of a religious and cultural figure in India that predates colonial rule and is connected to both Muslim and Hindu genealogies. Hijras were deemed criminal by British colonial law and within colonial travel writings, they were often represented as savage, against the assumed civility of European racial and sexual norms, and aesthetics. They were also understood as "born criminals" through a biopolitical reading of their bodies as deviant from a gendered, racial, and class-based system of hierarchy through which aesthetic difference from a white, masculinist, colonial body was equated with moral deviance (Rana). Hijras were seen to represent a sexual unlawfulness, an ostentatious and overly decadent pageantry of sex that also coloured colonial perceptions of Mughal courtesanship and harems in the Indian subcontinent. As already discussed, in 2014 the Supreme Court of India granted Hijras the legal right to declare themselves to be neither male nor female, recognizing them as Hijras. Slavoj Žižek has discussed the success of Haitian rebellions against French rule in which the use of French constitutional principles—"Fraternité, Equalité, Liberté"—served as a means of challenging colonial authority. Žižek suggests that Haitians did not mobilize this revolution based on precolonial ideals but based on French constitutional norms. Haitians used a distorted mirror of the blatant lies of European civility and governance to demand that the French empire follow their own rules, against the obscene underbelly of racist inequality (*Living in the End Times* 159). While Hijras do have a precolonial mythology, their recent victory in the Supreme Court of India in fact respects above all, the Indian constitution which grants dignity to all. Forms of political subjectivity that predate the rise of the occidentalist figure of "the citizen" as Western subject might also be valuable to chart contemporary sexual political struggles and ideas of a sexual citizenship beyond Orientalism. By asking for countenance as citizens within contemporary India, the Hijra body does not ask to mimic a Western LGBTQ identity as a marker of neoliberal "progress" but rather asks India to respect its own constitution and its queer history.

SLAVES TO HISTORY:

AGAINST A ROMANTICIZATION OF PRECOLONIAL INDIA

It is important not to romanticize sexualities in the precolonial period and to pay close attention to how precolonial cultures of religious rule in India also involved forms of sexual oppression often based in casteist lineages. Lower-caste women deemed to be adulterous were often used as slaves within precolonial empires and were also sold to European rulers. Sharmila Rege states, "Female adulteresses arrested as slaves of the government came mainly from the lower castes, since upper caste adulteresses were punished by excommunication from their caste" (Rege 26). Rege writes of how cultural forms of caste-based performance offer historical evidence of the discursive and ideological construction of lower-caste women as sexually deviant. Rege's research is situated in the state of Maharashtra and discusses the *lavani,* a public performance of lower-caste women who performed in sexualized ways, largely for male audiences. Rege argues that the lavani "became one of the modes of constructing the bodies of lower caste women as constantly either arousing, or satiating male desire" (25). She further discusses the relationship between the lavani and forms of sexualized slavery suggesting that "This construction was crucial to the pre-colonial Peshwa state's appropriation of the labour of lower caste women through the institution of slavery" (25). Rege further discusses the changes that came about through colonialism with folk performances usurping the lavani performances enacted by lower-caste women because a Victorian puritanical ideology valorized upper-caste forms of theatre and desexualized public cultures. The colonial period involved the moralizing and sanitizing of cultures of performance and dance that devalued the roles of lower-caste women as performers and cleansed the public sphere of sex.

LINGERING ANXIETIES:
THE LIBIDINAL DESIRES OF CASTE-BASED (IM)PURITIES

The nationalist period within India involved the rise of film culture in which the lower-caste woman was again constructed as an overly sexualized vixen, seen either as a figure to be reformed by an upper-caste male hero or as a character whose constructed evil was cast against the virginal figure of the upper-caste heroine (Rege 28-32). Despite narratives of illusory progress or celebratory readings of precolonial utopias, lower-caste women have been sexualized, exploited, and subjected to violence throughout the documented history of the Indian subcontinent and continue to be denigrated through processes of casteism and sexism. There is no romantic or simple story to tell regarding the complexities of caste-based sexualized exploitation that dates back to precolonial India. While precolonial Mughal courts and other dynasties exploited the bodies of lower-caste people as sexualized performers and slaves, colonialism and nationalism ushered in capitalist modes of production, creating separate spheres of bourgeois domesticity. Sexual labour was separated from the bourgeois home, quarantined in spaces of criminalized sex work and held at a distance through film screens, keeping the anxieties of caste-based mixture and female sexuality at bay. The rise of capitalism turned those who were owned as slaves, sold as commodities, and taxed for state interests into contractual labourers who would sell sex as performers and as sex workers whose labour was criminalized by colonial law (Rege). Rather than seeing one historical period as being superior to another or constructing precolonial state forms of ownership as better than the rise of contractually performed sexual labour, these processes should be viewed as complex stagings of sex that haunt the contemporary postcolonial moment. Although a full and comprehensive discussion of sexuality within precolonial and nationalist India is beyond the scope of this work, history shows that the construction of "sex in public"[2] was always a site of psychosocial ambivalence and political oppression. Sexualized performances in the public sphere have existed throughout Indian history, yet they have been denounced as the labour of those socially constructed as "impure," often owing to casteist and colonial moralities. The ideology of sexual "purity" continues to haunt the postcolonial psyche, explicitly informing the criminalization of sex work and implicitly informing cases such as the 2012 Delhi gang rape case, and other violent assaults against women and queers.

PRINCELY STATES OF SEXISM:
THE TAWA'IF AND GENDER IN MUGHAL INDIA

A detailed and thorough examination of Mughal patriarchy is also beyond the scope of this work. However, it is important to note that contemporary sexual politics envisioning political change cannot easily return to an idealized feminist and queer past that existed before British rule in the Indian subcontinent. O'Hanlon discusses the enforcement of masculine norms that structured Mughal kingdoms and the construction of women within precolonial India. O'Hanlon shows how the religious and cultural construction of embodied moralities within Mughal history imagined the body of an idealized man to be the epitome of humanity. O'Hanlon cites the thirteenth-century mystic Fariduddin Altar who asserted, "When a woman walks in the way of God like a man, she cannot be called a woman" (O'Hanlon, 54). O'Hanlon also cites the writings of Indian mystic Jamal Hainski who wrote that "The seeker of the world is feminine, the seeker of the other world is a hermaphrodite, and the seeker of the Lord is masculine" (O'Hanlon 53). While Hindu nationalism and colonial law espouse a rhetoric of misogyny and a violent regulation of queer desires, precolonial Mughal rule in India is not beyond feminist critique. O'Hanlon also suggests that while diverse enactments of sexuality were present within precolonial India, patrimonial authority structured processes of governance within Mughal kingdoms: "Patrimonial themes featured importantly in the public construction of royal authority: the king was at once father to all of his subjects and husband to the wider realm" (O'Hanlon 54). While scholars often write of precolonial cultures of courteseanship that did not limit female sexual expression to the domestic realm, these writers also note that such practices were often gendered through a determinant biopolitical scripting of women as providing sexual services to men. While practices of courtesanship can be juxtaposed to phantasmatic constructions of sexual deviance within colonial discourses of puritanism that associated localized sexual cultures with moral licentiousness, Mughal culture still remained dependent on existing structures of gender and class. An emphasis on searching for female, transgender, and queer agency within the precolonial period imagines an anti-oppressive utopia that has never existed outside of fiction. As Sameen emphasizes, "locating agency at the expense of sidelining hegemonic structures of power tends to produce inadequate understandings of historical processes" (Sameen 44). Sameen discusses forms of libidinal sexual agency that existed in the performative gestures and sexual labour of Mughal courtesans. However, the author veers away from a glorification of a time that existed before British colonial rule, which was free from exploitation and ideologies of gendered "respectability" tied to masculinist and patriarchal moralities. The author states that courtesans "remained embedded in their locality's patriarchal structuring, and their state of liminality between an underclass of common prostitutes and 'respectable' women forced them to walk the tightrope of political, economic and social vulnerability" (Sameen 44). Similarly, while Hijras within Mughal courts played a role within religious and cultural life, like the figure of the courtesan, their labour and social value was dependent on a fixity of gendered norms in which elite masculine bodies still had authority over them (Reddy). Sexual politics in postcolonial worlds involves a refusal to succumb to the fetishism of historical utopias and involves imaginative moments of protest that serve as history in the making. What might be unpredictable and promising about sexual politics in postcolonial worlds lies in the following: critiquing colonial law and morality, emerging and ongoing political movements in the Global South that do not strive to approximate Western history, and refusing to succumb to a delusional idea of essentialist precolonial culture. I suggest throughout this book that sexual politics in contemporary India are postcolonial hybrids of street-based activism, globalized media and technological tools of dissent, battles with state structures, and traces of anti-colonial mythologies retold today in a new urban grammar. José Esteban Muñoz discusses *disidentification*, a process through which minoritarian subjects work on and against the dominant social order to produce creative strategies of resistance (Muñoz 2-37). Contemporary feminist and queer politics in India do not wholly distance themselves from a history of political revolt in the subcontinent or from localized forms of gendered expression or precolonial cultures of sexual politics. These new enactments of desire are informed by precolonial history, the defiant spirit of anti-colonial resistance, and ethics embedded in the Indian constitution. Those who enact sexual politics in postcolonial worlds also disidentify with globalized cultures of transnational feminism and queer rights, using the tools of global media and queer and feminist networks worldwide to stage localized forms of resistance. What emerges is a challenge to the idea of fixity itself.

Romantic renderings of precolonial India attempt to essentialize the supposedly true nature of sexualities within the subcontinent by unearthing a "pure" precolonial past. Colonial law also attempts to hold bodies in place and to construct airtight coffins of "deviant" desire. Eurocentric feminist and queer histories and globalized branding schemes also essentialize the feminist and queer body in the Global South as ostensibly backwards but on an inevitable and necessary path towards universal secular-capitalist "progress." This book suggests that feminist and queer movements within India are as Homi Bhabha discusses in relation to postcolonial mimicry, "almost the same but not quite," (Bhabha 127) in their clever usage of all aspects of these competing totalities. The variant discourses that inform protest movements and cultures such as those that emerged following the 2012 Delhi gang rape case and 2013 decision to criminalize same-sex desire are as mixed and reinvented as words translated from the rush of the Indian street to the computer screen: Āzādī.

"WE ARE ALL ON A JOURNEY":
PIED PIPERS OF SEXUAL "RIGHTS" AND NEOCOLONIALISM

In 2011, Prime Minister David Cameron's "Gay conditionality" proposals suggested that British aid to countries in the Global South should be dependent on their institution of LGBT rights. In proposing that many formerly colonized countries that do not institute LGBT rights which mimic the West and Europe should not receive British aid, Cameron stated, "I think we are all on a journey, and we should help these countries on their journey" (Rao). This supposed journey begins with European systems of colonial law that first criminalized diverse enactments of sexual desire in the Global South, and ends with the assumed benevolence of European "rights" discourse. The wider structures of global governance tied to colonial histories of capitalist exploitation threaten to further impoverish postcolonial nations that were often initially exploited by colonial rule under the guise of sexual "rights." Rahul Rao discusses the critiques levelled against Cameron:

Warning that the refusal of aid on LGBT rights grounds could provoke a backlash against queers who would be scapegoated for reduced aid flows, the critics have pointed out the insidious ways in which such initiatives could drive a wedge between queers and a broader civil society in recipient countries, besides reinforcing perceptions of the westernness of homosexuality as well as the imperial dynamics already prevailing between donor and recipient countries.

From the obscured and partial perspective of neocolonial power and Hindu nationalist rhetoric, feminist and queer bodies in the Indian subcontinent do not exist. Yet on the streets of Delhi, following the Delhi gang rape case of 2012 and the 2013 decision regarding Section 377, many people engaged in processes of "world making" to redefine forms of juridical, state, familial, and colonial classification. Bourdieu states that,

> To change the world, one has to change the ways of world making, that is, the vision of the world and the practical operations by which groups are produced and reproduced.... The power to impose upon other minds a vision, old or new, of social divisions depends on the social authority acquired in previous struggles. (23)

Sexual political movements in India gain social authority from previous campaigns in 2009 that were successful in their contribution to the reading down of Section 377, by the Delhi high court. Queer people and allies continue acts of "world making" that alter universal understandings of desire globally and within the nation. Following the 2013 decision made by the Supreme Court of India to reinstitute the sodomy bill, David Cameron remained politically silent. Bloodsworth suggests that to maintain favourable economic trade relations with India, Cameron must forego any commitment to advocate for queer people. The author references a report issued by the UK Foreign Commissions Office following the decision to reinstitute Section 377, which states that "The actions of India's Supreme Court are a matter for India" (Bloodsworth). Yet no less than two years earlier, Cameron played the transparently self-serving role of knight in shining armour by using queer rights to justify cutting aid budgets to some of the poorest people in the world, who were, arguably, impoverished because of British colonial rule. The ambivalent contradictions within colonial discourse, those that declare British rulers to "be the father and the oppressor" (Bhabha 136) of India, emerge again in the gap between European governance as civility through aid conditionality schemes masking the economic imperatives of Western human rights interventions in a time of mass austerity.

"CRIMINAL" TRIBES AND "FAIR" AND LOVELY WHITE SETTLERS: TRANSNATIONAL ANTICOLONIAL POLITICS

Anticolonial political struggles are sexual-political struggles, embodied forms of oppression and revolt that resonate beyond the borders of nation and the reductive categories of colonial bureaucracy. The criminalization of "tribes" by colonizers in the Americas for example pathologized Aboriginal bodies in gendered and sexual ways, constructing those who did not conform to white European bourgeois family norms as deviant. Discussing the buried lineages of Two-Spirited people, Kerry Swanson states that,

> Prior to colonization, queer identity (known as Two-Spirit in honour of the existence of both male and female spirit in one body) was widely accepted among many different North American tribes, although this fact has been virtually eliminated from historical renderings of this period. (Swanson)

Similarly, in the Criminal Tribes Act of 1871, instituted in India by British colonial rule, some tribes were criminalized by birth: the Hijras, or what might be referred to as transgender persons, were one such tribe. Narrain and Gupta write,

> These communities and tribes were perceived to be criminals by birth, with criminality being passed on from generation to generation. It fit in well with the hierarchical Indian social order, in which some communities were perceived as unclean and polluted since birth.

The idea of sexual deviance as a biological trait passed through a lineage of "criminal tribes" discursively connects racial purity with heteronormative moralism in ways that speak to the relationship between race, sexuality, and colonialism. Within a great deal of colonial discourse, colonized peoples were associated with sexual licentiousness and "wild" expressions of desire (Puar; Young; Lewis). Within neocolonial discourse, colonized people are now scripted as being in need of sexual "liberation" by those in secular Western countries as a means of disavowing the gross imbalances of wealth that structure the lives of those in the supposed First World and those in the Global South.

MISSIONARY POSITIONS: THE BENEVOLENCE OF RACISM

While the skin of gendered and sexualized bodies in the Global South often appears scarred and battered within the globalized media, colonialism arguably continues to mark the skin of those who live in supposedly "progressive" and "free" places. David Cameron's "Gay conditionality" proposals were levelled in the wake of the London riots that followed the racist police shooting of Mark Duggan and the rise of border security measures in the UK. The will to construct political regimes in the Global South as oppressive and Europe as an imagined safe haven for the oppressed masks ongoing forms of racist systemic violence that exist in the UK, as evinced in the shooting of Black British men like Duggan by the British police (Bridges). There is an ambivalent and paradoxical slippage between the racialized body in and from the Global South as a victim of cultural barbarism, and as a deviant figure, criminalized within the racist gaze of the state when such a figure appears within Europe and North America. Foucault writes of "the species body," (139) a concept used to describe the political valorization of certain bodies that are imagined as those that can reproduce an idealized citizenry. Black bodies are constructed within imagined spaces of Western civility and freedom as being unable to reproduce a desired citizenry and as threats to idealized, white, and affluent Europeans and heteronormative European families. Similarly, women and queers in India who stray from Hindu middle class formations are not offered full countenance as citizens, as their bodies do not correspond to the biopolitical goals of nation building. Those marked as "dark stains" on flags become justified and excused targets of violence and exclusion. Shortly after the Supreme Court of India made the decision to recriminalize queer desire, Minister of Law Somnath

Bharti was embroiled in a scandal after accusing groups of Africans in India of being involved in the drug trade and in prostitution (Joshi). A raid occurred in Khirki village in Delhi—a community that is home to a large number of African migrants, transgender people, and Hijras, all of whom face police brutality brought about by the racist and homophobic complaints of neighbours. Heteronormative and middle-class Hindu families can pathologize those who are visibly marked as "other" in ways that warrant their exclusion from social space. Both the queer body and the African body hold no place within the imagined middle-class Hindu family and are, therefore, scripted as "anti-citizens," revealing the ruse of the secular state regarding biopolitical familial and nation building in Hindustan (Bhatia).

While the harassment of African migrant women in India may seem to be a world away from the European polis, the migrant body within Europe is also racialized in sexual ways. Jin Haritaworn writes succinctly of how queer politics within Europe explicitly and implicitly supports racism and xenophobia, with the imagined perpetrators of homophobia being scripted as racialized migrants. Haritaworn writes,

> If the queer lover has become recognizable through hir famil-
> iarity with trans/national neoliberal ideals of respectability and
> privacy, the hateful Other entered into the German landscape
> by joining a rich archive peopled by dysfunctional families from
> deficient communities in the degenerate "ghetto." (60)

Just as migrants in Europe are disciplined based on sexual norms, so too are racialized migrants within India subject to sexualized racism, which justifies their violent exclusion from the nation. Kavita Krishnan of the *All India Women's Association* writes,

> It is ironic that the rape of a Danish woman in Delhi is recognised
> as violence against a woman—a foreign guest in our country.
> But the violence and appalling violation of rights to which
> African woman were subjected isn't recognised by the Delhi
> Government as the same. (Krishnan qtd. in *Feminists India*)

Rape culture cannot be separated from colonial cultures transnationally. As discussed in an earlier chapter of this text, the inordinate

violence experienced by Aboriginal women and Two Spirited peoples in North America is, for example, implicitly and explicitly informed by colonialism and white-settler colonial ideologies. The extreme forms of sexual harassment experienced by African female migrants in Delhi and throughout India can also be considered as gendered and sexual expressions of racism, with African women being accused of being involved in sex work. The rhetoric of European "Gay conditionality" is also undercut by racism, as evinced in statements by political leaders such as British Prime Minister David Cameron who implicity constructs racialized people in formerly colonized countries as sexually "backwards" and ostensibly uncivilized in gendered terms. What both the Indian state's gendered violence against African migrants and Cameron's "Gay conditionality" proposals share is a sexist and implicitly homophobic (hetero) sexualizingof the Black body, a trope dating back to slavery that continues to colour perceptions of Blackness within mainstream political and popular culture (Wright and Schuhmann; Lee; Fanon).

WORLD MAKING: CREATING SUBVERSIVE SPACES

Although the raid on Khirki village and the subsequent protests and debates that followed were in some ways reminiscent of the Stonewall riots, in which racialized and transgender people were subject to police raids, they also spoke to the lingering histories of anti-colonial resistance that haunt India. B. R. Ambedkar's criticisms of brahmanical patriarchy and emphasis on human dignity and bodily integrity outside of one's utility for market and nation should be revisited in relation to the contemporary political moment in the Indian subcontinent. Ambedkar's thought informs the Indian constitution and contemporary political struggles. For example, traces of Ambedkar's thought can be found in the Delhi high court judgment of 2009 regarding Section 377. The court emphasized principles of bodily dignity beyond the imagined "purity" of bodies within the biopolitical ideals of an imagined Hindustan. The racialized skin of Africans—harassed, humiliated, and stripped of all countenance of humanity—and the gendered and sexed skin of queer bodies—made criminal for supposed "unnatural" desires—is also haunted by the deep-seated hatred that Ambedkar spent his lifetime fighting against. Ambedkar once stated that he "judged the progress made by a community, by the progress women have achieved" (Ambedkar qtd. in Kuber 287) and suggested that the relationship between husband and wife "should be that of best friends" (Ambedkar qtd. in Kuber 287). In an "India shining," with glaring violations of human dignity, with gang rapes and legalized marital rape, with queer bodies not afforded bodily integrity, Ambedkar's thought haunts the skin of a nation and all the anxious untouchabilities that it continues to produce.

One of the popularly publicized comments in the 2013 decision to uphold Section 377 of the Indian penal code was made by a Supreme Court judge who stated that he had "never met a gay person" (Justice Singhvi qtd. in Vij). The immediate and perhaps tactical reaction on the part of many queers in India was to publicize a knowable, nameable "rights" bearing "Gay" identity. While this judge's comments could be read as "backwards" in comparison to a reading of universal sexualities all striving to approximate the aesthetic and visible similitude of the "Legalize Gay" branding of North America, the scales of time and mapping of sexual knowledge itself can be problematized. Perhaps the "no going back" of queer temporality in India in fact suggest that one has not "gone back" far enough when knowledge of dissident desire and queer people is associated with something that is not foundational to the history of the nation. When a Supreme Court judge in the Indian subcontinent states that he has not met a queer person, he is in many ways in line with largely white, Western neoliberal political leaders and commentators who assume that "gayness" does not exist if it does not approximate sexualities in the West, and is not intelligible within the grammars of European and Western histories of sexuality. The irony is that the colonial Victorian puritanism of contemporary magistrates in India often makes for unlikely bedfellows with Orientalist and racist Western political leaders and queer movements. In discussing the 2013 demonstrations against the ruling regarding Section 377 alongside the 2012 Delhi gang rape protests, this book suggests that both events offer evidence of the meetings of bodies in the streets as living proof of infinite cycles of anti-colonial resistance. Protestors who participate in contemporary sexual politics in postcolonial worlds—many of them young, feminist, and queer—are haunted by the ghosts of revolutionary figures, those desiring embodied freedoms beyond translation. Āzādī.

TIME PASS:[3]

THE YOUNG AND THE RESTLESS—PRECARITY IN URBAN INDIA

Since the 2012 Delhi gang rape case and the following protests, young people within the Indian subcontinent and specifically in urban India have paradoxically been blamed for sexual violence and also heralded as a progressive vanguard. According to projections from the 2011 census, 20 percent of India's population is "young," as defined by the United Nations. When this youthful demographic is compared to other G20 nations such as Canada in which only 12 percent of the population is counted as young, the face of contemporary India and specifically urban India is a youthful one that is growing up in an increasingly globalized and technologically driven moment. The Justice Verma Commission, which was created following the 2012 Delhi gang rape case, blamed sexual violence in Delhi on a "mass of young, prospectless men" who are "fighting for space in an economy that offers mainly casual work" (Verma Commission qtd. in Subramanya "The Perils of an Unfulfilled Indian Youth"). Paradoxically, Justice Verma also praised the young for their political activism following the Delhi gang rape and murder case. Justice Verma specifically praised the youth movement, stating that,

> Much to learn from the youth, it is not possible to name every-
> one who contributed. Even when there was provocation, they
> did not react and continued to maintain calm. It was the young
> men who were conscious that this gender inequality has to be
> done away with. (Verma Commission qtd. in Subramanya, "The
> Perils of an Unfulfilled Indian Youth")

Discourses concerning young urban Indians are fraught with con-tradictions: political leaders seize on the energies of young people to support national interests while they also blame young people for their insecurity within a neoliberal economy. Subramanya writes that,

> India's youthful population is often portrayed as a "demographic
> dividend." Young people will become the workers of tomorrow
> and drive India's economic rise, so the story goes. But the dark
> side of this tale is the presence of large numbers of uneducated

or poorly educated young men who are, in many cases, unemployed or underemployed, unmarried and frustrated.

This "demographic divided" is also being divided in gendered terms: young women are praised as idealized neoliberal citizens and workers for the global economy, while young men are seen as potential threats to the "India shining" rhetoric of supposed capitalist progress. Orientalist ideas of Asian femininity often construct the Asian woman as submissive and easy to control making her an ideal exploited labourer in comparison to her young male counterpart who is vilified as being out of control, lawless, or lazy. I want to move away from psychologizing young Indian men in ways that hearken back to colonial discourse, describing poor and unemployed Indian men as savages from Jungle Book[4] tales of missionary civility. While "idle young men" are being blamed for sexual and physical violence, statistically, unemployment among young women in India is in fact higher than it is for men. Kunal Kumar Kundu writes that,

> The latest World Development Report by the World Bank says India's youth unemployment—as a percentage of the youth work force—was 9.9% for males and 11.3% for females in 2010. In 1985, the figures were 8.3% and 8%, respectively. Youth unemployment in India, like most countries, has consistently been above the national average. But of late, the data indicate rising youth unemployment, now virtually 50% more than the national average, or total unemployment rate.

The idea of *timepass*, an Indian term often used to describe unstructured time not fenced in by the working day or scales of the global economy, might offer the time and space for emancipatory politics, as evinced in the large numbers of young people who took part in the 2012 Delhi gang rape protests. One can ask how timepass relates to Benjamin's "messianic time," an idea that moves away from understandings of time as being structured by secular-capitalist orderings of bodies, lives, and life worlds.[5] Robinson discusses Benjamin's notion of messianic time stating that

Benjamin goes further than simply criticising capitalist forms of time. He suggests that excluded groups and revolutionaries can access another way of experiencing time, even in capitalist contexts. He suggests that the "messianic" moment exists as a form of time. This other kind of "messianic" time is associated with the experience of immediacy, and the creation of non-linear connections with particular, past or future points. The present revolt is connected in spirit to past revolts. The present generation of activists is always potentially the messiah which past revolutionary movements were waiting for.

To orient the gendered body away from the moment of time pass towards the homogeneous empty time of capital which Benjamin critiques, that which is reliant on "clock, calendar, and calculator," is to turn the desiring body into a productive and reproductive one that can fulfill the biopolitical aims of the nation ("Walter Benjamin: Messianism and Revolution—Theses on History"). Women and also men, as shown in the Delhi gang rape case of 2012, who are out "too late," who occupy public spaces outside of the "business day," whose bodies are "loose" property within the streets, can be regulated through the violence of harassment, abuse, and murder. Drawing on Phadke's writings regarding loitering and public space in the India, what might unite queer and feminist movements in contemporary India is the idea of pleasure within public space. Phadke, Ranade, and Khan write that,

> not only do we desire to loiter, we in fact believe that this act of pleasure seeking holds the possibility of not just expanding women's access to public space but also of transforming women's relationship with the city and re-envisioning citizenship in more inclusive terms. (Phadke, Ranade, and Khan 185)

They further state that "Even within the women's movement, the desire for pleasure has never been as legitimate as the struggle against violence" (3). The right to pleasure and the right to occupy public space offer new articulations of both feminist and queer citizenship. The authors discuss how discourses of protectionism imagine the perpetrator of gendered violence as a man associated with "the street." They write that,

> The struggle against violence as an end in itself is fundamentally

premised on exclusion and can only be maintained through violence, in that, it tends to divide people into "us" and "them" and actually sanctions violence against "them"in order to protect "us." The quest for pleasure on the other hand, when framed in inclusive terms, does not divide people into aggressors and victims and is therefore non-divisive. (Phadke, Ranade, and Khan 185-186)

The "right to pleasure" is central to an understanding of queer politics in contemporary India. As many have written about in regards to Section 377, India's colonial sodomy law, this piece of legislation implicitly polices pleasure as it criminalizes what are termed "unnatural acts," meaning sexual acts that are not aimed at familial reproduction, including masturbation and oral sex. The right to have sex for pleasure is curtailed by colonial laws and the Victorian moralities that inform their normalization. Similarly, the Delhi gang rape protests of 2012, while often reframed by mainstream political leaders to suit the protectionist policing of women's mobility, can be thought of in relation to this desire for freedom, or as heard in the city streets: Āzādī.

The Delhi gang rape case of 2012 spoke to the sheer vulnerability of human life, an expression of a time of global precarity. Similarly, the precarity of bodies and their desires were revealed in the decision to reinstitute Section 377, a ruling that many queers in India suggest came "without warning" and was both "shocking" and "terrifying" (Vij). The precarity of bodies is also reflected within times of economic insecurity, in which the guarantees of old, stable forms of social security once held in place by the social welfare state are no longer guaranteed. Rather, transnational businesses attempt to turn young urban Indians into captive consumers for global industry, while they simultaneously face a competitive global capitalist market and high rates of unemployment. The Delhi gang rape protests of December 2012 are an expression of a precarious feminism, as its organizing tactics and ideology cannot be separated from a global economy of increased uncertainty, including the insecurity of gendered bodies in public space and desiring bodies faced with the whims of legal authority. Judith Butler writes that, "precarity is, of course directly linked with gender norms, since we know that those who do not live their genders in intelligible ways are at heightened risk for harassment and violence" ("Performativity, Precarity, and Sexual

Politics"). Butler goes on to highlight the precarity of gender within public space. Butler argues that the body of the woman, queer, and transgender person is one that is made insecure within public space:

> Gender norms have everything to do with how and in what ways we can appear in public space; how and in what way public and private are distinguished, and how that distinction is instrumentalized in the service of sexual politics; who will be criminalized on the basis of public appearance, who will fail to be protected by the law or, more specifically, the police, on the street, or on the job, or in the home. ("Performativity, Precarity, and Sexual Politics")

The production of the insecure body can be thought of in relation to a wider moment of instability. Against narratives of the imagined progress of neoliberal capitalism in India and globally, many are not at home. Many are not at home in public space because of gendered vulnerability, not at home in the nation because of the perilous place of workers in an unstable global economy, and not at home in the world because of the growing numbers of stateless persons crossing borders to often appear on city streets as unfamiliar racialized migrants, subject to violence. Mainstream political leaders following the 2012 Delhi gang rape case tried to blame gendered precarity on poor and migrant workers within urban India. Yet a theory of precarious feminism serves to make connections between the heightened gender vulnerability of bodies in public space and the precarious lives of workers and migrants. Butler questions the relationship between gender performativity and precarity and suggests that,

> In the end, the question of how performativity links with precarity might be summed up in these more important questions—How does the unspeakable population speak and make its claims? What kind of disruption is this within the field of power? And how can such populations lay claim to what they truly require? ("Performativity, Precarity, and Sexual Politics")

Butler's questions highlight the tensions between gendered precarity and other precarious populations. Thinking about the Delhi gang rape

113

case and the protests that followed in relation to a broader moment of precarious politics throughout the world moves away from Orientalist readings of India that often rely on a timeless reading of culture that divorces political movements in India from a wider moment of global austerity and from precarious populations the world over. Rather than reading something quintessentially Indian in the protests of 2012 and 2013, these actions can be read as decidedly precarious, reflective of an India that is connected politically to a world of new social movements. The question becomes if and how the discourse of precarity that has become popular within Europe is applicable to the Global South and specifically the Indian subcontinent. Isabel Lorey writes that,

> precarization can be seen as a neoliberal instrument of governance. Neoliberal societies are now governed internally through social insecurity, which means providing the minimum possible social security. (Lorey)

The year preceding the Delhi gang rape case, activist Anna Hazare launched large scale protests against governmental corruption in the Indian subcontinent. The instability of neoliberal governance is compounded by the corruption of the postcolonial state and its inefficient forms of bureaucracy. The lack of security that defines neoliberal capitalism can also be thought of in relation to the increasing urbanization of the nation and a growing agrarian crisis that has led to the rapid dissolution of rural-based economies. The precarity within contemporary urban India can be seen in relation to not only state governance and market insecurity but a rapidly changing psychic, social, and political sphere. As Lorey suggests, the deep insecurity of the precarious body can lead to increased politicization. Lorey argues that there should perhaps be a unity in the growing *precariat*, one that unites those who are made insecure by neoliberal strategies of governance in disparate and yet interrelated ways.[6] Dividing issues of gender-based violence from issues of precarity serves to construct feminism as a neoliberal and legislative bid for "rights" that is separated from the wider instability of the global economy. The will to think about gendered violence in the context of precarity and the global recession in no way excuses reprehensible hate crimes such as gang rape and murder. This line of inquiry seeks to explain these forms of abhorrent violence in the economic and political context in which they take place rather than using quick and ahistorical psychological and cultural explanations of "Indian society" or the "Indian male psyche."

FEMINISM:

CHALLENGING THE TEMPORALITIES OF NEOLIBERAL "GIRL POWER"

The formation of feminism as a middle-class and educated movement informed by academic institutions and non-governmental organizations has often divided feminist politics from issues pertaining to the working class, both in India and transnationally. However, Lorey and other writers who centre the precaritization of life under neoliberal forms of governance point out that increasingly, the instability of the social welfare state is a condition that unites people across classes and embodiment. Bhabha suggests that an effective language of critique refuses to simplistically resolve contradictions. He writes,

> The language of critique is effective not because it keeps forever separate the terms of the master and slave, the mercantilist and the Marxist, but to the extent to which it overcomes the given grounds of opposition and opens up a space of translation: a place of hybridity, figuratively speaking, where the construction of a political object that is new, neither the one nor the other, properly alienates our political expectations, and changes, as it must, the very forms of our recognition of the moment of politics. (37)

Feminism often constructs clear divisions between powerful and powerless, particularly in cases of gendered violence. However, the contemporary political moment is beset by uncomfortable and complex truths of violence. The precarious nature of global capitalism and all the violence that engenders troubles both self-righteous outrage and trite justifications of the misogyny of poor urban men. The social antagonism of gendered precarity that often appears in spectacular and abhorrent ways through the magnified violence of young impoverished men speaks to a contradiction within feminist politics. There is a continued antagonism between pedagogies and political movements that triumph the oppressed while also critiquing and protesting against the misogyny of

115

the subaltern. Those who are interested and engaged in sexual politics globally must address the histories and ongoing gendered violence of the proletariat and today, the precariat.

OF MIGRANTS AND MEN:
GENDERED VIOLENCE AND THE 'FOOTLOOSE' MIGRANT

Hindu nationalist leader Raj Thackery pathologized migrants in the wake of the Delhi gang rape and other incidents of sexual violence in Mumbai and throughout India. Thackery, a member of the MNS (*Maharashtra Navnirman Sena)* party suggested that Bihari migrants were to blame for rising levels of sexual violence in urban India ("Thackery Blames Bihari Migrants"). Bihar, one of the poorest states in North East India and home to a large number of religious minorities, has been vilified previously by conservative political leaders. Due to the impoverishment of the largely agrarian state, Biharis are one of the largest migrant populations in Delhi and increasingly in Mumbai. Migrant rights activists in Delhi and Mumbai have documented the sickening living conditions that often define the lives of Bihari migrant workers. Bihari migrant workers often live without access to amenities such as proper housing, adequate food and water. In addition to this, Biharis are often stigmatized by middle-class urban Indians and are often scapegoated as criminals by the state and police (Atluri Personal interviews). The vilifying of migrant men is a political strategy that serves to colonize women's deaths to suit the interests of elite men. The scripting of the poor, migrant man as most likely to commit acts of sexual violence is yet another way in which feminism is appropriated to justify conservative political agendas that further hinder women's access to resources and sexual freedom. As mentioned in the introductory chapter of this work, the construction of the 2012 Delhi gang rape case as a case of poor men attacking middle-class urban women also ignores that the caste, class, and labour of Jyoti's family were not dissimilar to some of her assailants.

PRECARIOUS FEMINISMS:
CONTRACTUALLY BOUND LIVES AND FLEETING FREEDOMS

Precarious feminism is a theoretical, philosophical, and political position that centres the experiences, struggles, and politics of gendered and sexed bodies within times of austerity, precarity, and global recession. While neoliberal capitalism often purports to offer "freedom" in the form of capitalist consumerism, instability brought about by global austerity may in fact cause a further entrenchment of normative gender relations, the valorizations of heteronormative biopolitical scripts of the family, and sexism. In the context of contemporary urban India where employment and financial security are not guaranteed for impoverished, lower-class and lower-caste men, migrants, and women, an enforcement of patriarchal power relations may be reverted to in order to give the illusion of stability. Those without economic and political power may assert discursive and embodied power through physical and epistemic acts of violence, expressed in the minute performative staging of idealized gender roles and through extreme acts of sexual and physical assault. In relation to the previous chapter regarding sexual politics and cyberspace, the relationship between precarity, insecurity, and Internet-based technologies can be questioned. In a time when worlds of work, education, and interpersonal human relationships are often structured by technology, the high-speed world of online lives can produce a transnational anxiety. The click of the wrong button can have incalculable consequences beyond the likelihood of human error. Precarious feminism involves an apprehension of gendered and sexual politics in contemporary contexts in which technologically driven life worlds, economic, personal, and political futures can be as shaky as an Internet connection.

The precarity of the gendered body that is subject to abhorrent violence to the point of death can be contextualized within an overall crisis of all stable forms of life, times of deep personal, political, and economic insecurity exacerbated by financial austerity and increasingly few guarantees offered by the social welfare state. These are precarious times in which lives can be as unstable as contractual labour and wireless Internet connections. Theorists writing in regards to precarity and the growing global precariat have often used Europe and the Eurozone crises as their point of reference. However, theories of precarity can be applied to the Global South and specifically, to the Indian subcontinent. Those who have written about the European precariat have proposed a unification of precarious bodies across divisions of identity politics. Lorey writes that,

If we understand precaritization in this sense as the normalization and steering of differences in the midst of insecurity, then it becomes pointless to construct specialized groups with critical emancipatory intentions around notions of precarity, as divisions into "luxury precarity" and "impoverished precarity" ultimately only reproduce neoliberal dynamics of competitiveness between different degrees of precarization. (Lorey)

Yet the trouble with totalizing theories of oppression particularly in contexts such as contemporary India is that such approaches obscure the long histories of virulent misogyny produced through state policy, law and market forces and existent in all aspects of social life. Precarious feminism needs to account for how, within the context of contemporary India, the unity of precarious gendered bodies and the insecure bodies of the unemployed are being divided through gendered violence. Just as earlier waves of the feminist movement both in India and transnationally had to account for sexism, homophobia, transphobia, misogyny, and gendered violence among workers and subaltern movements, a feminism that addresses global austerity must also politicize the new forms of sexual violence that surface in a time of financial insecurity.[7] Lorey suggests that one must consider the multiplicities that are at play among a growing group of people who are produced as insecure bodies in different states of vulnerability, transnationally (Lorey). The collective "public judgment" exercised by protestors in India in 2012 and 2013 spoke to a commonality of political dissent against growing forms of gendered and sexual violence that shows not only the inability for feminist goals to be achieved by neoliberalism but the worsening conditions of feminist and queer lives as a result of precarization. Precarious feminism accounts for the impacts that the casualization of life has on the production of insecure gendered, sexual, and labouring bodies navigating precarious urban life worlds. Precarious feminism is a symptom of the instability of our times, a feminism that attempts to address the bodily violence of sexual antagonism that threatens to divide the global precariat from itself.

ENDNOTES

[1]The word "bus" loosely translates into "enough" in Hindi.
[2]Berlant and Warner offer an interesting discussion regarding "sex in

public." The authors suggest that "nothing is more public than privacy" and discuss the relationship between the policing of sexuality through zoning laws in New York City and through the implicit celebration of national heterosexuality. While their discussion focuses on North America, the authors theoretical assertions are still perhaps of relevance to the Indian subcontinent and transnationally (547-566).

[3] *Time Pass* is a term often used in urban India to refer to "hanging out." Since the Delhi gang rape, it has been largely used to in a negative way to refer to young men who are precarious and unemployed within cities and are being blamed for rising levels of sexual violence (Fuller; Jeffrey).

[4] *The Jungle Book* was originally a collection of stories written by Rudyard Kipling, a European colonial writer, who also wrote *The White Man's Burden*, a racist justification for colonial rule, which constructed white Europeans as missionary saviours of racialized people in the Global South. The book was later made into a Walt Disney film featuring a young orphan Mowgli, a brown boy left in the jungle and raised by wild animals. Brown bodies are associated with the wild and animals in ways that support colonial discourse. The "white man's burden" becomes one of saving brown people from a constructed savagery and the lawlessness of the jungle, inculcating them into Western systems of political governance, English language, and Christian norms (Kipling).

[5] Benjamin, Walter. "On the Concept of History." *Walter Benjamin: Selected Writings. Volume 4. 1938-1940.* Translated by Edmund Jephcott and Others. Edited by Howard Eiland and Michael W. Jennings. Cambridge: The Belknap Press of Harvard University Press, 2006. 389-400.

[6] Lorey further argues that neoliberal strategies of governance that threaten social security, stable forms of employment, and resources allotted to guaranteeing the freedoms of bodies in public spaces can be used to unite those who are made precarious in different ways. As the author states, "If precarization has become a governmental instrument of normalization surpassing specific groups and classes, then social and political battles themselves should not assume differential separations and hierarchies" (Lorey).

[7] While feminist and queer politics have often involved forms of "identity" politics in which the aesthetics, embodiment, and sexual desires and practices of bodies are used as forms of strategic essentialism, Lorey suggests that a time of global precarity can be utilised to generate new forms of social and political solidarity. As the author writes,

when it is a matter of searching for the common in the various forms of precarization, for possibilities of coming together to form alliances through difference, then identitary, subject-oriented politics are obviously not suitable for their hindering of what is common in difference. (Lorey)

Similarly, while therapeutic, medical, or social work discourses psychologize subjects and use familial history to explain psychic unrest, the precaritization of life within times of uncertainty can be seen as causing anxiety and aggression. As Slavoj Žižek writes,

Today, in the era of "risk society", the ruling ideology endeavours to sell us the very insecurity caused by the dismantling of the Welfare State as the opportunity for new freedoms. Do you have to change jobs every year, relying on short-term contracts instead of a long-term stable appointment? Why not see it as a liberation from the constraints of a fixed job, as the chance to reinvent yourself again and again, to become aware of and realize the hidden potentials of your personality? You can no longer rely on the standard health insurance and retirement plan, so that you have to opt for additional coverage for which you must pay? Why not perceive it as an additional opportunity to choose: either better life now or long-term security? And if this predicament causes you anxiety, the postmodern or "second modernity" ideologist will immediately accuse you of being unable to assume full freedom, of the "escape from freedom", of the immature sticking to old stable forms.... Even better, when this is inscribed into the ideology of the subject as the psychological individual pregnant with natural abilities and tendencies, then I as it were automatically interpret all these changes as the result of my personality, not as the result of me being tossed around by market forces. (Žižek *The Universal Exception* 237)

WORKS CITED

Ambedkar, B. R. *Annihilation of Caste: The Annotated Critical Edition.* Ed. S. Anand. Delhi: Navayana, 2014. Print.

Atluri, Tara. Personal interviews. 2012-2014.

Berlant, Lauren and Michael Warner. "Sex in Public." *Critical Inquiry*

24.2 (Winter1998): 547-566. Print.

Bhabha, Homi. *The Location of Culture*. London: Routledge, 2004. Print.

Bhan, Gautam, and Arvind Narrain. *Because I Have a Voice: Queer Politics in India*. New Delhi: Yoda Press, 2005. Print.

Bhatia, Gautam. "The Great Indian Racist." *thehindu.com*. The Hindu, 13 Feb. 2014. Web. 2 March 2014.

Bridges, Lee. "Four Days in August: The UK Riots." *Race & Class* 54.1 (2012): 1-12. Print.

Butler, Judith. "Sexual Politics, Torture, and Secular Time." *The British Journal of Sociology* 59.1 (2008): 1-23. Print.

Butler, Judith. "Performativity, Precarity, and Sexual Politics." *Revista de Antropología Iberoamericana* 8 June 2009. Web. 11 June 2015.

Bloodsworth, James. "Is the British Government Ignoring Gay Rights in India for Trade?" *Left Foot Forward*, 12 Dec. 2013. Web. 2 March 2014.

Bourdieu, Pierre. "Social Space and Symbolic Power." *Sociological Theory* 7.1 (Spring 1989): 14-25. Print.

Burke, Jason. "Arundhati Roy Accuses Mahatma Gandhi of Discrimination." *The Guardian*, 18 July 2014. Web. 21 Oct. 2015.

Chabot, Sean, and Jan Willem Duyvendak. "Globalization and Transnational Diffusion between Social Movements: Reconceptualizing the Dissemination of the Gandhian Repertoire and the 'Coming Out' Routine." *Theory and Society* 31.6 (2002): 697-740. Print.

Deftereos, Christine. *Ashis Nandy and the Cultural Politics of Selfhood*. New Delhi: Sage, 2013. Print.

Fanon, Frantz. *Black Skin, White Masks*. London: Grove Press, 1968. Print.

Faleiro, Sonia. "Modi Is No Champion of India's Women." *The New York Times*, 22 Dec. 2013. Web. 26 Feb. 2014.

Feminists India. "Women, Student Bodies Stage Protest in Delhi as AAP Defends Racist Action." *Feminist India*, 19 Jan. 2014. Web. 2 March 2014.

Fuller, Chris. "Time Pass and Boredom in Modern India." *Anthropology of This Century*, May 2011. Web. 7 Aug. 2015.

Foucault, Michel. *The History of Sexuality Volume 1: An Introduction*. Trans. Robert Hurley. New York: Vintage Books, 1990. Print.

Gatade, S. "Modis and the Art of Disappearing Untouchability." *Kafila*, 12 Feb. 2014. Web. 26 Feb. 2014.

Hawitorn, Jin. "'Beyond Hate': Queer Metonymies of Crime, Pathology, and Anti-Violence." *Jindal Global Law Review* 4.2 (November

2013): 44-78. Print.

Jeffrey, Craig. *Timepass: Youth, Class, and the Politics of Waiting in India.* London: Stanford University Press, 2010. Print.

Joshi, Malicca. "We are Stoned, Spat at on Roads: Africans in Delhi." *The Hindustan Times,* 18 Jan. 2014. Web. 2 March 2014.

Khanna, Ranjana. "Post-Palliative: Coloniality's Affective Dissonance." *Postcolonial Text* 2.1 (2006). Web. 11 June 2015.

Kipling, Rudyard. *The Jungle Book.* London: Macmillan Publishers, 1894. Print.

Kuber, W. N. *Ambedkar: A Critical Study.* Delhi: People's Publishing House, 1991.

Kumar Kundu, Kunal. "Young, Jobless, and Indian." *India Real Time,* 23 Nov. 2012. Web. 11 June 2015.

Lee, Shayne. *Erotic Revolutionaries: Black Women, Sexuality, and Popular Culture.* Maryland: Hamilton Press, 2010. Print.

Lewis, Reina. *Gendering Orientalism: Race, Femininity and Representation.* London: Routledge, 2013. Print.

Lorey, Isabel. "Becoming Common: Precarization as Politically Constituting." *E-flux,* 2015. Web. 11 June 2015.

McLelland, MJ, "Interpretation and Orientalism: Outing Japan's Sexual Minorities to the English-Speaking World." *After Orientalism: Critical Engagements, Productive Looks.* Ed. I. Boer. Amsterdam: Rodopi, 2003. 105-22. Print.

Munoz, Jose. *Disidentifications: Queers of Colour and the Politics of Resistance.* Minnesota: University of Minnesota Press, 1999. Print.

Nandy, Ashish. *The Intimate Enemy: Loss and Recovery of Self Under Colonialism.* Oxford: Oxford University Press, 1983. Print.

Narrain, Arvind and Alok Gupta. *Law Like Love: Queer Perspectives on Law.* New Delhi: Yoda Press, 2011. Print.

O'Hanlon, Rosalind. "Manliness and Imperial Service in Mughal North India." *Journal of the Economic and Social History of the Orient* 42.1 (1999): 47-93. Print.

Phadke, Shilpa Ranade, Shilpa and Sameera Khan. "Why Loiter? Radical Possibilities for Gendered Dissent." *Dissent and Cultural Resistance in Asian Cities.* Eds. Melissa Butcher and Selvaraj Velayutham. London: Routledge, 2009. 185-203. Print.

Puar, Jasbir. *Terrorist Assemblages: Homonationalism in Queer Times.* Durham: Duke University Press, 2007. Print.

Rana, Subir. "Nomadism, Ambulation, and the `Empire': Contextualising the Criminal Tribes Act xxvii of 1871." *Transcience Journal.* N.p., 2011. Web. 16 Oct. 2015.

Rao, Rahul. "On `Gay Conditionality,' Imperial Power and Queer Liberation." *Kafila,* 1 Jan. 2012. Web. 2 March 2014.

Ray, Sugata. "Darcy Grimaldo Grigsby and Sugata Ray in Conversation in Berlin." *Art History Berkely.* Berkely, 4 March 2015. Web. 21 Oct. 2015

Reddy, Gayatri. *With Respect to Sex: Negotiating Hijra Identity in South India.* Chicago: University of Chicago Press, 2005. Print.

Rege, Sharmila. "The Hegemonic Appropriation of Sexuality: The Case of the Lavani Performers of Maharashtra." *Contributions to Indian Sociology* 29.1-2 (1995): 23-38. Print.

Robinson, Andrew. "Walter Benjamin: Messianism and Revolution—Theses on History." *Ceasefire,* 15 Nov. 2013. Web. 24 Nov. 2015.

Sameen, Zoya. "Prostituting the Tawa'if: Nawabi Patronage and Colonial Regulation of Courtesans in Lucknow, 1847-1899." *Academia,* 2015. Web. 11 June 2015.

Subramanya, Rupa. "The Perils of an Unfulfilled Indian Youth." *India Real Time,* 28 Feb. 2014. Web. 11 June 2015.

The Jungle Book. Dir. Wolfgang Reitherman. Walt Disney Pictures, 1967. Film.

"Raj ThackeryBlames Bihari Migrants for Delhi Gang Rape Case." *The Times of India,* 6 Jan. 2013. Web. 20 June 2015.

Vij, Shivam. "The Dubious Arguments for India's Ban on Gay Sex." *The New Yorker,* 13 Dec. 2013. Web. 19 June2015.

Wright, Michelle M. and Antje Schuhmann. *Blackness and Sexualities.* Berlin: Lit. Verlag, 2007. Print.

Žižek, Slavoj. *The Universal Exception.* Eds. Rex Butler and Scott Stephens. London: Bloomsbury, 2006.

Žižek, Slavoj. *The Year of Dreaming Dangerously.* London: Verso, 2012. Print.

3.
JAIL BAIT

LEGALIZING DESIRE OR DESIRING
OUTSIDE OF THE LAW?

*F*AIR IS FAIR. *Fair enough. Fair and lovely. The white-wigged and white-skinned magistrates of a once great empire banged their mighty wooden gavels across the dark continents of the world. In the streets of something called a postcolonial city, barristers of many hues are dressed in legal regalia. Many famed nationalist and postcolonial leaders studied law, and they, too, once buried their heads in the books of Western legality. The fair is fair of a bureaucratic ordering of lives that catalogue bodies like files, according to number and name. The darkness of Dalit flesh, the flesh of a woman exposed to show the Delhi police her scars and bruises, evidence of violence beyond calculation. The flesh of a Hijra, a body and name carrying centuries of religious mythology, now often found begging in the traffic of Indian cities.*

Exhibit A. Exhibit B. Exhibit C. A Dalit. A woman. A Hijra. All are counted now as something called citizens, left to stand like statues exhibited in great colonial museums, bearing scars and bloodied limbs, bruises concealed with foreign-imported cosmetics and clothes. The haunting everyday violence is now catalogued and filed by uniformed men and Western-educated lawyers whose tongues click around the fair is fair grammars of legality like the imported Italian shoes of a barrister. Lawyers in city offices will receive details of the untranslatable violence done to bodies in a gmail inbox, with advertisements for home furnishings and romantic comedies, distracting them from the dull, dead words.

The law turns grief into grievance. Lawsuits to conceal the fair and lovely materiality of the skin of bodies, colonized by the grammars of bureaucratic violence. Lawsuits to conceal the scars of fair and lovely Hindu middle-class wives, not raped and beaten by the usual suspects, the dark and poor, but by rich and powerful men, as celebrated as colonial tales of happy provincial

124

families. She is counted as a citizen and now she is dead. Tortured and raped and murdered in ways that defy all legal grievance. A grief beyond all claims to something called justice. S/he is counted as a citizen. Fair enough. S/he is chased through the train station, a Hijra, marked by all the consummate anxiety of others. S/he tries to jump from one platform to the next to escape the attackers, college boys returning from good schools in long shorts and ties, the matching uniforms of prissy school boys bonding through violence as sport. S/he jumps, a risk, one beyond wager and calculation when chased by a group of boys who salivate like wild dogs at the sight of this body, one counted as citizen. The legs of a Hijra dressed in a cotton sari only spread so far when jumping like a Commonwealth games athlete. S/he lands on the train tracks. A city of commuters. S/he looks up, newly declared citizen of an India shining and sees the light of the train. They will take this supposed citizen to the hospital. They will fill out paperwork and photograph bruised and broken limbs. They will try to find the assailants in a city of millions. Perhaps there will be some legal action that could be taken by a citizen who now has trouble walking. Fair is fair. Fair enough. Fair and lovely.

The question of the law and its relationship to gendered violence, sexual politics, and the body have been at the forefront of the 2012 Delhi gang rape case and other related struggles regarding gender justice in India. The law and legality have always made for an awkward arrangement within sexual political struggles. I arrived in India in December of 2013 shortly after the Supreme Court judgment to uphold Section 377 of the Indian Penal Code, when the centrality of the relationship between law and sexuality in contemporary India was forcefully articulated. The relationship between law, sexual politics, and basic principles of justice for all minorities in India has been a central theme throughout Indian history. For example, influential activists and great thinkers such as Ambedkar were trained in the grammars and protocols of law through formal education in the legal field. As discussed throughout this book, there may be a limit to the language of law in fully articulating desire, in fully honouring embodiment, and in allowing for a space to envision sexualities outside of bureaucratic colonial grammar. However, the importance of the law within sexual politics in the subcontinent is politically strategic and offers evidence of the historical and ongoing work of inspiring political thinkers, who have invested in the language of law. Narrain and Gupta discuss the key role that law and legality have played in both criminalizing sex and sexualities and the importance of using the law as a tool of political change in India. They state that,

> It is impossible to contextualize the roots of homophobia in law without reference to colonial law.... It was only colonial law that introduced clear strictures against homosexuality. This is enforced by laws like the notorious Section 377 of the Indian Penal Code, Criminal Tribes Act, 1871, and numerous prohibitions under the broad guise of nuisance, obscenity and public morality, all colonial codifications, which seek to enforce a conservative hetero-normative sexual order. (xiii-xv)

The constitution of public forms of declared and enforced morality as well as the concept of "nuisance" already presuppose a unified consciousness regarding what constitutes morality and gesture to the policing of desire in public spaces through colonial norms. In this regard, in causing a supposed nuisance in public space and declaring a public morality not against the constructed "obscenity" or "unnaturalness" of queer rights but against the obscenity of everyday forms of heternormative masculinist violence the 2012 Delhi gang rape protests are implicitly be tied to Section 377. While seeing queer people expressing signs of romantic love in public spaces in the city of Delhi is often naturalized as "unnatural," violence against women in public spaces, ranging from staring to groping is shockingly common. While any public sign or even mention of queer desire is met with suspicion and constructed as "out of place" and against "our culture," the reduction of women's bodies to objects of the male gaze who are subject to gender-based violence comes to be a "normal" part of a Delhi day. Gender-based violence is often made sense of through questioning the imagined "naturalness" of the woman who survives violence rather than questioning her attacker. The question becomes how debates regarding Section 377 and the ideological norms it implicitly supports promote a certain gendered and sexual vision of society that cannot be divorced from the Delhi gang rape case. Law and legality are connected to broader colonial ideologies that mark queer and female bodies as already "guilty" in moral terms. Simultaneously, the violence of powerful men is often justified as innocent and harmless, as just boys being boys.

"UNNATURAL" DESIRES AND "NATURAL" RAPE:
THE BIOPOLITICAL FACE OF LEGALITY

Writing after the 2009 reading down of Section 377 of the Indian Penal Code by the Delhi High Court, Basheer, Mukherjee, and Nair discuss the relationship between ideas of the "unnatural" and colonial regulations of sexuality in India. While the authors praise the 2009 judgment, they critique terms such as "unnatural" which continued to be used even following this decision. The authors state that,

> The Naz Court endorses a line of Section 377 cases that embody a prudish Victorian morality, under which only "procreative" sex is seen as "natural." By this logic, even condom usage during sex would count as unnatural. (Basheer, Mukherjee, and Nair 433)

For my purposes, in discussing the relationship between the Delhi gang rape case of 2012 and Section 377, what is of interest from a theoretical perspective is how constituting certain sex acts and desires as "unnatural" naturalizes the female body as one lacking sexual desire, one whose embodiment is produced through law as a tool for the biopolitical aims of idealized nation building. The female body continues to be imagined as one whose sexuality is only important to the reproduction of future citizens of the nation state. Basheer, Mukherjee, and Nair state that "the word 'natural' is loaded with a positive evaluation, much like the word 'normal.' So, to call something 'natural' is not simply to describe it, but to praise it. Conversely labelling something as unnatural amounts to denouncing it[1] (Basheer, Mukherjee, and Nair 436). However, what constitutes natural in the Indian subcontinent cannot be understood through a Eurocentric paradigm of secular gender binaries. The recent 2014 decision by the Supreme Court to offer legal recognition to Hijras, which also involved proposed changes regarding toilets and health services for transgender people, offers evidence of how law is used in contemporary sexual political struggles to challenge colonial norms of what is assumed to be natural. What might also be of symbolic importance about the Delhi gang rape protests of 2012 and ongoing struggles regarding Section 377 is the Hijras' historical role as the protector of women and their ties to traditions of sexual sacrifice and renunciation. Rather than advancing a purely rights-based discourse that draws on a language of secular "progress," Hijras often emphasize their historical, cultural, and religious value as part of Indian history. In receiving legal countenance, the body of the Hijra does not become a "natural" body that approximates the cisgender male or female body, nor does it become an "unnatural" body that gains sympathy from others; rather, Hijras are counted in law as Hijras, a "third sex" that ruptures biopolitical constructions of "natural" male-female binaries. Foucault suggests that in eighteenth-century Europe the body begins to be framed as a state problem that requires an investment in the lives of certain bodies to support the economic[2] vitality of the nation. Foucault writes,

> the body of individuals and the body of populations appears as the bearer of new variables, not merely as between the scarce and the numerous, the submissive and the restive, rich and poor, healthy and sick, strong and weak, but also as between the more or less utilisable, more or less amenable to profitable investment, those with greater or lesser prospects of survival, death and illness, and with more or less capacity for being usefully trained. (Foucault qtd. in Smart 374)

The birth of the modern nation and modern capitalism coincides with the birth of the body as an object of state inquiry. The need to control and regulate bodies gains importance at the level of state power in order to reproduce a workforce. With the rise of industrial capital, bodies are translated into a language of capital. What is deemed as "unnatural" is sex that is ungoverned, as it serves no value for the state or market. In regards to the relationship between population and utility, Foucault states,

> The biological traits of a population become relevant factors for economic management and it becomes necessary to organise around them an apparatus, which will ensure not only their subjection but the constant increase of their utility. (Foucault and Gordan 172)

Sex for pleasure in the metropole and the colonies is haunted not only by the psychic and ideological fears and anxieties of Victorian moralism, but also by the presence of desires that are criminalized for having no role to play in the reproduction of an idealized "mother country." The "naturalness" of the body produced through laws such as Section 377 and the marking of "criminal tribes" normalizes the powers of the colonial empire to govern colonial subjects in ways that will reproduce its wealth. Similarly, the legalization of marital rape through the colonial countenance of woman as property within colonial law also serves a biopolitical function as it curtails the possible threat that comes from unregulated female sexuality, which could produce the "wrong" kinds of citizens, namely those who are not ideal workers or subjects for and of empire. As Foucault discusses, the regulation and criminalizing of certain bodies cannot be separated from the positive investments made in other kinds of sex. Foucault suggests it is not simply that discursive powers of sex articulated through institutions of disciplinary power weigh on people or are internalized; rather, a much more nuanced relationship exists between sex and power. He writes,

> What I want to show is how power relations can materially penetrate the body in depth, without depending even on the mediation of the subject's own representations. If power takes hold on the body, this isn't through its having first to be interiorised in people's consciousnesses. There is a network or circuit of bio-power, or somatopower, which acts as the formative matrix of sexuality itself as the historical and cultural phenomenon within which we seem at once to recognise and lose ourselves. (Foucault 186)

It is interesting to question what produces, regulates, and constitutes the "network or circuit of biopower" (Foucault *The History of Sexuality* 186) in contemporary India. How might people come to recognize and lose themselves and their sexual desires through this schema of regulatory power? How does the recognition of "natural" sex allow people to recognize themselves as citizens within contemporary India? Foucault's repression hypothesis regarding Victorian bourgeois moralism suggests that far from silencing sex, discourses of repression produce an endless litany of discussion and debate (Foucault). This book asks how sex came to be spoken about through a discourse of colonial legality that informs contemporary sexual politics in India. While there continues to be a great deal of discussion regarding queers and female sexualities, much of which began with the 2012 Delhi gang rape case and the 2013 decision to uphold Section 377, sex is often only discursively intelligible through ideas of biopolitial utility that have historical resonance in European colonial law. The simultaneous repression and obsession with queer desire and female sexuality by the Indian state speaks to the lingering ethos of bourgeois Victorian moralism, with its simultaneous aversion to and obsession with sex. Through existing grammars of colonial category, legality, and state power sexualities are often discussed in the mainstream public sphere. Hence, discussions regarding the normative queer body who is posited as being part of the nation and discussions regarding the "natural" versus the "unnatural" are often already framed within categories of disciplinary power. Similarly, within much of the mainstream writing concerning the 2012 Delhi gang rape case, sex was often again discussed in relation to its potential to destroy or erode the biopolitical aims of the nation state by defaming the alleged honour of the idealized Hindu middle-class woman as a future "Mother India" for the nation. While this chapter deals with strategic uses of the law by feminists, queers, activists, allies and everyday people in their bids for something that might be called Āzādī, it also asks a lingering question about what the law may not be able to calculate or contain.

OF GRIEF AND GRIEVANCE: THE ETHICS OF LAW

Many feminists in the Indian subcontinent have written of the centrality of the law in Indian feminist struggles. Farah Naqvi discusses how 1970s law reforms in India marked the emergence of the contemporary Indian women's movement. Yet Naqvi also problematizes this focus on law in a few important ways. First, Naqvi discusses the limits of the law in offering feminists the kinds of legal and political changes that they demand. The law often attempts to conserve tradition, meaning that feminists have to dilute their demands for radical political change in the language of legality. Naqvi asks, "In our search for the 'strategic' solution, are we losing sight of the ideal? Have we abandoned our search for that elusive outcome called 'legal justice?'" (Naqvi 43). In considering the limits of the law a placard carried by a young woman at the Delhi gang rape protests of 2012 comes to mind; it read: "Justice delayed means the justice denied." While law is a strategic tool that can support political victories of the present and garner media attention, how might the often slow moving bureaucratic temporalities of colonial legality evade the moment of public spectacle? Although new laws make headlines, the processes of justice that emerge through the often slow moving bureaucracy of the colonial state may prevent immediate and necessary action in cases of gender-based violence. This critique is applicable to the 2012 Delhi gang rape and murder case in which one of the major critiques of activists and commentators was directed against police corruption and the bureaucratic inefficiency of the Indian state. The idea of legalistic justice is of course related to feminism and specific crimes of sexual and bodily violence. In regards to campaigns concerning rape and sexual violence, Naqvi asks, "What does `justice' mean for an individual survivor? What does `justice' mean for activists?" (Naqvi 1). Naqvi further discusses the problems that arise when authority regarding gender justice is vested in a few individuals who occupy elite positions within court and state structures and asks, "Should the law not acknowledge the excessive power vested in an individual in a position of state authority?" (Naqvi 1). Naqvi's intelligent question is also relevant to the decision to uphold Section 377 of the Indian Penal Code by the Supreme Court of India. Commentators point to the discrepancy between the language and sensibilities of the judges who made the 2013 Supreme Court judgment and the judges who made the 2009 Delhi High Court (Ranganathan).[3] As discussed in the previous chapter, the gap in age and generational sensibilities that defines the landscape of sexual politics in contemporary India magnifies Naqvi's question even further. Naqvi problematizes the ability of law to ever fully contain the trauma of sexual violence and to offer a meaningful feeling of justice for survivors. In regards to Section 377, and as discussed in subsequent chapters drawing on interviews done in India, what does legalistic justice mean for many queer people whose relationships with family, within educational institutions, workplaces, and within the broader society have been physically pushed and pulled by the whims of the state and by the seemingly flippant whims of law makers? The decisions made by courts can produce feelings of insecurity in a group of people often already constructed as vulnerable.

Naqvi further discusses the ethical questions that arise when crimes of individual suffering are turned into political causes. Ethical questions can be posed about the 2012 Delhi gang rape case and 2013 decision to uphold Section 377, and the infringement of privacy that often occurs through public campaigns documenting homophobic assaults and sexual violence. Naqvi writes that "Law reform has been preceded by feminist-led campaigns centred around particular cases. These `trigger' cases continue to be critical for the women's movement" (Naqvi 2). Yet, Naqvi problematizes how these cases, while generating national and transnational attention, might further traumatize survivors because of media spectacle. Naqvi also discusses how in using certain cases to generate social upheaval and change, the individual wishes of survivors can be sacrificed in the name of greater political goals.

Recall, for example, the death of Dr. Ramchandas Siras who supposedly committed suicide after his dismissal from his position as a lecturer because of his sexuality, in the wake of the reading down of Section 377 by the Delhi High Court in 2009. The publicizing of same-sex desire in India might, in fact, make certain bodies more vulnerable. Furthermore, it can be asked how media spectacle causes survivors of gender-based and sexual violence to be vulnerable to further shame and debasement by courts and transnational media as evinced in the legal trial of those accused of murdering Jyoti and violently assaulting her companion Awindra. In the trial, Awindra has been subject to ridicule and public shaming by defence lawyers who have called him a "womanizer," with this being reported in the global media[4] ("Counsel Says Friend 'Womanizer'"). Far from being solely about this individual case or strictly about gender-based violence, the 2012 Delhi gang rape case and subsequent protests and trials have elucidated fundamental questions regarding governance, state, and judicial powers in India. Ram Singh, one of the accused in the 2012 Delhi gang rape case supposedly committed suicide in a Delhi jail during the trial. There are those who suggest that Singh was in fact killed by other prisoners and that the Indian police may have also been involved. Singh's death caused many to question the workings of the prison system within contemporary India. There have also been many allegations regarding the corruption and inefficiency of the Indian police[4] (Menon, "Why Was Ram Singh Killed in Tihar Jail?"). The mirror that was held up to the state structure not only offers a chance to question the corruption and negligence of the Indian state but a means through which one can pose questions regarding the hollow nature of legalistic rights and state power. Badiou suggests that true justice can never be achieved through the application of a pre-given political and legal code. He suggests that, every politics which is thought in actu entails, in proportion to its force and tenacity, serious trouble for the State. This is why political truth always shows up in moments of trial and turmoil … It follows that justice, far from being a possible category of statist and social order, is the name for those principles at work in rupture and disorder. (100)

The moments of rupture that occurred following the 2012 Delhi gang rape case and the 2013 decision to criminalize same-sex desire in the Indian subcontinent was an articulation of justice that happened in the streets, not only outside formalized state bureaucracies but often in direct opposition to police powers and empty grammars of legalistic right.

TO CALL A ROSE BY ANY OTHER NAME, TO CALL A RAPE BY ANY OTHER NAME: NAMING AS AN ACT OF POWER

Names. Victim. Survivor. India's daughter. Daughter. Daughter in Law. Student. Medical student. Nirbhaya. Damini. The fearless one. Courageous. Brave. Mutilated. Godless girl. Poor girl. Stupid girl. Unlucky girl. Dented and Painted Ladies. Bitch. Ugly bitch. Whore. Slut. Slag. Lesbian. Tranny. Traitor. Hero. National Hero. National Tragedy. Martyr. Feminist. Activist. Indian woman. Hindu woman. Brown woman. Foreign woman. Woman. Cisgender woman. Girl. Little girl. Friend. Girlfriend. Wife. Partner. Mother. Teacher. Fiancé. Sex worker. Colleague. Neighbour. Raped woman. Gang-raped woman. Walking corpse. The deceased. *Names.*

The will to find a name in which to speak the truth of power that marks the gendered body as one subject to rape, to torture, to murder is a constant refrain that translates the unintelligibility of bodies into discourses of legal right and market freedom. The legibility of some bodies is not simply a matter of representation but a matter of life and death. Butler suggests that the recognizability of forms of gendered and sexual intelligibility does not only determine who is counted politically but who is counted as human.[5] The battle regarding names within the 2012 Delhi gang rape case spoke to the complexities of gender, legality, and rights within contemporary India. Female protesters were, for example, publically referred to by political elites as "dented and painted ladies"[6] ("Sexist Comment `Dents' President's Son") to ridicule and moralize those participating in protests through a violent colonial epistemology. The lack of humanity that is afforded to those who are subject to violent rape and torture is expressed in the bureaucratization of pain by state power. What is unintelligible is both the subjectivity of those forever marked by the gender-based violence enacted against them, and the body itself, one carrying trauma that can never be fully captured in text, bill, or law. Gayatri Chakravorty Spivak writes that "translation is the experience of the impossible" (xxv). The impossible experience of translating grief into grievance, however, is one of the only possible means through which bodily violence expressed in textual writings and legal documents can enter into public, national, and transnational discourse.

The Times of India took an active role in covering the 2012 Delhi gang rape case and the protests that followed. The national newspaper gave Jyoti the name "Nirbhaya," loosely translated into "the fearless one." Other tributary names, often connoting bravery and courage, were also used to refer to Jyoti, before her name was revealed to the global media by her father. As Ravinder writes,

> Somewhere deep within our hearts, we were all hoping for a miracle for the nameless, faceless, brave heart girl. Yet, we called her by many names, Amanat, Damini, and Nirbhaya and probably more, I called her Shakthi.

These acts of naming can be read as an affront to discourses of female passivity and weakness that are often circulated to justify restrictions on women's mobility and sexual agency. This is especially true in contemporary India where conservative religious nationalist leaders used the 2012 Delhi gang rape case to justify further restrictions on women's mobility. Yet the idea of the fearless woman as national hero and national martyr can also be thought of in relation to competing histories of Orientalism, colonialism, and nationalism in the Indian subcontinent. The image of the feminized, weak, passive "Oriental" often reappears throughout colonial history to justify colonial rule. To counter this pervasive rhetoric of white male colonial power, nationalists often used signifiers of the feminine to connote national heroism. Images such as "Mother India" countered the Orientalist construction of the passive Indian woman assumed by colonizers to be a consummate victim by celebrating women as nationalist heroines (Sinha). Instead of debating whether the naming of a survivor of sexual violence by the national press was appropriate, I want to ask how the bodies of Indian women are consistently used within bids to colonial power, national sovereignty, and neoliberal branding. Whether or not women are afraid in the face of rampant violence or "fearless" in accessing public space seems to be of less interest than the competing uses of narratives of gender-based violence in different bids for political power and competing versions of history.

In her iconic postcolonial work, "Can the Subaltern Speak?," Spivak discusses the inaudibility of the brown woman caught between competing authorial voices of male power. Nirbhaya, the fearless one, becomes fearless within a long colonial and Orientalist genealogy that constructs the Indian woman as one who lives in perpetual fear of brown male barbarism; brown men are constructed as holy "terrors" to justify the salvation narratives of white colonial men and women (Spivak 28-38). Badiou suggests that "whenever there is a genuinely political event, the State reveals itself" (101). In December 2012, with water cannons, with tear gas, with brute force, the Indian state revealed itself. The state also reveals itself in more insidious ways, at the level of names. The naming of Jyoti as "the fearless one," and as "India's daughter," reveals how the bodily violence enacted against women is always produced through histories of colonialism, nationalism, and the different claims to speak on behalf of the imagined Indian woman to cast her as a character in a script of governance used to justify competing visions of the nation. The sexual agency of Indian women is an impossible name often buried in the names of fearless daughters, martyrs, Mother Indias, and racist global spectacles of poor, colonized brown women from poor, colonized places. Phadke argues that,

> questions of violence and safety in public space, especially for women, are inevitably placed in fallacious oppositional binaries: private versus public, safety versus violence, safety versus risk, rational versus risky, where one is cast as the antithesis of the other. (Phadke 44)

The naming of Jyoti as "the fearless one" also expresses this binary construction. The will to offer women agency beyond their constructed victimhood leads to the valorization of women as survivors and heroines. The image of eternal Indian female suffering, often popular within colonial discourse, meets its binary opposite: the image of heroic Indian women as nationalist martyrs. Kalpana Kannabiran writes of what she terms, "the violence of normal times" (Kannabiran 3). The violence of the everyday is what is never named as nationalist heroism or Third world tragedy. The endless search of names shows how the state and media revealed itself at the event of the political moment and seized on the discourse of violence against women in the Indian subcontinent to support wider political interests. The subsequent naming of Jyoti by her father placed her within the narrative of the family, while her given name also placed her within a system of caste and religion. Butler discusses of the lack of intelligibility of the gendered body as that which can never be fully contained by the state and bureaucracy. Similarly Butler discusses translation as an impossibility that can never fully capture the materiality of gender and gender based violence in written and spoken language alone. This is perhaps clearly felt in these impossible translations of violence into law and human subjectivity into names. Names that make the gendered body intelligible to the mainstream are uttered through previous injunctions of patriarchal power. Names of survivors of gender-based violence and for those who do not survive are also found in genealogies of religious and political nationalisms that are ironically often part of the violence that strips women and sexual minorities of political subjectivity. Rather than dismissing this will to call Jyoti by her "real" name, a more interesting dialogue is being staged regarding the secular and affective, and the role that both play in the inability of gender-based violence to ever be fully contained by law. There is a competition of discourses of religion, nation, and law that is expressed in these acts of naming. Talal Assad discusses the relationship between "free speech" and law, and distinctions between the religious and secular. Assad states,

> The wilful destruction of signs—that is to say, the assault on images and words that are invested with the power to determine what counts as truth—has a long history of transcending the distinction between the religious and the secular.[7] (Assad 33)

The naming of Jyoti moved her away from the grammars of secular statehood that would have erased her name as it is common not to disclose names of those who are subject to sexual violence because of legal injunctions. By defying the state injunction on naming "survivors" or "victims" of sexual violence, the use of the name Jyoti, meaning "light" in Sanskrit, brought to light the ongoing dialogue between the supposedly secular state, colonial history, religion, and familial discourse in contemporary India. These acts of naming reveal how the body becomes intelligible in words that never fully articulate the corporeal pain and resistance that defines the fatality and vitality of a body on a city street.

COMMITTEES, CORPSES, AND CANDLE LIGHT VIGILS: THE VERMA COMMITTEE REPORT

The Verma Committee report was drafted in the wake of the 2012 Delhi gang rape case and the massive nationwide demonstrations that followed. Arvind Narrain wrote optimistically about the initial recommendations for legislative change:

> The Verma Committee Report most fundamentally alters the public discourse on crimes against women by placing these crimes within the framework of the Indian Constitution and treating these offences as nothing less than an egregious violation of the right to live with dignity of all women. What is particularly moving and inspiring about the Report is that it does so by placing the autonomy and indeed the sexual autonomy of women at the very centre of its discourse.

What the initial report also offered was a definition of rape that moved away from a patriarchal heteronormative paradigm toward an understanding of rape as a crime inflicted against the human body.[8] The normative ideology of sexual violence in India as a crime against a woman's virtue, which is implicitly enforced within Indian law, serves to produce supposedly "impure" gendered bodies constructed as being incapable of experiencing sexual violence. Those who are ideologically constituted as impure within wider societal discourses are often offered little empathy from the state. The discursive construction of sexual impurity implicitly woven into the fabric of law also enforces a puritanical and misogynistic protectionism towards female sexuality. By moving the focus away from sexual morals to the basic entitlements of bodily integrity, the Verma Committee recommendations challenged colonial constructions of gender. As Narrain writes,

> The Committee, based on an understanding of equality in the Indian Constitution comprehensively rebuts Sir Matthew Hale's outdated declaration in 1736 that the *"husband cannot be guilty of rape committed by himself upon his lawful wife"* [author's emphasis].

Making note of the uses of rape and sexual violence by the Indian army and police force, the report also highlights the state's active role in perpetuating sexual violence against minority women. The uses of rape against tribal and Adivasi women in India and against women in the Northeast, as part of the covert tactics of occupation and land seizure, were also mentioned and vilified by the Verma Committee. While some commentators suggested that the 2012 Delhi gang rape protests would only lead to changes that would benefit urban, middle-class women, the report sought, by highlighting state sexual violence, to implement broad-based legal changes that would support the bodily integrity of the poor, the rural, and the landless. In addition to troubling the law of the father within the home, the report also questioned the patriarchal authority of the state in its lawless use of sexual violence as part of routine military and police operations. The initial report offered an optimistic turn to the unspeakable tragedy that defined the gang rape and murder of Jyoti. Furthermore, the committee sought to change understandings of sexual violence. The recommendations would have not only offered the promise of protection, power, and freedom to women but also acted as a means through which those who were subject to gender-based and sexual violence could have found some measure of intelligibility and some hope for justice.

On February 1 2013, less than two months after the one year anniversary of the tragic death of Jyoti and the waves of mass mobilization that followed, the president of India signed an ordinance amending the Verma Commission report. Under the ordinance many of the potentially radical suggestions made by the Committee were altered, causing a great deal of outrage and disappointment, particularly among feminists and activists. In the words of activist Vrinda Grover, "the impunity of every citadel ... family, marriage, public servants, army, police" remained

out of the purview of feminist critique and legal changes pertaining
to the criminalization of sexual violence (Grover qtd. in Menon "The
Impunity of Every Citadel Is Intact"). The Verma Committee report's
subversive elements were swiftly rewritten by the state. The idea of rape
as a gender-neutral crime was challenged by the ordinance with rape
continuing to be defined as a crime of male violence against women.
The ordinance therefore serves to reinforce a patriarchal heteronormative paradigm that implicitly allows for the silencing of sexual violence
against queer and transgender persons, and continues to construct sexual violence as a crime against a woman's imagined sexual honour and
chastity. Nivideta Menon cites the work of feminist scholars regarding
the relationship between narrow definitions of rape and patriarchal
constructions of gender:

> One important suggestion for rape law reform is to remove
> narrowly defined "rape" (which is defined only as penile pene-
> tration of the vagina) and replace this with a series of degrees
> of "sexual assault", the punishment increasing in severity with
> the degree of physical harm caused. As Flavia Agnes has
> pointed out, only in sexual assault is harm caused by a part of
> the human body considered to be more grievous than harm
> caused by a weapon. The reason why in patriarchal law, penile
> penetration of the vagina is considered more grievous than
> penetration by say, an iron rod, is obvious. Rape is considered
> to be a harm against the honour of the woman's family, and
> the purity of her womb. ("The Impunity of Every Citadel Is
> Intact")

The ordinance sought to make rape law into a conservative set of maxims
that would implicitly support women's idealized roles as mothers and
wives, which would fulfill the biopolitical aims of the state. This will to
preserve conservative gender and sexual norms is made more apparent
in the legalization of marital rape. The ordinance went so far as to justify marital rape by stating that the will to criminalize men for sexual
violence against their spouses would "break up a family." (Menon "The
Impunity of Every Citadel Is Intact.") Finally, the ordinance altered the
Verma Committee's attempts to hold military, state, and police forces
accountable for their active use of rape against minority women. Me-

non discusses the documented uses of rape and sexual violence against women in Chattisgarh, Adivasi, and tribal women, women in Kashmir, and activists throughout the Indian subcontinent. She asks, "Is the Indian state making it quite explicit that rape is a weapon of war, and that its coercive apparatus will continue to use it with no compunction?" (Menon "The Impunity of Every Citadel Is Intact"). The ordinance diluted the initial findings by the Verma Committee to the point that the implicitly patriarchal and misogynistic ideology underlying colonial moralities regarding gender and sexuality in India continue to be instituted in law. The decision to alter many of the decisions made by the Committee underscored the state's need to manage the potentially radical moments of protest in December 2012. The spark that lit the eyes, candles, and raucous cries of many people in the Indian subcontinent in December of 2012 were drenched in conservative semantics, with as much routine aggression as the rush of a police water canon in a nation where so many go thirsty.

MARCHING PAST THE COURTHOUSE:
READING GENDER JUSTICE IN THE STREETS

Alan Badiou writes of justice not as that which is meted out by state power through a series of pre-existing rules. Drawing on the work of political philosophers and theorists, I am interested in how the protests of 2012 that occurred throughout India following the gang rape and murder of Jyoti can be read as both an expression of the state's failure to offer meaningful forms of justice and as a testament to the will of people to actualize their own means of redress and declarations of judgment through political action. What does it mean to actualize principles of justice through public action? In the last few years, throughout the world, new collectives of people have gathered in streets, in squares, in public parks, and in other public spaces to both declare an action-oriented politics and to question the absence of true democratic principles at the level of statist and legal bureaucracy. From global Occupy movements to protests against austerity throughout Europe to the revolts of 2010 in Tahir Square, forms of political action have been born that cry out for the most basic political rights and protections, not in the language of the state but in the language of collective action. Badiou suggests, "Justice, which seizes the axiom latent in a political subject, necessarily designates what is, rather than what should be" (100). He further argues that the modern state has nothing to do with justice. In fact, Badiou suggests that the modern state in its will to harmonize conflicting interests in the service of capital is in fact an affront to any meaningful idea of justice. Badiou writes that,

> every programmatic or statist definition of justice changes it into its opposite: justice becomes a matter of harmonising the interplay of conflicting interests. But justice, which is the theoretical name for an axiom of equality, necessarily refers to a wholly disinterested subjectivity. (100)

Badiou's idea of the disinterested subjectivity of gender justice can be considered in relation to debates concerning the Verma Committee report. The initial report declared sexual assault as a crime against "bodily integrity," (Narrain) upholding the embodied rights of the subject against their biopolitical utility as a woman or man. The ordinance, which altered the initial Verma Committee report, maintained gender based binaries in service of the biopolitical goals of idealized nation building, apart from any respect for universal bodily integrity. The state-led ordinance highlighted the misogynistic ideology that not only exists on the streets of India but is implicitly and even more insidiously expressed at the level of law. Alan Badiou further discusses the shifting names that are attributed to the political subject. Writing specifically in regards to Europe, but perhaps making a generalizable point regarding names, he writes,

> The political subject has gone under various names. He used to be referred to as a "citizen." ...He used to be called "professional revolutionary." He used to be called "grassroots militant." We seem to be living in a time when his name is suspended, a time when we must find a new name for him.[9] (102)

The search for names to ascribe to "victims" and "survivors" of gender-based and sexual violence meets the search for names to ascribe to "feminists" and "activists." Following the Delhi gang rape protests of 2012, some feminists and activists writing in the Indian subcontinent suggested that the protests should not be read as serious political action, as many people who participated did not have the pointed political agenda of left-wing activists who often spearhead protests in Delhi and throughout India. However, drawing on Badiou, I suggest that it was precisely in the lack of succinct declaration, agenda, and nomenclature of bodies in the streets that these protests were reflective of a politics not predetermined but actualized through a political event. The politicization of people in this case was instructive, not only in revealing the failures of the state but in revealing the failures of past social movements to offer any meaningful feeling of justice to the extreme forms of bodily violence that define gender-based violence in India.

Some of the most striking images that defined the protests of December 2012 involved allusions to violence. Many people brought nooses to demonstrations, and written on placards and heard in the streets was the refrain "Hang the rapists." I want to move away from discussing the merits of the death penalty. Within the context of India, corruption, state inefficiency and casteism-classism could lead to chilling forms of extermination of lower-caste and lower-class people that give the illusion of justice if the death penalty were implemented. Yet, there was something striking about the visceral rage that protestors expressed. The death of Jyoti struck a nerve. There was something inexpressible in text and bureaucracy about the bodily violence that defined this case. The narratives of her torture with a metal rod, of her intestines unravelling because of the assault, of the inhumane violence she experienced, moved people into the streets and moved many to question the limits of bureaucratic justice. Badiou writes that "even by drawing on a history, albeit without continuity or concept, of what `justice' was once able to designate, we still have no clear idea of what this word means today" (102). Those who marched in the streets of India in December 2012 and those who cried out in a frustrated rage for the death penalty were perhaps asking a question regarding what a just punishment or response could be when faced with such basic affronts to bodily integrity and human dignity.

Drawing on the political uprising of Paris 1968 as an example, Foucault suggests that while the court could be read as an institution that served to represent the interests of popular struggle it could also be seen as an institution that served to co-opt popular struggles:

It is not so much that the court is the natural expression of

popular justice, but rather that its historical function is to en-
snare it, to control it and to strangle it, by re-inscribing it within
institutions which are typical of a state apparatus. (Foucault
and Gordan 1)

Foucault's ideas can be revisited in relation to the popular uprisings
that followed the Delhi gang rape case of 2012 and the state's subsequent use of this case and systems of legality to posit this case as a
spectacle of "failed" and pathological migrant masculinities, seen to
hold no place within the biopolitical aims of the state. Simultaneously,
state power used the popular uprisings often led by the vital political
bodies of many women in the Indian subcontinent to justify a moralizing
rhetoric. This was evinced in mainstream political and public discourses
that emphasized the "protection" of the middle-class woman from the
imagined aggression of men "of the street." Simultaneously, legal ruling
and conservative political leaders and commentators supported the
ongoing erasure of sexual agency within the system of marriage and in
public space. Within mainstream thinking, the courts and systems of
law are imagined as neutral. However, Foucault argues that these are
not neutral institutions; they are already imbued with political aims.
He suggests that true justice within popular uprisings is thwarted by
the state and that the seizure of popular struggles by the law is "not the
setting up of a neutral institution standing between the people and its
enemies, capable of establishing the dividing line between the true and
the false, the guilty and the innocent, the just and the just" (Foucault
and Gordan 1). Foucault asks whether institutional redress for popular
protest is not then,

> a way of resisting popular justice.... A way of disarming it in
> the struggle it is conducting in reality in favour of an arbitration
> in the realm of the ideal.... I am wondering whether the court
> is not a form of popular justice but rather its first deformation.
> (Foucault and Gordan 2)

The construction of the Justice Verma Committee was an attempt to set
up a mediatory body that addressed the wider questions raised by this
case and posed by many people in the streets. However, the dismissal
of the criminalization of marital rape, and the striking down of gender

neutrality within rape cases spoke to the disarming of this moment and movement of its potentially radical aims. The patriarchal upper-class and upper-caste Hindu male figure of husband and father remains as a little India version of what McClintock refers to as the "white Imperial family man," one whose control over property and nation is imbricated with his power over the bodies of women and children (McClintock 232-258).

The mass mobilizations that happened throughout India following the Delhi gang rape case in December of 2012, the mass outpouring of attention the world over, and the initial response by the Verma Committee all point to a political vitality not contained in the bureaucratic language of state power—a political vitality that shouts out in the face of chilling fatality, Āzādī. As Badiou writes,

> Justice is a wager on the immortal against finitude, against "being towards death." For within the subjective dimension of the equality we declare, nothing is of interest apart from the universality of this declaration, and the active consequences that arise from it. (104)

Āzādī.

ENDNOTES

[1]The authors discuss the term "natural" that is utilized in criminalizing same-sex desire as one that derives from colonial history and discourse. They state that,

> The wording of Section 377 is an instance of the naturalistic fallacy described by the British philosopher G. E. Moore. 23 There is no reasonable basis for classifying an "unnatural" act (where unnatural may be understood in any of its various meanings) as being illegal, unacceptable or wrong, and a 'natural' act as legal, acceptable or good. (440)

They further discuss the use of the words "unnatural" and "natural" as providing little justification for criminalizing sexual desire, thus demonstrating the invocation of such concepts as a tactial political strategy by state power. As the authors further state,

> Diseases, droughts, natural disasters are all instances of natural

occurrences which humans have tried their best to eliminate or avoid as they present dangers to the society. From the fact that something occurs naturally, it does not necessarily follow that it is socially desirable. Similarly, acts that are commonly perceived to be "unnatural" may not necessarily deserve legal sanction. (440)

[2]Foucault, Michel. *The Birth of Biopolitics: Lectures at the College de France, 1978-1979* (Lectures at the Collège de France). London: Picador, 2010.

[3]Ranganathan discusses how the judges in the Koushal judgment, which upheld Section 377 of the Indian Penal Code, made this ruling based on narrow technical grounds and ignored the many testaments offered by queer activists and allies. As the author states,

At the Supreme Court, Koushal's side argued that homosexuality was against Indian culture. He was joined by various religious groups and the Delhi Commission for Protection of Child Rights and an AIDS denialist organization. Supporting Naz Foundation India as respondents in defense of the lower court's ruling were parents of LGBT persons, mental health professionals, legal academics, and noted filmmaker Shyam Benagal. The testimonies by the parents recorded as affidavits stated that their children are law-abiding citizens and are far from being criminals. Further, they stated that they enhance the social fabric rather than destroying it. The mental health professionals submitted that homosexuality is no longer considered a mental disorder. Despite shocking testimonies by persons who faced persecution as a result of 377 and the voluminous literature—cultural, literary, and scientific—placed before the Supreme Court, the Court reversed the judgment of the Delhi High Court and recriminalized homosexuality on December 11, 2013. The court refrained from their role of judicially reviewing the validity of Section 377 and instead pushed the onus to amend the law onto the Parliament to dispose of as it deems fit. Thus the judges arrived at the conclusion on narrow technical grounds, turning a blind eye to the material placed before the court.

[4]Discussing the death of Ram Singh in Delhi, Nividetia Menon writes,

Yes, Indian prisons are violent and brutal, and the police callous and vicious. Yes, there should be an enquiry to assign responsibility. But I'm pretty certain I know who killed Ram Singh—some other prisoners. And I think that they did it on orders from the police. So what could Ram Singh have revealed if he had his day in court? What could he have said to deflect attention away from his own crime? ("Why Was Ram Singh killed in Tihar Jail?")

[5]Discussing the relationship between the recognition of gendered and sexual bodies and precarity, Butler states,

the terms of recognition—and here we can include a number of gender and sexual norms—condition in advance who will count as a subject and who will not ... it is on the basis of this question, who counts as a subject and who does not, that performativity becomes linked with precarity.

[6]As a journalist writing in *The Hindu* reports,

President Pranab Mukherjee's son Abhijit Mukherjee on Thursday found himself in the thick of a controversy over his remarks that "dented and painted" women protested against the gang rape in New Delhi. Calling the anti-rape agitation a nautanki (drama), he said the women protesters were good looking but did not exactly look like students. "Students walking the streets with candles ... going to discotheques ... our days as students were different. These people did not look like students to me" Mr Mukherjee told a TV channel. He also said that the agitators had little connection with ground realities. ("Sexist Comment 'Dents' President's Son")

The Hindu further reports that Mukherjee's comments "remarks were quickly criticized by the political opposition as well as the civil society" ("Sexist Comment 'Dents' President's Son"). After a great deal media attention and criticism and public opposition from feminists, activists, and the general public throughout India, Mukherjee later issued a public apology.

[7]Assad writes specifically about blasphemy, free speech and competing meanings of the religious and the secular and discusses the controversy that arose in Europe regarding a series of Danish cartoons depicting Muslim signs and signifiers. However, for my purposes, what is of interest is how ideas of censorship and freedom of speech are themselves expressions of competing discourses of religion and secularism. The naming of "Jyoti" gestured to the inability to separate secular statehood

from other competing discourses of nationalism, religion, and family that also claim the right to name the gendered body within the Indian subcontinent. As I discuss throughout this book, the inculcation and naming of the body marked as "woman" within nationalist, religious and familial narratives is not innocent or celebratory. In this contest of names ascribed to bodies that are subject to sexual violence, one perhaps bore witness to how women's bodies and the claiming of ownership over them is expressive of different bids for power on the part of variant political forces and competing narratives of "India," "Hindustan," and "Indian culture" (Assad).

[8]Arvind Narrain discusses how the understanding of rape as a violation of bodily integrity in the Verma Committee report challenges existing discourses that construct rape as a crime violating the honour of the one subjected to harm. As Narrain writes,

> In the Committee's thinking rape is a form of sexual assault like any other crime against the human body in the IPC. According to the Committee it is 'the duty of the state as well as civil society to deconstruct the paradigm of shame-honour in connection with a rape victim.

[9]Badiou's use of the pronoun "he" is questionable, and may be reflective of the assumption that the political subject is a masculine subject. However, Badiou's political insights and his philosophical approaches to political culture are deeply important and should not be flippantly dismissed because of language. It is also important to note that the works of Badiou I am citing are English-language translations of texts originally written in French.

WORKS CITED

Assad, Talal. "Free Speech, Blasphemy, and Secular Criticism." *Is the Critique Secular?* Eds. Talal Assad, Wendy Brown, Judith Butler, and Saba Mahmood. California: University of California Press, 2009. 20-64. Print.

Badiou, Alain. *Metapolitics.* Trans. Jason Barker. London: Verso, 2005. Print.

Basheer, Shamnad, Sroyon Mukherjee and Karthy Nair. "Section 377 and the Order of Nature: Nurturing 'Indeterminancy' in the Law." *NUJS Law Review* 433 (2009): 433-443. Print.

Butler, Judith. "Performativity, Precarity, and Sexual Politics." *Revista de Antropología Iberoamericana* ,8 June 2009. Web. 11 June 2015.

"Counsel says Gang-Rape Victim's Friend 'Womaniser.'" *IndiaTV*, 10 May 2013. Web. 12 June 2015.

Datta, Bishakha, Ed. *Nine Degrees of Justice: New Perspectives on Violence against Women in India.* New Delhi: Zubaan Press, 2015. Kindle Edition.

Foucault, Michel and Colin Gordan. *Power/Knowledge: Selected Interviews and Other Writings, 1972-1977.* London: Harvester Press, 1980. Print

Foucault, Michel. *The History of Sexuality. Volume One* Trans. Robert Hurley. New York: Random House, 1980. Print.

Kannabirān, Kalpana. *The Violence of Normal Times.* New Delhi: Women Unlimited, 2005. Print.

McClintock, Ann. *Imperial Leather: Race, Gender, and Sexuality in the Colonial Contest.* New York: Routledge, 1995. Print.

Menon, Nividetia. "'The impunity of Every Citadel Is Intact'–The Taming of the Verma Committee Report, and Some Troubling Doubts." *Kafila*, 3 Feb. 2013. Web. 12 June 2015.

Menon, Nividetia. "Why Was Ram Singh Killed in Tihar Jail?" *Kafila*, 12 March 2013. Web. 20 June 2015.

Narrain, Arvind. "Alchemizing Anger to Hope." *The Hindu*, 25 Jan. 2013. Web. 12 June 2015.

Narrain, Arvind and Alok Gupta, eds. *Law Like Love: Queer Perspectives on Law.* New Delhi: Yoda Press, 2011. Print.

Naqvi, Farrah. "This Thing Called Justice: Engaging With Laws on Violence against Women in India." *NineDegrees of Justice: New Perspectives on Violence Against Women in India.* Ed. Bishakha Dutta. New Delhi: Zubaan Press, 2015. Kindle Edition.

Phadke, Shilpa. "You Can Be Lonely in a Crowd: The Production of Safety in Mumbai." *Indian Journal of Gender Studies* 12.1 (2015): 41-62. Print.

Ranganathan, Gowthaman. "Ruling in India Not the Last Word." Alternative Law Forum, 25 June 2014. Web. 20 June 2015.

Ravinder, Sharmila. "The Death of India's daughter." *The Times of India*, Dec. 2012. Web. 20 June 2015.

"Sexist Comment 'Dents' President's Son." *The Hindu*, 28 Dec. 2012. Web. 12 June 2015.

Sinha, Mrinalini. *Specters of Mother India: The Global Restructuring of an*

Empire. Durham: Duke University Press, 2006. Print.

Smart, Barry,ed. *Michel Foucault Critical Assessments.* New York: Routledge, 1995. Print.

Spivak, Gayatri Chakravorty. *The Spivak Reader.* New York: Routledge, 1995. Print.

4.

CARS, COLONIES, AND CRIME SCENES

SPACE, GENDER, AND VIOLENCE

THE PRESIDENT of the United States of America is Black. Gay television, transgender supermodels, multi-ethnic cuisine and Barbies with bindis. Last decades civil rights movements are this decade's branding. This is what people sometimes term "progress."

Sammy Yatim was shot to death at close range on a streetcar in Toronto. They say that he had a knife. They say that he was troubled. They say that the police officers were only doing their jobs. Everyone these days is often only doing their jobs. He is dead now. A teenage boy with a whole life of possibility was murdered in a matter of minutes on a Toronto streetcar. Now he is forever immortalized in a YouTube video in which his life is snuffed out in grainy images with the repeated sound of bullets ringing in my ears through the Internet screen. This is what people sometimes term progress.

A girl in Delhi is gang-raped, tortured, and murdered on a bus. Her male friend is also severely beaten. They say that this is a problem of Indian men, migrants, culture, religion, poverty, misogyny, class antagonism, hatred. Like a boy lying dead on a street car in Toronto, she was a body marked as citizen, one called free, one dead in the streets of cities. Cities full of business elites taking taxis past public buses, streetcars, and crime scenes.

It was on the train. Audrey Lorde wrote of being a child on a train in New York City. The old white woman pulled her expensive coat away from the young black girl's body. Was there dirt between them? A bug? What had happened? Lorde wrote that her mother knew in that moment what had happened and quickly ushered her child away from the cold condemning stare of that rich white lady in her beautiful, expensive coat. Lorde later recalled the incident as a Black woman in America. She recalled learning what it meant in that moment to be Black in America. To be untouchable. To be considered

*a dirty, contaminated stain on the lily white dreams of bourgeois purity. To
occupy the same space and to touch the darkness of Black bodies was so feared
by white racists that the entire fabric of American cities came to be designed
to keep darkness at bay.[1]*

*Separate water fountains, segregated schools, slave quarters. Now there are
projects, gated communities, and gentrification that divide in casual ways.
Now there are boys dead on YouTube for riding streetcars and girls gang-raped
on buses. There is no branding, no television show, no beauracratic paperwork, and no puppet forms of representation that can replace the experience
of bodies in streets, on trains, on buses, in public spaces. Bodies marked as
flesh and skin, bodies marked for death. The body in public space—the Black
boy shot at close range by police on his way to the candy store, the Arab boy
beaten outside of some "world class" university after two towers fell and every
young girl's hair from Jersey to Hackney to Kabul went up in flames in some
gesture they call democracy.*

The body of a woman on a bus in Delhi, India, in December of 2012.

*The buses of America are haunted by Black bodies, ghostly reckonings of the
ruses of liberal enlightenment ideals that haunt the back of every bus. The
buses of Delhi now too feel haunted.*

Space. The question of space and its relationship to power, to violence,
to justice is one that has been posed repeatedly by many different philosophers. Michel Foucault, defined the anxiety of "our time," the time
of capitalist modernity as a spatial anxiety. Foucault argues that,

> the anxiety of our era has to do fundamentally with space, no
> doubt a great deal more than with time. Time probably appears
> to us only as one of the various distributive operations that
> are possible for the elements that are spread out in space. (23)

As I discuss throughout this chapter, sexual politics in India is both
spatialized and temporally constructed. The space of protest at Jantar
Mantar following the Delhi gang rape case of 2012 was a temporally
determined event, perhaps as contained and illusory as the elevation
of women to goddesses in temples, as the celebration of Hijras and
feminine heroines in Bollywood film. Once the time passes, once the
camera turns, once Jantar Mantar is cleansed of the reminders of the
everyday atrocities of India, the time and space of just another day in

Delhi remains. To name the violence of the everyday is urban spaces as violence may seem overly critical when faced with the statistical truths of bodily and sexual violence that Indian women experience by state persecution and in the home, those without laptops, foreign currency, and Western passports. Yet, as Žižek makes clear, and as I discuss throughout this work, the obscene spectacles of violence framed by the global media can mask the structural, epistemic, and ideological foundations of cases such as the 2012 Delhi gang rape. Conservative publics who grieve for deaths that gain transnational media attention can weep for the dead in similar ways as they weep for characters in television tragedies. The viewers of this publicly staged grief are not, however, made to question how their ideologies implicitly valorize the conservative moralities that make graves out of women's lives (Žižek *Violence*).

The real time of city spaces of urban India are always set to multiple meandering clocks—to the time of Macaulay's colonial minutes; to the time of Google and the sounds of cash registers chiming in Silicon Valleys overseas; to the time of temples and calls to prayer, breaking the banal sounds of the emotionless everyday of market-driven publics with resonant overtures of faith. The hum of old songs in dead and dying languages competes in city streets with the sound of chiming ring tones. Calls to prayer, calls to arms, calls to Samsung and Telus all marking the uneven rhythms of the temporalities of a subcontinent of as many female deities as dead women. The rapid pace at which sexual politics unfolds in the real time and everyday spaces of India speaks to the impossibility and inevitability of discussing sexual politics and its relationship to space. As discussed, months after arriving in Delhi, India, Minister of Law Somnath Bannerjee was implicated in a scandal that received international attention when he is reported to have arranged a raid on the homes of African female migrants in Delhi's Khirki village. The Delhi police raided the homes of several African female students who were assumed to be involved in prostitution and drug trafficking, owing perhaps to anti-Black racism. African migrants in Khirki village say that they are constantly harassed by neighbours and residents who accuse them of criminality, accusations that are often coupled with blatantly racist comments (Taraporewala and Negi). Some residents are reported as saying that they think African people are "cannibals," conjuring up blatantly colonial constructions once purported by European explorers (Vasudeva, Joshi, Mondal, Kohli). The racism experienced by

Black bodies within India cannot be divorced from colonial history, just as the increased migration of Africans to India is not born out of individual will but informed by neocolonial politics. As Taraporewala and Negi state,

> one must contextualise the sudden rise of African migrants in Delhi. While historically India has had ties with African countries based on shared beliefs in anti-imperialism and anti-racism, since the turn of the century, India has increased the engagement with the continent manifold. This is clearly illustrated by the increase in the value of trade between the two regions from USD 7.5 billion in 2000 to USD 66 billion in 2013. Trade is estimated to touch USD 100 billion by 2015.

The authors further discuss the relationship between African migration to India and global politics: "India is competing with China by positioning itself as a hub for educational and medical support for Africans. These international policies have increased people's movement between both the regions" (Taraporewala and Negi). The racism of the street and the bodies who occupy it are microcosms for wider structures of economic and political power. The haunted skin that divides people in the postcolonial city is marked by the ghosts of colonial dominance and its new translations of neoliberal capitalist exploitation.

Journalists in India who have interviewed Africans and African-Americans throughout the Indian subcontinent state that,

> Racial stereotypes are also clearly divided along gender biases. While African men are stereotyped as "dumb", "dangerous" and "prone to violence", the women are branded as sex workers. Significantly, instances of discrimination and violence are felt not just by African nationals but also by African-Americans. They reveal that they too have been subject to comments about their skin-colour, been questioned about their country of origin, and in extreme cases, faced physical violence on the streets. (Vasudeva, Joshi, Mondal, and Kohli)

One month after the racist attacks in Khirki village—which magnified the everyday violence that African migrants face and specifically the

153

sexual and-gender based violence that Africans in India experience—many Africans living in Khirki village fled their homes (Taraporewala and Negi). Valued gendered bodies are counted like coins within the national biopolitical scripts of an "India shining." The wives of rich men are valued as prized and polished property. The countenance of women and queers "citizens" is as unstable as the lives of African migrants in the country that Gandhi was born in and the country that Gandhi was killed in ("Africans Decry 'Discrimination' in India"). The Delhi gang rape case of 2012 cannot be divorced from the violence that oppressively marks certain bodies because of their aesthetic difference from the idealized figure of a normatively gendered body imagined to hold a rightful place within the idealized Hindu middle-class family, a microcosm for the nation. There is perhaps a connection between the rape, torture, and murder of a woman in public space in Delhi and the everyday persecution of queer and racialized migrants in contemporary India. These acts of exclusion all offer evidence of an inability to insure bodily integrity outside of heteronormative, familial, racially, and religiously "pure" understandings of the family. Those who murdered Jyoti on a bus in Delhi, India, in 2012 are reported to have ridiculed the couple with insults about their occupation of space and the time of day in which they appeared together in city streets ("Delhi Gang Rape-Victim Narrates the Tale of Horror"). What are you doing out so late at night with this woman?[2] It was implicitly a question of both space and time that was asked in regards to what connotes "appropriate" gendered and sexual occupations of public space, with the time of the night being associated with social deviance. The psychic and symbolic associations made between darkness and deviance cannot be separated from colonial discourses and Hindu nationalist ideologies which construct blackness as sexually and morally suspect.

TRAFFIC AND TRAFFICKING:
RED LIGHTS, RULES, AND RACISTS

The associations made between the imagined sexual and moral deviance of certain women, of queer people, and of migrants in public spaces, particularly at night, are perhaps informed by a deeper anxiety concerning sexual labour in India. While there was a great deal of mainstream press and attention surrounding the Delhi gang rape protests of 2012 and the decision to uphold Section 377 in 2013 by the Indian Supreme Court, the regulation of bodies that stray from gendered and sexual norms cannot be divorced from the policing of sex work. Shah discusses the policing of public spaces in Mumbai with reference to a wider global discourse on human trafficking that has emerged in the Indian subcontinent in the last decade. Shah discusses the relationship between the policing of sex work in India and a wider process of mapping deviance onto certain bodies in the streets. She writes that,

> soliciting clients for sex in urban areas has been criminalised through anti-nuisance and anti-solicitation laws that target street-based solicitation of sexual services. These laws serve a broader purpose of policing public urban spaces in general. (273)

Shah suggests that the anxieties concerning sex work and trafficking within contemporary India cannot be divorced from those that pervade public spaces within India. Making reference to the *Immoral Trafficking Prevention Act*, Shah states that "These laws serve a broader purpose of policing public urban spaces in general" (273). The author suggests that the appearance of women on balconies and in public spaces at night within certain areas of Mumbai is shadowed by a deeper psychosocial anxiety concerning sex. She writes that,

> Examining the ITPA, helps to situate the state's idealised vision of the ways in which urban public spaces in India may be used and inhabited. For example, the language of the ITPA expresses a subtext of anxiety regarding interactions between men and women in public that may be unmediated by kinship and other regulatory networks. (Shah 273)

While the rise of a neoliberal India of "youth" consumerism in the form of bars, dance clubs, and other social spaces has emerged, these spaces are also tainted by anxieties regarding sex work. Feminists, for example, discuss the policing of dancers and other women working in bars and night clubs in Mumbai. "Bar girls" are often migrant women whose sexual labour is legally policed by the state, and morally policed and denigrated by urban elites who partake in neoliberal forms of consumer excess, while distancing themselves from labourers who service their weekend past times. To go to a bar in urban India is often a sign of "progress," of excess wealth, and of the privileges of being able to mimic the assumed "freedoms" of North America and Europe. However, to work as a "bar girl" is to be stained with a moral and sexual deviance that make one's labour and dignity subject to regulation (Shah 274). Drawing on extensive research done with "bar girls" in Mumbai, the Forum Against the Oppression of Women (FAOW) states,

> In contemporary social and economic circumstances, women are seeking livelihoods within extremely constricted options, determining for themselves where and how they will work. At such junctures, when the state as well as sections of society seek to control and arbitrate women's lives, feminists have to confront not just patriarchy, but a morality that benefits only the powerful. (48)

To be associated with public sexuality is to touch a space of darkness that many impoverished migrant women who labour in industries of sex work and spaces associated with sex already occupy. There is therefore not only a regulation of spaces and how sex appears in public but a self-policing that women often learn and use against one another to distance themselves from other supposedly deviant women. As Shah writes,

> With its references to "loitering" and "molestation" as well as balconies and windows from which women may "expose themselves" to men walking by on the street, the text of ITPA's anti-solicitation clause actually provides a fascinating insight into the reproduction of dichotomies between "good" (honourable, respectable) and "fallen" (dishonourable) women. (273)

The threats of public violence that haunt Hijra bodies and the bodies of certain women and queers might also be seen as corresponding to the simultaneous production of commodified spectacles of Bollywood film and global media, which use images of "others" as a source of cinematic pleasure. Difference at a distance makes for a fascinating show, while the streets are often cleansed of all traces of imagined deviance and those that are associated with sex in the public imaginary. [3]

POMMANA LEKA POGA PETTINATTLU:

Far from being specific to India, as Berlant and Warner discuss, the United States has also seen an erosion of queer public space that perhaps corresponds to the rise of privatized queer branding in the form of television and consumer culture. Berlant and Warner state that "There is nothing more public than privacy" (247) and subsequently discuss how ideas of sex and privatized sexualities are mediated by the general public and within material spaces. Berlant and Warner argue that "national heterosexuality" is constructed as a space of protected and "pure citizenship" that is valorized at the same moment that queer spaces are policed and made invisible. They go on to discuss legal ordinances in New York City that implicitly criminalize sex publics that do not correspond to the imagined "pure citizenship" of national heterosexuality. The 1995 ordinances passed by the city council of New York involved a series of zoning amendments that explicitly targeted adult sex stores and other public spaces marked with allusions to sex. The indirect forms of spatial oppression that exclude and malign certain bodies across borders resonate with this Telugu proverb: *Pommana leka poga pettinattlu*. In English, the proverb can loosely be translated as: Instead of asking someone to leave, one can make them leave by starting to smoke. In other words, if one is unable to directly exclude someone through verbal and authoritarian injunction, they can indirectly create a situation that is not hospitable, covertly forcing someone to vacate a certain space. Berlant and Warner discuss the implicit removal of non-heteronormative sex publics through the cleansing of city streets of queer sex. Discussing the effect that these zoning laws had on sex publics in New York City, the authors write,

> Now gay men who want sexual materials or who want to meet other men for sex will have two choices: they can cathect the privatised virtual public of phone sex and the internet; or they can travel to small, inaccessible, little-trafficked, badly lit areas, remote from public transportation and from any residences (Berlant and Warner 551)

The valorization of spaces of "national heterosexuality" as those of "pure citizenship" is also connected to cases such as the Delhi gang rape case of 2012 and the 2013 Supreme Court of India decision to uphold Section 377, criminalizing same sex desire. If there is as Berlant and Warner suggest, "nothing more public than privacy" (247), then the publically, legally, and culturally sanctioned privacy of the Hindu family, including its "marital rape," corresponds to the erasure of bodies that do not compliment images of "national heterosexual" branding within an "India shining" moment. It is through the imagined fantasies of intimacy that mainstream publics are often made to ignore the structural inequalities of the political and the public sphere in favour of spaces of pastoral and "pure" familial bliss, imagined to be untainted by the oppression of politics. Berlant and Warner state that "Heterosexual culture achieves much of its metacultural intelligibility through the ideologies of intimacy" (551). Zones of intimacy and heterosexual sex are conceived of as those that are untainted by the political. Berlant and Warner suggest that heterosexual culture involves imagining

> a home base of prepolitical humanity from which citizens are thought to come into political discourse and to which they are expected to return in the (always imaginary) future after political conflict. (553)

The construction of spaces, bodies, and desires representative of a politically convenient image of a "prepolitical humanity" in the home also corresponds to the inhumanities experienced by women, queers, and racialized people. For every "happy home" of female citizens who can never be raped as "wives," a home of an African migrant woman is raided by legally sanctioned orders. For every "happy family" that exists in a space of delusional pre-political humanity in which male rape and the abuse of a "wife" as property exists outside of basic constitutional principles, a body of a queer Indian is made illegal.

STUCK IN TRANSIT:
ORIENTALIST WILLS TO HOLD BODIES IN PLACE

Bishakha Datta discusses the will to hold Indian women's bodies in place through spatialized practices of confinement and through a temporal violence that involves constructions of timeless notions of "culture" used to justify misogyny. The author poses a seemingly innocuous question regarding the idea of movement. Datta asks, "If we can move, travel, migrate from one country to another, why can't we move from one gender to another? That too is movement" (Datta 1). The fluidity of bodies is also deeply tied to questions of sexuality in contemporary India; Section 377 has been used to criminalize same-sex desire and non-reproductive sexuality, while the recent NALSA (The National Legal Services Authority) ruling has ironically afforded legal protection and countenance to Hijras and transgender persons. The word "Hijra" in fact also means "pilgrimage" within Islamic discourse and is often used to discuss religious pilgrimage (Reddy). The ability to move in public space and to express sexuality, gendered performance, and fluidity outside of rigid understandings of gender is also a matter of both space and time. The will to hold the body in place against the currents of physical and transnational movement that define contemporary India is a testament to the enduring fictions of occidentalist citizenship that define gender within the subcontinent. The subjectivity of the gendered body is territorialized in the same way that the so-called Orient is fixed within a certain spatial imaginary. Orientalism holds the bodies of so-called "Orientals" in place through an unchanging ideology from which the occident gains its "superior positionality" (Said 73). Similarly, the spatial anxieties of a contemporary urban India, in which the movement of Indian women and queers across national and transnational borders and within public space is increasingly the norm, is met with an anxious will to fix the body through static colonial moralities.

"THE CITY AIR MAKES MEN FREE"[4] BUT, WHAT IS IT DOING TO OUR WOMEN? GENDERED ORIENTALISM AND URBAN SPACE

While the gendered body cannot be held in place physically because of the need for growing numbers of Indian women of all classes to exist in public urban spaces due to urbanization and transnational flows of labour, fears of gendered transgression are managed ideologically by domesticating the sexual and political positions Indian women occupy. Shilpa Phadke discusses the discourse of protectionism, used to prevent women from accessing public space and from showing public displays of bodily pleasure and agency, as a form of violence. Phadke states that,

Denying women the right to be in public spaces, to access public services and amenities, to seek pleasure in the simply act of walking their city, I argue, is not just a denial of their citizenship rights, but a form of violence that is especially violent because it is not even recognized as such ("You Can Be Lonely in a Crowd" 42)

Just as Said suggests that imperialism constructed a discourse in which the "Oriental woman" was not given the agency to author her experience and to enact authority over history and her place in it, discourses of protectionism also involve the stripping of agency and voice from women. Phadke states,

Even when women flout restrictions on clothing, speech, and mobility, similar accusing looks and comments from the family and community stigmatize women's reputations and are a form of psychological violence. In the interests then of both achieving respectability and safety, women often restrict their movements and "choose" not to venture out on their own. This is a form of self-policing, even imprisonment, that gets defined as a rational choice, not as violence, even though it violates a woman's right and desire to access public space ("Dangerous Liasons" 1512)

Phadke also suggests that narratives decreeing public spaces as being unsafe for women are largely authorized by fearful elites.[5] A panic regarding women "trespassing" within darkened public spaces in India emerged following the 2012 Delhi gang rape case. A wave of stories erupted in the press, often focusing on the sexual assault and rape of women in public spaces. Religious fundamentalist groups and political leaders seized on this moment to further conservative and moralistic discourses that valorize women's safety in the private sphere and in the family.

ROSA PARKS AND PUBLIC PARKS: SPACE, OPPRESSION, AND PROTEST

The Black body is one that has also historically been subject to grotesque forms of violence, organized spatially through explicit forms of segregation and the implicit violence of whiteness found in contemporary processes of gentrification. The bus boycotts of the 1960s as well as student movements against segregated eating areas demonstrated how minute forms of daily life for Black people were tied to a racist management of space. Cornel West discusses how at an ideological level, the new Black student movements and civil rights organizing of this period challenged a depoliticized class of petite bourgeois African-Americans. West discusses the activism of the Student Nonviolent Coordinating Committee (SNCC) and suggests that this student-based movement, while largely financially privileged themselves, "epitomized this revolt against the political reticence of the "old"black middle class"(245). West highlights the issues of segregation of public spaces as being central to sparking the student movements that informed the radicalization of Black middle-class students. He writes,

> The spontaneous rebellion of young black people against the southern taboo of black and white people eating together exemplified a major component in the first stage of the black freedom movement: the emergence of politicized,black parvenu, petit bourgeois students. (245)

He further writes that these students,

> would give first priority to social activism and justify their newly acquired privileges by personal risk and sacrifice. So the young black student movement was not simply a rejection of segregation in restaurants. It was a revolt against the perceived complacency of the "old" black petite bourgeoisie. (244)

While the civil rights era politicized young Black students, the protests that followed the gang rape and murder of Jyoti can be read as a politicization of young, middle class people in the Indian subcontinent. Like earlier waves of social movements transnationally, these protests also centred issues of oppression and bridged divides between the personal and political, the bodily and the spatial. The collective occupation of space that followed the 2012 Delhi gang rape case is reflective of responses to oppression that cannot be solved by the ethos of individualism that increasingly defines commonsense cultures of neoliberalism globally. Yet when drawing parallels between histories of African-American civil rights movements and their politicization of the body in public space and sexual politics in India, it is important to question the complex role that women's moral and sexual agency play within the history of Black liberation. The tenuous role of sexuality within previous civil rights movements transnationally, might be instructive to contemporary political struggles about space in urban India. West writes of the importance of the case of Rosa Parks in 1955:

> The arrest of Rosa Parks on December 1, 1955 in Montgomery's bus line that year—led to the creation of the Montgomery Improvement Association (MIA), adoption of a citywide black boycott and the placement of King at the head of the movement. After nearly a year of the boycott, the U.S. Supreme Court declared Alabama's state and local bus segregation laws unconstitutional. (245)

The case of Rosa Parks and the 2012 Delhi gang rape case raise questions regarding the role that female sexuality plays in public space. Writing in *The Nation*, David Zirin recounts the work that Parks did in politicizing sexual violence against African women as a definitive issue within the civil rights movement. Zirin writes,

> In 1944, 23-year-old mother and sharecropper Recy Taylor was gang raped by seven men and left for dead. The NAACP sent Parks to investigate. Rosa Parks's investigation and activism against rape, recounted in Danielle L. McGuire's brilliant book *At the Dark End of the Street*, presents an alternative history of the civil rights movement as something that had roots in resistance to the sexual violence perpetrated on African-American women. (Zirin)

Movements regarding civil rights and questions of public space and racism were always also movements regarding the conjoined experiences of racial and sexual violence in public space. The politicization of the 2012 Delhi gang rape case draws on the most extreme cases of physical and sexual violence against the body in public urban space to pose broader questions about the relationship between the individual postcolonial "citizen" and the urban polis.

OF BUSES AND BABIES:
WHERE TO CAST(E) THE GENDERED BODY

Ghosh discusses the class dynamics of the 2012 Delhi gang rape case and protests and suggests that the structure of class and its relationship to state power must be questioned. Ghosh problematizes how a moralistic and legal-juridical approach to cases of rape not only supports a patriarchal capitalist judiciary but also valorizes the normative familial model. He writes,

> those citizen-subjects, who turn agents of such legal-juridical approach to anti-systemic politics, live in the neurotic comfort of condemning rape and baying for the blood of rapists even as they perpetuate the gender-unequal structure of social power through their agency as citizen-subjects of civil society and its constitutive unit: the family. (Ghosh)

The murder of Jyoti was often narrated by mainstream media in ways that valorized the normative, patriarchal Hindu family and attending systems of caste and class hierarchy (Roychowdhury). However, behind this focus on the family as with many of the other interpretations made of the case is the question of space. The 2012 Delhi gang rape and murder happened in a moving bus on the darkened street of urban India. Yet within mainstream media narratives and even among the most empathetic writers, a constant effort to move the story from the street to institutionalized space was perceptible. Jyoti needed to be relocated to the family unit for her case to be taken seriously. To be constructed as an idealized victim of sexual violence, her narrative could not remain in the street. The narrative was also spatialized through institutions of disciplinary and capitalist power by discursively placing her within the space of the school. The constant mention that Jyoti was a medical student and the focus on her family moved this case away from the darkness of the Delhi street and into the spaces of enlightenment education and the heteronormative home. Through the explicit spatialization of this case, a connection between the workings of gendered "citizenship" within the Indian subcontinent and the anxieties of space that Foucault wrote of can be seen. There is an assumed depravity to the image of women's bodies moving in public space in the darkened streets of urban India.

163

This image is juxtaposed with the lightness of a romanticized family unit and the assumed pristine spaces of enlightenment education. Ashwini Tambe discusses how British colonial law privileged the rights of the bourgeois male property owner to own women as property. Tambe writes that,

> The East India Company upheld the right of husbands to buy wives and parents to sell children, and it targeted the `enticing' of children and women into prostitution as an infringement on these property rights of husbands and parents. The law thus largely enshrined male private property rights in women and children in such measures that apparently targeted prostitution. (28)

By enshrining the rights of male private property owners, the East India Tea Company turned the rights of women into the rights of the men who were thought to own them. The gendered forms of citizenship accrued to men are also then dependent on their spatial location vis-à-vis the bourgeois home and institutions of disciplinary power. Men associated with the street are constructed as the likely perpetrators of sexual violence, while men who occupy interior spaces as familial patriarchs and as authorities within ivory towers and courts of law are often absolved of culpability.

HAPPY HOMES AND DARK CONTINENTS: DOMESTICATING "WILD WOMEN"

Michel Foucault discusses the construction of the "non-space" that women must occupy to be sexualized. He discusses the space of the "honeymoon" in which the newlywed couple must flee to a "non-place" that exists outside of the reproductive time of the bourgeois home and the productive time of labour. To be "deflowered," Foucault suggests that women need to be taken to a nether region of what he terms a "deviant heterotopia" (Foucault qtd. in Reis and Bastos da Silva 239). In this regard, the woman who occupies the "deviant heterotopia" of the street becomes sexualized through a moralistic reproductive bourgeois framework. Within the dominant paradigms of spatial sexualization and segregation, women exist outside of the home only to be claimed and conquered for marriage, or "deflowered" by legally recognized husbands

164

in the liminal temporalities and spaces of honeymoons. The woman who crosses borders, who strays from the "happy home" into the street and beyond the "pure citizenship" of "national heterosexuality" is an exiled body within the patriarchal, heteronormative, colonial imaginary. The deep irony of the will to spatialize narratives of "perfect victims" of sexual violence, as those who are at home within the normative family and the nation-state, against those associated with public space lies in how the home is sanctified in ways that make it unhomely for women. By imagining women to be at home in a patriarchal nation and family, their sexual violation and abuse within the domestic realm is often made unintelligible, inaudible, invisible, and unspeakable. The imagined innocence and lightness of the interior as opposed to the darkness of exteriors constructs home as a space in which misogynistic violence has no name. Gendered bodies gain empathy and the right to have bodily rights as citizens[6] within the public and political sphere only by suspending all entitlements within a familial system of legislated sexism, a domesticated version of a larger masculinist nationalist imaginary (Das and Arendt qtd. Benhabib 49).

FLESH BORDERS:
GANG RAPE AS A MARKER OF BOUNDARIES

Writing in the wake of the Delhi gang rape case, Arvind Narrain discusses how sexual violence must be reconfigured outside of a patriarchal heteronormative framework that sees rape as existing on a continuum with sexual desire. Narrain suggests that sexual torture should be seen as a tactic of state and patriarchal violence: "These acts of brutality are often executed in situations of armed conflict; sexual assault is woven into the very fabric of military conquests" (18). The construction of group spaces of masculinist violence that function according to their own built-in codes resonate with mainstream articulations of nationalism. Codes of overarching morality and legality are breeched in these spaces, and men perform for one another according to norms of masculinist honour that often glorify misogyny. As Narrain argues, the marking of borders of nation-states have always involved using women's bodies to define and demarcate boundaries, often through the use of sexualized torture. The image of the gang or group of men travelling to a space that they use to commit sexual and physical crimes resonates with tales of colonial explorers who construct liminal spaces of travel to engage in misogynistic and racist fantasies. Razack writes of the spatialization of white-settler violence and discusses sexual violence against Aboriginal women by white-settler Canadian men who travel to Aboriginal reserves to rape, abuse, and murder Native women. The author further suggests that while white-settler men commit deplorable acts of rape and racist assault when far from home, they often act in "civilized" ways when in domestic spaces and elite workplaces. By constructing Aboriginal territories as "wild" and lawless spaces, white-settlers who commit acts of racist and sexist violence cartographically, can subsequently justify their crimes. The spatial politics of violence across borders continues to be defined and determined by the haunting of colonial history and its obscene nationalist expressions (Razack 121-144).

In considering the transnational ways in which sexual violence is often justified through nationalist discourse, the scripting of the 2012 Delhi gang rape case as a quintessential problem of "Indian culture" is not only deeply Orientalist but also; it is deeply ahistorical and myopic. For example, the U.S. State Department issued a medal of courage in honour of Jyoti, even though crimes of sexual torture have been a well-publicized part of the U.S.-led global "war on terror," and the torture of African immigrants such as Abner Louima by the New York City Police Department are foundational to American national-ism (Narrain). Žižek writes of the relationship between the everyday workings of American culture and practices of torture. Following the release of the photos of tortured prisoners at Abu Ghraib, many of which came to haunt the general public in their infinite reproduction through Internet technologies, Rush Limbaugh minimized the torture committed by U.S. soldiers by comparing these acts to "hazing rituals." Discussing Limbaugh's comment, Žižek argues that the resemblance between American military torture and hazing rituals does not reveal them to be minimal but actually reveals the extreme perversions that lie at the core of North American patriotism. Žižek writes, "What we get when we see the photos of humiliated Iraqi prisoners is precisely a direct insight into 'American values,' into the core of an obscene enjoyment that sustains the American way of life" (*The Parallax View* 372). More-over, not long after the international media coverage and outpouring of sympathy from the United States government regarding the Delhi gang rape case of 2012, the Steubenville rape case occurred. The case involved the gang rape of a 16-year-old woman by a group of North American high school athletes. The case gained international attention when it was alleged that the educational institution in which the young men played football attempted to protect them from legal prosecution for rape, because of the ways in which the prowess of university athletes often supports the branding of North American educational institutions. Teachers and university administrators who are reported to have tried to shield the accused from criminal prosecution as valued sports heroes who generate lucrative revenue for schools were privileged over the bodies of raped and dehumanized women. Much like the 2012 Delhi gang rape case, the disturbing details of the Steubenville case involved an alcohol-fuelled "party" and acts against the survivor that involved ridicule, obscenity, and public shaming, mimicking the sickening under-belly of jockish fraternity and "party" culture[7] ("High School Football Player Convicted"). Before the world's cameras turn, Western nations wave medals of courage in the name of dead brown women. Yet at the same moment, soldiers are also celebrated for torturing Arab prisoners far from the "happy homes" of colonizing white settlers. So too, are gold medals pinned on sporting young men whose crimes of rape are justified as just another North American pastime.

GUIDING LIGHT: JYOTI AND GLOBAL POLITICS

Drawing on the work of Frantz Fanon, Homi Bhabha asks how the postcolonial subject might act as a guiding figure in regards to global politics. Bhabha asks, "In what way, then can the once colonized wom-an or man become figures of instruction for our global century?" (xix). The extreme violence experienced by Jyoti and countless other women and queer people within the Indian subcontinent speaks to a sense of political urgency and begs a series of questions on the limits of liberal discourses of "rights" and developmental ideas of "progress." Bhabha discusses the timeless quality of the psychosocial forms of oppression that Fanon wrote of that move outside of a normative order of temporality and space by attacking the bodies and minds of the oppressed. Bhabha writes that "A psycho-affective relation or response has the semblance of universality and timelessness because it involves the emotions, the imagination or psychic life" (xix). The centring of psychic and bodily oppression that cuts to the very core of the humanity of the colonized is

167

acutely expressed in cases of sexualized violence against gendered bodies in postcolonial space. The lack of state accountability, infrastructure, and economic stability creates conditions of extreme vulnerability in which bodily integrity is violated to the point of death in the Indian subcontinent. The gendered and sexualized body in postcolonial space becomes a figure that instructs against a fetishization of "rights" and a developmentalist paradigm, which purports to offer justice in the form of neoliberal capitalist advancement that will benefit the very elite and masculine body of the city.

Bhabha suggests that Fanon's centring of the postcolonial subject and context leads to asking how turning one's gaze to the postcolonial body can shape how one envisions global politics. The colonized, gendered body in the Indian subcontinent that is subject to extreme sexual and bodily violence might offer instruction for global politics by drawing attention to forms of routine bodily degradation that are part and parcel of the everyday. Bhabha writes that for Fanon, "the colonized acquire a peculiar visceral intelligence dedicated to the survival of body and spirit" (ix). This visceral intelligence is clearly expressed in the narratives of protestors in the Indian subcontinent, following the Delhi gang rape and murder case of 2012. Narratives erupted everywhere in the Indian and global press where women, queer, and transgender persons told stories of their embodied lives in India. One Mumbai student commented, "To be a woman in an Indian city is to live in constant paranoia" ("Women Are Taught to Live in Paranoia"). This hypersensitivity was also what Fanon wrote of when he discussed the experience of Blackness in a white world.

"LIKE BUSES": WHERE/WHEN HISTORY BRAKES/BREAKS

"Men are like buses"[8] is an old adage that women often hear. In December 2012, Jyoti and Awindra caught a bus, a bus full of men who committed unspeakable crimes of rape, torture, and murder. A bus full of men who mercilessly killed Jyoti and left Awindra severely beaten, with incalculable psychic trauma. If men are like buses, then women it seems are always being taken for a ride. There are no words to capture the magnitude of violence and loss that defined this case. Yet the Indian subcontinent is still being taken for a ride, on a collision course of history that violently threw the country into something called "modernity." Said's Orientalist narrative was always a gendered tale in which the parable of rape was used to describe the pillage of colonized places by imperialist explorers. While celebrated male postcolonial theorists have written lyrically about decolonization, to stop the train-wreck of late capitalist modernity and (neo)colonial plunder, one must begin with the story of a woman on a public bus in India who did not live to tell her own story. As with Said's analysis of Flaubert who spoke for the silent, passive "Oriental woman" with no consent, Jyoti, too, has been silenced (Said). Her story is left to be narrated through the mouths, pens, and computer clicks of others. Undoing Orientalism and reimagining the figure of "the citizen" beyond Orientalist narratives of masculinist authority can begin here, with the troubling absence of those whom history has always silenced and continues to silence in the most despicably common ways. In the spirit of justice, this moment can be marked by moving in a new direction. As Slavoj Žižek suggests, "The task of the leftist thinker today is, to quote Walter Benjamin, 'not to ride the train of history, but to pull the brake'" (Žižek qtd. in O'Hagen).

ENDNOTES

[1]Lorde lyrically writes of her experiences of racism on a New York City train:

> The AA subway train to Harlem.... My mother spots an almost seat, pushes my little snow suited body down. On one side of me a man reading a paper. On the other, a woman in a fur hat staring at me. Her mouth twitches as she stares and then her gaze drops down, pulling mine with it. Her leather-gloved hand plucks at the line where my new blue snow pants and her sleek fur coat meet. She jerks her coat closer to her. I look. I do not see whatever terrible thing she is seeing on the seat between us—probably a roach. But she has communicated her horror to me. It must be something very bad from the way she's looking, so I pull my snowsuit closer to me away from it, too. When I look up the woman is still staring at me, her nose holes and eyes huge. And suddenly I realize there is nothing crawling up the seat between us; it is me she doesn't want her coat to touch (147-148).

[2]In an interview done with the BBC regarding the case, one of the accused

remains unrepentant and continues to site the time of day that Jyoti and Awindra were on the streets as a justification for the brutal assault, gang rape, and murder. As *The Times of India* reports,

> One of the main accused in the Nirbhaya gang rape gave a shocking interview recently blaming the victim for the fatal sexual assault, "Women who go out at night have only themselves to blame in case they attract attention of male molesters," Mukesh Singh, driver of the bus in which the rape took place, said. He recently gave an interview to British Broadcasting Corporation [BBC] from jail, which will be aired on March 8, which is also celebrated as International Women's Day. (Sinha)

[3]Stuart Hall discusses the management of anxieties, aggressions, and repressed desires that are managed towards "otherness" spatially. Drawing on the writing of Julia Kristeva, Hall states,

> Symbolic boundaries keep the categories "pure," giving cultures their unique meaning and identity. What unsettles culture is "matter out of place"—the breaking of our unwritten rules and codes. Dirt in the garden is fine, but dirt in one's bedroom is "matter out of place"—a sign of pollution of symbolic boundaries being transgressed, or taboos broken. What we do with "matter out of place" is to sweep it up, throw it out, restore the place to order, bring back the normal state of affairs. The retreat of many cultures towards "closure" against foreigners, intruders, aliens, and "others" is part of the same process of purification. (236)

While spectacles of Hijras, queers, sex workers, and women—marked as "other" to the dominant middle-class, heteronormative Hindu ideal—may appear as entertainment in film and television; these same bodies may be implicitly and explicitly barred from social and public space through unwritten codes of exclusion and acts of physical and sexual violence. [4]Park and Burgess cite this old German adage, "the city air makes men free" [*Stadt Luft macht frei*]. The authors state,

> This is doubtless a reference to the days when the free cities of Germany enjoyed a patronage of the emperor, and laws made the fugitive serf a free man if he succeeded for a year and a day breathing city air. (12)

In this idiom and many writings regarding those thought to occupy city space, there is often little mention of women in the city or of those whose "freedom" and survival in urban space is tied not only to economics but to patriarchal and heteronormative violence and exclusion (D'Souza and McDonough).

[5]Phadke further discusses narratives of protectionism in which conservative political elites use cases of gendered violence in public space to support an ideology of fear, one that supports the barring of women from accessing city spaces. As Phadke writes,

Conservative voices tend to directly blame women for the violence committed against them. However, the tone of even the most liberal media narratives is one of "the city under siege" and "women in danger." All of these narratives of danger contribute toward the evocation of a sense that women are unsafe in the city. (Phadke 1513)

[6]The concept of "the right to have rights" was one that was first articulated by philosopher Hannah Arendt in discussing citizenship and exile (Arendt qtd. in Benhabib 49).

[7]At the time of writing the accused in the Steubenville rape case was released from juvenile detention after serving less than two years in prison. One of the other people convicted in this case received a lesser sentence and has also been released from prison (Kutner).

[8]Renderings of the image of "the bus" by political leaders can be found transnationally. For example, the former Prime Minister of Britain Margaret Thatcher once stated that "any man over the age of twenty-six who finds himself on a bus can consider himself a total failure in life" (Thatcher qtd. in Mason). Thatcher's comments are perhaps reflective of the ways in which mobility in public space is tied to social mobility. The relationship between masculinity and capitalist ideals of achievement, and the state's lack of investment in public transport can be read as an expression of indifference and implicit hostility towards working-class and lower-income people.

WORKS CITED

Benhabib, Seyla. *The Rights of Others: Aliens, Residents, and Citizens.* Cambridge: Cambridge University Press, 2004. Print.

Berlant, Lauren, and Michael Warner. "Sex in Public." *Critical Inquiry* 24.2 (1998): 547-566. Print.

Bhabha, Homi K. "Foreward: Framing Fanon." *The Wretched of the Earth.* By Frantz Fanon New York: Grove Press, 2004. vi-xliii. Print.

Das, Veena. *Life and Words: Violence and the Descent into the Ordinary.* California: University of California Press, 2007. Print.

Datta, Bishakha, Ed. *Nine Degrees of Justice: New Perspectives on Violence against Women in India.* New Delhi: Zubaan Press, 2015. Kindle Edition.

"Delhi Gang Rape-Victim Narrates the Tale of Horror." *The Hindu.* 23 Dec. 2013. Web. 9 Aug. 2015.

"Delhi Gang Rape: 'Women Are Taught to Live in Paranoia.'" British Broadcasting Corporation, 20 Dec. 2012. Web. 13 June 2015.

D'Souza, Aruna and Tom McDonough. *The Invisible Flâneuse?: Gender, Public Space and Visual Culture in Nineteenth Century Paris.* Manchester: University of Manchester Press, 1999. Print.

Forum against the Oppression of Women." Feminist Contributions from the Margins: Shifting Conceptions of Work and Performance of the Bar Dancers of Mumbai." *Economic and Political Weekly* XLV. 44-45 (October 30 2010): 48-55. Print.

Foucault, Michel, and Jay Miskowiec. "Of Other Spaces." *Diacritics* 16.1 (Spring 1986): 22-27. Print.

Ghosh, Pothik. "Delhi Gang Rape and the Feminism of Proletarian Militancy." *Radical Notes,* 28 Dec. 2012. Web. 13 June 2015.

Hall, Stuart. *Representation: Cultural Representations and Signifying Practices.* London: Sage Publications, 2012.

"High-School Football Player Convicted of Steubenville Rape Is Released." *The Guardian,* 6 Jan. 2014. Web. 13 June 2014.

Kutner, Jenny. "Convicted Steubenville Rapist Trent Mays Released from Juvenile Detention." Salon Media Group, 7 Jan. 2015. Web. 11 Nov. 2015.

Lorde, Audre, "Eye to Eye: Black Women, Hatred, and Anger." *Sister Outsider: Essays and Speeches.* Berkeley: Crossing Press, 1984. 145-175. Print.

Mason, Mark. *Move Along Please.* London: Cornerstone Press, 2013. Kindle Edition.

Narrain, Arvind. "The Violation of Bodily Integrity." *Economic and Political Weekly* 48 (2013): 17-19. Print.

O'Hagan, Sean. "Slavoj Žižek: Interview." *The Guardian,* 27 June 2010. Web. 14 Sept. 2014.

Park, Robert E. and Ernest W. Burgess. *The City: Suggestions for Investigation of Human Behaviour in the Urban Environment.* Chicago:

University of Chicago Press, 1984. Print.

Phadke, Shilpa. "Dangerous Liasons: Women and Men Risk Reputation in Mumbai." *Economic and Political Weekly* 42.17 (Apr. 28 - May 4, 2007): 1510-1518. Print.

Phadke, Shilpa. "You Can Be Lonely in a Crowd: The Production of Safety in Mumbai." *Indian Journal of Gender Studies* 12.1 (2005): 41-62. Print.

Razack, Sherene. *Race, Space, and the Law: Unmapping a White Settler Society.* Toronto: Between the Lines, 2002. Print.

Reddy, Gayatri. *With Respect to Sex: Negotiating Hijra Identity in South India.* Chicago: University of Chicago Press, 2005. Print.

Roychowdhury, Poulami. "The Delhi Gang Rape": The Making of International Causes." *Feminist Studies* 39.1 (2013): 282-292. Print.

Said, Edward. *The Edward Said Reader.* Edited by Moustafa Bayoumi and Andre Rubin. New York: Vintage Books, 2000. Print.

Shah, Svati P. "Producing The Spectacle of Kamathipura: The Politics of Red Light Visibility in Mumbai." *Cultural Dynamics* 18.3 (2006): 269-292. Print.

Sinha, Kounteya. "Nirbhaya Gang-Rape Convict Blames Victim for the Fatal Assault." *The Times of India*, 2 March 2015. Web. 9 Aug. 2015.

Soumya, Elizabeth. "Africans Decry 'Discrimination' in India." Aljazeera, 2 Dec. 2013. Web. 13 June 2013.

Tambe, Ashwini. *Codes of Misconduct: Regulating Prostitution in Late Colonial Bombay.* Minnesota: University of Minnesota Press, 2009. Print.

Taraporewala, Persis and Rohit Negi, "Criminalising Africans in Delhi's Villages." *The Hindu*, 27 Feb. 2014. Web. 13 June 2015.

Vasudeva, Ravinder, Joshi, Riddhi Mondal, Sudipto, and Namita Kohli. "Their Indian Horror: Africans Recount Everyday Racism." *The Hindustan Times*, 12 Oct. 2014. Web. June 13, 2015.

West, Cornel. *Keeping Faith: Philosophy and Race in America.* New York: Routledge, 1993. Print.

Zirin, David. "No for the Love of God Johnny Manziel Isn't Rosa Parks." *The Nation*, 11 Aug 2013. Web. 14 Sept. 2014.

Žižek, Slavoj. *The Parallex View.* Cambridge: MIT Press, 2006. Print.

Žižek, Slavoj. *Violence: Six Sideways Reflections.* New York: Picador, 2008. Print.

II.
IN THE STREETS

5.

"LOVE BEGINS HERE"

DIAMONDS AND THE MINEFIELDS OF ROMANCE

ADJACENT TO the Saket city bus stop outside of a shopping complex where two people saw a film in December of 2012, an evening which ended in a horrific gang rape and murder, an advertisement for a diamond wedding ring can be seen by passersby. It is in many ways, a cruel joke. Commenting on the commodification of human love through market values, Friedman points out that the genealogy of the diamond wedding ring can be traced back to the British mining of diamonds in South Africa in the nineteenth century[1] (Friedman). In a time of technologically powered globalization, metaphors of "love" are used to increasingly sell products, with iPhones being sold through branding campaigns that declare that 99 percent of iPhone users truly "love" their phones (Matyszczyk). The critiques of capitalism made by the 99 percent that took to the streets in global Occupy protests, and the many Chinese workers committing suicide in apple factories are often invisible within these celebratory narratives of market-based "love" as property.

The "love begins here" branding of diamond wedding rings outside of shopping malls in Delhi is haunted by a young girl's hands that will never wear a wedding ring, that will never raise in a fist against a lingering patriarchal ideology of state power that values and valorizes women as the property of men, as existing only within the domestic sphere where they can be legally raped by men named as "husbands," and left for dead on city streets. Yet the irony of the image of branded romance found in a public space marked by the haunting of the Delhi gang rape case lay in a love not beginning or ending in material possessions; rather the Delhi gang rape protests offer evidence of a politicized love that begins in the streets and will perhaps forever echo in the streets.

JEWELS IN CROWNS AND WEDDING BANDS:
"LOVE" AS COLONIALISM

The idea of love as pre-discursive and innate, as a universal apolitical idea that is without history can be critiqued through the English-language use of the word "love," the relationship between ideas of romantic love and colonial history, and how the concept of love is now manipulated within global capitalist branding. Betsy Bolton discusses the relationship between love and colonialism. Bolton cites the writings of Frederic Jameson who discusses uses of love within nineteenth- century Europe as a means of masking class antagonism. As the author states, "Frederic Jameson suggests that romance originates with a class conflict not yet articulated in terms of class or conflict" (3). Sara Suleri argues that the romantic genre within eighteenth- and nineteenth-century Europe emerged at a time of nationalist conflict in which romantic love became a metaphor for the love of the nation. The love of the "mother country" corresponds with idealized forms of heteronormative, monogamous familial love. The popularization of romantic Anglo-Indian fiction within the empire reflects the use of romantic narratives to evade material questions of capitalist and colonial power. Relationships laden with oppressive hier-archies of power were celebrated through metaphors of love, romance, and benevolent scripts of salvation. Suleri discusses how the conventions of the romance genre were used to stage scenes of imperial domination as love stories. The affective sentiments of desire and longing scripted the relationship between colonizers and the colonized as a tender affair. The obvious capitalist exploitation, racism, and violence of colonizers were masked in a trite narrative of love. As Suleri states,

> In negotiating between the idioms of empire and of nation, the fiction of nineteenth-century Anglo-India seeks to decode the colonised territory through the conventions of romance, reorganising the materiality of colonialism into a narrative of perpetual longing, and perpetual loss. (11)

Within the mirage of romantic longing produced through imperialist genres of romance, colonized countries such as India become the absent other that is longed over. The colonizing power loves the colony in the way that an abusive patriarch turns power into romance. As Suleri writes,

India becomes the absent point toward which nineteenth-century Anglo-Indian narrative may lean but which it may never
possess, causing both national and cultural identities to disappear
in the emptiness of a representational mirage. (11)

Homi Bhabha's writings regarding the psychoanalytic dimensions of
colonization make reference to the deep-seated narcissism of empire. As
the "jewel in the crown" of the British Empire, the Indian subcontinent
is desired for and "loved," in similar way as capitalism turns the ownership of women's bodies within heteronormative patriarchal narratives
of conquest and projections of the male gaze onto the female body into
something called love (Suleri 126-131). In tales of missionary salvation
and Victorian moralism, the colonies are represented as savage and
in need of the maternal love of "mother countries" to turn the brute
aggression of colonization into a relationship of care. As Bolton states,
"the sentimental mode of late imperial romance attempts to resolve
this tension by translating the materiality of colonialism into an appeal
to sensibility and moral right" (4). Bolton draws on Rudyard Kipling's
canonical colonial writings about the racist construct of the "white
man's burden" to discuss how the material exploitation of colonialism is
rewritten as romance. Making reference to the farcical nature of colonial
romance scripts, Bolton asserts that

Taking power in the name of history coincides with a turn from
farce toward sentiment and romance: the white man's burden
is yet another variant on the knight's quest to save the forms
of civilisation for humanity. (5)

While Bolton focuses on romantic fiction, McClintock's writings on
advertising and imperialism offer another farce of commodified and
colonized love. McClintock discusses the rise of commodity fetishism
and spectacle through advertising, which began in the nineteenth
century. McClintock talks about Pears soap ads that became popular
in nineteenth-century Europe; the ads visually depicted a white child
washing a black child with soap accompanied by the slogan, "The first
step towards lightening the white man's burden is through teaching the
virtues of cleanliness" (32). Domestic products provided a means for
turning the supposed domestic bliss of the home, a cite of imagined

pastoral romance into one that taught the illiterate masses of Europe that racism was a matter of moral virtue and salvation. Love became associated with forms of domestic, heteronormative, and familial bliss that turned the wretched project of racist and capitalist domination into one of care and moral salvation. Bolton illustrates how the domestic scene within European colonial fiction masked oppressive gendered power dynamics in the home, and the violence of imperial conquest that put the tea into the cups of "happy" colonial families. Bolton cites writings from the colonial period in which the "longed for domestic space cramped and invaded by labour, poverty, tears, illness and physical abuse represent an ideal family intimacy" (6). Nineteenth-century fiction and advertising turned colonialism into a narrative of romance in which the "fair and lovely" colonial "mother country" imagined itself as performing a benevolent gesture of salvation through attempting to domesticate the imagined savages in the colonies. The capitalist power dynamics of colonial pillage, slavery, and the use of the colonies to produce the enrichment of empire were both naturalized and made sentimental in these romantic narratives. Similarly, contemporary globalized branding also tells a "love story" that masks its inherent violence.

PUT A RING ON IT?
DIAMONDS, SLAVE LABOUR, AND THE BRANDING OF "LOVE"

Contemporary nationalist romance solidified through the purchase of diamond rings also conceals the material and political violence that produces the love object, with diamonds found in wedding bands being excavated by new-fangled slaves in African diamond minds. As discussed in a report by researchers at Harvard Law School, child labour is often used within diamond mines throughout the Global South to produce symbols of "romantic love" for affluent consumers. Making specific reference to child labour in the diamond mining industry in post-civil war Sierra Leone, the authors state, "hundreds of children and youth are exploited daily as they labour in open-pit diamond mines" (International Human Rights Clinic iv). The heteronormative middle-class family conceals the exploitation that produces its ostensibly innocent images of love. In the shadows of sparkling family portraits are the small hands of "other" darker and poorer children that dig diamonds for the wedding fingers of "fair and lovely" socialite wives. Just as the history of imperial bourgeois domestic scenes of familial bliss concealed the forced labour and economic impoverishment of colonies that sweetened the lives of European families with plantation sugar, the national romance of heteronormative, upper caste and upper class Hindu narcissism conceals its dark underbelly. As noted throughout this book, sexual politics in postcolonial worlds should be considered in relation to the violence of contemporary globalized capitalism and its historical relationship to colonialism. Furthermore, I also argue that the racial, sexual, caste and class-based anxieties produced among an idealized and heteronormative Hindu middle class are haunted by colonial ideology. This "fair and lovely" image of Indian nationalism is produced through the dark shadows of history concealed in the *nouveau riche* glare of traffic and mall lighting, obscenely banal spectacles of love as wealth in an "India shining."

The "love begins here" advertisement for diamond wedding rings that appears outside of a mall in the city of Delhi—a reference point to an appalling case of a gang rape, torture, and murder—markets domestic bliss to an idealized urban Hindu middle class. Simultaneously, as discussed, a woman in contemporary India can be legally raped by her husband, treated as his disposable property. The genealogy of love that appears within the contemporary branding of consumer goods resonates with the history of empire. Just as the sentimental paternal and maternal stories of romantic love and uses of advertising in the nineteenth-century masked the material and psychic violence of colonization, the contemporary branding of "love" removes the truth of power from its narcissistic image. In the gleam of the diamond ring in neoliberal advertising found outside of Taj Mahal malls, there is no trace of the blood of a woman tortured to death or the mangled hands of labourers in diamond mines whose bodies are sacrificed to the ruthless tyrannies of global capitalism. In the gleam of the diamond ring, now used to sell secular ideals of love and marriage to the Indian middle class, the woman who is legally raped as "wife" becomes a love object whose ownership is celebrated in foreign-made products from economies fuelled by newly legislated forms of slavery and forced labour. The "love begins here" of expensive diamond rings is an unattainable love in a nation with just as many newly erected slums as billboards.

If the European empire turned its masculinist hold over colonies into a tale of a "white man's burden" to enact a paternalist violence masking itself as care, nationalism also serves to domesticate bodies through narratives of romance. The idealized middle-class Hindu woman is confined within the romantic narratives of the idealized middle class heteronormative marriage, now solidified by secular-capitalist branding. She is a captive consumer for foreign made products associated with romance, while colonial laws and patriarchal sexual mores discipline her bodily desires. Abhigyan Sarkar draws on writings regarding affect and consumerism to suggest that companies often use ideas of love to produce brand loyalty among consumers. Sarkar cites research which suggests that secular romance narratives are often utilized by advertisers to sell products, producing emotions of desire, longing, and fidelity in consumers. Sarkar states that "interpersonal love consists of three highly correlated dimensions: intimacy, passion, and decision/commitment" (83). Sarkar further argues that "the structure of consumer-object (the object can be a brand) relationship is very similar to the structure of interpersonal love as stated by Sternberg" (82). In contemporary India, narratives of secular romance and romantic agency are often seen as "progressive" compared to religiously informed structures of arranged marriage. However, ideas of love are increasingly bound to neoliberal capitalist economies. While Western neoliberal discourses of feminism often imagine agency and choice to be beneficial to women as desiring agents, the idea of "choice" within the context of postcolonial nations can be questioned in relation to colonial history and the glaring inequalities of global capitalism. Those who begin love with an imported diamond ring produced in slave labour conditions in a nation of glaring gaps between the rich and the poor are among the chosen few. Furthermore, the imagined agency of the consumer who loves the brand and the obvious lack of agency of the woman who can be legally raped by her husband, make the obvious lack of choice afforded to captive consumers and women in India clear. The illusory freedoms of choice within an India bound to colonial legality and hurtling towards secular capitalist futures is challenged, however, through the "Āzādī" of protestors in the streets, a passionate cry that cannot be captured in insipid, apolitical love stories.

WHITE WEDDING DRESSES AND BLOOD RED POLITICS: CONSUMER DRIVEN ROMANCE AND GENDER BASED VIOLENCE

Ideas of love, globalized branding, and changing articulations of femininity are not specific to urban India but reflect a wider process of change in Asia. The articulation of "romantic love" through secular capitalism and its relationship to performances of class-based femininity is also expressed in contemporary, post-socialist urban China. Interviewing young women in urban China, McWilliams sees the white wedding dress as a marker of "new Chinese femininity" that is tied to capitalist ideas of "freedom." McWilliams discussion surrounding consumerist femininities in China resonates with Chowdury's discussion regarding the "New Indian woman" of consumer power (145-183). For many middle class urban Asian women, national belonging is expressed in acts of commodity consumption. In China for example, the store bought wedding dress has replaced the traditional Chinese garments worn by earlier generations of Asian women (McWilliams). Whereas arranged marriage structures and those tied to agrarian systems of land once determined women's sexual, reproductive, and marital roles, many women in contemporary urban China now are part of a "choice"-based generation. The wearing of the white wedding dress is, therefore, symbolic of the complex relationship between individualistic ideas of agency, consumer capitalism, and globalized ideals of feminine performance that often derive from secular Western media. As McWilliams states,

> the white wedding gown symbolizes the emergent present linked to a romanticized ideology of globalization, female worldliness, and heterosexuality ... contemporary Chinese femininity is in a state of flux. Critical attention to gender and sexuality throughout these vestimentary markers of the material culture of modernity provides us with a richer knowledge of how market capitalism and consumption function as crucial aspects in the construction of an uneasy set of Chinese female subjects. (163)

Commodity fetishism produces idealized symbols of "new femininity" in China, but these images of capitalist freedom do not provide meaningful solutions for high levels of gender-based violence in Asia (Yang). Furthermore, the images of consumer-driven pleasure and freedom sold to women in urban China are ones of heteronormative and class-based desire, which make the bodies and lives of queers, transgender people, working class, and migrant women invisible. The assumed love expressed in white wedding dresses and diamond rings offer women in urban Asia a supposed liberation from older traditional systems of marriage and reproduction defined by religion and culture. Yet, within contemporary secular capitalist culture new hierarchies and systems of oppression emerge. Women are increasingly inculcated in conservative, heteronormative ideologies of middle-class "family values" and market-based desires to consume products branded as symbols of love. The ostensible innocence of products such as white wedding dresses and diamond wedding rings conceals the grotesque exploitation of workers in mines and textile factories and the corpses left to haunt city buses.

On December 16, 2013, a protest marking the one year anniversary of the Delhi gang rape case was organized outside of the Saket City Bus stop in Delhi. From my interviews with protesters, feminists, activists, and people at the demonstration that day, I was struck by the inability of those who were there to fully articulate the meaning of these protests and the totality of demands that are definitive of what many term a new "movement" within urban India concerning gender, justice, and Āzādī. Drawing on writings regarding other new global social movements such as Occupy and the Arab Spring protests, I suggest that the inability and unwillingness of people to articulate their desires and demands within a language of state power and narrow patriarchal scripts of gender is in fact one of the greatest strengths of this movement. The actions were organized under the name of "*Jurrat*," meaning courage. This was the courage of people, young and old, of all genders, races, faiths, and per-suasions who gathered at a bus stop in a city to mark all the losses that haunt this time and all that drives us forward beyond commemoration and towards a love that has no ring or tagline or perhaps even a name. The constant refrain of those who came to the protest, to mark the day as a day of unspeakable violence and to remember the year as one of political fallout, slow and steady change, and ongoing resistance was Āzādī—freedom. People cried out again and again. Āzādī. It was heard in every song and cheer. Āzādī.

UNROMANCING THE STONE IN THE STREETS:
FOR THE LOVE OF POLITICS

If love begins here, it does not end when wedding rings are placed on young women's hands, transforming women from people into property. It does not begin on one day and end when the world's cameras turn away. It begins in the streets, just as the fateful torture, gang rape, and murder of a young woman began in the streets. It begins in the streets, just as the unprecedented levels of protest in Delhi, throughout India, and throughout Asia often began in the streets. It begins with the resilience of people who, like all those who embark on consolidating, building, and envisioning struggles for justice, begin with a beautiful inability to ever fully articulate the spirit and will that carries revolutionary demands. The true meaning of any social movement lies in what cannot be branded or articulated. Love for those selling diamonds dug up in Africa by shackled slave wage labourers is a contractual obligation. It is a piece of property. It is a financial deal. For political leaders, politics is an easily articulated set of demands and rights. It is laws and bills passed. Yet for people embarking on a new vision of society, the truly revolutionary thing, which frustrates journalists, academics, political leaders, and media pundits, is the inability to fully name what one wants and what one is in fact doing. Writing about the Occupy movements that began in New York and spread throughout the world, Slavoj Žižek discusses a similar quality that could not be fully articulated. He writes,

> In the psychoanalytic sense, the protesters are indeed hysterical actors, provoking the master, undermining his authority; and the question with which they were constantly bombarded, "But what do you want?" aims precisely at precluding the true answer—its point is "Say it in my terms or shut up!" In this way, the process of translating an inchoate protest into a concrete project is blocked. But the art of politics is also to insist on a particular demand that, while thoroughly "realistic," disturbs the very core of the hegemonic ideology, that is, which, while in principle is feasible and legitimate, is de facto impossible. (*The Year of Dreaming Dangerously* 83-84)

The blanket cries of "Āzādī" reflect an impossibility of gendered freedom. The desire for Āzādī points to the lack of freedom afforded to gendered bodies under the chokehold of bureaucratic corruption and lingering colonial laws, the lack of freedom afforded by law, and the suffocating ways that gender itself attempts to hold bodies in place in symbolic prisons of discursive and legal categorization. When speaking to people at these protests, what was striking were their utopian demands of a freedom, not only from violence but from the often-invisible, ideological bars of gender itself.

On December 16, 2013, we meet in the streets. The glare of mall billboards selling shiny things has faded. Pavel[2] identifies as a queer men based in Delhi, who is "out and proud." Yet the constant thread that runs through our conversation is one of gender as a limit, a barrier, a form of oppressive and repressive control. As Pavel puts it,

> They [the protests] aren't only about passing a law that will take care of this issue but also we're having conversations about how gender impacts upon our lives everyday lives. That has shown up, this discussion about gender is now very much being had in many places, by many people. You go out in the city and everyone is talking about it. Well, not everyone is talking about it but the number of people talking about it has increased.

The idea of moving beyond gender is a constant and perhaps never fully translatable desire, reflected through what many people gathered today at the Saket city bus stop term "a movement." Nandita, an activist and feminist who has been part of struggles against gender-based violence in the city for years makes a similar comment when asked what change she would like to see in Delhi and throughout the Indian subcontinent. She suggests that she would like to see a move away from an apprehension of the body in the street through the narrow lens of gender binaries that subsequently regulate bodies based on their appearance within a male-female structure of powerful and powerless. Nandita states,

> Everytime a woman walks out no one sees that she is a person, a citizen. She should be looked at in the same way that any person is looked at. With the same respect, with the same dignity. And for the service providers, for the laws, we want her to be treated with the same yardstick that we use to treat anyone else. It is a big change, but a step that has to be made.

The Āzādī that is articulated by those whom I speak with is a freedom that can never be fully captured within the language of gender or within the language of the state. The constant cry of Āzādī is not just a cry for freedom from the violence of the street or from the violence of the home; it is reflective of a concomitant desire for freedom from gender as a structuring, defining, and ordering principle. Much like the utopian and intangible freedom from capitalist violence that was articulated by Occupy protesters—leading to their ridicule, dismissal, and condemnation by many conservative politicians and mainstream media commentators—those who see themselves as part of this growing movement critique not only state and legal structures but underlying societal norms. Protestors, activists and everyday people constantly point to the need to question the larger ideologies of gender and sexuality that permit, excuse, and legislate violence in its most insipient and grotesque forms in Delhi and throughout the Indian subcontinent. As with Occupy, the "hysterical" cries of a new social movement, always on the verge of both revolution and co-option, begin with the smallest of demands and move to a radical questioning of the entirety of the social structure.

PARTNERS IN CRIME:
UNITING TRANSNATIONAL DISCOURSES OF PROTEST

Only a few days prior to the anniversary of the Delhi gang rape and murder case, the Supreme Court of India made the shocking decision to uphold Section 377 of the Indian Penal Code, India's sodomy bill, despite the 2009 decision by the Delhi high court to read down this old colonial law, what many in the region saw as a gesture that would lead to the lasting decriminalization of same sex desire throughout India. Many of the activists at the anniversary protests make reference to this decision and see it as being tied to a broader struggle for gender justice at the level of not only law but ideology. Aaliyah, a protestor at the demonstration, states,

> These struggles are connected. Like a lot of other movements, like the Arab Spring and yes, even Occupy, I think people are just fed up with so much. So when you see all these people coming with different signs to things like a Section 377 protest or a gang rape protest it's not always bad or not organized. I think it just means that people are now seeing that all issues are connected and even if it's not your son or daughter, these

187

things are about everyone. They are about how the country works and if you are going to call it a democracy then yes, fine, let's make it a democracy.

Aaliyah also discusses the commonalities of these movements in reference to an overall desire for freedom from violence. She discusses the decision regarding Section 377 of the Indian Penal Code and how her participation in feminist protest is connected to her participation in demonstrations against the criminalization of same-sex desire. As she states, "I think that the 377 ruling was a very unfortunate judgment. On Sunday there was a huge gathering that I also joined. It's about refusing any form of violence. All violence must be protested against." Protesters whom I speak with continually discuss the need for freedom from succint gendered and sexual categories, which many suggest are implicitly used to justify violence. What is striking about the conversations I have with protesters on the one year anniversary of the 2012 Delhi gang rape case in India is that they move beyond solely focusing on commemorating the tragic 2012 Delhi gang rape case to a wider focus on a reorganization of social and political structures, which can only be brought about through an ideological shift.

Writing in regards to the Occupy protests and anti-capitalism today, Žižek suggests that there is a litany of "anti-capitalist" rhetoric that often ironically accepts capitalism as an unchanging truth that cannot be challenged:

There is no lack of anti-capitalist sentiment today; if anything we are overloaded with critiques of the horrors of capitalism.... But what is never questioned is the democratic institutional framework of the (bourgeois) state of law itself. This remains the sacred cow that even the most radical of these forms of "ethical anti-capitalism" ... do not dare touch. (*The Year of Dreaming Dangerously* 83-84)

Parallels can be drawn between Žižek's reading of "anti-capitalism" and many anti-sexism movements, and specifically anti-violence against women movements globally. A critique of the violent workings of gender and patriarchy is accompanied by an often silently accepted belief that normative gender roles and patriarchal models of family and property ownership will continue. What is striking to consider in reference to the anniversary protests of December 16 2013, a year after the Delhi gang rape case and shortly after the reinstitution of Section 377 lies in the willingness of those involved in what they term a "new movement" to question the workings of gender. There is an overarching will to shift normative thinking pertaining to gender and sex that unites feminist and queer struggles in urban India. Āzādī, freedom, is articulated not just as freedom from the violent regulation of gendered bodies at the level of rape and domestic abuse but also freedom from categorization itself. This is an Āzādī" that protestors cry out for, asking to be free from the colonial confines of gender and from the reductionist categorizations of social movements. Protestors continually express the desire to be free from violence outside of gendered norms and argue that freedom from gender-based violence cannot occur without a change in the judgments made based on the surface reading of bodies.

ENGLISH WORDS, UNTRANSLATABLE PASSIONS: REFRAINS OF COMMITTED STRUGGLE

What is exciting and perhaps confounding about the beginnings of movements, which are of course always tied to longer genealogies of activism and the genealogies of nations and their margins, is their ability to be both everything and nothing. While the Delhi gang rape protests of 2012 can be seen as part of the "feminist movement," the cries of those involved seem to move beyond gendered language. Rather than discussing patriarchy or men, many of the people I met in the streets speak in universal terms about ideas such as freedom, justice, dignity, and even love; they also implicate state power as a source of gender-based oppression. Like the Occupy movements which were often led by disgruntled middle classes who were faced with austerity measures and the collapse of the social welfare state, protests following the 2012 Delhi gang rape case and 2013 decision to criminalize same sex desire involve a broader questioning of the social structure, often by many young relatively middle class urban people. The extreme violence inflicted on the body of this woman serves as a metaphor for a wider sickness within the body politic. Fathima is a Delhi student who participated in protests that took place in December of 2012. She discusses the attitudes of police and law enforcement as a key problem that will not be changed by only making demands for legalistic amendments. "Yes, the government will make changes. They will have to make changes. But there is still the problem with the attitude of the police." The question of an inefficient and corrupt state that is out of touch with the sensibilities of the people, particularly among what protestors call a "new generation," is another common thread that runs through the divergent voices of those who gather at the Saket City bus stop to mark the anniversary of the gang rape and murder of Jyoti. Many of the protestors are not shy about pointing to the state, political leaders, and police as allowing and even promoting gender and sexual violence. Fathima discusses the use of feminist issues by politicians as a bid to gain votes for the upcoming election. She further suggests that while many leaders are increasingly vocal about gender-based violence in India, this may be an attempt to win votes that does not translate into a real commitment to politicize gender. She reflects on the sense of disillusionment that many feel in Delhi following the Delhi gang rape case and the recent elections:

> I am so sad, because even one year after this case—we recently had the elections. And so many of these parties tried to cash in on this case and make big posters about it. I didn't see any statement by any of these parties today. It's the one-year anniversary of this tragic case and where are these politicians who supposedly care so much? And more importantly, where is the real prioritization for women? Where is the importance? Where is the move to make changes? And I think the sad thing is, this is the same thing we see everywhere. And that is what I want to see happen, a political change. And that is why I am here.

State power at the level of local and national governance is questioned by those whom I speak with who make reference to the 2012 Delhi gang rape case and the Supreme Court of India's 2013 decision to reinstitute Section 377, despite a long campaign by *Voices Against 377* in Delhi in 2009 and other queer activists within India and transnationally. There is a growing sense of cynicism not only regarding the arcane colonial laws that are still used in India but their application by corrupt and often bigoted police. Protestors question the role of the state and state power itself, expressed in an liberatory cry of Āzādi. One can perhaps read the ambitious and broad desires of protestors as radical and utopian visions that often surround the beginning of any new form of social movement that has not yet had to articulate itself in narrow ways. Much like Occupy movements and the Arab Spring, there is an inspiring feeling of possibility and imagination that colours the beginning of these emerging articulations of resistance. Saat, a protestor who identifies as queer and has been part of demonstrations regarding the 2012 Delhi gang rape case and Section 377, discusses the relationship between law and expressions of sexual desire:

> In some ways, it really doesn't matter. Does law impact on my daily activity and everything I do? No it really doesn't. But is there a threat? Is there a threat looming over me because of the existence of this law? Yes, there is. So, one can't give a clear idea of how the law impacts on my life. But there is a threat that looms there. The fact that a law like 377 exists means that there is a threat that looms in my head. It effects upon your psyche, your liberty, your dignity. In one way it doesn't really change. I'm queer and I'm proud and I'm out. So, does a law really change that? No. There are enough spaces that I reclaim for myself. Does the law change that? No. But if the authority in power wanted to do anything to me because of the spaces that I am claiming, then they can force certain things on me.

Saat goes on to suggest that the forceful will of the state on desiring bodies might cause one to question governmental authority, "At this point, I think after everything that has happened this year, people are questioning the state itself."

"Love begins here." The advertisement for diamonds was arguably the sick joke of a foreign advertiser working for a multinational corporation. A corporate salesman of neo-colonial "love" paid more money than many in the Indian subcontinent can even comprehend to affix a billboard for a diamond wedding ring to a bus stop outside a Delhi mall, where two people ended an evening not with love but with a hateful night of sickening atrocity. Yet the words were not wasted on diamonds or branding. Love perhaps did in some small and untranslatable way begin here, in the building of new movements for justice and for politics—what Badiou terms an act of collective, "public judgment" in which many people experience the heinous nature of this case as a breaking point (10-26). One young woman I speak with suggests that the extreme forms of sexual and physical violence that were definitive of this case "expressed the limits of humanity." The idea of the human, of the human body, and of some sense of universal ethics is also themes that run throughout my discussions with Āzādī protestors. Rather than humanity beyond sexism, many of them discuss humanity beyond gendered and sexual categorization, rigid coffins of name and skin that often bear traces of the haunting ethos of colonialism and the narrow minds of patriarchal elites. "Love begins here." On December 16, 2012 the whole world watched as a nation grieved, as courts and lawmakers clamoured to turn grief into grievance, as cameras clicked and candles burned. Every day in the Indian subcontinent, the ink of the daily press reports another story of another woman or Hijra or transgender person or queer person that has died or is dying in what has been termed "the world's largest democracy." Yet can the sheer visceral love of global media spectacle lead to a lasting social movement, to lasting political, structural, and ideological change? Swati is young and fierce in her cheers of Āzādī, of freedom. I ask her what if anything has changed in the year following the 2012 Delhi gang rape protests. There are others who answer this question by citing the gaps between the statistical truth of violence and the inaction of the state: "We all know that a woman is raped this many minutes in India. But is there any justice for these people? For those whose names and cases gain no attention?" There are others who point to the recent changes in sexual harassment law in India but also to the contentious decision by the Indian government to continue to legally sanction marital rape. Yet Swati sees optimism in the spaces of dialogue and chance meeting that happen in the streets:

> This case has changed things. They used to tell you not to say anything, not to tell. That it would be your fault. There is a very long way to go. People need an education in values. I am not sure how people have lost any sense of values and ethics. Maybe it was always this way and we looked the other way. But things are different now. I really believe so. Things have changed because we are here having this conversation.

Love begins here.

ENDNOTES

[1]Friedman discusses the origins of the diamond wedding ring as lying in consumer-based advertising campaigns. The tradition of romance signified by the wedding ring was one that was invented to boost sales. Friedman cites Epstein who traces the origins of the diamond to the discovery of massive diamond mines in South Africa in the late nineteenth century, which for the first time flooded world markets with diamonds. The British businessmen operating the South African mines recognized that only by maintaining the fiction that diamonds were scarce and inherently valuable could they protect their investments and buoy diamond prices. The author shows how diamonds were marketed as being tantamount to "love" and "romance" in North America during the Great Depression. Friedman states that marketers set out to persuade young men that diamonds (and only diamonds) were synonymous with romance, and that the measure of a man's love (and even his personal and professional success) was directly proportional to the size and quality of the diamond he purchased. Young women, in turn, had to be convinced that courtship concluded, invariably, in a diamond (Friedman). The rise of diamond sales in contemporary India is emblematic of neoliberal capitalist globalization, which attempts to sell ideas of universal love and romance to those in the Indian subcontinent through transnational corporate advertising.

WORKS CITED

Badiou, Alain. *Metapolitics.* London: Verso, 2005. Print.

Bhabha, Homi. *The Location of Culture.* London: Routledge, 1994. Print.

Bolton, Betsy. "Farce, Romance, Empire: Elizabeth Inchbald and Colonial Discourse." *Eighteenth Century Theory and Interpretation* 39.1 (1994): 3-24. Print.

Chowdhury, Kanishka. *The New India: Citizenship, Subjectivity, and Economic Liberalization.* New York: Palgrave Macmillan, 2011. Print.

Friedman, Uri. "How an Ad Campaign Invented the Diamond Engagement Ring." *The Atlantic.* Atlantic Magazine, 13 Feb. 2015. Web. 28 Nov. 2015.

Matyszczyk, Chris. "Apple Claims that 99% of iPhone Users Love their iPhone." Cnet, 10 July 2015. Web. 10 Aug. 2015.

McClintock, Anne. *Imperial Leather: Race, Gender, and Sexuality, and the Colonial Contest.* Routledge: New York, 1995. Print.

McWilliams, S. "'People Don't Attack You If You Dress Fancy': Consuming Femininity in Contemporary China." *Women Studies Quarterly* 41 (2013): 162-183. Print.

Sarkar, Abhigyan. "Romancing With a Brand: A Conceptual Analysis of Romantic Consumer-Brand Relationship." *Management & Marketing Challenges for the Knowledge Society* 6.1 (2011): 79-94, Print.

Suleri, Sara. *The Rhetoric of English India.* Chicago: University of Chicago Press, 1992. Print.

The International Human Rights Clinic. *Digging in the Dirt: Child Miners in Sierra Leone's Diamond Industry.* Boston: Harvard Law School, 2009. Print.

Yang, Mayfair Mei-hui. "From Gender Erasure to Gender Difference: State Feminism, Consumer Sexuality, and Women's Public Sphere in China" *Spaces of Their Own: Women's Public Sphere in Transnational China.* Ed. Mayfair Mei-hui Yang. Minneapolis: University of Minnesota Press, 1999. 35-67. Print.

Žižek, Slavoj. *Violence: Six Sideways Reflections.* London: Picador, 2008. Print.

Žižek, Slavoj. *The Year of Dreaming Dangerously.* London: Verso, 2012. Print.

6.

HAUNTED CITIZENS

GHOSTS THAT CROSS BORDERS

ĀZĀDĪ: SEXUAL POLITICS BEYOND NATION-STATES

T HERE ARE MOMENTS in which citizenship erupts as a mode of political subjectivity that ironically enacts the utmost political gestures by
refusing to follow the rules. The story of the 2012 Delhi gang rape case
is as much a story about citizenship as it is about postcolonial history.
While a neoliberal discourse of "India shining" posits the "new urban
Indian woman" as free because of market vitality, arguably, meaningful
freedom, that challenges Orientalist evocations of citizenship, is best
expressed by the constant call of protesters heard in the streets: Āzādī.
This book is a story of Āzādī. A story of how an idea and a refrain heard
throughout history is translated within the contemporary moment
through the defiant tongues and spirits of gendered bodies in urban
spaces. How and why does Āzādī articulate itself in gendered terms?

Rather than offering an exhaustive history of Āzādī, I focus on its
contemporary usage by offering a genealogy of the limits of gendered
citizenship in India. I trace the history of the archetypal Indian woman:
First constituted within colonial discourse and law, she is reimagined
to support fantasies of cultural "purity" in the nationalist period and
is violently marked by histories of partition. I then follow her into the
streets of contemporary urban India where she embodies the new in-
carnation of Āzādī: a language resonating with political acts that have
always been breathed outside of cramped visions of colonialism and
Hindu nationalism. Contemporary Āzādī, however, finds new grammars
of articulation through feminist, queer, and largely urban enactments of
citizenship that engage with technology, media spectacle, and global queer

and feminist discourse. Indian life worlds cut across Internet wires and through lines of transnational labour that are structured by oppressive workings of capital (Žižek, *Violence*). However, I suggest that the skewed space and time of a technologically driven urban India might enable new grammars of gendered and sexual citizenship after Orientalism.

OF CITIZENS, SARIS, AND SERVANTS:
THE COLONIZED WOMAN AS "ANTI CITIZEN"

In "Citizenship After Orientalism," Engin Isin discusses the making of the modernist citizen as a project that is tied to colonialism and Orientalism:

> the occidental tradition has constituted the Orient as those times and places where people have been unable to constitute themselves as political precisely because they have been unable to invent that identity the occident named as the citizen. The figure of the citizen that dominated the occidental tradition is the figure of that sovereign man (and much later woman) who is capable of judgment and being judged, transcending his (and much later her) tribal, kinship, and other primordial loyalties and belongingness. (32)

The making of "the citizen" had implications for the simultaneous construction of the imagined Indian woman as anti-citizen. If, as Isin suggests, the constitution of the occidental woman as citizen came "much later" (Isin 32) the temporal mappings of the so-called Oriental woman as citizen may have never arrived. The writing of Partha Chatterjee clearly identifies the relationship between colonialism, and the figure of the "unfree" Indian woman. Chatterjee states,

> By assuming a position of sympathy with the unfree and op-pressed womanhood of India, the colonial mind was able to transform this figure of the Indian woman into a sign of the inherently oppressive and unfree nature of the entire cultural tradition of a country. (622)

Chatterjee further discusses how Indian nationalists promoted a reverse

Orientalism to glorify "Indian womanhood" and specifically upper-caste Hindu womanhood as a sign of imagined cultural superiority. As Sangeeta Ray states,

> the discursive construction of the Indian nation by both nationalists and imperialists was often inseparable from their idealisation of a Hindu India epitomised in a particular Hindu female figure. (Ray qtd. in Daiya 4)

The constitution of the Indian woman as a national symbol of "culture" informs cases such as the 2012 Delhi gang rape case and debates regarding the criminalization of queer desire in the region in 2013. The intelligibility of female sexuality, only to the extent that it corresponds with violent patriarchal ideologies of bodily and cultural "purity" counts women as citizens in relation to sexist fantasies, thereby excluding subversive sexual desires.

SLY SEXUALITY:
THE BLOOD OF BORDERS AND THE SURVIVAL OF RESISTANCE

The relationship between the 2012 Delhi gang rape case and citizenship in India lies in the histories of partition that mark the making of postcolonial India with the blood of women. Kavita Daiya suggests that sexual violence in South Asia is haunted by the 1947 moment of partition between India and Pakistan: "if there is a singular moment in the history of South Asia and Britain that had a profound and lasting effect on the politics and societies of many of the nations that make up contemporary South Asia, it is the 1947 Partition" (5). Drawing on postcolonial feminist scholarship, I discuss feminist and queer struggle in relation to the sexual violence that was integral to Indian nationalism. There is an irony to the reclaiming of Āzādī by Delhi gang rape protesters and by those protesting against the criminalization of queer desire in the Indian subcontinent. The feminist and queer Āzādī speaks to how the freeing of postcolonial nations such as India from British rule did not involve freeing the citizen from gendered and sexual norms, shaped by British colonial law and by colonial moralities. The cries of freedom— Āzādī!—that echo in the ears of all who bear witness to emerging feminist and queer movements is a cry for freedom that might not fully translate into text, a bodily and psychic freedom removed from the colonial baggage that drags at the heels and souls of the nation. There is a long history of mapping colonized people as non-citizens, a history that gestures to the ambivalence of empire. Homi Bhabha quotes an essay by Lord Macaulay—a colonial officer who was responsible for drafting Section 377 of the Indian penal code, India's sodomy bill, a law that now continues to criminalize queer desire and people. Bhabha states that, "It is probable that writing 15,000 miles from the place where their orders were to be carried into effect ... [Lord Macauley and his colonial compatriots] never perceived the gross inconsistency of which they were guilty" (135). Bhabha further states that,

> Whoever examines their letters written at that time, will find there many just and humane sentiments...an admirable code of political ethics...Now these instructions, being interpreted, mean simply, "Be the father and the oppressor of the people; be just and unjust, moderate and rapacious." (135)

Bhabha reads these moments for their signs of inherent ambivalence, for their psychic and social anxiety:

> "Be the father and the oppressor ... just and unjust" is a mode of contradictory utterance that ambivalently reinscribes, across differential power relations, both coloniser and colonised. For it reveals an agonistic uncertainty contained in the incompatibility of empire and nation; it puts on trial the very discourse of civility within which representative government claims its liberty and empire its ethics. (136)

What is of interest is how the utterance "Be the father and the oppressor" speaks to the duplicity of colonial rule as the duplicity of patriarchal power. Years after Lord Macaulay wrote these words, his colonial laws were upheld by the Supreme Court of India to criminalize queer desire. The Indian state uses the colonial law and ideology of Macaulay and other British colonial ideologues to enact a fatherly injunction against desire. Much like the protectionist narratives regarding female sexuality that emerged following the 2012 Delhi gang rape case, injunctions against desire are acts of injustice against bodily integrity masked in narratives of heteronormative, sexless moralism. The imagined "humane" care of the patriarchal father figure of state power conceals its violent enforcement of biopolitical ideologies of "pure" bodies and families, microcosms for the nation-state. In *The Location of Culture*, Bhabha discusses the ambivalent position of the colonized civil servant who works for the British government during colonial rule. Bhabha argues that those who were subjected to colonial violence within British India employed a "sly" mode of obedience to authority, much in the way that children of patriarchal families publically obey the rules of the father to reap the material benefits of the heteronormative family (132-145). The workers who labour for their fatherly oppressor, much like the free-spirited child, never fully believe in the authority and rules that they are subject to. Similarly, many feminists and queers whom I spoke with in Delhi work in national courts of justice as lawyers and for state-funded human rights organizations; their labour power is tied to the same state that enacts gendered violence against their basic bodily integrity. Contemporary queers and feminists in India often enact forms of sly civility that may involve publically obeying state power in worlds of work while organizing politically and personally to create new visions of sexual politics and postcolonial worlds. Sly civility now emerges not only through protest but through everyday acts of deviance that ironically enact political citizenship by laughing in the face of the law. In the smallest of gestures—of queer people loving one another, of women occupying public spaces, of working people reclaiming the commons—the inability of the bureaucratic word to contain the body is expressed.

"INDIAN CULTURE" AS POLITICAL CULTURE: RE-MAPPING DISSIDENT DESIRE

Rather than seeing feminist and queer movements as being at odds with Indian culture, these movements may be expressions of Indian culture as political culture. While there were many who tried to turn the Delhi gang rape case into a chance to assert protectionist and patriarchal narratives regarding women "in danger," the Āzādī moments that erupted in the streets instead revealed how the city of Delhi and the South Asian subcontinent are haunted by histories of revolt. As discussed in the introductory chapter of this book Avery Gordon suggests that haunting is not necessarily melancholic but reflects something to be done (Gordan, *Ghostly Matters,* Gordan; "Some Thoughts on Haunting and Futurity").

The haunting of histories of political violence that inform what Walter Benjamin once termed the everyday emergency that defines the pedagogy of oppressed peoples also produces long histories of resistance(Benjamin). This idea of everyday oppression and ongoing political struggle is a common refrain among those who are active in feminist, queer, and social justice movements in Delhi and through-out India. At a protest following the decision to reinstitute Section 377, I meet Abhishek, a queer and feminist activist who discusses the politically charged space of Delhi. Abhishek discusses the love-hate relationship that many who are involved in emerging movements regarding gender justice speak of:

> Every place has its pros and cons. But the pros of Delhi—in the entire country, this is the place that is most political. So if you belong to a marginal community, Delhi provides a space to voice your opinions and concerns. It's also the capital of the country, so there are a lot of people coming in, a lot of cultural intermingling. So, I love Delhi for that reason. I know there are a lot of problems with Delhi in that it's not safe for women. But I wouldn't leave Delhi for that, I would like to change Delhi. That's more important. Rather than just quit Delhi, change Delhi.

Satish, a member of an organization that works with men to chal-lenge hegemonic masculinity and to promote feminism among men in India, also discusses Delhi as a place of both abhorrent violence and enduring resistance. Contemporary neoliberal feminism, often aligned with the *NGOization* sexual politics, often turns "gender justice" into a bureaucratic exercise that works with and through the state and its colonial machinery. However, in the violence of street spectacle and in the epistemic, psychological, and cultural struggle to alter norma-tive understandings of gender that enable violence, the anticolonial political movements of today resonate with the Āzādī of feminist and queer movements. Satish sees Delhi as a place that is paradoxically known for both violence against women and organized collective actions regarding feminism, queer politics, and other broader social movements. He states,

we have to understand that Delhi has become a capital of protests concerning violence against women. So all of the issues
about violence against women are being highlighted. So, some
people are saying that Delhi is the global rape capital. But we
are saying that you could also see this the other way, that Delhi
has become the global protest capital against rape.

I want to suggest that the making of the city of Delhi as both the
site of publicized cases of sexual violence and publicized protest is tied
to the history of the subcontinent, the erection of borders, narratives
of religious violence, and ongoing anxieties and debates regarding conceptions of "purity." The violence of conservative religious nationalists
and patriarchal political figures who forcefully attempt to contain the
body of the citizen as a figure of national purity is tied to the will to
construct a "pure" gendered body. Yet this space of policed bodies also
gives way to resistance, to what Isin terms "activist citizens," figures that
might defy category.

Isin discusses the making of the "activist citizen" as being tied to the
making of other new bodies within the polis, those that defy countenance through stable national categories. Within the context of the
Indian subcontinent, a cyclical pattern of efforts to repress bodies that
defy colonial categorization emerges; simultaneously, cyclical forms of
emergent postcolonial political defiance erupt again and again across
time and space, haunted as much by colonial authority as by anticolonial
resistance. Isin highlights the relationship between bodies that cannot
be succinctly categorized and bodies that are politicized. He writes that
the unnamed figure within the polis is making its appearance on the
stages of world history and argues that the inability to fix categories
of emergent political subjectivities gives way to emergent political acts
that signal the need for new vocabularies of what constitutes "citizenship" itself. Figures who cannot be counted and categorized easily by
state power alter the boundaries of political subjectivities and the polis
itself.[1] Isin goes on to say that emergent figures that unsettle attempts
to stabilize national bodies are also "implicated in the emergence of
new 'sites,' 'scales,' and 'acts' through which 'actors' claim to transform
themselves (and others) from subjects into citizens as claimants of rights"
(Isin "Activist Citizens" 368). Emergent forms of sexual politics in the
Indian subcontinent gesture to new understandings and enactments

of gender and sexual acts that challenge the narrow countenance of gendered bodies by the Indian state, often rooted in a heteronormative and patriarchal Hindu model of the family. Contemporary feminist and queer political movements in urban India can be thought of in relation not only to topical issues and cases such as the Delhi gang rape case of 2012 and the 2013 Supreme Court ruling regarding Section 377 but as part of a longer and broader genealogy that moves outside of a teleological idea of "progress."

HAUNTINGS: SEXY AND UNSEXY GHOSTS

The political movements of today and the constitution of "activist citizens" and political acts cannot be divorced from what authors discuss as being foundational political histories that are specific to the Indian subcontinent, namely those of partition and colonialism. Mushiral Hasan states that,

> No other country in the twentieth century has seen two such contrary movements taking place at the same times. If one was a popular nationalist movement unique in the annals of world history for ousting the colonisers through the non-violent means the other, in its underbelly was the counter movement of Partition marked by violence, cruelty, bloodshed, displacement and massacres. (Hasan qtd. in Viswanath and Malik 61)

The haunting ethos of partition in India returns time and again through its subtle and poignant appearance in the world of Hindi film, which several authors suggest is a genre that is essentially about partition. The ghostly appearances of bodies that symbolically evade borders also appears in the in the "sly civility" (Bhabha 141) of sexual subjects whose acts cannot be subsumed within the grammars of nationalism. Finally, partition haunts contemporary India through acts of gender-based violence. As postcolonial feminists assert, partition involved violent abductions and rape of women as a means of marking national borders between India and neighbouring nations such as Pakistan (Daiya; Butalia). Narratives of rape and specifically communal enactments of sexual violence were part of the making of the modern nation. While histories of anticolonial struggle often involved the construction of alternative masculinities and the active role of many female political activists, partition expressed a violent assertion of heteronormative masculinity that was deeply tied to modernist understandings of nations and bodies. The group, gang, and communal assault of women marked as "other" during partition served as a symbolic form of power that expressed nationalist superiority through masculinist sexual violence. Women's bodies, both Hindu and Muslim, were used as objects to express a war between men and between nations. The 2012 Delhi gang rape case—an act of group sexual violence committed by men in a vehicle moving through the streets of Delhi—resonates with this history of communal uses of rape as a tool of power and the marking of territories by men through the bodies of women.

While those accused and convicted of the crimes committed in 2012 Delhi gang rape case were also Hindu, they were marked as outsiders to the city, as migrants bearing lesser entitlements to masculinist power because of their class position and displacement within the urban sphere. In marking the body of the woman, who perhaps exemplified the emerging middle-class urban face of India, there was a violent use of her body to claim patriarchal ownership not only of her individual life, but of city space itself. The citizen of India became a man and the man became a citizen often through asserting nationalist aggression, masculinity, and entitlement to land against his distant Pakistani cousins and siblings. The brutality of sexual violence in contemporary India, its often group and communal nature, cannot then be divorced from the making of India itself. There is a resonance to these genealogies of historical trauma that defies ideas of linear time. For example, memories and narratives of partition continuously emerged in the Indian subcontinent during the Gujarat riots of 2002. As many feminists, queers, and activists with whom I spoke in Delhi and throughout India suggest, the notion of honour and communal respect is deeply tied to the everyday workings of gender, sexuality, and violence in the region. Gordan writes about the experience of haunting as one in which the concept of home is thrown into question. For her, the term "haunting" means

> to describe those singular and yet repetitive instances when home becomes unfamiliar, when your bearings on the world lose direction, when the over and done comes alive, when what's been

in your blind field comes into view. (Gordan "Some Thoughts on Haunting and Futurity")

The street scene of a young woman in Delhi being driven through the city in a moving bus, and then being tortured, gang-raped and eventually murdered is an image that points to the homelessness of gendered bodies in India. The experience of abhorrent gendered, sexual, and physical violence that displaces the body offers evidence of the inherently uncomfortable place of women's bodies within nations, a form of misogyny that gives way to a loss of bearing. Yet, what might be specific to the ritualistic enactment of gender-based and sexual violence by groups of men within India is perhaps the historical haunting of partition. It was through making women unhomely, through gendered displacement, kidnapping, and violent forms of sexual marking that men within partition narratives expressed a masculinist and nationalist idea of "home." Furthermore, the experience of warring men claiming an entitlement to women's bodies in city space also resonates with colonial narratives where men became citizens through the marking of territory across women's flesh, symbolically planting flags of phallic power through acts of violence.

The eeriness of this case, and its ability to resonate with so many people throughout the Indian subcontinent, is demonstrative of the haunting histories of both partition and colonial rule and their relationship to histories of sexual communal violence. Yet reading Isin's understanding of the activist citizen alongside Gordan's notion of haunting and the understanding of Delhi as a space of political protest might also speak to the haunting resonance of anticolonial struggle in India. Isin suggests that political acts build upon political acts; "activist citizens" enact political subjectivities within genealogies of dissent (Isin "Activist Citizens"). And as discussed in the introductory chapter, Gordan also argues that haunting can produce political will.

The cries of Āzādī that could be heard in the streets following the 2012 Delhi gang rape case and the 2013 decision to reinstitute Section 377are indicative of the relationship between colonial haunting and an anticolonial futurity, expressing a need for different forms of gendered and sexual politics in the region. The anticolonial cry finds new expression, new translation in a generation of feminist and queer activists whose bodies and lives continue to be haunted by the violence of colonial rule and the marking of nationalist boundaries through sexual violence. The "to be done" of the contemporary Āzādī speaks to something that haunts in the form of colonial and nationalist markings that construct some bodies as less than citizen, as less than human. Yet the "to be done" also lies in a gendered and sexual politics in which women and queer people come to occupy city spaces to enact new forms of political intelligibility, "citizenship," and gender identity. The language of haunting that Gordan writes of moves outside ideas of secular time, reflecting how the sacred and the psychological inform contemporary political movements (Gordan *Ghostly Matters*).

The urgency of what is "to be done" was expressed in my conversations with a new generation of feminist and queer activists in India. Abhishek discusses the decision to reinstitute colonial sodomy laws as a moment of haunting futurity, a moment haunted by colonial rule yet a moment that propels him towards the something "to be done" of contemporary political activism. He states,

> Before this judgment I was very proud about my sexuality or whatever but I was not someone who was going to do anything about it. But now, suddenly your country shuns you, and you suddenly feel this need to go out and say something against it. And I think that is something remarkable, the activism that has come out since 2013. Of course before 2013 there was a lot of activism. But since 2013 I think people have started realizing that we can't keep fighting amongst each other because the bigger aim is something else. And I see this now. Before this ruling there used to be protests held by one organization and people from the other organization would not attend. Before, people who attended something for feminists would not attend something for queers. But now, this is going away. I see people coming forward and saying, "okay, let's just all work together." And it's beautiful to see.

The unhomely hauntings of a brutalized gendered and sexual body that can be left without bearings gives way to feminists who find their bearings in the streets. The streets of contemporary India that contemporary feminists and queers occupy are haunted by histories of anti-colonial rebellion that inspire the politics of the present. The rather unsexy ghosts of Lord McCaulay meet the historical resonances of passion, which haunts the political subject in inspiring ways.

UNTOUCHABLE DIGNITY:
AMBEDKAR AND BODILY INTEGRITY

Many activists make reference to the concept of dignity. Time and again in conservations, at meetings, protests, lectures, and panel discussions the word "dignity" is used to discuss sexuality, desire, gender, and violence in the region. It is important to see the futurity of dignity as being tied to the haunting of anticolonial struggles of the past. The enshrinement of dignity within the Indian constitution and in the Indian psyche can be traced back to revolutionary figures such as B.R Ambedkar, anti-caste activist, barrister, and political leader. Ambedkar writes of the individual as an end in itself: individuals are granted certain inalienable rights under the Indian constitution that cannot be interfered with or curtailed. The words and philosophy of Ambedkar challenge communal and colonial understandings of gender and sexuality, which threaten the ability of individuals to express themselves outside of familial, communal, and nationalist norms.[2] Cases such as the 2012 Delhi gang rape offer evidence of the lingering haunting of communally enacted sexual violence against women in public space, while the upholding of Section 377 is reflective of colonial laws and ideologies that haunt the nation. Yet in speaking with many who are involved in contemporary gender-based political movements in India, the inspiring work of Ambedkar and others also haunt the futurity of feminist and queer movements. The notion of the individual body as carrying a certain right to dignity is connected to histories of anti-caste activism in which the integrity of the body and the ability of Dalits to inform political change resonate with all con-temporary movements for bodily integrity in the Indian subcontinent.

While the case of the 2012 Delhi gang rape was clearly vested with caste and class ideologies of sexual "respectability" and the victimization of a Hindu woman constructed as "middle class" by the mainstream press, there was something about how the violence enacted against her body moved so many to political action and resonated with ideas of bodily integrity across time and space. Again and again, in the streets of Delhi, on the anniversary of the 2012 Delhi gang rape case, protes-tors make reference to the extreme forms of bodily violence enacted in the Delhi gang rape case, discussing the overarching lack of humanity that defines this case. The politicizing of basic bodily integrity for all breaks from typical feminist scripts regarding women's rights to a larger questioning of dignity beyond gender. Such questioning and the return to concepts of bodily integrity resonate with Ambedkar's writings regarding bodily respect and dignity used to champion the rights of Dalits (Rege). The emotive ways that the Delhi gang rape case touched people and generated such a visceral political outcry cannot be divorced from the sickening violence of partition and colonial history, and the return to bodily integrity that has been central to anticolonial struggles throughout Indian history.

The day before the anniversary of the Delhi gang rape case, I am walking in the streets of Delhi. I am walking past a local park that is close to where I live. A man is following me, at a close enough distance that I am aware of his gaze and his body at every turn. I stop in the streets and wait for him to pass. He is gone, lost to the city street, a strange ghost whose menacing stare chills to the bone. As I walk past the park, I hear someone cry out, an unintelligible muttering. I look up and find him there again, masturbating in full view, looking at me dead in the eyes, a grin stretched across his face. The irony of this moment is that the masturbation of this man within contemporary India is now a crime because of the Supreme Court of India's decision to uphold Section 377, criminalizing sexual acts deemed to be "unnatural," including masturbation. Non-reproductive forms of sexuality are criminalized, while patriarchal structures of power are upheld by the paternalistic gaze of state power, wedded to the Victorian moralities and laws of colonial rule. The body of a woman in the streets can be constructed as "loose" in ways that are used to justify sexual harassment, while the woman "at home" can be legally raped by a man named as a "husband." The body of the woman on the street is an object of surveillance, just as non-heteronormative, non-reproductive sexuality is also policed. The deviance is mapped onto the sexual act, while the power of men to objectify women through an obsessive heteronormative, masculinist gaze is normalized.

This is an "India shining," one of broadband connections and narrow paths, one of women gang-raped, tortured, and murdered on public buses and memorialized the world over through the flickering screens of computers, shining like candles at yet another vigil, for yet another murdered woman, on just another day in "the World's largest democracy." I awake the next day and the day after to attend demonstrations, meetings, gatherings, events, and discussions regarding the Delhi gang rape protests of 2012 and something called "justice." When speaking to people who are not affiliated with feminist, queer, or activist movements, I mention the story of the man masturbating in the park. The reactions are telling in how the general population often understands patriarchal violence. The incident for many is "funny;" it is a story of just "boys being boys"; someone even tells me that I should be "flattered." The other reaction, often from older women of a certain class and caste, is one of deep colonial outrage. The incident is "dirty" and "disgusting," and is reflective of the behaviour of a "certain type of man," a "certain type of person" in Delhi, one from a "bad community." I will return to the figure of the masturbating man later in the chapter dealing with desire, which discusses the relationship between sexual acts marked as "impure," casteism, and sexuality in India.

In the gap between the experiences of the gendered body—apprehended in city streets through a disciplinary power that justifies and informs violence, and colonial histories of shame and anxiety—lies a dream of translation. It is a dream of translating bodily shame and violation outside of the categorizations of gender, class, caste, and colonial history that turn certain bodies into targets of mockery, citizens who bear the brunt of epistemic and material violence. In the streets of Delhi, one year before the masturbating man entered the scene as an object of scholarly inquiry, the Delhi police fired water cannons at protestors, wasting water in a country in which many still die of dehydration. The police shot water into the crowds, using the money and resources garnered from the labour of "citizens" to blatantly attack people protesting in the name of something called justice. At the time, I could not help but think of the similitude between the image of men masturbating all over the streets of Delhi, haunting the days of women in India, and the Delhi police shooting off their water cannons like bored boys spraying an impotent power into crowds.

NO SPACE CALLED HOME: UNHOMELY BODIES, ESTRANGED CITIZENS

What emerges as a constant refrain in conservations had in Delhi and throughout urban India is the disdain regarding the uncomfortable spaces that gendered and sexual bodies occupy within Indian cities. In increasingly class-divided, financially driven, and overcrowded cities, the feminist and queer body is often violently haunted by colonial rule and narratives of partition, simply through everyday acts of trying to live a life. Malik, a young migrant man from Uttar Pradesh who works at the multinational coffee chain Café Coffee Day states that he feels "disgusted" by the 2012 Delhi gang rape case and discusses common assumptions about who has the right to occupy public space in urban India. He states quite clearly that, "For a long, long time the problem has been in India that the space, all the space belongs to men." A migrant man to the city, he fights against the desire to pathologize young migrant men as the enemies of women by affluent political elites, and he understands himself to be in solidarity with women. "The city does not belong to me either. But it belongs to women even less." Kai, another person with whom I spoke in Delhi discusses the spatialized fears of queer people following the institution of Section 377. We discuss fears of queer couples who worry about expressing desire and romantic love both within public space but also as part of communities and neighbourhoods where extortion, harassment, and the threat of state power can be used to discipline desire. We further discuss the case of a queer couple who have been together for three years, during which the Delhi high court judgment of 2009 offered them protection. Kai states,

> They've been living together for 3 years now after the ruling to keep 377 in 2013, they think what if they tell the neighbours to not park their car here or there and the neighbours get pissed off and call the police. And the maid who works for them might say, "oh I've seen them sleeping together in the bed." And then, before you know it, the police might stop them and say we are stopping them from doing an offense against 377. And maybe the police will file a charge or rough them up or ask for a bribe. This is how 377 works.

Shilpa Phadke has written extensively about the relationship between gender, sex, and public space in Indian cities. Her work and the work of her colleagues is exemplary in arguing that pleasure, desire, and the right to risk are central to sexual politics. I speak with her in Mumbai where she teaches at the Tata Institute of Social Sciences. She suggests that there were competing narratives of public space that emerged following the Delhi gang rape case of 2012, those of protectionism and those of a radical reclamation of the commons as a pleasure seeking commons. Phadke states,

> Often in India the understanding of public space is very much structured around safety. And I think now, because it is out there among the general public and there is a discussion happening on the streets, there is a space for "Back Off Āzādī" movements. There is an idea for fun and loitering which my colleagues and I have tried to advance. I think that what the last year has done is to create these little spaces for Back Off Āzādī and to offer a chance to talk about what we have been doing, which is to speak about and politicize fun and loitering. The idea of a right to public space. (Phadke, Personal interview)

While she is optimistic and hopeful after years of researching and writing about gender and public space in India, she like many other feminists and activists is also worried about continued policing and the erasure of gendered bodies in city spaces. Phadke makes the astute observation that the Delhi gang rape protests have generated a dialogue about public space, without necessarily altering the ways that bodies move within space. The disjuncture between the written word and the spatialized anxieties of bodies discussed earlier resonate in our conversation. She states that,

> in many ways this case changed the ways we talk about public space. I don't know though, if it's changed how we inhabit public space, if you know what I mean. We might speak differently and behave in the same ways. Still, at least public space is an actor in this conversation. (Phadke, Personal interview)

Within the gap between the conversation about gender and sexuality and the reluctance or inability of bodies to move freely in city spaces, cyberfeminism can be useful.

NARROW PATHS AND BROADBAND CONNECTIONS: ĀZĀDĪ.COM?

Through a dimly lit computer screen, flickering like candles sheltered from the wind at protests held one year ago, after a woman, yet another woman, was raped and murdered in "The world's largest democracy" I receive a message. It reads only, "My country sucks!" The attached PDFdocument is marked by all the terms of legality, of bureaucracy, of the vicious tongues of civility imposed in a chillingly cold Queen's English. The Supreme Court of India has struck down all petitions made against the criminalization of queer desire in India through the upholding of Section 377 of the Indian Penal Code, India's colonial sodomy law. These were petitions filed by scholars, feminists, activists, artists, lawyers, judges, petitions filed by "citizens," petitions filed by criminals. Since Lord Macaulay first decreed these old colonial laws, the Indian body has been pushed, pulled, and prodded by text. Yet how might the Internet world open up the possibility for new worlds and new words of dissent? While there are ongoing debates surrounding the digital divide in India, Rosi Braidotti, Donna Haraway, and South Asian cyberfeminists such as Radhika Gajjala discuss the important role that the Internet plays in feminist and queer movements in India and beyond borders (Braidotti "Cyberfeminism With a Difference"; Haraway; Gaijala). The Internet played an important role in organizing demonstrations following the 2012 Delhi gang rape case and in globally disseminating information about these protests. Moreover, the Internet played a large role in generating global support for queer people following the decision to reinstitute Section 377, with "days of rage" being held worldwide ("Protests across the Globe"). In her 2011 Reith lectures, political leader and dissident Aung San Su Kyi states,

> The freedom to make contact with other human beings with whom you may wish to share your thoughts, your hope, your laughter, and at times even your anger and indignation is a right which should never be violated.

In contemporary India, freedom to make contact with others can be violated in sickening ways, as evinced in the brutal gang rape and murder of Jyoti in 2012 and countless other cases of chilling, ghostly violence. Queer people's freedom can be legally violated, leading to police harassment, violence, and psychic trauma all of which has risen since the decision to reinstitute Section 377, as reported by Queer activists. The rise of Internet counter-publics reflects the lack of freedom offered by the state and the hostility of the public sphere. Yet cyberactivism also expresses the resilience of those who ironically become the most political subjects because of their exclusion from formal rights of citizenship.

As discussed, the Arab Spring protests of 2011 gave way to an inspiring moment of resistance, largely witnessed by much of the world outside of Egypt through the Internet. While the digital divide still operates within India, largely dividing urban publics from rural areas where Internet access is often not always available, the space of the Indian city is increasingly one in which many people have access to mobile phones and Internet mediums across class. Often the digital divide in cities such as Delhi is based on generation rather than on class. NGO activists who work with youth in the slums of Delhi say that young men and women in slums have access to mobile phones and Internet technologies, often accessed through large cultures of digital piracy that make such tools increasingly accessible. The availability of globalized technology in slums may also correspond to the lack of basic infrastructure available within a neoliberal "India shining" moment. According to recent statistics, 63 percent of those living in slums have access to a cell phone, while only 34 percent have access to toilets (Vishnu). Transnational globalization clearly affects the lives of young workers and students unevenly in cities such as Delhi and increasingly throughout an urbanized India. The rise of neoliberal models of business and the outsourcing of call centres have led to the proliferation of Internet-driven industries and forms of labour, in which young workers are becoming literate in Internet mediums. The material violence of globalization that ushers in Internet-based technology and exploitative industries of transnational labour, which often do little to address a lack of basic living amenities in India, can ironically be protested against using these same technological tools.

The cries of Āzādī that were tweeted and "shouted" online are indicative of the lack of freedom afforded to the body on the city street, while also offering evidence of how Internet spaces and temporalities can be used to assemble bodies in the streets to protest against everyday atrocity. The use of water cannons against protestors in December of 2012 by the Delhi police, and the subsequent closing of the Delhi metro, which trapped protestors at India gate and prevented protests from growing in size and challenging constitutional rights of freedom of mobility and assembly, offers evidence of the material violence of state power. Against all bureaucratic and textual "rights" of the Indian constitution, the state manipulated, curtailed, and imposed violence on the bodies of people and the body politic of material spaces. The Internet, however, can record and broadcast these abuses of power throughout the world, shaming the state in its flagrant abuse of power.

One year after the Delhi gang rape case of 2012, I return again to Delhi. In 2012, the year ended with a haze of sprayed water, fired with the force of bombs into crowds of everyday people protesting against bodily injustice. In 2013, the old ghosts of Lord MacCaulay were back again, as the Supreme Court of India made the shocking decision to uphold Section 377 of the Indian Penal Code. I stood in the streets, yet again, feeling haunted by the weight of history and by the propelling force of resilient postcolonial publics. Many of the protests regarding the 2013 decision to uphold Section 377 and actions following the 2012 Delhi gang rape case have been organized online, through listservs, social media, emails, and text messages. The Internet has functioned as the medium that creates and supports the staging of political events and speaks to the ironies of postcolonial cities that are marked by all the repressive haunting of imperial history. Interviews with feminists and particularly with newly "criminal" queers are often organized online, and the question of one's safety and freedom in public space is still a gaping one in the minds, lives, and political tactics of feminists and queers. This is in an India that is supposedly "shining" with mall lighting, yet the streets remain minefields of darkened paths haunted by the chilling normalization of the daily gendered violence that marks just another day in Delhi.

AN ONLINE POSTCOLONIAL FUTUR?
THE TOOLS OF A POLITICAL OCCUPATION

The use of social media by protestors in the 2012 Delhi gang rape protests and the 2013 queer protests against Section 377 in India resonates with Arab Spring protests that gained global recognition in Egypt in 2011. Titzmann argues that the role of the Internet and social media in both these global protests was similarly used as a means of organizing street-based actions, often comprised of youth in urban postcolonial cities. The majority of India's increasingly urban population is under the age of thirty-five and the face of contemporary Egypt and many other cities in the Middle East is also young compared to many Western and European countries. In cities in Asia, the Middle East, and throughout the Global South, this media-savvy Internet generation is deftly using tools of technology as tools of political dissent. Drawing on research pertaining to digital activism in both the Middle East and India, Titzmann states that researchers have found a connection between digital mobilization and political mobilization in social movements throughout the world. Titzmann draws on the writing of Saskia Sassen who discusses the "toolness" of Facebook in the context of the Tahir Square movement in Egypt(85). Sassen's analysis suggests that the tools of social media are neutral and depend on the ways that users utilize them. However, using critical writings in technology in the Global South, Titzmann further notes that the Internet within postcolonial contexts such as India can predetermine the nature of political struggle in regards to the class-caste status of those who have access to these tools of dissent. Titzmann cites the research of Holst who argues that "the impact of new media content and debate rests essentially upon technological structures that are not always adjusted to local environment" (Titzman 85). She further states that "Issues of language and script for example, may provide technological disadvantages for many nations in the Global South. Multilingual India is one of the best examples" (85). However, the crucial comparison to be made between the 2012 Delhi gang rape protests, the 2013 Queer Āzādī struggles in India, and the Arab Spring protests of 2011 is that these movements are at the same moment local and global.

There is a relationship between the use of social media and the actual occupation of public spaces within cities, and a further relationship between localized events of political outrage and a global media that is used to turn localized political unrest into moments of globally trans-lated appeals for justice. Titzmann discusses the "Indian Spring" of 2012 and the "Arab Spring" of 2011 to suggest that, "While incidents happen outside of the digital space and consequentially trigger online outrage, debates, and mobilization, they are in the course of a protest movement brought back to the streets" (86). While Titzmann critiques the "slacktivism," often defined by the clicking of "like buttons" and the circulation on online petitions, in the political struggles being waged in both the Middle East and contemporary India, the streets are not separated from the tweets. She cites Egyptian artist-activist Bahia

Shehab who discusses the "'full circle' of mobilization in the case of Egypt's revolution in 2011" (Titzmann 86). Shehab refers to "'media mobilization inspired by real-life events that led to street protests and their return into social media through documentation in the form of recordings, images, and reports that again incite mobilization'" (Shehab qtd. in Titzmann 86). A similar "full circle" use of the Internet to organize demonstrations and to subsequently document protests and create further political campaigns occurred following the 2012 Delhi gang rape case and following the 2013 Section 377 decision. Titzmann cites the writings of Castells who

> identifies a space of autonomy which he refers to as the "third space" between communication networks and physical sites of action. On account of mutually taking inspiration from other movements around the world he states that movements are local and global at the same time. (Titzmann 85)

Without uses of Internet-based technology, the localized events of politics that occurred on the streets of Delhi and throughout urban India in 2012 and 2013 would not have reached global importance. In a panel discussion regarding cyberfeminism in Delhi, one cyberfeminist makes the point that Internet activism is often appealing to women and queer people in Delhi because of its ability to level the material power of bodies. "You have women saying that they are free online, because no man is bigger than them online, no man can crowd them out of the space." While she went on to discuss cyberharassment and cyberbullying, she remained adamant that many women with access to the Internet in Delhi and throughout urban India often see it as liberation from the bodily bullying that occurs in public space. Over Internet wires, she subsequently wrote, "Online I am as big as any man, and I can SHOUT JUST AS LOUD."

FROM AVENIR TO ĀZĀDĪ:
SIGNS FROM A FUTURE OF TRANSLATIONS

As discussed in an earlier chapter of this text, Žižek discusses the possibility of a radical openness towards the future, an *avenir*, foretold in what appear as outbursts within our contemporary political moment. He states that, "We should fully accept this openness, guiding ourselves on nothing more than ambiguous signs from the future"(134). In reading the 2012 Delhi gang rape protests and 2013 protests against Section 377 as "ambiguous signs from the future" it is important to consider how these political movements are all connected to a broad critique of state power. Rather than being solely aimed at critiquing patriarchy or homophobia, the Delhi gang rape protests and those against the Supreme Court of India's decision to criminalize same-sex desire, involved a political struggle that was enacted against the state. Ronojoy Sen discusses the Delhi gang rape protests as events of the political that are connected not only to feminist struggles but to other contemporary bids for justice, such as the Anna Hazare movement against state corruption. Hazare staged an anti-corruption protest in 2011 by going on a hunger strike to pressure the Indian government to enact strict anti-corruption laws (Sen). In comparing the Delhi gang rape protests and protests against the Supreme Court of India's decision to criminalize same-sex desire to the Hazare movement, all of these political struggles interrupt colonial history through ongoing forms of anticolonial and postcolonial revolt. These moments of political insurrection are not disconnected from the history of the Indian subcontinent but still offer an unpredictable political future. Hazare's protests, for example, were said to be inspired by those of Mahatma Gandhi; he used Gandhi's tactics against British rule to protest the corruption of the neoliberal Indian state (Sen). Similarly, those protesting against gender-based and sexual violence in India also opposed the callous nature of the state. Protestors exposed the Indian police as corrupt figures whose interests do not lie in protecting the lives of everyday people. Political citizens also challenged the failures of the Supreme Court and political leaders to reflect the sexual sensibilities of many within the subcontinent. If contemporary India is troubled by the ghosts of Lord Macaulay and the haunting rapes and tortures of partition, the ghosts of anticolonial politics still linger in the streets and in its timeless translations of Āzādī.

The Occupy movements, which began on Wall Street, can also be compared to the Delhi gang rape protests and to the Hazare movement as they also involve an overarching critique of both capitalist "freedom" and state negligence towards the majority. Like the circular nature of social media discussed by Egyptian activists, Occupy movements much like cyberfeminist movements in India use media and technology to disseminate information regarding protest and to document narratives and images that turn what may seem like the demands of a minority into moments for global solidarity. Contemporary sexual politics in urban India are also comparable in the mobilization of what might be termed the "middle class," transnationally. Writing in regards to the 2012 Delhi gang rape protests, Titzmann states, "What struck many observers was that the mass protest was led by the educated urban middle classes who are often deemed as apathetic, hedonistic, and apolitical" (81). In discussing the 2012 Delhi gang rape case in comparison to the Hazare anti-corruption demonstrations, Sen also points out the "middle-class" nature of these actions. Sen suggests that there is

> a continuum with the anti-corruption protests led by Anna Hazare. A striking similarity between the crowds milling around the Ramlila grounds during Hazare's 13-day fast in 2011 and the protesters in Raisina Hill was the number of middle class people who had turned up. As was the constant presence of television cameras.

Similarly, the Occupy protests were often led by those who were not necessarily among the poorest of the poor. The Occupy protests in North America were often not organized by Indigenous people or those who are wholly economically and politically disenfranchised in North America and Europe, but by many whose "middle-class" status was expressed in their ability to use social media to mobilize large sections of the population outside of identity-based categories and gain attention from mass media. Some critiqued Occupy in North America as "white" and "middle class," but as with the 2012 Delhi gang rape protests and the Arab Spring revolts, these struggles signify the politicization of those often thought to be apathetic citizens. Žižek writes of the Arab Spring and other comparable contemporary political struggles often organized and enacted by privileged classes:

> it is clear that the huge revival of protest over the past year, from the Arab Spring to Western Europe, from Occupy Wall Street to China, from Spain to Greece, should not be dismissed merely as a revolt of the salaried bourgeoisie.... One could argue that the uprisings in Egypt began in part as a revolt of the salaried

bourgeoisie (with educated young people protesting about their lack of prospects), but this was only one aspect of a larger protest against an oppressive regime. (Žižek "The Revolt of the Salaried Bourgeois")

While other protest movements such as those aimed at affording women the right to vote or demonstrations staged by labour unions often have clear goals and make succinct pleas to state authority, these contemporary social movements involve a deeper critique of power structures themselves. The 2012 Delhi gang rape protests much like Anna Hazare's anti-corruption protests in Delhi, global Occupy movements, and the Arab Spring revolts express an untranslatable anger on the part of many regarding the emergency of the every-day. As Benjamin writes, *"The tradition of the oppressed teaches us that the 'emergency situation' in which we live is the rule"* (Benjamin). The commonplace callousness towards gender justice and the corruption of state power makes violence and rape an often unremarked upon reality within urban India. Similarly, the indifference to the majority by wealthy power holding elites is also an accepted violence made into a momentary global spectacle. Contemporary protesters open the windows of Internet browsers to occupy the streets. Movements against everyday oppressions inspire the opening of computer windows across borders to an undetermined *avenir.*

JAHAN KAHIN BHI ZULM HOGA, HUM AWAAZ UTHAYAENGE: AFFECTIVE AND POLITICAL RESONANCE ACROSS BORDERS

The borders of India have always been haunted by the blood of wom-en and the lingering heteronormative sexual anxieties that define the making of modern nations. While narratives of partition rape haunt the subcontinent, anticolonial sexual politics also travel across borders. Journalists discuss the protests that took place in Pakistan regarding the Delhi gang rape case stating that

Members of Pakistan's civil society held an hour-long can-dlelight vigil here on Monday for the Delhi gang rape victim in solidarity with the protests in India against the culture of violence against women. Braving the evening cold of Islamabad, a small clutch of men, women, and children gathered outside a shopping arcade as the sun went down for the last time this year. Holding placards—some of which said "sisterhood goes beyond boundaries"—they urged shoppers to join in the vigil for an issue that affects all of womankind. ("Pakistan Groups Hold Candle Light Vigil")

Through the use of social media and the global media coverage of these events of the political, the publicity garnered was used to draw attention to sexual politics in neighbouring Asian countries. As one article states,

In the neighboring Nepal, students of National Medical College [NMC], Birganj protested with a rally and marched through the main roads of Birganj town which lies along the Indo-Nepal border. According to media reports, some housewives too joined the rally. Nepal too has witnessed troubled times as its women have fought for a life of dignity. (Kumar)

The media throughout Asia utilized this case as a springboard for high-lighting gendered and sexual violence. Journalist Aela Callan states that

Gang rape hit the headlines last year after the brutal attack of a woman on a bus in India's capital, Delhi. But new research suggests that gang rape is a wider problem across Asia - with some of the highest recorded levels of violence against women in the world to be found within the Asia-Pacific region.

Despite many campaigns by the United Nations, local feminist groups, and other activist-based organizations, sexual violence continues to be normalized throughout much of Asia. Callan cites the research of the United Nations: "Four UN agencies interviewed 10,000 men across seven countries in the Asia-Pacific, with startling results. One in four said they had raped a woman or girl, while one in 25 admitted to taking part in gang rape" Callan further discusses cultures of gang rape in Cambodia as an expression of normative ideas of masculinity and sexuality in the country:

In December 2012, a horrific gang rape on a bus in Delhi led to the victim's death and sparked global outrage. But more than twice the percentage of men in Cambodia admitted to gang rape compared to India (post-conflict sites in the Pacific are likely to be even higher).

The author also discusses the relationship between Cambodian nationalism and rape culture. Much like the history of Indian nationalism, born out a violent separation from Pakistan and a colonial history in which postcolonial masculinities are often hyperbolically performed as a means of countering the emasculating history of colonialism, the histories of Asian nationalisms and the feminized role that Asian nations play in the global capitalist economy can also be considered in regards to gendered violence. Callan discusses gang rape culture in Cambodia as being tied to a history of civil war and competing nationalist masculinities:

> Then, there is the effect of civil war. These are the sons and grandsons of people who suffered through the unimaginable horrors of the Khmer Rouge. This exposure to extreme violence, as well as the absence of positive influences and effective parenting practices, may have in some way warped perceptions of what it means to be a man.

Journalists, feminists, and activists throughout Asia make reference to the 2012 Delhi gang rape protests and protests against the 2013 decision to uphold the criminalization of same-sex desire in India as moments of spectacle that were useful in highlighting both sexual violence and sexual political movements in Asia. The violence of global capitalism, which often turns the hands and bodies of Asian workers into exploited labourers for Western multinational IT companies, also produces an Internet-savvy generation of people throughout Asia and a globalized media through which localized tragedy inspires global protest. The Asian woman labouring to build MacBooks to line the pockets of Silicon Valley executives overseas can also click on keys to unlock the possibilities of sexual politics in a transnational world. A body held prisoner in an American-owned factory, building computers used as toys—appendages of wealth and tools to support exploitative Western corporations—can deftly use the grammars of cyber feminism to actualize a freedom extended beyond borders of skin and nation and to find a common grammar for common causes. At a vigil and protest held in neighbouring Pakistan following the death of Jyoti, the crowds chanted in unison:

> *jahan kahin bhi zulm hoga, hum awaaz uthayaenge* [We will raise our voices wherever there is an atrocity]. *Jab take auratzulm sahegi, hum awaazuthayaenge* [We will raise our voices as long as crime is committed against women].(Joshua)

While there are no words to fully describe the material and psychological violence enacted onto bodies and minds through acts of sexual violence, there is a space opened up in these moments for a transnational language of protest. Āzādī.

In conducting fieldwork in Delhi, I meet Vish, a Delhi-based queer and feminist activist at a protest against sexual violence and state negligence in India. Vish states,

> I think things have changed. Now when you speak to your friends, your colleagues, your classmates, things like gender are being spoken about. That to me is what the protests were about. Not just about this case but about raising awareness about how gender comes to act upon all our lives. And we are now talking more about it. Gender is a controlling aspect. Whether man or woman, everyone has felt the controlling aspects of gender. And this is a time for everyone to come together and say we won't go through this control ever. But it also has to come not just on days of protest but in your everyday engagement with life, in your every day cognizance of life.

Vish further suggests that the Delhi gang rape protests and queer movements in contemporary India are connected:

> The anti-rape protests are very much connected to the queer rights movement. Whether it's a fight for gender equality, sexuality, caste, it's about basic dignity. To be able to live with dignity, to have the liberty to be who you are. On another level, it's also against a certain harassment and a certain suppression

you go through. So really it's about protecting the integrity of the person, whether that individual be Dalit, be queer, working class. It's about a struggle for dignity for everyone.

The countenance of "citizenship" through colonial classification makes individuals intelligible and valuable to the nation in gendered terms. The Āzādī of contemporary sexual politics in Delhi and throughout Asia ironically often enacts a politics of bodily integrity through dis-embodied worlds of cyberspace, as safe spaces of translation, turning bodies marked by ghostly violence into unpredictable agents of political vitality. Homi Bhabha writes,

> If hybridity is heresy, then to blaspheme is to dream. To dream not of the past or present, nor the continuous present; it is not the nostalgic dream of tradition, nor the Utopian dream of modern progress; it is the dream of translation as "surviv-al" as Derrida translates the "time" of Benjamin's concept of the afterlife of translation, as *survivre*, the act of living on borderlines (321).

The work of translation as survival is felt in the Āzādī of feminist and queer movements and lives in India. To live on borderlines is the reality for those who live with the illusory freedoms of formal citizenship, haunted in chilling ways by histories of masculinist violence and the tight lipped rage of Victorian sexual moralities. These borderlines of belonging are excessively policed by state power to discipline sexual political struggles and offer few guarantees of freedom from gender-based violence in the streets. To live on borderlines is to live somewhere between inhospitable material spaces and a global cyberfeminist and queer community that is supported by the labour of captive workers. Internet-based tech-nologies are powered by exploited labourers transnationally while also paradoxically enabling a liberation from gendered hierarchies of the body. Making desire translatable through cybernetworks enables the survival of political movements and the psychic and social survival of those who are often alienated in their supposed "homes." Yet translation is a two-way street that traffics in multiple mythologies. In translating feminist and queer politics into the language of Āzādī, traces of anti-colonial resistance also survive.

The political significance of the language of Āzādī lies in its ability to speak in a grammar outside of teleological conceptions of "progress," in which feminism and queerness are often associated with Western secular capitalist modernity. An Āzādī that resonates across the borders of India, Pakistan, and beyond challenges the figure of the archetypal "homonationalist" body, a queer and feminist subject aligned with nationalist interests (Puar). A gendered Āzādī lives on borderlines and defies the nation's investments in the imagined "purity" of culture and of people.

While we labour and dream of spaces not haunted by the violent histories of colonial rule, we gather strength and solidarity, sharing new words for old desires. Āzādī.

ENDNOTES

[1]The emergence of new populations of the foreign and stateless correspond to emerging activist movements that create new vocabularies of "political subjectivity" that both challenge the bureaucratic and reductive imaginings of what constitutes an act of "citizenship," and also expand categories of national belonging. Isin writes,

> We have categories to describe this figure: foreigner, migrant, irregular migrant, illegal alien, immigrant wanderer, refugee, émigré, exile, nomad, sojourner and many more that attempt to fix it. But so far this figure resists these categories not because it has an agency as such but because it unsettles the very attempt to fix it. (Isin 367)

[2]In *Against the Madness of Manu,* Sharmila Rege writes on the relationship between brahminical Hindu masculinity and patriarchal and sexual violence in detail. While a detailed discussion regarding the relationship between the violence of caste hierarchy and the normative gendered and sexual violence that exists within India is beyond the scope of this work, Rege's text offers a detailed analysis of the historical and ongoing imbrications of casteism, sexism, and heteronormative patriarchal politics. While mainstream feminist analysis often ignores the writings of revolutionary anti-caste leaders such as B. R. Ambedkar and the ways in which Dailt activism is foundational to sexual politics in the Indian subcontinent, Rege offers a much needed scholarly intervention, as she discusses how the writings of Ambedkar informs anti-caste feminism and many other social movements in India (Rege).

WORKS CITED

Ambedkar, B. R. *Annihilation of Caste: The Annotated Critical Edition*. Ed. S. Anand. Delhi: Navayana, 2014. Print.

Benjamin, Walter. "On the Concept of History." Marxists Internet Archive, n.d. Web. 15 June 2015.

Bhabha, Homi. *The Location of Culture*. London: Routledge, 1995. Print.

Braidotti, Rosi. "Cyberfeminism with a Difference." *New Formations* 29 (Autumn 1996): 9-25. Print.

Braidotti, Rosi. *Nomadic Theory: The Portable Rosi Braidotti*. New York: Columbia University Press, 2011. Print.

Butalia, Urvashi. *The Other Side of Silence: Voices from the Partition of India*. Durham: Duke University Press, 2000. Print.

Callan, Aela. "It's a Man's World." Aljazeera 101 East, 8 March 2013. Web. 15 June 2015.

Chatterjee, Partha. "Colonialism, Nationalism, and Colonized Women: The Contest in India." *American Ethnologist* 16.4 (1989): 622-633. Print.

Daiya, Kavita. *Violent Belongings: Partition, Gender, and National Culture in Postcolonial India*. Philadelphia: Temple University Press, 2011. Print.

Gaijala, R. *Cyber Selves: Feminist Ethnographies of South Asian Women*. Oxford: AltaMira Press, 2004. Print.

Gordan, Avery. *Ghostly Matters: Haunting and the Sociological Imagination*. Minnesota: University of Minnesota Press, 2008. Print.

Gordan, Avery. "Some Thoughts on Haunting and Futurity." *Borderlands* 10.2 (2011): 1-21. Print.

Isin, Engin. "Citizenship After Orientalism: Ottoman Citizenship." *Citizenship in a Global World: European Questions and Turkish Experiences*. Eds. Fuat Keyman and Ahmet Icduygu. New York: Routledge, 2005. 31-52. Print.

Isin, Engin. "Citizenship in Flux: The Figure of the Activist Citizen." *Subjectivity* 29 (2009): 367–388. Print.

Joshua, Anita. "Candlelight Vigil in Pakistan." *The Hindu*, 1 Jan. 2013. Web. 15 June 2015.

Kumar, Ashok. "Protests Over Brutal Delhi Gang Rape Seize South Asia." *One World South Asia*, 2 Jan. 2013. Web. 24 June 2015.

Menon, Nividetia. "The Impunity of Every Citadel Is Intact"–The Taming of the Verma Committee Report and Some Troubling Doubts." *Kafila*, 3 Feb. 2013. Web. 12 June 2015.

Phadke, Shilpa. Personal interview. 2014

"Pakistan Groups Hold Candle Light Vigil for Delhi Gang-Rape Victim." *DNA India*, 1 Jan. 2013. Web. 15 June 2015.

"Protests Across the Globe Against Indian Supreme Court Judgment on Section 377." *Galaxy Magazine: Empowering Expressions*, 2014. Web. 16 Feb. 2014.

Puar, Jasbir. *Terrorist Assemblages: Homonationalism in Queer Times.* Durham: Duke University Press, 2007. Print.

Rege, Sharmila. *Against the Madness of Manu: B.R Ambedkar's Writings on Brahmanical Patriarchy*. Delhi: Navayana Press, 2013. Print.

Sen, Ronojoy. "The Delhi Rape Protests: Observations on Middle Class Activism in India."The International Relations and Security Network, 2013. Web. 28 Nov. 2015.

Su Kyi, Aung San. "Liberty Lecture One." British Broadcasting Corporation, 28 June2011. Web.16 Feb. 2014.

Titzmann, Fritzi-Marie. "*The Voice of the Youth*': Locating a New Public Sphere between Street Protest and Digital Discussion." *Studying Youth, Media and Gender in Post-Liberalisation India: Focus on and beyond the Delhi Gang Rape*. Eds. Nadja-Christina Schneider and Fritzi-Marie Titzmann. Berlin: Frank and Timme GmbH, 2015. 79-113. Print.

Vishnu, Uma. "34% in Slums Have No Toilet, but 63% Own a Mobile Phone." *The Indian Express*, 22 March 2013. Web. 25 Oct. 2015.

Žižek, Slavoj. "The Revolt of the Salaried Bourgeoisie." *London Review of Books*, 26 Jan. 2012. Web.15 June 2015.

Žižek, Slavoj. *The Year of Dreaming Dangerously*. London: Verso, 2012. Print.

Žižek, Slavoj. *Violence: Six Sideways Reflections*. London: Picador, 2008. Print.

7.

A JEWEL IN THE CROWN

CAPITAL, LABOUR, AND PROTEST

CARS, CONDOMS, AND COFFEE
THE "NORMALCY" OF NEOCOLONIALISM

Sumita, an upper middle-class professional in Delhi was shocked, just as many people throughout the Indian subcontinent and particularly those among the Indian middle class, were outraged by the brutal gang rape and murder case that gained worldwide attention in December of 2012. Talking with her in a middle-class suburb of Delhi about the case and its significance, the constant refrain is that of "normalcy." She discusses the "ordinariness" of the victim, and stresses the new norms of gender, consumption, and pleasure that are now definitive of the new Indian middle class. She states,

> It was just such an ordinary day, such an ordinary thing for a girl to do.... After work, you go for a movie with a friend. You chat, you get onto a bus, you go on the metro and you come back home. Such a normal day and then for something so extraordinary to happen, and the way it happened was so disturbing.

While one could, in a surface reading of this case, see the massive Delhi gang rape protests that spread throughout Indian cities as an expression of newly "liberated" middle classes who were articulating a secular, "free" attitude towards sex, sexuality, and desire, I want to suggest that how sexuality operates among a new grouping of Indian "middle-class," consumer-driven publics who act as embodiments of transnational globalization is more complex. There is a great deal of work that goes into producing the figure of the "ordinary" girl in contemporary urban India; it involves a careful management of consumer desire, Hindu nationalist and familial expectations, and sexuality. This also involves what Leela Fernandes terms a "politics of forgetting" that defines India's new urban middle class. This politics of forgetting entails an erasure of the bodies of the poor within the national imaginary. Fernandes suggests that the focus on the urban, Indian middle class as idealized and visible citizens of India is a state driven and enforced ideology that seeks to cleanse India of poverty within the global imaginary (Fernandes). The reductive and classist reading of poor migrant men as posing a threat to the supposedly enlightened values of middle-class urbanites conceals the complex web of colonial power, shame, class purification, and adherence to nationalist ideals of gender that inform middle-class sensibilities and politics in contemporary India.

What defines the narratives of shock and awe on the part of the many Hindu middle-class people I speak with in Delhi is this constant discourse of the "ordinary" and often the "common sense," largely among upper-caste and upper-middle-class Hindu publics for whom gender involves a series of very careful negotiations of Western consumerism, Hindu norms, colonial moralities, and often contradictory ideas of "freedom." There is a certain image and ideal of sexual- and class-based respectability that women must mimic in contemporary India to become a survivor of sexual violence who garners sympathy from what is often termed the Indian middle class, that encompasses a great deal of urban India. The segment of the urban Indian population who are termed as "middle class" often remain caught between dreams of multinational capitalist power, the moralities of colonialism, and upper-caste Hindu ideology. The idea of the "ordinary" girl is constructed against the bodies of lower-caste women, queers, Hijras, supposed foreigners, and impoverished men. The "ordinary" girl follows certain codes and norms that are seen to be "common sense" within urban India and among people of certain classes and castes. The mass attention that the gang rape and murder of Jyoti caused expressed an outrage that feminists suggest challenges the myths that often surround rape among upper-caste and upper-middle-class Hindu publics. Nirali works with a Delhi-based organization offering counsel and other forms of support to survivors of sexual assault in Delhi and throughout India. She discusses how the 2012 Delhi gang

rape protests challenged certain ideas that still colour perceptions of
rape and sexual assault in India. She states,

> The incident that happened on December 16 was not new. It
> was not one of the rarest of rare cases that happened. What was
> new was that people came out and protested. This particular
> incident turned into a people's movement. It became a people's
> movement because the case broke certain myths that people
> have around incidents of rape. Say for example, the idea that
> a girl is generally raped when she is out at night alone. Or
> she is out at night at a particular time. But here, this girl was
> out at 9. And because this is a metropolitan city, 9:00 p.m. is
> not late. She was with her friend. She was decently, modestly
> dressed. She was travelling in a public transport. She was not
> pulled into a private car. So these myths that people have were
> challenged. There was no alcohol attached to the incident. This
> was an instance in which the middle class realized that if it can
> happen to this girl, it can also happen to them.

Many feminists and activists suggest that this case garnered a great deal
of attention because it momentarily shocked the middle classes out of
complacency and their moralistic judgment of survivors of sexual assault.
However, the violence done to the supposedly ordinary and sexually
respectable girl, which is seen by many as extraordinary, can mask the
routine sexual violence that many "other" women, Hijras, transgender,
and queer people experience. The case also points to the class dynamics
that inform mainstream, middle-class outrage in contemporary India,
which focuses on the crimes of poor and migrant men but obscures the
violence committed by elite men. Nirali discusses the class dynamics of
the case and the magnitude of outrage that it generated:

> One of the reasons that this case caused so much outcry was that
> the men who committed the rape on December 16 belonged
> to a lower economic class. And there was an idea among many
> people that crimes are committed by a particular class of people,
> so the anger was also against that particular class of people.

Jyoti was constructed as being supposedly middle class, while her attackers were perceived as impoverished migrants. The perception of Jyoti's seemingly middle-class status overshadows the caste origins of her family, which are similar to some of her attackers: her family's migration to the city, and her working-class roots—her father worked menial jobs in Delhi to pay for her education (Roychowdhury 284). Nirali further argues, however, that the severity of the torture and the gender-based violence that defined this case and the growing anger regarding governmental failure and corruption should be thought of as informing the mass protests that took place throughout India regarding the 2012 Delhi gang rape case:

> Given the facts, and the inaction of the police and state in so many of these cases, maybe it was high time that something caused people to take notice. There was a growing anger and people needed an outlet, so they took to the streets. There is a long history of this in India.

Saleema, who also works for a feminist NGO that offers support to survivors of gender based-violence and programs to promote gender justice in India, critiques an often "common sense" classist idea equating misogyny with the poor and "progressive values" with the rich. From her experiences working with survivors of sexual and gender based violence in India, she instead suggests that poor women are much more likely to publically discuss violence when compared to middle-class women. Having worked for over a decade with organizations in India that combat gender-based violence Saleema says,

> Women from the middle and upper class are more apprehensive to talk about the violence they are experiencing because they have a particular social status to maintain in the society. Middle-class women have appearances to maintain. We see this from our experiences. Women from a lower economic background would say, "Didi, what do we have to lose if we say something? If the husband beats us, the husband beats us. What do we have to lose in telling the truth?"

Saleema challenges mainstream discourses espoused by many politicians who attributed the brutality of the Delhi gang rape case and the rising rates of rape in Delhi to "wayward," unemployed, poor, migrant men—"footloose migrants" in ManMohan Singh's phrasing— whom politicians continue to blame for rising reports of sexual assault in Delhi. On the contrary, as Saleema suggests, many of the silent, rarely publicized, yet deeply oppressive forms of gendered violence in India take place in the middle-class home. Saleema relates that,

> A middle-class woman would come and complain about a case where she is violated by a man from a lower economic background. If it took place in the family—she would not talk about such things. The middle classes would say—"We are from a very good family and such things do not happen to us, it happens to them." Yes, if a man from a lower economic status violated a middle-class woman she would report it. If a rape is committed yes, they would file a complaint. But, if it was a husband or someone in the family they would try to sort if out outside of court to avoid any attention.

The politics of class, caste, and gender in India are broad issues that seem to touch every aspect of the feminist movement, attitudes towards sexuality in the region, and the mainstream media's reporting of events. For my purposes, the Delhi gang rape case expresses both a rupture in the moralistic, colonial silences that largely inform middle-class attitudes towards sexuality and a continued effort to censor discussions about sexual politics by political leaders, conservative male authorities, and commentators through using the divisive rhetoric of class and caste.

Sita attended the protests that followed the 2012 Delhi gang rape case. She is active in grassroots feminist politics in urban India and is hopeful about the Delhi gang rape protests. She discusses the largely youthful demographic of protestors and the dynamism and vigour with which many young feminists and queer activists politicized this case:

> There was this constant talk of how unsafe things are. It's been a long-standing frustration that's been going on. It was just at this point when these frustrations were already running high that this case happened and people realized that this could happen to anybody. There is no way to protect yourself, to

isolate yourself from violence, other than to not go out of your house, which is just ridiculous. So, it was time.

Sita sees these protests as being important outside of this singular case, to a wider moment of political reckoning and awakening in Delhi and perhaps the nation:

In terms of perception, with this case, there was nothing that one could do to protect themselves. So that was the best thing about the protests. As much as there was a protectionist approach from politicians and some other people, at the same time, there were an equal number of people articulating a desire for freedom. Of course there was the usual "protect our women" rhetoric but it was also about the freedom to move. It's my right to be free and I have a right to be free from violence. And I shouldn't be protected; someone shouldn't have to protect me. I shouldn't need any protection to freely move in the city. Everyone was saying this. One could see that this usual protectionist approach was being challenged.

I want to suggest that the protests might have expressed new understandings of "freedom" and desire on the part of India's younger generation, a generation influenced by global capitalism, affected by growing unemployment, and marked by a willingness to question colonial sexual moralities. Yet following the case, discourses of protectionism still emerged as did attempts to understand the case in class-based terms, locating "justice" in the proposed hanging of poor migrant men while locating imagined safety within the middle-class home. There was an effort on the part of conservative forces to forego a politicization of sexual violence, which feminists and activists say often goes unreported by middle-class women when their attackers are middle-class men, particularly those in their family or social circle.

In this chapter, I discuss the Delhi gang rape case and the decision to reinstitute Section 377, India's sodomy bill and how it relates to neoliberalism, capital, and labour. I draw on the work of Fernandes who suggests that what undercuts the ethos of the urban middle class in India, which has risen in size and national focus since economic liberalization policies of the 1990s, is a callous indifference to the nation's massive numbers of impoverished people. Furthermore, Fernandes suggests that fantasies of national and economic betterment for the Indian middle class involve a wilful amnesia regarding the countries ongoing problems of gender based, religious, and political violence. The writings of Chatterjee and Fernandes can be used to analyze the Delhi gang rape case as an expression of a public act of remembering, a spectacle that served as a reminder of all the traumatic aggression that lingers below an India of shining new malls and transnational corporations. This act of remembering also resonates with the earlier discussion regarding the haunting nature of contemporary sexual politics in India, as always being marked by lingering traces of the past. The act of remembering that occurred in the 2012 Delhi gang rape protests and in other moments of epistemic state-led violence that criminalize desire through colonial law is a forceful, traumatic, and violent memory of historical antagonisms. In these moments, the gross discrepancies of power that are often silenced in the blinding lull of consumer power and pleasure that defines the new Indian middle class become visible. Instead of understanding protests regarding sexual politics as solely being about gender, I suggest that they express deeper frustrations concerning the discrepancy between neoliberal forms of "freedom," and the freedom to consume transnational products as compared to meaningful forms of political freedom. Mainstream commentators often asked how the Delhi gang rape case could have happened within an "India shining"? I suggest that the events of December 2012 are the result of an "India shining," where the harsh glare of fluorescent mall lighting obscures a larger political vision.

POLITICAL AMNESIA: THE CLEANSING OF "BRAND INDIA"

Scholars have written extensively about the rise of a class of conspicuous consumers within urban India who have access to luxury items such as colour television, Western food imports, Western clothing, and other lifestyle-based products that mimic Western middle-class consumption patterns. Reading the Delhi gang rape case of 2012 in regards to growing consumerism in India rather than being solely about patriarchy offers insight into how this case touched on lingering class antagonisms that are often blinded by urban India's towering skyscrapers. Leela Fernandes writes that,

The visibility of the urban middle class is marked by changing consumption practices and lifestyles. The visibility of the urban middle classes sets into motion a politics of forgetting with regard to social groups that are marginalised by India's policies of liberalisation. (2415)

Fernandes sees the contemporary Indian middle class as being a discursive and ideological construct, actively supported by state forces to give an image of a "new India," without class antagonism and where upward mobility, akin to the "American dream," is possible. The urban Indian middle class Fernandes refers to is decidedly wealthy because of class and caste position; but it is constructed as an aspirational object that lower middle-class people and migrants are encouraged to emulate. Fernandes argues that the centring of the Indian middle class as the defining image of India causes the erasure of other bodies through symbolic processes of national branding and practices of spatial segregation. Fernandes writes that, "The politics of forgetting refers to a political-discursive process in which specific marginalised social groups are rendered invisible within the dominant national political culture" (2415).

Fernandes sees the production of the new Indian middle class as being tied to the construction of nouveau rich classes throughout Asia, an expression of the rise of Asian tiger countries within the global economy:

This production of the new Indian middle class paralells comparative trends in the construction of the "new rich" as a social group that is the prime beneficiary of globalization. This middle class is the visual urban embodiment of globalization that appears to dispel fears that places in late industrialising nations like India will remain forgotten on the routes of capital movements. (2416)

With the rise of new middle class norms of femininity that often turn around normative forms of gendered consumption and entertainment, the branding of India's middle class has specific gendered implications. The bodies of poor migrant women—whose labour in the city often produces the effortless appearance of the rising middle class—are forgotten in this feminine image of neoliberal India. Lingering colonial anxieties concerning gender and sexuality that emerge alongside new economic freedoms are also made invisible through this focus on the Indian urban middle class. While one can find a litany of advertising images, online branding campaigns, and new forms of consumer culture that herald the "new Indian woman" as supposedly being more liberated than her mother—interviews with feminists, queers, Hijras, and several activists in India point to the continued sacredness of the upper-caste Hindu family, in which the bodies of women exist as the property of men. The construction of the body of the woman as property of the Hindu family is also enforced in law through the legal sanction of "marital rape" as discussed in earlier chapters of this text.

Nirali discusses the decision not to criminalize "marital rape." She stresses that rape committed by men named as "husbands" will take a great deal of time to reach the status of the law because of the glorification of marriage, particularly by the Hindu middle class. When I ask her why she thinks that the government of India was quick to strike down the idea of criminalizing marital rape, she states,

> This is India. And of course, marriage is considered to have social and religious sanctity. Unlike Christianity and Islam where marriage is considered to be a social contract, in Hinduism it is a sacred institution. Marriage is considered to be God knows what? It is seen as everything that matters in a woman's life, the centre of her existence. It is so glorified. I mean marital rape? So many of the Indian women I speak to have been raped within their marriages. It's not like it's a new thing. In fact, it's only new in the sense that one would even think it's possible for a husband to rape a wife. Unlike the term "partner" used in the West and among a very small segment of intellectuals and activists, a man is a husband and a husband can do what he wants to his wife. She belongs to him.

Sanctioned and glorified domestic violence within India and among the Hindu middle class can be thought of in relation to colonial history and histories of partition. To define themselves against Christianity and Islam, Hindu nationalists valorized the family unit as one that gained a resonance outside of law and civil society. The family unit for "Hindustan" comes to take on a life of its own, lying outside of rationality, legality, and "rights" despite constitutional discourse. Nirali's comments resonate with an earlier discussion in this text regarding imagined "pre-political" spaces of heteronormative romance and family. Partha Chatterjee discusses the role that the home and ideas of culture played within late-colonial and early-nationalist India. The home became a sacred and valued space in which Indians could practice culture, imagined as pure and free from contamination. The idealized Hindu middle-class home was a space in which religion and culture were overemphasized in their importance as an affront to forced Westernization in the public sphere brought about by colonization. I want to suggest that Chatterjee's writings are of relevance to contemporary India in which, increasingly, transnational corporations produce public spheres of global consumption and competition. What remains "sacred" are narrow gendered norms that valorize the Hindu middle-class family. The illusion of gendered freedom brought about by consumerism does not touch the core of this private-public division produced by nationalist efforts to counter colonial imposition with sacred evocations of the domestic sphere.

EXTRA(ORDINARY) WOMEN: JUST ANOTHER DAY IN INDIA

The 2012 Delhi gang rape case was demonstrative of the hollow nature of the freedoms of middle-class consumerism in the context of the gross divisions in class and normative misogyny that define contemporary India. The collective forgetting of large segments of India's population such as migrant workers, the rural poor, and others stricken by poverty was violently remembered in this case. The body of the aspirational, supposedly middle-class woman, consuming "ordinary" products and engaging in "ordinary" pleasures, was falsely constructed as being one that is threatened by the extraordinarily common yet increasingly forgotten bodies of India's migrant poor. Furthermore, the Delhi gang rape case offered evidence of how the seemingly ordinary lives of gendered and sexualized bodies in India are subject to extraordinary misogyny, and breathtaking violence that can become as unremarked upon and basic as breathing. Yet the marking of this case as a defining political moment within the history of the city of Delhi and the Indian subcontinent was extraordinary. The unprecedented levels of protest that erupted following the gang rape and murder of Jyoti also spoke to a collective act of remembering. A remembrance that commemorated the loss of not only this one woman's life but of all of those lives that fall into darkness within an "India shining," without so much as a glance. Yasmin, a student in Delhi who attended the commemorative protests held one year after the 2012 Delhi gang rape case, sees this case as significant in relation to sexual politics in Delhi and throughout India. Like many of the protestors and activists I spoke to, she asserts that the level of mass mobilization and attention that this case received is striking:

> I think there are a few things that need to be noted about that day. One thing is how heinous the crime is. But because it is so sickening, it affects the level of awareness that has come about among people of the country and people of the entire world, and this is a way to enter into dialogue with a lot of other broader issues. Issues that are developing throughout the world. And one of the entry points into thinking about a lot of what happens in India and globally is violence against women in all its forms.

Yasmin understands this case and the level of outrage that emerged as relating to a broader set of frustrations about governmental corruption and the dissolution of the social welfare state. She also suggests that emphasizing class dynamics hides larger questions regarding normative levels of gender and sexual violence that exist in urban India. When asked about politicians who scapegoated migrant men from Bihar as the causes of sexual violence, Yasmin argues against classification:

> It's not about men from Bihar or any class or caste of men. That is just people classifying. You have cases of the most elite journalists, jurists, political leaders. You have the chief justice up on charges of assault. It is pervasive through all of society, through all societies. The problem is the attitude. You have to change the attitudes of men towards women and that takes several generations.

Yet she remains optimistic about the protests that occurred in Delhi and throughout India in December of 2012:

> This case will make a change. You need to have some event to turn to as a moment, a reference point in history. Before this, we all knew about it. We just chose to shut up unless it involved

us or someone we were close to. And even then, people are ashamed of being associated with sexual violence because it's connected to sex. It's the whole attitude and mentality of the society that needs to change.

While Chatterjee's idealized middle-class woman of the nationalist period was a privatized consumer who expressed all wants and needs through domestic consumption and exercising power in the home, the Delhi gang rape protests made the bodies of many women in India visible as political agents of change. Kanishka Chowdhury writes of "new Indian citizenship" and its relationship to economic liberalization and state power:

Even as India, the largest democracy in the world is being trumpeted as an emerging economic superpower, a majority of its citizens continue to endure the legacies of colonialism and the policies of ruling governments that primarily protect the interests of the privileged. (1)

A recurring theme in speaking with many people in Delhi and throughout urban India is the tension between the image of India as an "economic superpower" and the daily realities experienced by those who are not among the most elite. From the grinding poverty of migrant auto rickshaw drivers, to the never ending work schedules of young urban workers, to the experiences of women from divergent backgrounds who all have stories of sexism, to the lives of queer Indians made criminal by state power, there are growing frustrations regarding the glaring gap between every day violence and the rhetoric of neoliberal "progress."

OF GOLD FLAKES AND GOLD MEDALS: FROM "COMMONWEALTH" GAMES TO TRANSNATIONAL CORPORATIONS

In conducting interviews on the streets of Delhi, at protests, and in public spaces such as coffee shops, market streets, malls, and public parks, I discover that the younger demographic—students and young workers—are more willing to talk about this case and sexual politics in India. Because the victim of the Delhi gang rape was a student in her twenties and many of the protests were organized by students and young activists, this reality has not been surprising. Yet I was not expecting the high numbers of young men interested in discussing the case. Young male labourers working in an economy of an "India shining," often for major Western multinational companies selling products that define middle-class consumerism repeatedly express strong opinions regarding this case, often placing it within a broader political discourse apart from solely feminist- and gender-centric language. Many of the young men I meet speak English and consume many of the Western lifestyle products that define the urban middle class. However, their labour positions are precarious as are their claims to property and wealth.

Prakash and Raj are both in their twenties and work for a multinational corporation doing market research. Their labour position exemplifies the role that multinational consumerism plays within contemporary urban India by the disseminating of a series of lifestyle brands that define consumer habits and labour. Their understanding of the Delhi gang rape case emphasizes state corruption and class, in contrast to the gendered arguments espoused by feminists and queer activists. While many women and queer activists draw on a language of feminism, Prakash and Raj relate this case to their experiences as workers in Delhi and to larger problems of political corruption and systemic poverty. Raj explains that

> The first thing is the system is totally corrupt in India. Secondly, the police are also corrupt. And education is so poor and people are illiterate. Anyone with money can bribe and any poor person can attack another poor person and no one will stop this. That is why so many of these awful things are happening in India.

Prakash cites cases of corruption within the Indian government, specifically among political leaders in Delhi:

> I would like to tell you, the last chief minister of Delhi, Miss Sheila Dixit, she has done fifteen years of the job of CM in Delhi, but corruption is getting worse and worse and worse. And now, we hope because of the election of new political leaders like Arvind Kerjiwal it will be stopped.

The Delhi gang rape protests that followed the anti-corruption protests of Anna Hazare have offered an entry point into discussing many of the everyday political assaults endured by people in Delhi and throughout the Indian subcontinent. While many of the women whom I speak with discuss the pervasive cultures of sexism and misogyny that inform cases such as the 2012 Delhi gang rape case, Prakash and Raj point to the corrupt face of state power and institutional failing as the cause of violence. Raj states that "The Delhi police are not available. They and the government protect the business interests, not the people. Definitely not the women." Prakash and Raj are positioned at the nexus of forms of "new Indian citizenship" that Chowdhury sees as defining contemporary urban India since the economic liberalization policies of the 1990s were instituted. On the one hand, Prakash and Raj ostensibly benefit from transnational flows of global capital because of their employment for multinational companies that sell middle-class lifestyle brands. At the time of the interview, both were conducting market research about a new Greek version of *Gold Flake* cigarettes that will be sold in India. Yet they also express the common frustrations of an Indian public who are increasingly dissatisfied by the lack of state accountability, corruption, growing class divisions, and the disintegration of the social welfare state. Chowdhury discusses the effect that economic liberalization has had on contemporary India. He states that since the 1980s, India's ruling parties have pursued an agenda of economic reforms that have largely benefitted the country's ruling classes and the interests of transnational corporations. He writes that India's ruling parties,

> have "liberalized" the economy, meaning that largely deregulated foreign investment has been zealously pursued; public sector industries and financial institutions have been denationalized; the pool of reserve labour has been made available to multinational companies; large-scale social programs, especially in the agricultural sector, have been curtailed; and the public sector has been cut off from state budgetary support. (1)

Prakash and Raj are representative of the reserve labour that has become available to foreign multinationals. Not among India's elite upper class and castes, but young, English speaking and representative of a generation raised with secular urban norms, their labour now becomes used by major transnational corporations selling products like cigarettes and cellphones. Prakash and Raj's knowledge of transnational branding and popular culture, secular mores, and the English language is reflective of a globally savvy and perhaps cynical generation within neoliberal urban India. Like many of those whom I speak with both Raj and Prakesh have enough access to information with which to understand their labour exploitation by Western companies, and to comment on the inability of the Indian government to offer them meaningful forms of political redress. Much like many of the feminists I speak with in Delhi and throughout urban India, both Prakash and Raj believe that the sexual violence of elites is often concealed. Just as many feminists suggest that upper-class and upper-caste women do not report sexual violence in order to maintain the illusions of caste- and class-based respectability, Raj also argues that affluent men are often able to commit sexual violence without penalty because of police and state corruption: "If you have money, you just bribe. So if you are rich, you can rape." Many of the debates and conversations that arose in the wake of the Delhi gang rape case are reflective of the precarious balancing act between Westernized "consumer power" as a sign of class-based agency and the marking of the middle-class woman's body as an object of anxiety requiring paternalistic care. While both young men work for a multinational cigarette company, they also draw on a discourse of protectionism, specifically regarding the time bars are open in Delhi, which they believe is relevant to sexual violence. Prakash uses a language of protectionism as a means of compensating for the state's failure to meaningfully address gender-based violence in Delhi:

> I think pubs and bars should only be open until 12 p.m. because there is no protection in our city if you are not very, very rich. In the night, you are not safe in Delhi. Mostly its girls who are really not safe in the night, unless they are very wealthy.

There is a conflicting discourse of consumption, pleasure, labour, and what constitutes tradition that emerges repeatedly in my conversations with young workers in Delhi and other urban cities in India. On the one hand, many young people are employed by multinational corporations that sell products associated with Westernized lifestyle branding such as speciality Western food, forms of entertainment, and imported clothing. Yet they also express an apprehension towards what they see as the gendered and sexual impact of globalization on an imagined idea of tradition. The idea of ostensibly cleansing public spaces of what are seen to be Western pleasures to stop sexual violence against women is fiercely opposed by many researchers and feminists in the Indian subcontinent. Citing her in-depth research, Shilpa Phadke argues that closing bars earlier and creating cultures of protectionism makes cities less safe for women:

> It's completely wrong headed. Everything our research suggests is that the more shops are open, restaurants are open, the more bars are open, the safer cities are. Shutting things down earlier not only doesn't work, it makes things worse. (Phadke Personal interview)

Phadke also adds that preventing women from taking risks, from seeking pleasure and joy in their cities and in their lives is itself a form of violence:

> It's deeply problematic to not be able to take certain kinds of risks. To have certain risks be made unavailable to you which is how both infrastructure and ideology work. So in many contexts it's a question of whether there is transport available. In many contexts, it's also a question of whether there is lighting on the street. It's also how much agency you feel to report this violence and to be taken seriously, which is connected both to class, to temporality, to what time of the day and where the assault happens. (Phadke, Personal interview)

Phadke discusses how understandings of sexual violence in urban India are based on predetermined understandings of who has the right to occupy public space; seen as out of place in the city, the body of the woman is implicitly imagined to belong in the home:

> This is an example I often use. If you walk out on the street late at night and get hit by a bus, all kinds of processes of law and medical processes will happen. But if you walk out on the road and get sexually assaulted, before anything happens people will want to know why you were there in the first place. (Phadke Personal interview)

A "citizen" of a city, of a country who experiences certain forms of violence is afforded certain rights as a citizen, as a human being. However, a person who experiences sexual violence is understood firstly as a woman and is subsequently made sense of as a "certain kind of woman," who is either a "good victim" deserving of empathy or a "bad woman" who is assumed through a deeply misogynistic rhetoric to have invited gender-based violence. In these discrepancies between the bodily integrity of "citizens" as compared to "women," discourses of protectionism emerge as a means through which gendered bodies are counted not as citizens but as bodies whose value lies in their moral intelligibility and biopolitical value within an idealized, heteronormative, Hindu family.

The relationship between gender-based violence and essentialist ideas of "tradition" is discussed by young men whom I speak with in Delhi. Prakash suggests that the reason sexual violence is growing in India is because of multinational flows of culture, including sexualized forms of media:

> It's not Indian tradition that is the problem. Times have changed. Because of the Internet, you can see lots of porn. Think back to ten years before in India, the only things you had were CDs and DVDs. But now, you can see anything on the Internet. So, things will be changed with how people think about women and think about sex, because they see sex all the time. It has changed the mentality of the people. Now crazy people and crazy men have all these ways to get information and even worse ideas.

The belief that open displays of sexuality are tied to gender-based violence is prevalent within many of the narratives of both young workers and older middle-class professionals. The visibility of sexuality through globalized images, fashion, and nightlife in urban India is imagined to lead to sexual violence in ways that continue to glorify the space of the familial unit and an imagined culturally "pure" Hindu nation. Such a reading is challenged by many feminists and activists in the region who argue that gender-based violence is more likely to happen in the home, and often in the purportedly good Hindu middle-class home where cases of sexual violence often go unreported. Many who support a pastoral and romantic image of supposedly traditional Hindu middle-class family values associate late capitalist modernity with sexual deviance and criminality. Paradoxically, transnational flows of labour and capital are also associated with a rhetoric of "progress"; mainstream Hindu middle-class families desire Western products as a marker of upward mobility. In this contradictory discourse emerges a wish to manage sexual desire, specifically female and queer desire. While the idealized, middle-class Hindu citizen is produced within an "India shining" as a shameless consumer, the sexuality and the body of both the woman and the queer subject who defies familial norms and occupies public space can be constructed as an object of shame, as a body that is out of place within the nationalist imaginary. This "common sense" rhetoric that many of my interviewees espouse suggests that gender-based violence occurs because of transgressions of "culture" by those who are not able to strike the often impossible balance between appearances of consumer-based agency and public appearances of sexual repression. The gendered citizen in a neoliberal India is ostensibly free to consume sexy products, but is not afforded freedom from sexual violence.

Adya, an activist who works with a Delhi-based feminist organization, maintains that ideas of the "good woman" in India predate flows of multinational capital and globalized media and are part of the history of postcolonial India. She argues, however, that these attitudes are changing. The 2012 Delhi gang rape case protests and the subsequent worldwide media attention have opened spaces for dialogue and debate and have led many survivors of gender-based violence to report assaults and demand state accountability:

> It is not like things haven't changed. They are changing. But these attitudes we are talking about are like a thousand years old. And you cannot just change it overnight. It's not going to happen that way. There have been changes. Women are coming out and reporting incidents since December 16 and with fast track courts, changes to the law, and emphasis on police accountability, things are changing. Women feel that they are going to get support. So, they are aware that they can get justice because of this case. They might feel now that what has happened to them will be taken seriously and they can get justice.

When asked about the responsibility placed on men within India, Adya answers that while many families try to limit their daughter's mobility in public space to prevent sexual violence, they simultaneously protect their sons by excusing their sexism and hiding their crimes of sexual violence:

> It has never been the case that stigma becomes attached to men, not really. It depends on the parents; if the parents are sensitive and they are sensitive to women's rights, they would want the son to be punished because he violated someone's rights. But, in most of the cases, the family tries to shield their son from any blame.

The family unit becomes an institution governed by its own codes of morality, respectability, and honour—above the law. The idealized Hindu middle-class family, often a space of misogyny and silenced rape, is valorized against the conceptions of dignity and bodily integrity that are in the spirit of the Indian Constitution.

HUNG GOVERNMENTS AND PUBLIC HANGINGS:
POVERTIES OF JUSTICE

Amit, Anand, and Samir are in their twenties and early thirties. They work for a large Western cellphone company in Delhi. Like Prakash and Raj their lives and labour are expressions of the flows of transnational labour and capital to India. They too sell products that are expressions of new, urban, Indian middle-class "lifestyles," driven by technological tools such as cellphones and computers. Yet they too express concern and disillusionment over the failures of an "India shining" to offer meaningful judicial freedoms, as opposed to the freedoms bought and sold through consumerism. Regarding the Delhi gang rape case of 2012 and changes to the law, Samir is skeptical about the abilities of the Indian legal system to produce meaningful forms of redress concerning gender violence:

> I don't expect a lot of change in law. Not really. Some small changes, but not a lot. The law doesn't work here the way it might work some other places. The judges do what they want. The Indian government is trying to make changes, but the whole thing is really not working properly.

The routine failure of governance is a common criticism on the part of working people and women in India. Adya discusses the uses of patriarchal ideology by institutions of disciplinary power such as the police force, judiciary, and medical system in their dealings with survivors of sexual violence:

> It's not just the Delhi police, it's police all over the country that are the problem. They are part of the society. They have the same patriarchal mentality. And not only the male police officials but also the female police officials. Their entire attitude, when a survivor of sexual assault comes to file a complaint is bad. Their attitude has always been the same. They are not sensitive towards the woman who makes the complaint. They would ask her questions that are not in any way related to the case. For example, why are you out this late at night? And it doesn't matter. It doesn't matter how you are dressed. It is in no way connected to an assault. Time and again, the law says, various judgments say, the woman's supposed character, what she was wearing, it doesn't matter at all. But they keep repeating these questions.

She further discusses how the medical system in India, when treating survivors of sexual assault, is also guilty of an explicit sexism and a moral policing of female sexuality:

> Doctors still use the two finger test to check the virginity of survivors of sexual violence. The Supreme Court has struck this down saying the two finger test is not acceptable. It violates the dignity of the survivor and is not connected to rape. But time and again it is still going on.

Young workers and feminists also often make reference to judicial failing in relation to the Supreme Court's decision to uphold Section 377 of the Indian Penal Code, India's sodomy bill. In an interview following this decision, author and activist Gautam Bhan states:

> The gay movement was one of the few issues on which there was some progressive movement. This judgment has misread the

mood of India's young population. It has affected our standing
as a democracy in the world. It has betrayed the idea of India.
(Bhan qtd. in Vats)

From my interviews with young labourers in Delhi, both men and
women, Bhan's suggestion that the judgment misreads the mood of
India's young population appears to be very true. While Amit says that
he is not queer, he also states that the decision regarding Section 377 was
"annoying" and "made India look really bad, and really unfair, again." Amit
went on to cite the recent Delhi elections and the problems of political
representation in the city: "The election in Delhi just came. Last month
there was some voting in Delhi. So, the election is now declared a tie.
Now there is no major government. It's a big mess." Anand interjects
with a joke, referencing the decision to hang four of those accused of
the Delhi gang rape and the recent Delhi elections, "Hung government,
public hanging. Welcome to India!" He stops laughing to state that the
Delhi gang rape case was serious and saddening, "No, but don't get me
wrong. The whole thing was sad." "Yes," Samir agrees, "It was very sad."
They all go on to locate sadness not only within this case but within
the larger failures of the political system. "What's sad though," Samir
says, "is that the people care, but not the government. And so you can
protest and talk about all this, but in the end will they fix anything?"
    Chowdhury discusses the branding of a "new India" that began in the
1990s and has aggressively continued:

> The branding of the New India is intended in large measure
> to assure foreign investors and financial organizers that India
> is "on the right track" and has jumped on the global corporate
> bandwagon. Quite simply, such national branding is the way
> for developingcountries like India to become part of the "global
> community." (2)

The new "brand India" image masks the growing divisions between
rich and poor, and the grotesque living conditions that inform most
people's existence within the Indian subcontinent. Chowdhury continues,

> While propagating the New India brand, corporate and state
> interests also attempt to elide the grim realities—especially

the poverty and inequities—that confront the vast majority of India's people. The government is less inclined, for instance, to report that structural inequities at the national level are at critical levels. In 2009, India was ranked at 134 on the UN Human Development Index. (2)

The gendered dimensions of normative suffering and violence within India as well as state and bureaucratic inefficiency came to the forefront of media attention and public debate following the Delhi gang rape protests, thereby shining a light on the darkness of "brand India." Amit discusses his own labour in Delhi and the relationship between state corruption, brand India, and the struggles of city workers:

Actually, if you want food three times a day in India, you have to work more than twelve hours. And that's why we have not much time to think about the country. Every person in India has no time to think about his country or think about another person. We are so busy. And it's not because we work in technology, it's because we live in India. That's why the system doesn't work and the government can do what they want. Who has the time to complain apart from one week of protest? Who has the time to make a legal claim when it will take forever to be heard and when the judge will do what they want and everyone takes bribes?

He goes on to discuss the men accused of the Delhi gang rape and the growing numbers of impoverished migrant workers displaced within Indian cities. While not justifying their actions, he points to how the case is connected to the failures of an "India shining":

There are so many people in Delhi who come here and are too poor and starving and don't have any future. And they do nothing. And they go mental. Then the rest of the people just have too much work and are just trying to stay alive so they can't think about the future of India. So the government and really rich people can make all the decisions for India. But they do things for the rich and not for the average person. This is the problem. It's not people. It's the government.

247

While many women interviewed regarding the 2012 Delhi gang rape case and subsequent protests discuss patriarchy and sexism at the level of ideology, many of the young male labourers whom I speak with place the case within the context of state failure and globalization. This could be seen as an inability on the part of men to apprehend the deeper workings of patriarchy within India. Yet one could also see a focus on "universal patriarchy" as opposed to class, caste, and labour issues as informing the gender-centric lens of many upper- and middle-class feminists. While some feminists suggest that changes regarding the routine violence in urban India will come only from generational shifts in ideologies pertaining to women and sexuality, for young men labouring in the city, these changes cannot occur until broader political and economic oppression is addressed.

SACRED COWS AND HOLY TERRORS:
WAR- AND CASTE-BASED VIOLENCE

Smita Narula discusses the relationships between the imagined progress of neoliberal capitalist growth in contemporary India, militarism, and the ongoing abuse of Dalits. Narula compares the violence of American nationalism with that of Indian nationalism:

> The militarism and agnostic nationalism of both governments has also depleted state coffers in the name of ensuring "national security" and fighting the global "war on terror"—a fight in which both states are now staunch allies—to the detriment of the poor in both countries who enjoy neither physical nor economic security. (269)

Arvind Narrain writes of the use of rape as a tool of state power and an expression of nationalism. Narrain discusses uses of rape by the American state and the rape of Adivasis, Dalits, Muslims, and others deemed to be "minorities" by the Indian military and other forces of state power. Narrain compares the torture and sodomy of African immigrant Abner Louima by the New York Police Force to the 2012 Delhi gang rape, both of which led to large public protests:

> To understand gang rape, one must take the group seriously as

a space for a competitive masculinity with each member daring the other to outdo him. In this competitive excess, the issue is not sexual pleasure but sexual humiliation. The gang may come together for many reasons; sometimes it is bonding of racial superiority, at others the gang is formed for the sole purpose of acting out communal or caste hatred. (18)

The depoliticization of the 2012 Delhi gang rape case as an issue only regarding violence against women in India allows conservative forces to colonize the issue for their own purposes. Understanding sexual violence as linked to the workings of normative cultures of masculinist violence offers a means of politicizing gender-based violence as being interwoven in the overarching authority of state structure. Such a reading unites discussions regarding state violence and sexual violence.

POLLUTED DIGNITIES:
CRIMES AGAINST THE BODILY INTEGRITY OF DALITS

Hindu patriarchs also employ tools of sexual violence against the bodies of Dalits as a statement of their own investment in masculinist nationalism. The use of bodies of "others" to solidify the boundaries of a group, gang, or nation through competitive cultures of masculinity is expressed in acts of caste-based sexual violence and torture. Sharmila Rege has written of the sexual abuses that Dalit women and men experience in the work that they must do—often working as maids and servants in the homes of upper-caste and middle-class Hindu families; their bodies are subject to unspeakable acts of violence by these Hindu families, whose imagined civility and colonial puritanism masks the everyday atrocities experienced by Dalits (Rege *Writing Caste, Writing Gender; Against the Madness of Manu)*. Much like the routine rape of African-American women and men by white masters during slavery, the backs of kitchens and servants quarters contain the sickening secrets of sexual violence. The imagined morality of the "good" heteronormative "fair and lovely" upper caste family, much like the white colonizing family is shadowed by the violent truths of power. While an "India shining" moment has been used to brand a "progressive" vision of history tied to capitalist narratives of development, Narula suggests that caste-based violence continues to be prevalent within contemporary India. Just as the global "war on terror" solidifies the white masculinist power of American nationalism against the tortured Arab male body, the Dalit body is also stripped of all bodily integrity through celebrations of Indian nationalist militarism. Narula states that,

> caste-based inequality, like racial inequality survives dramatic economic growth. Even as India celebrated its triumphant testing of nuclear weapons, exploding them underground in the deserts of Rajasthan, Dalit manual scavengers were being manually lowered into open sewers without protective gear to unblock toxic and noxious sewage. In India, the rise of a nuclear state and a technological powerhouse has been accompanied by the rise of the number of manual scavengers in the country today. (269)

If, as Narrain suggests, rape is a crime that is not a gendered act of "men" against "women" but rather a crime against bodily integrity, Dalit bodies, lowered into pits of noxious sewage within an "India shining," are vulnerable to sexualized violence across gender lines. The inability to conceive of Dalits beyond casteist and colonial hierarchies of skin enables the basic integrity of lower caste people to be routinely trampled over. The sexualized abuse of Dalits is part of a larger ideology of bodily hierarchy definitive of ideologies of caste, class, and nationalism in which one's place in a group is solidified through their violent exclusion of others. The body of the Dalit, like the body of the racialized African migrant, the slave, and the Muslim man within a contemporary global "war on terror" is a feminized body, subject to torture and violence definitive of the macabre underbellies of nationalism.

Sharmila Rege's *The Madness of Manu* offers an exemplary reading of the relationship between patriarchy and caste, with the patriarchal authority of the upper-caste Hindu male serving as a microcosm for Hindu nationalism. Rege's writing is particularly important in a contemporary India that has elected Hindu nationalist Narendra Modi to the post of prime minister. While Dalit feminists have widely documented the madness of caste and its relationship to the commonplace abuse, torture, rape, and murder of Dalit women in India, the bodies of Dalit men are also subject to gross debasements of life and bodily integrity. Numerous cases continue to occur in contemporary India in which Dalit men, children, and women undergo forms of unfathomable cruelty—forced to eat human feces and subjected to bodily torture and sexual crimes beyond human comprehension (Narula). The sexual violence enacted against Dalits historically and its relationship to Hinduism is beyond the scope of this work. However, it is important to note that neoliberal narratives of economic "progress" have not stopped the debasement of Dalit lives. While Puar suggests that due to the Islamophobia of a Global "war on terror," Muslim bodies in North America are made queer to the nation, within contemporary India the Dalit body is also constructed through Hindu nationalist ideology as a monstrous figure. The Dalit body within "Hindustan" is often subject to sexualized abuse that resonates with acts of racialized sexual violence against African bodies haunted by slavery, and Muslim men terrorized by homonationalist American soldiers as part of an ongoing "war on terror." The implicit and explicit cruelties of nationalism justify violence against bodies marked as "other," globally.

"ALOT CAN HAPPEN OVER COFFEE": MIGRANT LABOUR, GENDER-BASED VIOLENCE, AND THE CITY

The visibility of India on the global stage and within the global imaginary shines a spotlight on transnational flows of investment and consumerism through the glare of mall lighting. However, the bodies of migrant labourers whose exploitation produces the seamless spectacle of the "world class" city are often invisible. The thankless work of dark hands digging ditches for the Commonwealth Games after the sun has fallen makes India "shine." Yet the narratives and images of migrant workers, Dalits, and impoverished and exploited workers are often nowhere to be found in lush advertising images of "world-class" Indian cities. While the gates of India are open for business, inviting transnational corporations and Western products into the nation, an increasingly urban India is also beset with growing numbers of migrant workers who are exiled in urban space and subject to brutal working and living conditions.

I meet Hazrat, a young man from Uttar Pradesh. The anniversary protests regarding the 2012 Delhi gang rape case and the protests against the 2013 Supreme Court decision regarding Section 377 have just ended. Hazrat works at *Café Coffee Day*, a major multinational coffee chain that now owns coffee shops throughout urban India. The "ordinary" lifestyles of young urban people in the city often revolve around a series of normative social and entertainment practices that mimic forms of Western secular-capitalist sociality in cities and suburbs. The café in which one can access Wi-Fi and order European-style products costing almost ten times what Indian chai or coffee at a roadside canteen would cost is a marker of India's new English-speaking middle class. Yet the seamless ease of middle-class entertainment is supported by the labour of migrants and the often unremarked on violence that they incur.

While some have read the gang rape and murder of Jyoti as expressing the rage and hopelessness of impoverished migrant men, Hazrat, a migrant labourer in Delhi, talks about the gendered violence enacted against migrant women. He tells me of the sexual harassment that many migrant female workers experience in the city and comments on the relationship between migration, class, and the family:

> Some rural girls are working in Delhi, for *Café Coffee Day*, and another person, well honestly, the boss of the coffee shop, tries something with them. Yeah, they complain and then they are terminated from their job. If you complain, you get fired. Poor girls have no choice. Poor girls are here for money to send home. They are working for their whole family. And it's not good that they have to put up with abuse. I can understand every poor child and poor girl who is working for her family. These girls should not be harassed. I am working alone too, also towards a secure future for me and so my family is secure, back home. I save money and send money to family. I will work the overtime for our family.

He says that he is religious and will have an arranged marriage in Uttar Pradesh; he works continuously and has few friends and no family in Delhi. He is lonely, but he will make sacrifices regarding his personal and psychological and emotional well-being in the interests of his family. The family unit, much like Chatterjee's reading of its role during the nationalist period, becomes the sacred space that he clings to, to deal with his public life of performing alienating labour for a transnational corporation. Regarding the 2012 Delhi gang rape case, he states that he "felt sorry for Damini's family" and that he "will pray for her family." When asked about the Supreme Court decision to uphold

Section 377 of the Indian Penal Code, Hazrat tells me that he has no time to follow politics:

> I am working seven days a week and any time I have, I need to sleep. I don't have time to really follow politics. I only heard about the case of the gang rape because it was talked about everywhere and always on the Internet and television. Mainly, I just have to think about working and then working more, and then sending money home. Then I think about how to save enough to pay for my bed and to eat something.

While the "brand India" dream sells gendered "freedom" to middle- and upper-middle class women through transnational flows of products, Hazrat points to the abuses of rural migrant labourers pouring lattes and cappuccinos for India's new "cosmopolitan" crowds. He also discusses the privileging of familial and gendered norms as a continued result of neoliberal capitalist expansion in which migrant workers often only find solace and a justification for their exploitative labour conditions through privileging their familial, religious, and cultural duty. The "ordinary" entertainment of the Indian middle classes in malls and cafés offers an entry point into thinking about the equally ordinary gendered dynamics of the middle-class Hindu family as a space of excused and often glorified gender violence, and as a space that is simultaneously valorized by many migrants in the city who are alienated from consumer-driven forms of sociality. Migrant labourers are invited to clean the coffee cups and scrub the malls of neoliberal urban India, yet their personal bodies and desires stand apart from images of the supposedly cosmopolitan middle-class Indian citizen. When asked if he likes coffee, dressed in a *Café Coffee Day* uniform adorned with the slogan of the multinational corporation "A lot can happen over coffee," Hazrat—who speaks with passion, rage, and loss regarding the commonplace sexual harassment of migrant women labourers in Delhi—responds with the slow and steady voice of a village man turned displaced migrant: "No, actually I prefer tea."

WORKS CITED

Chatterjee, Partha. "Colonialism, Nationalism, and Colonialized

Women: The Contest in India." *American Ethnologist* 16. 4 (1989): 622-633. Print.

Chowdhury, Kanishka. *The New India: Citizenship, Subjectivity, and Economic Liberalization*. London: Palgrave Macmillan, 2011. Print.

Fernandes, Leela. "The Politics of Forgetting: Class Politics, State Power and the Restructuring of Urban Space in India." *Urban Studies* 41.12 (2004): 2415-2430. Print.

Narrain, Arvind. "The Violation of Bodily Integrity." *Economic and Political Weekly*. 48.11 (2013): 17-19. Print.

Narula, Smita. "Equal by Law, Unequal by Caste: The 'Untouchable' Condition in Critical Race Perspective." *Wisconsin International Law Journal* 26 (2008): 255-343.Print.

Phadke, Shilpa. Personal interview. 2014.

Puar, Jasbir. *Terrorist Assemblages: Homonationalism in Queer Times*. Durham: Duke University Press, 2007. Print.

Rege, Sharmila. *Against the Madness of Manu: B. R. Ambedkar's Writings on Brahmanical Patriarchy*. New Delhi: Navayana, 2013. Print.

Rege, Sharmila. *Writing Caste, Writing Gender: Reading Dalit Women's Testimonios*. New Delhi: Zubaan Press, 2006. Print.

Vats, Vaibhav. "A Conversation with Lawyer and Activist Gautam Bhan." *The New York Times*, 11 Dec. 2013. Web. 15 June 2015.

8.

RED LIPS, RED LIGHTS, AND
SCARLETT LETTERS

FASHION CRIMES:
FROM ORIENTALIST ASCETICS TO SEXUAL AESTHETICS

EVEN THE MOST inconsequential of things, a tube of red lipstick for example, offers inroads into thinking about the complexities of desire in contemporary India. Mitra, a Delhi student, speaks to me about all of the nuanced ways that sexuality and desire are managed through daily gestures of the body in contemporary urban India:

> You can wear red lipstick, but usually on the weekends. At a party. You wear it when you are with friends, at a market in South Delhi. Or going to a night club on a Saturday night. Well, you see, certain women wear it in the day. But then they are from somewhere else. Or they work for a makeup brand. Or they are the ones you see in the traffic, the cross dressers. Or the ones you hear about who are selling sex. This is why you have to be careful how you look in India. But I don't worry that much, because people can tell the difference between one kind of a woman and the other. You know the one who has money or the one who really needs it.

Other female students whom I meet further debate the tube of red lipstick in a Delhi market full of fashion knockoffs haggled over with market *wallas*—migrant men who work as street vendors in the city, selling the latest-imported Western goods, smuggled across borders and now peddled by textile merchants in a neoliberal India teeming with shopping complexes. Žižek discusses the use of signifiers of feminine excess in class-based terms and points out that elites often prefer austere aesthetics, while the poor prefer images of luxury. Žižek's discussion regarding feminine excess and global capitalism can be understood in reference to the imagined sexless asceticism of India, which Western tourists often romanticize.[1] While working women in India mark their lips in red, Western tourists and consumers of "Incredible India"[2] buy luxury tours and items of sexless spiritual piety that resonate with Orientalism and its construction of a submissive East in both sexual and political terms. Orientalist evocations of a "natural" India shown in images of asexual yogic piety are juxtaposed to the red lips of the street. Wealthy tourists often seek an escape from worldly desires in their travels to an India of ashrams and store-bought sacrifice. In these branded constructions of the Indian subcontinent, Orientalist ideology comingles with neocolonial expeditions of "world class" travellers. Conversely, many women in contemporary urban India express sexual desire with imported red lipstick used to make them seem like experienced consumers of ostensibly worldly products. Red lips for women on the streets of urban India are used to connote sexual expression as consumer power or are used by sex workers as a symbol of their labour power. As Slavoj Žižek writes making reference to an ironic quip made by an observer during the reign of Yeltsin in Russia,

> ordinary women who wanted to appear attractive dressed like (the common idea of) prostitutes (heavy red lipstick, cheap jewels, and so on), while real prostitutes preferred to mark their distinction by wearing simple but expensive "business" suits. Indeed, as a saying popular among the poor who participate in carnivals in Brazil goes: "Only the rich like modesty; the poor prefer luxury." (*Living in the End Times* 249)

The red lips of Indian students, Hijras, and sex workers all connote different markers of class-based feminine excess. While these visual markings appear immodest, the seemingly austere yoga pants of affluent Western tourists often reflect an obscene Orientalist desire to construct the Global South as a timeless apolitical playground for neocolonial expeditions costing a great deal more than a tube of red lipstick.

In speaking with students and young urban workers such as Mitra regarding sexual desire and aesthetics, we discuss walking the tight-rope of acceptable gendered and sexual performance that middle-class women in contemporary neoliberal India often walk. This often impossible balancing act involves consumer-based performances of mall-chic Western female agency, and the maintenance of an image of upper caste and upper class female sexual respectability. Women whom I speak with in neoliberal India express supposed freedom through mall chic aesthetics, but such performances of feminine excess also risk crossing the line, traversing into spaces of danger where bodies of poor, lower-class, lower-caste women and Hijras are located within the gendered Indian imaginary. As discussed earlier regarding laws concerning balconies and "bar girls," the body marked with traces of that which might connote sex in public is anxiously policed through everyday self regulation, familial regulations of gender, and by the disciplinary powers of the state. To be associated with sex in neoliberal India, often means being associated with economic empowerment and "progressive" understandings of choice. However, a body can easily slip, take the wrong path and end up in the traffic of cities, in red light districts associated with a dangerous sex, with a sexual economy that tells a different story than the bedtime tales of billboard branding now lulling middle-class consumers to sleep.

What does desire mean for young women negotiating the time and place for red lipstick in an India where red lips are used to sell Diet Coke to a country that still has so many craving water? What does desire mean for young women who anxiously police their bodies and the ways that they appear in public space so as not to be stained by the darkness of impoverishment, the condition of the majority of people within a nation? What does desire mean for young women who are as desperate to seem "free" as they are bound by all of the lingering trepidations of the middle-class Hindu family and affected by patriarchal and caste-based neurosis? What does desire mean when red lips are a branding tool signifying wealth, but also a branding tool through which sex workers are read as selling criminalized yet widely known forms of embodied labour? What does desire mean in the context of the 2013 decision to criminalize what are deemed to be "unnatural" sexual acts in India and in the aftermath of the 2012 Delhi gang rape case?

The desire to be seen is complex and never fully intelligible in Indian cities where how a person is seen and sees others can never be fully known or calculated. The signification[3] of sex can easily slip across class, caste, religious, and linguistic lines (Hall 31). The signification of a feminine performance is met with a host of unexpected audiences, all of whom might misread the play of signs. Yet it is here—in the most seemingly unremarkable decisions, activities, and street scenes that encompasses the everyday in urban India, days of red lipstick and girls gang-raped and murdered on the way home from malls and film theatres—that the question of desire is posed. Desire lingers in the faint imprint of red lips, a filmic image of sex—like the red lipstick that stains coffee cups of South Delhi students and the chai tins of Hijras, waiting at the roadside for their next street scene of Bollywoodesque begging to begin. Desire is a haunting question that hangs in the arid heat of the city air, on another day in Delhi.

NEW WOMEN, NEW CLOTHES, OLD PUNCHING BAGS: IMAGES OF SEXUAL "FREEDOM"

The Indian subcontinent is still haunted by the question of desire. Desire within a neoliberal India, selling sex in mall-chic products while criminalizing sex through colonial laws, is still deeply unstable. Sex is an anxious stammer, a nervous joke that highlights the insecurities of an India that connotes Westernization through "sexy" products while still clinging to fantasies of female chastity as virtue. Kanishka Chowdhury discusses the marketing of films by disaporic female filmmakers such as Deepa Mehta and Gurinder Chadha. He argues that these artists are examples of globalized, transnational, and neoliberal feminist subjects who advance notions of Western sexual agency that imagine the "Indian woman" to be passive in Orientalist ways (Chowdhury). He suggests that films such as *Fire* and *Bend it Like Beckham*, both of which gained huge popularity in the West, are born out of a neoliberal conception of desire that sidelines class politics and political struggle in favour of individualistic conceptions of sexual agency. Chowdhury points to a 2007 issue of a popular Indian magazine *The Week* that devoted an entire issue to what it termed the "new woman" within contemporary urban India. The "new Indian woman" is an upper middle-class career woman depicted as having escaped from the restraints of sexism and now enjoys equality through capitalist success and increased consumer power. As Chowdhury states, "Political empowerment and bourgeois individualism seem to be conflated by many of these women" (145). The author provides a compelling critique of this "new woman" within an "India shining," both in terms of the actual statistical realities regarding economic opportunities for women in India and the ways that poverty systemically and structurally affects women more than men. Within this phantasmal image of the "new Indian woman," depicted not only in *the Week* but throughout media and popular culture in urban India, there is a denial of everyday forms of oppression that are definitive of daily life in the subcontinent:

> No mention is made of unequal wages, gender discrimination, caste, and religious injustice, housing expenses, or the enormous rise in the cost of living. All that we need to know is that the "new woman"—a consumer, an empowered free agent, and an equal of men-has arrived on the scene. (Chowdhury 145)

The arrival of this mythical "free agent" is divorced from long histories of feminist struggle within the subcontinent that have always been divided along class lines.

Conducting interviews in Delhi, I speak with Harish, an activist part of an organization that works with men to stop violence against women and to challenge hegemonic masculinity throughout India. He discusses the difference between the model of individualism and collective ideas of empowerment in the context of feminist history. Harish states,

> The Western feminists talked about individual rights, which is actually a neoliberal language. When the feminist movement went to the rural areas in the early '80s, women talked about collective empowerment and well-being. And this is a large paradigm shift in India's feminist movement. Urban middle-class women or South Extension Delhi women, which I call them [laughter], they spoke about individual rights, while rural women spoke about collective rights. And rural and poor women were empowered through the building of effective and sustainable collective structures.

The notion of individual rights often popularized by white, Western, middle-class feminists in North America and Europe is challenged by many Indian feminists who point to the glaring realities of poverty, which make "rights" futile without economic reform. The notion of collective rights as opposed to narratives of individual empowerment also remains deeply important in India because these communal entitlements reflect the reality of discrimination within the workforce. Barbara Harris White problematizes neoliberal assertions of women's political power as buying power by pointing to the statistical truth of women's economic status in India. As Harris-White states,

> Indian women's participation in the labour force remains low at just 36 percent compared to 84 percent of men... India is ranked as one of the worst ten countries in the world in terms of the gender gap in economic participation. (Harris-White qtd. in Chowdhury 146)

What is also startling regarding the media-driven and consumerist rhetoric of "gender freedom" in India is the continued use of sex selection to abort female foetuses. Activists in Delhi discuss the preference for male children, often among middle-class urban populations. Bipin, an activist whom I spoke with regarding gender in contemporary India, explains the secretive nature of violence that takes place in the Hindu middle-class home. He asserts that a clear indicator of misogyny within Hindu middle-class and upper caste households is the male to female sex ratio of children:

> You see, middle-class men in India are very secretive. They have big houses in which to bury their secrets. But the poor chap has no space [laughter]. He has only an auto rickshaw or maybe a bicycle. There is no place to hide [laughter]. I mean seriously, the kind of abuse and violence that middle-class and upper-class men do in this country is shocking. In so many rape cases, middle- and upper-class men buy the law and never see any repercussions for their disgusting behaviour. It's very secretive but one indication of the misogyny of the middle class is there in the statistics. The child sex ratio is going down statistically among the middle classes, who are

aborting female children. They are the ones who can afford the medical procedures to find out whether they are having a girl or boy child. Middle-class women bargain for their material comfort vis-à-vis their reproductive rights.

The language of bargaining with bodies for material comforts among the middle class is often discussed by those who advocate for sex worker rights and the decriminalization of sex work in India. Sex workers have long pointed out the hypocrisies of middle-class moralism. Middle-class women often bargain with their bodies to solidify caste- and class-based marriages to wealthy men (Shah). The imagined sexual freedom of the "new Indian woman" through consumer power can be considered in relation to those cast(e) in her shadow: abject bodies of poor women and Hijras whose sexuality is often threatened with violence and criminalized when used as a source of labour power through sex work.

MASTURBATION, MALLS, AND MONEY: CLASSED BODIES AS SEXED BODIES

Chowdhury critiques Deepa Mehta's film *Fire* and its depiction of desire within the film: it is expressed individually as an appendage to economic power among the Indian middle class. He states that,

> Desire ... becomes something that can be satisfied purely at an individual level, and fulfilling that desire is a step toward attaining liberation. The accumulation and expression of desire constitutes the attainment of freedom. (147)

Chowdhury also discusses the lack of class analysis within the film and highlights Mehta's privileged position as a non-resident Indian and a Western feminist who depicts an India where women lack sexual agency. For my purposes, it is interesting to question the relationship between desire and neoliberalism that the film offers an entry point into discussing within an India of sodomy laws and women gang raped to death on buses. Sexuality and desire at a bodily level are increasingly policed to allow for the capitalist illusion of freedom at an aesthetic level, while sex continues to be stained by the constructed darkness of

class, caste, religious, and colonial-nationalist "impurity." Chowdhury
offers an interesting analysis of the character of Mundu, a servant, in
Mehta's *Fire*, the only lower-caste character in the film and who is seen
masturbating. He writes that,

> Mundu is presented as being entirely without scruples; not
> only does he masturbate in the presence of the matriarch, he
> also spies on the sisters in law. The lack of sexual fulfilment
> and the projection of sexual desire (the principal characters are
> united by their denial or celebration of sexual desire) become
> the symptomatic variants in the household. (147)

For Chowdhury, these "symptomatic variants" overshadow the economic dimensions of Indian life and create a space in which desire exists
outside of economic power relations:

> The vagaries of predatory capitalism and the economic concerns
> of everyday life… play a minor role in disrupting the lives of
> the family members. The Indian family once again occupies an
> ahistorical space where ungoverned passions are the only causes
> for the disruption of the domestic space. (147)

Yet Chowdhury's reading of the space of the family presupposes that
sex is divorced from economics within the family. There is an implicit
assumption, in many Marxist writings that sexual acts are ahistorical
when they are not explicitly made sense of within a strictly Marxist
framework. Reading the figure of Mundu, in a time when colonial
laws have recently been reinstituted in India to criminalize "unnatural"
sexual acts including masturbation, sex itself has been classed and
denigrated by state power. Sex is associated with dirt, impurity, and
darkness in ways that mark the lower-caste servant in sexual terms.
Similarly, queer people and certain women who stray from idealized
roles of upper caste female sexual respectability are often described
in a casteist language of imagined filth, dirtiness, and colonially constructed impurities of the body.

I meet with Jai, a Delhi student who has been heavily involved with
queer activism since the 2013 decision by the Supreme Court of India
to reinstitute Section 377. He discusses the criminalization of all sexual

acts that are deemed to be "unnatural" under Section 377:

We're not saying that bestiality or sodomy should be okay. We're just saying that consensual sex should be okay. So under 377 you are making all of these sex acts that happen every day wrong. You are making blow-jobs between a man and a woman illegal. You are making hand-jobs wrong. Are you telling me that the judges on the Supreme Court have never had a hand-job or a blow-job in their lives? You make masturbation for a man illegal. So every day when I masturbate—well I don't do it every day [laughter].... But anyway, every time I masturbate, I'm a criminal?

The criminalization of certain sex acts considered to be "unnatural" stems from lingering colonial and class-based anxieties within the "New India." The image of an "India shining" produces a paradoxical stringent regulation of bodily desire that continues to be marked by the darkness of upper-class, upper-caste Hindu moralities and their regulation through colonial laws. While Chowdhury offers a necessary critique of the capitalist dynamics that enable diasporic filmmakers such as Deepa Mehta and others to speak on behalf of "Indian women," enacting a native informant position, the ideologies pertaining to sex in the Indian subcontinent should perhaps be understood in the context of colonial history and Hindu nationalism. It is precisely through the marking of Mundu as the masturbator, the one whose body is sexually public outside of the reproductive family, that he becomes the queerest character in *Fire*; his impurity is both criminal and culpable at the level of servitude and "deviant" sex. The relationship between sexuality and the underbellies of the Indian economy through the sale of pornography depicted in the film is also of importance. The upper-caste elite male lead in the film is shown selling illegal pornography to customers through the family's restaurant. Just as the fantasies of Hindu middle-class purity are upheld through the exploitation of the bodies of masturbating Dalits, the paradoxes of economies of sex that define neoliberal urban India and the ruse of colonial appearances are revealed. The minefield of "sexual morality" that many must traverse is a narrow-minded path marked by the ruse of appearances, secrecy, and the ghostly presence of colonial history.

"ALMOST THE SAME, BUT NOT QUITE": APPROXIMATIONS OF
PHALLIC POWER AND POSTCOLONIAL MIMIC WOMEN

Lucie Irigray discusses how women enact feminine performances in ways that turn the constituted disadvantage of feminine embodiment into a performative mode of resistance against the authorial norms and values of masculinist systems of power. As Irigray writes:

> There is in an initial phase, perhaps only one "path," the one historically assigned to the feminine: that of mimicry. One must assume the feminine role deliberately which means already to convert a form of subordination into an affirmation and thus to begin to thwart it. The mimicry of femininity make(s) "visible," by an effect of playful repetition, what was supposed to remain invisible: the cover up of a possible operation of the feminine in language. It also means to unveil the fact that, if women are such good mimes, it is because they are not simply reabsorbed into this function. They also remain elsewhere: another case of the persistence of "matter" but also of "sexual pleasure." (qtd. in Bolton 6)

Homi Bhabha's reading of mimicry uses the Freudian theory of castration to discuss colonialism as a discourse of deep seated ambivalence, one in which the narcissism and anxiety of empire are managed through processes of mimicry and irony. As Bhabha states,

> colonial mimicry is the desire for a reformed, recognizable other, as the subject of a difference that is almost the same, but not quite ... the discourse of mimicry is constructed around an ambivalence in order to be effective, mimicry must continually produce its slippage, its difference, its excess. (qtd. in Bolton 6)

Bolton suggests that Bhabha's idea of the "mimic man" is gendered, constructing colonial processes of mimicry as those enacted by men. Bolton states,

> Bhabha's analysis of colonial mimicry is itself constructed around an ambivalence, producing or replicating a slippage

between gender and race. Black men under colonialism and white women in psychoanalytic theory mark a difference that is almost the same-but not quite. (6)

If all the imagined women of psychoanalytic theory are white and all the colonial subjects of postcolonial theory are men, the body and desires of the colonized woman and her role in the psychic and socio-symbolic world of language and power are made invisible.

CASTRATION ANXIETIES AND BRAHMANICAL LADIES: THE AMBIVALENCE OF AUTHORITY IN THE IDEALIZED HINDU HOME

The marking of the female body as always being elsewhere within language and existing in a libidinal economy of sexualized desire is also informed by the racialization of colonized women. Laws pertaining to "criminal tribes," same-sex desire, and sex work were informed by puritanical discourses of empire, through which British laws constructed the bodies of women, queers, and Hijras in India as sexually depraved. As discussed earlier, Chatterjee argues that nationalists responded to the colonial markings of deviance onto the bodies of colonized women by constructing the idealized Hindu middle-class woman as a figure who mimicked the idealized European mother and wife of empire but who would impart upper-caste values to children and reproduce the culture of "Hindustan." The "Hindu woman" of the postcolonial nation state is at the same time "almost the same but not quite" (Bhabha qtd. in Bolton 6) in relation to the male body who holds authority over her in the domestic sphere and through the patriarchal and masculinist power relations of state governance. The colonized woman in India is also "almost the same but not white" in relation to an idealized European image of femininity. Postcolonial India female mimicry is therefore enacted not only through race and gender but through hierarchies of caste, class, and religion. The upper-caste and upper-class woman can mimic the "almost the same but not quite" authority of nationalist men through her ability to claim power over lower-class and lower-caste figures and through "others" marked as sexually "deviant." In the coveted space of the Hindu home, she is reformed as an ideal mother and wife in ways that resonate with Irigray's concept of female mimicry. Yet the mimicry of women operates alongside and in relation to Bhabha's concept of "mimic men" by considering the phallic authority that upper-caste and upper-class women wield over lower-caste men and women, particularly in the home (Bhabha).

In the film *Fire*, the body of the Dalit man is symbolically castrated through a process of phallic power based not in hierarchies of gender but those of caste-class. In the masturbation scene in *Fire*, Mundu watches the "illegal" and pirated pornographic films that the upper-caste family sells under the table. Mundu does not have the phallic power to reproduce idealized upper-caste and upper-class children and his body is therefore marked as symbolically feminine, which is associated with the elsewhere of materiality, a sex that cannot be named and ordered to suit the biopolitical aims of nation building. One of Mundu's main functions in the household is to serve the mother of one of the male heads of the household, an aged widow who is stripped of all sex, dressed in the traditional white sari that widowed women often wear to signify mourning, purity, and sexlessness. The aged widow in white, Biji, also has no reproductive role left to play. Her body is marked by disability in ways that further construct her as asexual within a normative, bio-political conception of desire that is ageist, ableist, and heteronormative in its scripting of sex as something that women provide as a service to men and the nation through their reproductive capacity. Biji, however, commands a phallic authority over the lower-caste man. While Biji is paralyzed and can no longer speak, her role in the household affords her an authorial power that speaks louder than words, solidified in the casteist and patriarchal system of the normative Hindu middle class family. Without the linguistic authority of voice or an ability to reproduce any more citizens for "Hindustan," Biji mimics a postcolonial authority through her role as an upper-caste mother-in-law whose power comes from her "mother India" relationship to the eldest male son, the figure of nationalist, class-caste, patriarchal, and heteronormative authority in the household.

CHURCH BELLS, SCHOOL BELLS, AND THE MENACE OF DISCIPLINARY POWER: THE VIOLENCE OF CASTE-BASED MIMICRY IN THE FILM FIRE

Biji is given a bell to ring when she needs something which she shrilly commands over Mundu and the daughters in law. Biji's bell echoes through the house, a jarring sound of implicit violence to which others must respond. Mundu, the Dalit man, and the daughter-in-laws, who engage in a queer relationship with each other in the film, are left to jump to her aid when she rings her authorial bell. Without the powers of linguistic speech or embodied reproductive capacity, Biji speaks not with the mimicry of colonial language or the feminine language of the body but through the language of bureaucratic authority. The ringing of the bell signifies her caste- and class-based power, which mimics colonial modes of disciplinary order. Much like the chiming bells of Hindu temples which often bar the entry of Dalits, colonial church bells, and the bells of elite schools born out of colonial histories of Queen's English, her bell is an "almost the same but not quite" mimicry of colonial forms of governance. Like a magistrate banging a gavel to criminalize masturbation and queer desire, the bell is a phallic symbol of power that she wields over the lower-caste servant and queer daughters-in-law, who are left to curse her under their breaths throughout the film while they publicly kiss her brahmanical feet. Mundu is left to masturbate in front of her while Biji rings her bell in protest, a comical scene reflective of the divergent forms of impotent phallic authority produced by Dalit men and aged widows, both "almost the same but not quite" in relation to the idealized symbol of authority, the upper-caste, able-bodied, heteronormative Hindu man (Mehta).

In the final scene of *Fire*, it is the widow, Biji, who tries to set the two female lovers on fire, attempting to burn them alive. While Biji is supposedly "innocent" and is visually represented as being in need of care because of illness, age, and an embodied lack of mobility, she mimes the phallic power of "purity" afforded to upper-caste women by Hindu nationalism. Her violent and murderous gesture of tipping over a torch to set the queer female lovers in the film on fire, in an act of homophobic hatred justified through religious sacrifice, echoes with the cruelties of casteism performed in the implicit violence of her ringing bell to discipline the body of the Dalit man. Postcolonial female mimicry is depicted as a violent enactment of the cruel powers of authority enacted through caste by the upper-caste woman against her male servant and through the violence of Hindu nationalism enacted against those whose desires are constructed as being "impure." The release of the film *Fire* was met with similar acts of setting fire to theatres by Hindu nationalists, many of whom were women. The religious imagery within *Fire* that led to protest and public controversy throughout India offers evidence of forms of colonial mimicry that are offered to the Hindu woman through casteist, classist, heteronormative discourses of religion. The image of the "pure" Hindu woman within religious texts constructs a body that is "almost the same but not quite" in relation to the phallus of Hindu masculinity, depicted in the figure of Ram, a masculinist symbol whose image is constructed against that of the virginal feminine figure of Sita. However, the "purity" of the Hindu woman within a casteist economy of representation and political authority can also be used by women in postcolonial India as a means of asserting phallic power over the bodies of Dalits and queers, left with the sounds of bells ringing in ears and the scars of kitchen fires.

DESIRED DAUGHTERS AND DEAD DAUGHTERS: SEX, "RESPECTABILITY," AND SEXUAL VIOLENCE

I meet inspirational people in Delhi. Yet if inspiration is like taking a breath of fresh air, the remarkable courage of so many of the people I meet is also produced by a wider climate of fear and rage that chokes and suffocates like the exhaust of the Delhi traffic. I meet Rani, an activist who works with a feminist and queer organization based in Delhi. We discuss the relationship between the 2012 Delhi gang rape case and the 2013 decision made by the Supreme Court of India to uphold Section 377. She discusses how certain norms of caste-based sexuality, respectability, and heteronormative moralism were used to narrate the Delhi gang rape case:

> The Delhi gang rape case appealed to everybody, everybody could easily empathize. Nobody throughout the case could say—which of course always, always wrong to say—she was inviting it. But no one in this case could say that she was inviting it. And this mentality of "she is inviting it" always comes from a certain idea of the "respectability" of the woman. If something like this happens and say I that I smoke and they find cigarettes in my bag, my "respectability" quotient will automatically reduce. And if I've had a few drinks, and if I'm wearing something else, like I'm out for a party and I'm dressed differently, then my "respectability" will also reduce. And then my caste will come into play.

Much like the red lipstick example, there are other consumption habits and appearances that express the confounding paradoxes of gender and sexuality within a time of neoliberal capitalism in India. The appearance of "freedom" regarding clothing marked as "Western" as well as consuming alcohol and smoking is often connected to class mobility and the power to consume imported products that are expressive of a neoliberal urban economy within contemporary India. Yet when it is women who consume these products, they can easily fall into the space of darkness associated with lower class-caste behaviour that constructs them through casteist and misogynistic ideology as deserving victims of gender violence.

Rani and I continue to talk about the making of the 2012 Delhi gang rape case as an attack against "India's daughter" in regards to the metaphoric equation of the nation with the idealized Hindu family and woman. Rani asserts that,

> The woman in this case became the symbol of all of those ridiculous names that people came up with. And I do think those names were ridiculous, but she was used as the symbol of these names. The daughter of the nation as the nation would like to see their daughter. If she was a queer woman, a Dalit woman, a sex worker, a woman who drinks and smokes, she would not be a daughter that the nation would want to claim, except for maybe a very few people.

Chowdhury's reading of *Fire* as expressing desire outside of questions of economics is relevant to Rani's assertions. While Chowdhury rightly argues that films like *Fire* support Orientalist understandings of women in the Global South as sexually repressed and in need of benevolent Western feminist salvation, the relationship between sex and the family is often already structured and upheld through an implicit economic rationale tied to colonial history and Hindu nationalism. The child that the nation would not want to claim that Rani refers to, is a sexualized child constructed through class- and caste-based moralisms that advance a certain image of "freedom" at the level of consumption patterns, while an obsessive focus on colonial discourses of bodily "purity" is maintained. Through classist and casteist discourses Jyoti, the 2012 gang rape victim, was constructed as the "perfect victim" in ways that stripped her of sexual agency and saw her gross violation as a loss of gendered Hindu respectability.

Kiran, a queer activist in Delhi, suggests that lingering shame often prevents overt discussions of sex and sexuality within India. Kiran discusses intergenerational shame that is often passed from parents to children. Kiran further suggests that being actively involved in the queer movement and campaigns to repeal Section 377 have made them politically active in regards to feminism, sex work, and other struggles in the region. Kiran discusses generational shifts of attitudes regarding sex and the continued difficulty of discussing desire in contemporary India:

> My generation is maybe becoming better ... But even among my generation it's difficult. I think among the general population, fifty percent of people would rather not talk about sex. Because we are not taught like that and our families are still the same. We are still often raised in joint families and there is a lot of pressure to maintain appearances and to obey our elders. Topics of sex are not discussed, so that kind of awareness has still not reached our country. So that is why this whole 377 issue is very, very important.

Kiran's overarching suggestion is that the politicization of sexuality, its discussion, and questioning offer an entry point into thinking through a broader set of minute political performatives that are microcosms for larger political struggles and challenges. They state,

> I think being part of this movement [the queer movement in India] has made me much broader in my thinking. I think it has changed the way I perceive things. I think it has changed how I think about things like sexism and patriarchy and lots of things that we take for granted that are going on around us every day. It gives us an idea of everything that is wrong in society. When we start talking and thinking about gay rights, it allows us to start thinking about so many other things, about gender and transgender people. In the end, it is the society that is wrong. And it is the society that needs to change. And we end up talking about every problem in India when we begin by talking about sexuality. When we discuss sex and relationships

we begin thinking and speaking about sex workers, about sati.[4]
I've read so many things that have sati and sexuality in the same
bloody paper. And so we have to consider sexism and feminism
and sexuality as all being connected.

Kiran talks about a common refrain that is often heard regarding the
relationship between caste-based and sexual politics, or lack thereof. Kiran
has a professor who suggests that queer rights are "five star rights" as
opposed to the violation of Dalit rights, which are fundamental breaches
of the Indian Constitution but often do not garner global attention, or
transnational solidarity. As an activist who is engaged in ongoing movements to repeal Section 377 and is part of broader left-wing movements
in Delhi and throughout India, Kiran troubles this division at the level
of political strategy. Much like the intersectional approach advanced
historically and transnationally by African-American feminists, women,
and queer people of colour, Kiran's analysis demonstrates the problems
of solely politicizing a singular form of oppression:

> There is a professor of law and politics in my college and he
> talks about Dalit rights. And he is a Dalit himself. When he
> was talking about homosexuality in class he said that gay rights
> are five star rights and so when it comes to human rights, we
> don't need to focus on this. And he says Dalit rights are the
> foremost rights. And I think this is the mentality that exists
> among different groups. So, if I am a Dalit, I think that I am
> already fighting for my rights and I see gay people and gay
> rights as infringing on this. It's the same with women and
> women's rights. They don't want something else to come in and
> take the spotlight, they want their rights coming first. So this
> is where class and caste becomes a factor. So we talk to these
> people and say, what about Dalits who are gay? Are you not
> concerned about them at all? Are you saying that they are not
> doubly marginalized by being both Dalit and gay?

Kiran further remarks upon the existence of queer people and politics
across class lines. Yet at an ideological level, I want to suggest that apart
from politicizing queers across class and caste lines, there is a deeper
relationship between sexuality, class, caste, and colonial ideology in

India. This separation of rights not only is politically divisive but fails to consider how class and sexually are mutually constituted. We can return to the figure of the masturbating servant in Deepa Mehta's *Fire*, one whose overt non-reproductive display of sexuality further marks him as exiled from biopoliotical ideals of the normative family, upper caste and class identity, and an idealized version of the nation. Chowdhury states that Mehta produces a gender-centric text in which alliances regarding gender, sexuality and a deeply flawed discourse of "universal female subordination" serve to erase a politicization of class and caste. Chowdhury writes, "In an effort to show solidarity along gender lines in the relationship between the sisters-in-law, Mehta trivializes the class relations that exist in the household" (147). I agree with Chowdhury's problematizing of the diasporic, middle-class feminist narrator as a privileged native informant called on to narrate stories of gender-based oppression on global stages. However, while class should not be trivialized, the interconnectedness of sexuality, class, caste, and colonial ideology in contemporary India should also be taken seriously. "Sex," when it appears outside of the idealized reproductive unit of a Hindu family is already classed, often in pathological and untouchable ways. Simultaneously, the sexual crimes concealed within the Hindu middle-class home are often expressive of incomprehensible violence, hidden behind the thinly veiled rhetoric of family values.

DENATURALIZING THE "HAPPY HOME": THE "RIGHTS OF THE CHILD" AND RAPE CULTURE

While a comprehensive discussion regarding sexual violence against children in India is beyond the scope of this book, it is important to note that children suffer a great deal of documented sexual abuse and rape. Recent changes to law have attempted to create new legal measures for dealing with the extreme amounts of sexual violence committed against minors in India. Following the release of a national report titled *Study on Child Abuse: India 2007*, the Protection of Children against Sexual Offences Bill (PCSOB) was passed in 2011. Researchers state that PCSOB is an "attempt to protect children against sexual abuse, sexual harassment, and child pornography" (Kumar et al.) and is unprecedented in dealing exclusively with sexual offences against children and in imposing harsher penalties such as longer prison sentences and higher fines for those convicted. The high rates of sexual violence against children in India is deeply disturbing and the passage of the 2011 bill is perhaps a sign that the issue is being taken seriously by those in positions of power. However, given the Supreme Court of India's 2013 decision to uphold Section 377 of the Indian Penal Code, it is important to consider how a discourse of "children's rights" can be used to further criminalize and pathologize queer desire and people. Writing in regards to the 2009 petition by the Naz Foundation to "read down" Section 377, several authors involved in queer and feminist movements in India discuss how the "rights of the child" were used to justify criminalizing same-sex desire by equating consensual sexual practices between adults with child abuse, through the concept of "unnatural acts" ("Rights for All"). The passage of the special bill dealing with the protection of children now criminalizes child abuse separately, thereby offering no justification for upholding Section 377 in the name of the child. Authors writing in regards to child sexual abuse, the rights of the child, Section 377, rape law, and rape culture all discuss the need for a broader critique of the social structures and systems of power that often normalize and justify sexual violence. Researchers maintain that as with other national contexts, the majority of sexual abuse committed against children occurs within localized contexts such as homes and schools and that the perpetrators are often known to children. Researchers further argue that codes of familial, caste, and class-based respectability often contribute to the silencing of the sexual abuse of children (Kumar et al.). The justification of criminalizing same-sex desire and the equation of non-heteronorma-tive sexualities with crimes against children masks the violence of the patriarchal home and the statistical likelihood that many children will experience abuse at the hands of supposedly "normal" and "respected" patriarchs and matriarchs.

STOLEN INNOCENCE AND ABDUCTED JUSTICE: UNMASKING THE OBSCENITIES OF PATERNAL-MATERNAL POWER

While research has shown that children are more likely to be abused within the family home or within institutions of disciplinary power such as schools, the "rights of the child" can continue to provide a convenient tool for justifying violence against sexual minorities. For example, while their precolonial role involved blessing children in religious ceremonies, many Hijras in India are now accused of "abducting" children, legitimizing transphobic violence by the state. Writing in regards to recent accusations of child abduction against Hijras in Bangalore, researcher Dipika Nath argues,

> Because of prevailing myths that hijras habitually kidnap young boys, reports of the arrest of two hijras on criminal charges are a convenient excuse to target the entire community without arousing public outcry.

Pitting the "rights of the child" against queer, transgender persons, and Hijras does little to stop sexual violence against children but does provide a means through which the state can police those who fall outside of heteronormative kinship structures, the same structures in which children are often abused. As researchers state in reference to the 2011 Bill,

> Child sexual abuse is a dark reality ... but in a majority of cases it goes unnoticed and unreported on account of the innocence of the victim, stigma attached to the act, and the callousness and insensitivity of the investigating and the law enforcement agencies, etc. Merely enacting legislation will not be enough unless this is followed by strict enforcement of the law with accountability defined.(Kumar et al.)

Activists writing about Section 377 of the Indian Penal Code suggest that a broader critique of sexual ideologies is needed to prevent the manipulation of discourses of children's rights for conservative political aims. As Voices Against 377 writes,

> There is ... the need to locate csa (childhood sexual abuse) in the larger social and cultural contexts. If sexuality continues to be a taboo subject, with certain expressions of sexuality being virtually demonized, we are working against the possibility of a child being able to protect herself/himself from abuse.

Researchers further note that despite the often gender-centric reading of sexual violence as a crime that men commit against women, male children experience sexual abuse at the same rate as female children, as concluded in the 2007 national report regarding childhood sexual abuse. While male children face the same high levels of sexual violence as female children do, the stigma surrounding same-sex desire may contribute to the inability of boys to report sexual abuse committed by male adults, specifically older members of the family and other authorial "father" figures such as police officers and religious leaders (Kumar et al.). Furthermore, the sexualization of female children can be thought of in relation to a broader sexist and heterosexist ideology in which very young women and girls are sexualized to the point that rape culture and child abuse exist on a continuum, part of what Kannibaran terms the "violence of normal times."

RAPED PROPERTY AND PERFECT VICTIMS:
TROUBLING DISCOURSES OF SEX, COMMUNITY, AND POWER

I meet with Ajay, an activist in Delhi, who has been part of the feminist movement in India for decades. Rather than discussing the Delhi gang rape case solely in terms of gender, he makes explicit reference to class:

An aspiring middle-class girl is being raped. It must be contested. She was raped by a low class of downgraded Bihari migrant men. The Delhi middle classes got angry. The boys started feeling like if this continues we will not have girlfriends when we are visiting malls. Jokes apart, that is one of the real reasons this case got attention. The class dynamics of this case cannot be denied. Why is it that when Soni Sori, a tribal activist, has stones inserted into her vagina, Raisina Hill[5] does not belong to her? Raisina Hill does not belong to a girl who got raped in a bmw. She is also middle class, but the rape took place within the bmw and the man who committed the assault is rich so there is nothing said. A girl in the slums of Delhi, Dalit women in Haryana get raped, Raisina Hill doesn't belong to them. When does Raisina Hill ever belong to them? Who does it really belong to?

In reading the criminalization of same-sex desire alongside the Delhi gang rape case, sex itself can be seen as a tool of power to both constitute marginality and to police bodies in class, caste, and religious terms. The 2012 Delhi gang rape case appealed to the Indian middle class because the body of Jyoti was discursively "purified" while her attackers were associated with darkness and deviance. Disturbingly, in interviewing men and women in Delhi, the Delhi gang rape case is at times equated with sex itself. I speak with young men who work at a local market about my Non Resident Indian (NRI) status, and they suggest that Canada must be a "clean" place, a place where "there is no sex." When I ask what this means, they reference the 2012 Delhi gang rape case and the high levels of rape in India. Rape and violence come to be associated with public, non-reproductive forms of sexuality. The Delhi gang rape case is turned from a gross violation of power and affront to bodily integrity to a denigration of a middle-class woman's imagined sexual "purity" and "cleanliness." By focusing on fantasies of female respectability and chastity, gender based violence is conceived of as a crime against women who are valued as the communal property of men, religious authorities, and nations.

I meet with Madhu, a remarkable feminist and activist who works with a major feminist organization in Delhi. She offers counselling to survivors of domestic violence, rape, and other forms of gender-based violence. When discussing the role that religion, culture, and mainstream ideas of community play in structuring sexual violence in India she highlights the abuse of women during communal riots throughout the country. She states,

> Yes, religion plays a huge role. Not only in terms of the law but look at what happened in Kothra, what happened in Kandamar, what is happening in Kashmir. Muslim women were being sexually assaulted and violated by Hindu men during these riots. Rape is all about power. During these communal riots, the men did not rape a woman because they were sexually aroused; it was an act of communal power.

Madhu states that rape itself is often mystified as being worse than death because of its association with sex and the defaming of women's supposed honour:

> I keep saying this, if I am raped in a locked room and then if I am slapped in a public place, somehow the rape is seen to

be more shameful. Why? Why don't I see these two issues as being the same? Rape has been graded at such a high level in our society. This whole concept of honour and virginity, and the woman being totally violated as a person to the point that many women who are raped try to commit suicide is connected to a very patriarchal mindset. There is such a burden on the woman to "save herself," meaning to preserve her virginity or else she is forever marked as being a "bad" woman. That is why rape in this country has become such a common tool of power.

The 2012 Delhi gang rape case and the mainstream discourse concerning rape, violence, power, and desire is connected to an overarching structure of community, caste, family, and sex as a tool of power in India. The bodies of Dalits, queers, lower classes, and other "others" are already marked as beyond honour because of their distance from the idealized Hindu male patriarch. Their sexual violation is disturbingly normalized and often expresses routine forms of state violence against those deemed to be minorities.

There is a marking of certain bodies as having privatized as opposed to public sexualities in ways that turn certain cases of sexual violation into national tragedies. The exclusion of queer sexuality by law within contemporary India and the growing fear and reports of queer bashing that activists report, implicitly pose lingering questions concerning privatized versus public desires. Bodies seen as "walking sex," because of the imagined space that they occupy outside of the bourgeois Hindu family, are marked for violence, often for death. Beyond the gated malls, beyond the gated communities of "good families" and their "good daughters," the street becomes associated with sex. However, such an association masks the statistical truth that more women in India are often raped and experience domestic violence in the family home rather than outside of it ("100 Women 2014: Violence at home is India's failing"). A privatization of desire and a publicization of certain violence can be read as supporting a certain class and caste agenda. The division of interior from exterior space, of reproductive from non-reproductive sex offers inroads into thinking about the relationship between desire and power within neoliberal India. Far from being a simple privatization of desire through neoliberal capitalism for the middle classes, expressions of desire as consumerism versus non-reproductive desire continue to be stringently regulated at the level of law, state power, and psycho-social norms.

MALL CHIC, GANG RAPE BUSES, AND CRUISING PARKS: SEX, PUBLIC SPACE, AND (IN)SECURITY

The spatial mapping of desire expresses the power of transnational capital to offer middle classes "freedom to" consume, yet freedom from violence is not guaranteed within public space. Chowdhury draws on the early writings of Marx and Engels and their understanding of capitalism in England as leading to the dissolution of the commons, specifically, regarding the aspirations of the bourgeois and the destruction of local systems of trade in favour of global markets. This dissolution of the local can be seen in contemporary India: transnational products and the creation of spaces such as shopping complexes increasingly threaten local systems of agriculture, street markets, and the livelihoods of street vendors and hawkers (Chowdhury). How should the articulations of desire and understandings of gender and sex within the lived spaces and skewed temporalities of a globalized India be read? The India of today advances a certain biopolitics that corresponds to a *necropolitics* (Mbembe). While new forms of capitalist masculinity are celebrated as the norm, farmers throughout the region commit suicide at a startling rate. Indian farmers are emasculated to the point of death in contemporary India, while non heternormative queer masculinities are also excluded from national images of patriarchal success. The bodies of queer people sit somewhere between illusory Internet-based acceptance through neoliberal images of gay branding and the damning material fears of sodomy laws, policing, and the erosion and invisibility of queer public cultures because of threats of violence. Gendered bodies in the material spaces of the village, the city, and the nation continue to be regulated in ghastly ways while private expressions of "freedom" are often articulated superficially through consumer power.

In discussing the Marxist concept of "spatial disruption" Chowdhury states that, "If expansive and destructive policies are inherent to the logic of capital, as Marx and Engels suggest, then the accumulation of capital is inevitably linked to a variety of spatial disruptions" (183). He further suggests that these spatial disruptions can now be seen within contemporary globalization, with the metropolis in the Global South offering an exemplary case of the spatial antagonisms generated by flows of transnational capital. He continues, "Spatial disruptions and increased class antagonisms are similarly an integral part of contemporary capitalism, masquerading in its benign Universalist designation, globalization" (183). As discussed throughout this book, there is a lingering question regarding the relationship between desire and public space within the Indian city. Chowdhury discusses the "globalized" third world city as containing "the worst excesses of globalization," which he suggests are "often most perceptible, because limited space is appropriated at the cost of a majority of the cities populations" (183). The fetish of the commodity, of red lipstick bought in shopping malls and worn at private parties, can be juxtaposed to the erosion of public spaces and practices of desire within the commons.

Rishi, a Delhi-based queer activist, discusses the increased policing of cruising parks for queers, particularly lower-class queers within Delhi, since the 2013 decision to uphold Section 377, India's sodomy bill. Rishi makes reference to the 2009 decision by the Delhi High Court to read down Section 377 and the impact this had on public spaces in Delhi. He further comments on the impact that the 2013 ruling to uphold Section 377 will have on public spaces of desire:

Being gay in India is not a crime. It's just the act of sexual intercourse that is not penal to vaginal that is a crime. After the 2009 judgment, I came to Delhi. And so I've only seen Delhi after this judgment. After this 2009 judgment a lot of things came out in the open and people were okay with talking about it because they felt that they were not doing something legally wrong. And a lot of people used to be harassed by the police—there's a gay cruising park right here in CP [Connaught Place]. What used to happen before the 2009 judgment is that the police would stand outside and when gay men would enter, the regulars, they would take twenty or thirty bucks from them and say, okay we won't pick you up, we won't arrest you if you just give us twenty or thirty bucks. After 2009 this stopped, so people who didn't have the money could cruise or even make-out in the park. You also didn't have to fear being harassed by the cops. And since 2013, the police are now standing outside these places again and are extorting money again. After the

2013 judgment, things like public spaces to cruise if you're gay are very much vanishing from the public open areas.

Drawing on interviews regarding the 2012 Delhi gang rape case, Section 377, and sexuality in contemporary India, I argue that normative desire is regulated within the Indian metropolis spatially. One can read the cultural capital[6] accrued to those who can purchase sexualized consumer objects in relation to the paradoxical violence of the street. The ongoing erasure of basic entitlements to bodily freedom and desire that occur in urban India, offers evidence of the ruses of social mobility through consumer power (McRobbie).

On the night of the gruesome 2012 Delhi gang rape and murder, the young couple were returning from seeing a foreign film in a gated shopping mall, guarded by security guards and electronic surveillance, which exemplifies the consumer-driven freedoms of the neoliberal Indian city. Yet the space of the street that gendered bodies must navigate functions as a site of abhorrent violence. The ironies of desire within contemporary India are further found in the Supreme Court's criminalization of same-sex desire as an affront to "Indian culture" and the declaration that criminalizing rape within a marriage would "threaten the Indian family." At the same time, the Supreme Court of India also promotes the dissolution of local culture in favour of transnational corporatism. The ironies of the Indian state's rhetoric of safeguarding India "culture" are evinced in legal decisions such as the Supreme Court's ruling to support the destruction of local textile mills to make room for the development of shopping malls and other similar policies that promote global capitalism yet construct desire as an affront to national mores (Chowdhury 183-211).

The desire to buy and to visually and aesthetically consume products that are coded as symbols of "freedom" and agency meets the simultaneous enforcement of heteronormative sexual moralities that curtail the sexual freedoms of desiring bodies in the streets. Chowdhury writes of the shopping mall boom within India as being

one representation of the fruits of globalization. As resplendent new buildings packaged with consumer goods, they symbolize private spaces that offer entertainment and luxury products and shield consumers from the vicissitudes of the world outside. (183)

The coding of "the world outside" as one that can and should be kept at bay has specific implications for desiring bodies.

At a protest following the Supreme Court ruling on Section 377, Vanita, a young queer woman, tells me that the Internet is now the main way in which she dates within Delhi and other Indian cities. She states, "Before this, I might have gone to parties or even tried to meet people at college or in certain areas outside. But now, I'll only try on the Internet and I'm kind of scared to do this as well." The upholding of Section 377 of the Indian Penal Code, much like other instances of gender-based violence, constructs the public sphere as an object of fear. While the Internet provides a means of expressing desire, the public nature of online life worlds can also cause anxiety among desiring publics. Furthermore, the use of the Internet as a means of expressing queer and female sexual desire in the city is implicitly informed by class divisions that bar many from access and literacy. Those who are privileged enough can access the Internet and often English-speaking queer and feminist websites, while bodies in and of the streets are increasingly constructed as objects of fear. This erosion of public spaces that carry resonances of sexual desire offers evidence of the contemporary biopolitical workings of transnational capital.

The appetite for sexual desire and pleasure can be satiated in middle-class consumers through the fetish of commodities and sexualized film and advertising images. Yet the body in and on the street of the city comes to be a target for both violence and state protectionism. Krishna, who works with an NGO that runs programs to discuss feminism with men and help prevent violence against women, reflects on the problematic narrative of protectionism that surfaced following the Delhi gang rape case:

I think protectionism is another denial of responsibility. And it comes up quite a lot because within patriarchal norms, men are given the role of protector. And now if violence is coming out in the public sphere it sends this message that you bloody men are unable to protect your women. And it's this narrative of gendered extremes. So it becomes very easy to spin this as a ways to reinforce gender roles. And again this idea of trying to make women afraid is not very new. In 2004, this Delhi police officer, yet again, said that if women are walking alone at night or out late at night, they are provoking violence. We came out very strongly against this. I'm sorry you cannot say this! The state is unable to fulfil its responsibility so they are diverting responsibility by blaming women and even blaming men who are supposed to protect women while the government and police do nothing.

Within a time of privatized neoliberal "freedom" at the level of consumerism, basic constitutional rights are increasingly eroded, while gender and sexuality are spatially regulated. Women are instructed both covertly and overtly to police their own behaviour within public spaces as they cannot rely on empathy or justice from state and police powers. Krishna further states:

We came up with another idea that if you want to be protected, more and more women have to come into the public sphere at all times rather than staying in the house because this type of luxury is not available for all women or men. The luxury to stay in a room or house is not there for women who have to work outside the home. Many women have to be on the road, for work, for survival, for migration. Also, many women don't have shelter or nice living conditions. So if you are walking on the road at nine or ten at night, more women on the road actually creates safety. This creates a safe feeling for other women also. The woman is not alone or stigmatized if lots of women are there.

Krishna went on to critique the role of protector that many middle-class Hindu men adopted following the 2012 Delhi gang rape case:

I think this case has advanced the wrong idea of safety as fear and protectionism. We strongly oppose protectionism. Even when working with men, we say that your role is not to protect. Your role involves fair, responsible behaviour. Your role is to work with other men and to teach those men not to protect women but to respect those women's human rights and their constitutional rights. If a woman is walking on the road then this is her constitutional right. There should be no need for protectionism; men have to learn to respect the constitution. The state and police have to learn to respect their own constitution.

The right to embodied enactments of sexual desire in the public sphere in urban India are often sublimated and projected onto forms of privatized and illusory "consumer power." The threat of violence that faces those who stray from heteronormative Hindu nationalist scripts can cause desiring publics to buy "sexy" products in lieu of sex. Transnational brands of red lipstick are sold by Western multinational corporations, whose global branding is celebrated by the state as a sign of supposed "progress" as economic growth, while the narrow paths that women must walk in urban India are haunted by death. A lack of public space as feminist space can also force women into the interior zones of the family, which is often a site of hidden and excused violence. In the final section of this chapter, I turn to the regulation, erasure, and desire of Hijra bodies within Indian cities.

THE GOLD HAS COME, THE HIJRAS HAVE GONE: THE TRAFFIC OF MYTHOLOGIES

Between the lines of the law are assumptions regarding what sexual violence connotes and who its imagined antagonists and protagonists are. The imagined perpetrator of sexual violence within mainstream discourse is often constructed as a man attacking a woman, outside of the space of heteronormative spousal relationships and the family home. Such a scripting ignores the commonplace acts of sexual and physical violence experienced by transgender persons in India, particularly lower-class and lower-caste Hijras and those engaged in sex work. Devinder, a queer activist, asserts that the gender neutrality of rape law in India is a key legal and political issue that is part of not only the feminist movement but the queer movement:

> If you say it's only women who are raped, where do you put Hijras and transgenders? We recently had a roundtable on sexual offences and we talked about when a transgender person goes to the police station and says that she or he was raped, and Hijras state that the police are always taking off their saris to see if they were raped, inspecting them, and then trying to see

if they have certain genitals or not. That is a violation of their rights. If I am a man and I am raped, I should be respected regardless of gender. If they question me on my identity it's very, very abusive and very violative. That is why the women's organizations always hesitate and there are arguments regarding putting these two categories together in the rape law—women and rape. While it is fine to address the reality of male violence, if rape is considered as a crime of men against women where do you put those who are a third gender or what about gender neutrality? What about gay men who are raped and male sex workers?

The conflicts regarding gender neutrality within rape law in India speaks to deeper ideological tensions between a gender-centric feminist movement and wider struggles for sexual liberation that move outside of strict male-female binaries, not only in India but transnationally. Far from being new, the body of the Hijra—as one that crosses religious and cultural mythologies, that crosses sacred and secular space, that crosses rural and urban life worlds, and that crosses male-female binaries— challenges a modernist form of gender politics that invests in gender binaries and concepts of desire rooted in the patriarchal familial model and a discourse of universal agency. While Hijras have recently been included as members of the "third sex" within the Indian constitution, the 2013 decision made by the Supreme Court of India to criminalize same-sex desire in the region continues to make Hijras vulnerable to abuses of state power. Devinder states that the criminalization of sex and sexuality by Section 377 is often felt most acutely by sex workers and Hijras:

It is often Hijras, transgender people, and others who are visually different and not in positions of economic power that will feel the effects of Section 377 in terms of police harassment the most, I think. I mean, if you look at me on the street, you can't tell that I am gay. If you look at your average gay man or lesbian, people often can't tell who they desire or what kind of sex they have. And if you are upper-class or upper-caste then even if they can tell, they probably won't harass you or will try to get money from you by bribing or threatening you. But Hijras and trans people and poor gay and lesbians who visually look different face on-the-ground harassment from the police. It will only get worse now that this 377 law is in place.

At the time of my interview with Devinder, the Supreme Court of India had struck just down all of the petitions filed by activists, feminists, scholars, and queers against the Supreme Court decision regarding Section 377. Devinder tells me that the next step is the use of a curative petition which would not only critique this legal judgment on Section 377, but offer a broader societal context regarding the effects that the reinstitution of Section 377 has had:

> We gave the court eight different review petitions from eight different people stating all of the problems they had with this decision. And in twenty minutes they supposedly read through four thousand pages and said no. So they basically got on this defensive front where they just wanted to prove the Supreme Court is right. So, we only have one option, which is the curative petition, and when you talk about the curative petition in India, well, it's never been used.

Devinder further discusses the silence and shame surrounding cases of rape and sexual violence against transgender people and queers and its effect on the petition, which the Indian government is now considering. The silence around sexual violence is a further obstacle in proving the societal ramifications of Section 377 as one of its effects has been to prevent queers from speaking publically about their sexuality and sexual violence that they have suffered because of fears of further stigmatization and brutality. As Devinder states,

> So, a review petition is filed a month after a judgment comes out. And a review petition discusses everything that is wrong with a judgment. It just focuses on the judgment. In the curative petition one tries to give accounts of how a judgment has impacted upon the society at large, and the ethical and moral wrongs that have been caused as a result of a judgment. So we'll be talking about how after the 2013 decision to uphold 377 this man in Ahmadabad was raped. He is a thirty-year-old

man who was raped. A transgender woman was raped in Kolkata. We will discuss how homophobia has become rampant.
And those that were always homophobic now have a judicial
and political backing to support them. So this will all be in
the curative petition. But it's very difficult. Because you don't
have a lot of witnesses, you don't have people who are willing
to come forward. Because it's all very, very private. And also,
these things are very hard to prove.

There is a deep difficulty in documenting the routine violence that
queer people in contemporary India endure, making the fight that queer
activists face a very complex one. Yet it is a fight that many activists
are courageously committed to. There is a desire for change on the part
of many feminist and queer activists in contemporary India, many of
whom are often part of an emerging generation that can be counted
as among the majority of the population who are under the age of
thirty-five. Many activists are optimistic about what they see to be a
"changing India" and discuss shifting norms of gender and sexuality
brought about by Internet literacy, migration, education, and a loosening
of the religious conservativsm of their parent's generation. However,
queer and feminist activism is not historically new, nor is it a Western
import or the product of an "India shining." As I have discussed with
reference to Chowdhury's writing regarding the rise of mall culture
and neoliberalism within India, globalization does not necessarily offer
any meaningful change in the lives of the majority of working women
and queer people. The majority of women and sexual minorities in India—those who do not occupy the privileged position of patriarch of
an upper-class and upper-caste Hindu household with ties to financial
capital—will not benefit from an "India shining."

FROM TRAMPS TO TRAMPS:

HIJRAS, SEXUAL ANXIETIES, AND THE POVERTY OF HISTORY

The illusions of sexual "freedom" through the visual fetish of the commodity threaten to displace other histories of desire in the Indian
subcontinent. Manoj, an activist in India, discusses what he sees as the
shifting position of Hijras between feudal and capitalist patriarchy. He
states that the increase in transphobia, impoverishment, and rates of

HIV/AIDS that Hijras face as well as their turn to sex work in India is a relatively new phenomenon:

> In the last decades Hijras are facing problems. Always in history there was a religious space for them. They were in the security system. They were in charge of the security of women. This was two hundred years ago in South Asia. Now that job has gone. Earlier in the feudal system there was some system for the survival of all these various people. Now that system has gone. In the feudal system, the landlord was providing lots of services. Now those services have stopped. In the feudal system, landlords had the responsibility to take care of health, to buy cloth for marriage, to organize all these things. The landlord could also of course beat his people, but no other could beat them. This was the feudal system. That system is gone. The control now becomes one of the state. But now the state has stopped all the services and social welfare for people like the Hijras, but they can still come out and beat the people.

Without romanticizing feudal patriarchies, one can ask how the gendered body within a neoliberal capitalist economy of globalized queer branding becomes a commodity fetish, with the images of sex being used to sell neoliberal products outside of the guarantees of economic vitality and respect in public space for bodies marked as sexually "other." Contrary to the discourse of neoliberal capitalist "progress," figures such as Hijras, who historically performed certain ceremonial rites that insured their economic survival in India, are often no longer afforded respect or financial security. Manoj discusses his memories of Hijras in rural India and the ways in which neoliberal urbanization has affected Hijras:

> When I was young, twice a year for one month so many Hijras would come to my village. The whole community fed them and every year when a son was born or there was a marriage, each family fed them and gave them lots and lots of gifts. There was this very, very pretty relationship with the Hijras. But now, the economic thing has come and this is gone. Marriage is still there, lots of gold has come to the village, lots of expenses, a

big market, but the Hijras have gone. Now the Hijras, what can they do? How can they live? They only have the chance to survive by going out onto the road and begging.

There is an emotional tone to his language, which resonates with all of the incalculable losses of neoliberal globalization. Rather than fulfilling a desire for meaningful relationships and embodied connections with others, the violence of transnational global capital can displace Hijras from their historically intimate and intersubjective connection to many Indians. Hijras within the burgeoning spaces of cities often enter into sex work, which is criminalized by the Indian state and into economies of begging, which can be economically precarious. Economies of sex work and begging can also create contexts in which Hijras are subject to police harassment and abuse. Within the everyday spaces of streets haunted by Victorian moralism and populated by many whose thinking relies on modernist divisions of gender, Hijras can also face both physical violence and forms of epistemic violence that construct them as objects of pity and ridicule. Manoj further states:

I don't know why Hijras have become these outcasts. That I am unable to understand. You know, sometimes I feel very emotional when I remember the Hijras coming there when I was a boy and staying in my village. I remember how nice we treated them and everybody paid them so much respect. And now when I think of them begging and being treated badly, I don't know what has happened to our society.

The respect that was afforded to the Hijra as Hijra declares itself through a different grammar of desire. As I will discuss in the forthcoming chapter regarding masculinities, the loss of this grammar perhaps resonates with constructions of "new masculinities" in contemporary India. The rise of transphobic and homophobic masculinities that draw upon secular language, images of neoliberal machismo, and discourses of nationalist power to classify, defame, and inflict violence on bodies should be seen not as a lack of "progress" within contemporary India but as being reflective of colonial and capitalist ideology. Manoj goes on to discuss Hijras in Mumbai and changing constructions of masculinity in relation to consumer capitalism:

So there was one day when a Hijra died on the road in Mumbai and no one wanted to be associated with it. And this man was saying oh no, I do not know anything about it and said this Hijra is just some beggar so their death does not matter. And then his boss said, no actually I gave you a job on her request because I am old enough to remember when the Hijra had respect. So, many people in our history were supported by Hijras but do not support them today. And maybe part of the problem is that people have become superficial about looks. Maybe they fear that Hijras are aggressive people because of the way they look. Or sometimes maybe they just hate them. Sometimes some religious people might still fear their curse and when they see them begging, they give the Hijras five or ten rupees. There are still some religious people who believe in this religious power of the half male, half female. Vishnu is a half male and half female God. The old forms of masculinity actually said this third gender is a higher, sacred figure. But the new capitalist masculinity says that these Hijras are lower persons who do not deserve respect because of their appearance and maybe because they do not have a lot of money.

Manoj relates how his boyhood village changed over the years. He laments that the rise neoliberal globalization has detrimentally affected Hijras. He says that in this village, "People have cars now. They have money. The gold has come in, but the Hijras, the Hijras are gone." This disappearance of the Hijra from village spaces of sacred ceremony and the transphobic violence of city streets reflect the damaging effects of spatial practices of globalized capital in contemporary India. Yet if spaces are never finished, if cities are never finished, and if the stories and histories of both are never absolute, in the lingering narratives that many still remember, there is an inspirational haunting of revolutionary political work, still yet to be done (Gordan).

In the streets of Mumbai, in an afternoon of traffic, s/he greets me in the city street. S/he is dressed in a cotton sari lined with gold. S/he asks for change. I think of the feminists and activists whom I spoke with in yet another day spent in the exhaust of city smoke. Cities of exhausting rape statistics and colonial laws, of endless rushes of traffic washing over history. I think of the haunting look of both loss and hope in a person's eyes as he recalled all the timeless beauty that he once saw in Hijras as a village boy.

S/he blesses me in the traffic.

[1]Mainstream branding culture often attempts to market South Asian or brown femininities through peace loving, new-age products such as yoga, organic foods, and other appendages of saleable health and healing for the affluent. The relationship between Orientalism, sexism, and racism is apparent in the film *The Darjeeling Limited*. In the film, a group of white men travel to India as part of a spiritual sojourn. The love affair between one of the men and an Indian woman is part of his new-age, therapeutic, and neocolonial journey. Both the Indian subcontinent and the body of the brown woman are used to fulfil apolitical Orientalist fantasies and heal the souls of white men whose fantasies are marked across world maps and the bodies of brown women in ways that are reminiscent of colonial history. As with Said's discussion of the masculinist nature of occidental power over the feminized Orient, the sexual desires of the "Oriental" women are nowhere to be found as the Indian women only exists to serve the fantasies of white, Western men (Weiner).

[2]The phrase "Incredible India" has been used to brand India through tourist advertising by both the Indian government and transnational corporations. Amitabh Kant places the "Incredible India" moment in the context of global politics. The author states,

In 2001-2002, after the destruction of the World Trade Centre, the war on Afghanistan and the attack on Indian Parliament, tourism was down in the dumps in India. It was at the peak of this crisis that the "Incredible India" campaign to position India as a tourist destination was launched. (Kant 1)

[3]Stuart Hall discusses processes of signification where signs come to signify meaning within a sign system in which objects, images, words and other signs convey meaning. The meaning of the sign depends on its difference from others. The sign system in which signs function is derived from specific and shifting histories of meaning. Hall draws on the writing of Jonathan Culler who discusses signification in reference to the linguist Saussure,

For Saussure, according to Jonathan Culler, the production

of meaning depends on language: 'Language is a system of signs.' Sounds, images, written words, paintings, photography, etc. function as signs within language 'only when they serve to communicate ideas…. Material objects can function as signs and communicate meaning too. (31)

Stuart Hall's writing regarding processes of cultural signification are foundational to studies of difference, as Hall uses semiotic and linguistic theory to discuss how embodied, cultural, and class based differences are signified through signs and how these meanings shift across time and space. Furthermore, Hall discusses how the ways that we come to signify and understand ourselves and others is never fixed as signs may not be read in the same ways by different spectators. How people come to signify sexual desire in contemporary urban India may be read in different ways by those whom they encounter in public space, owing to shifting lexicons of gender, sex, sexuality, and urban aesthetics.

[4]Sati is a practice of self immolation in which Hindu women set themselves on fire after the death of their husbands, by throwing themselves onto the funeral pyre of their deceased spouses. Sati is said to have been most prevalent in the 19th century in India and was criminalized in the 1800s. There are several debates regarding the depiction of Sati by British colonizers and Western feminist commentators as a sign of India's supposed cultural and religious tyranny. Orientalism is often used to explain gender based violence and to simplify the complexities of religious practices (Mani).

[5]Raisina Hill makes reference to the space where governmental power rests in India, a spatial metaphor for state authority.

[6]McRobbie draws on Bourdieu's notion of cultural capital as non-financial assets that connote class to specifically discuss the relationship between women's clothing and consumer purchases as significations of economic and social position.

WORKS CITED

Bhabha. Homi. *The Location of Culture*. London: Routledge, 1995. Print.

Bolton, Betsy. "Farce, Romance, Empire: Elizabeth Inchbald And Colonial Discourse." *Eighteenth Century Theory and Interpretation* 39.1 (1998): 3-24. Print.

Bourdieu, Pierre. *Outline of a Theory of Practice*. Cambridge: Cambridge

University Press, 1977. Print.

Chatterjee, Partha. "Colonialism, Nationalism, and Colonialized Women: The Contest in India." *American Ethnologist* 16. 4 (Nov. 1989): 622-633. Print.

Chowdhury, Kanishka. *The New India: Citizenship, Subjectivity, and Economic Liberalization.* London: Palgrave Macmillan, 2011. Print.

Fire. Dir. Deepa Mehta. Zeitgeist Films, 1996. Film.

Gordan, Avery. *Ghostly Matters: Haunting and the Sociological Imagination.* Minneapolis: University of Minnesota Press, 1997. Print.

Nath, Dipka. "Indian police accused of social cleansing after another attack on trans community." *Pink News,* 19 Nov. 2008. Web. 15 June 2015.

Hall, Stuart. *Representation: Cultural Representations and Signifying Practices.* London: Sage Publications, 1998. Print.

Kannibaran, Kalpana. *The Violence of Normal Times: Essays on Women's Lives and Realities.* Delhi: Women Unlimited Press, 2006. Print.

Kant, Amitabh. *Branding India: An Incredible Story.* London: Harper-Collins, 2009. Print.

Kumar, Alok, Asha Pathak, Sandeep Kumar, Pooja Rastogi, Prateek Rastogi. "The Problem of Child Sexual Abuse in India Laws, Legal Lacuna and the Bill—PCSOB-2011." *Journal of Indian Academy of Forensic Medicine.* 34. 2 (April-June 2012): 170-175. Print.

Mani, Lata. *Contentious Traditions: The Debate on Sati in Colonial India.* Berkley: University of California Press, 1998. Print.

Mbembe, J-A., and Libby Meintjes. "Necropolitics." *Public Culture* 15.1 (2003): 11-40. Print.

McRobbie, Angela. "Notes on 'What Not To Wear' and Post-Feminist Symbolic Violence." *The Sociological Review* 52.2 (2004): 97-109. Print.

"100 Women 2014: Violence at Home Is India's 'failing.'" British Broadcasting Corporation, 29 Oct. 2014. Web. 1 Dec. 2015

Said, Edward. *Orientalism.* New York: Vintage Books, 1978. Print.

Shah, Svati P. "Sex Work and Women's Movements." Crea: Count Me In Initiative, 2009. Web. 13 Aug. 2015.

Voices against 377. "Rights for All." *Voices Against 377.* Voices against 377, 2009. Web. 19 May 2015.

Weiner, Jonah. "How Wes Anderson Mishandles Race." *Slate Magazine,* 27 Sept. 2007. Web. 6 June 2015.

Žižek, Slavoj. *Living in the End Times.* London: Verso, 2011. Print.

9.

BETWEEN "HOLY" WARS, HYENAS, HYUNDAI CIVICS, AND A HIJRA

POSTCOLONIAL MASCULINITIES

MODI, MUSLIMS, AND MONSTERS:
GHOSTLY DISTURBANCES

A T THE TIME of writing, Narendra Modi, leader of the Bharatiya Janata Party, a Hindu right-wing fundamentalist party, which has not held a prominent mainstream national political role in India in decades, has been elected as Prime Minister of India. As Jason Burke reports, "The Congress party, which has been in power since 2004 and for all but 18 of the last 67 years, appeared to be heading for its lowest ever tally" (Burke). Living in Delhi leading up to the election of Modi and travelling throughout the Indian subcontinent to conduct interviews for this book, I can sense the emotive resonance of the political that surrounds Modi's campaign and recent, shocking victory. In Kolkata, in Delhi, in Mumbai, and in rural Indian villages, the topic of Modi causes reactionary outbursts of anger, joyous almost religious fervour, and the implicit haunting of partition violence and colonial history that I comment on in earlier chapters of this text. As I discuss throughout this book drawing on the writing of Avery Gordan, haunting and ghostly matters are a serious part of our everyday personal and political reality.[1] In a small effort to use Gordan's exemplary work and the questions posed by haunting, I have drawn on a range of theoretical and methodological frameworks to discuss how gendered violence in India cannot be divorced from the ghostly resonances of colonial, nationalist, and partition history. As Kavita Daiya argues, the partition riots of India and Pakistan were an immediate image and reference point that came to the forefront of public discourse during the Gujarat riots of 2002, which involved religious violence between Hindus and Muslims. Contemporary political anxieties and aggressions resonate with the collective unconscious of an always haunted postcolonial nation.² Modi's role in the Gujarat riots and the unspeakable religious violence that ensued between Hindus and Muslims is deeply disturbing. This election was haunted by the partition of India and Pakistan and bloodshed in the name of flags and faiths in chilling ways. Gordan writes that "The ghost is not simply a dead or a missing person, but a social figure, and investigating it can lead to that dense site where history and subjectivity make social life" (8). Modi's campaign, the divergent emotive and political reactions to this campaign from Muslims and Hindus throughout India, his reference to colonial partition, and his rhetoric and threats regarding deporting Bengali Muslims to Bangladesh are all haunted by histories of violence that simmer below the surface of the everyday in the Indian subcontinent. The social figure of "the Muslim" much like "the queer" or "the woman" can be exploited at divergent moments as a scapegoat to support political whims that generate a mass outpouring of attention, collective emotion, conflict, and pleasure among the mainstream national public. The discursive construction of these social figures in cases such as the 2012 Delhi gang rape case, the 2013 decision by the Supreme Court of India to uphold Section 377, and in Narendra Modi's references to terror in political speeches and in interviews with the press point to the lingering haunting of colonial, nationalist, and religious tensions that simmer as ghostly apparitions beneath the surface of the every day. What was also unsettling to witness was how the truly eerie and potentially frightening election of a man who has been deemed "Israel's best friend in South Asia," (Ronen; Tharoor) who threatens feminist and queer activism in the subcontinent, and whose image projects a decidedly Hindu nationalist face of the nation has been tolerated by so much of India's middle class.

To say Modi's name to many middle-class urban Indians in a neo-liberal "India shining" often led to a litany of jokes. Even after Modi's historic victory, the use of humour was used to manage Modi's deeply controversial election. Many tweeted and blogged about catching flights to Pakistan, and there was an effort to turn this moment of political melancholy into a moment of laughter.³ The use of laughter, a psychosocial device often employed to relieve emotional and political stress, resonates with Gordan's understanding of haunting as unresolved tensions that unsettle our contemporary lives. As psychoanalytic thinkers argue, jokes offer a momentary collective release of latent anxieties and aggressions (Freud). Disturbing histories of partition violence that cannot be reconciled and that still linger in contemporary India are ghostly reckonings, managed by psychosocial tools such as humour. I will discuss the use of humour and comedic discourse throughout this chapter in reference to masculinity in India. What is of interest in the wake of Modi's victory is how his contentious campaign, persona, and election to the post of prime minister reflect an uncanny and often paradoxical political moment in the Indian subcontinent. A thorough discussion of what Modi's victory might mean is beyond the scope of this book, as much of this text was written during Modi's election campaign, before his election to the post of prime minister. Despite press in the Indian subcontinent suggesting that many wealthy sections of the Muslim population voted for Modi, others suggest that India's poor Muslims, often those in villages and smaller states, will be further marginalized by Modi. Writing in *The New York Times*, Gardiner Harris states,[4]

> Now, after a landslide electoral triumph Friday by the Bharatiya Janata Party of Hindu nationalists, some Muslims here said they were worried that their place in India could become even more tenuous.

The tenuous place of the Muslim, the queer, and the woman who stray from Hindu nationalist reproductive ideals is expressive of the relationship between an "India shining" moment and the making of a biopolitical "New Indian citizen" that is implicitly gendered, racialized, and classed.

Puar and Rai write of the discursive and political linkages between the figures of "monster, terrorist, and fag" within the global "war on terror." Drawing on Foucault's writing on monstrosity, the authors discuss how the monster in Foucault's historic writing is a figure of sexual and moral perversion, one that exists to be both exterminated and corrected. Puar and Rai argue that the discursive construction of terrorists as monsters within the global "war on terror" queers Muslim bodies, making them perverse to the nation-state through a discourse of constructed monstrosity that is implicitly sexualized. The authors write,

Today, we find the two figures of the monster and the person to be corrected in some ways converging in the discourse of the terrorist-monster. Which is to say that the terrorist has become both a monster to be quarantined and an individual to be corrected. It is in the strategic analyses of terrorism that these two figures come together. (121)

While Puar and Rai make explicit reference to the American political landscape, the language of monstrosity used by American leaders to refer to Osama Bin Laden has also been recently used by Narendra Modi to discuss the figure of the terrorist within India. Modi's comments concerning terrorism are disturbing because the figure of the terrorist is both associated unapologetically with the Pakistani body and with unidentified objects of otherness. Modi's constructed terrorist could easily be conflated with the Muslim. Modi states that terrorism is "a hydra-headed monster" that must be tackled "through multi-pronged strategy." Modi also draws on metaphors of the terrorist as not only a non-citizen, but a non-human ("We Shall Overcome"). In the context of Modi's new India, queerness, Muslimness and monstrosity attach themselves to certain bodies and acts, producing a biopolitical face of "Hindustan" that is racialized, gendered, sexualized, and classed with "failed" queer masculinities and "failed" Muslims being violently excluded and disciplined.

This violent exclusion and torture of "the other" happens in ways that demonstrate the relationship between sexual, moral, and national forms of supposed perversion that construct some as monsters to strip certain bodies of not only citizenship rights but basic claims to humanity. Discussing terrorism, Modi further states,

Terrorism has no boundaries such as national, geographical, social or emotional. This is a ruthless and callous manifestation of a sick mind whose only intention is to acquire political power so that he can rule. ("We Shall Overcome")

Modi's biopolitical invocation of the terrorist as someone with a "ruthless and callous manifestation of a sick mind" points to the construction of a subhuman or inhuman monster figure that is repeatedly referred to as being afflicted with a "sickness." When this language of monstrosity is coupled with Modi's support of the American-led war on terror, his mention of Pakistan, and references to Islam, one can see how Rai and Puar's arguments regarding the construction of "monsters" as "terrors" and "terrors" as "Muslims" through a historically gendered language of deviance become exceedingly determinative of how the bodies of "others" are constituted within contemporary India.

Rai and Puar discuss how the civilizational anxiety, which is at-tached to the body of the non-normative sexual subject, and figure of the terrorist are part of the same modernist ethos. They discuss how the language of American terrorism attaches itself to bodies across national lines: "In the contemporary discourse and practice of the war on terrorism, freedom, democracy, and humanity have come to frame the possibility of thinking and acting within and beyond the nation-state" (139). This possibility of thinking and acting beyond the nation-state and rights of citizens is clearly seen in the detention of prisoners in Guantanamo Bay, a prison facility that exists in a lim-inal space outside the boundaries of America, imprisoning citizens deemed to be terrorists from many countries throughout the world. Modi implicitly creates an image of the terrorist as existing outside of national borders and claims to citizenship through his statement that: "Terrorism has no boundaries" and further constructs this figure of the terrorist as a subhuman, monstrous figure. In a speech regard-ing "monster terrorists," Modi made comments at a rally in Bengal, suggesting that Bengali Muslims could potentially face deportation to Bangladesh. At the rally preceding his sweeping landside victory he stated, ""You can write it down. After May 16, these Bangladeshis better be prepared with their bags packed" (Ghosh "Come May 16"). He went on to suggest that Muslim voters were being targeted as "votebanks" and stated, "You are spreading the red carpet out for the Bangladeshis for the sake of vote bank politics"(Ghosh "Come May 16"). For my purposes, what is of importance regarding Modi's threat to potentially deport "Bangladeshis," which commentators suggest also refers to Bengali speaking Muslims (Murshid) is how—much like the figure of the "international terrorist" constructed by the United States government to justify detaining, torturing, and deporting Muslims post-September 11 despite having national citizenship—the Indian Muslim can quickly be constructed as a non-citizen who can be forcibly removed from the nation.

These incidents, coupled with public statements made regarding "monster terrorism," offer evidence of how a Muslim within the contemporary political moment in India cannot be an Indian and an Indian cannot be a Muslim. Navine Murshid argues,

> At a time when Hindu nationalism is on the rise ... it is perhaps not surprising that anti-Muslim sentiments, whether anti-Pakistani or anti-Bangladeshi, find support among Indian politicians as well as the Indian masses. (Murshid)

Modi's comments regarding Muslims and Islam at recent public rallies and in the Indian press can be read in relation to the following: The Gujarat riots of 2002, which involved horrific Islamophobic violence; Modi's role in orchestrating these riots; his refusal to publically apologize; and a global "war on terror," of which Modi is an active supporter. The disturbing ways that monstrous "subhuman" deviance attaches itself to Muslims became apparent even less than a week into Narendra Modi's term as prime minister of India.

The "hydra-headed" monster that is referred to in Modi's rhetoric resonates with George Bush's propaganda regarding Islam and Bush's construction of "the Muslim" as one that cannot correspond to the figure of "citizen." Rai and Puar assert that this is a deeply modernist construction of Islam that does a deep injustice to the rich complexity of Islam and its many genealogies, which span continents and pre-date Orientalism. As I discuss making reference to the contradictory ethos of the "No Going Back" refrain uttered by queer activists and the precolonial genealogies of Hijras and queer desire in India, modernist constructions of political subjectivity and identity do a deep disservice to the history of India itself. For example, as Flood notes, the city of Delhi has a long Sultanate Princely history of Mughal rule that predates colonial rule. Rather than being a "minority," the Muslim body plays an integral role in Indian history and in the making of spaces in urban Indian cities. The language of monstrosity is not specific to Indian history but to colonial forms of disciplinary power that rely on Western imperialist categories of science to apprehend "non-normative" bodies that are antithetical not to India and Indian history but to an idealized European colonial subject. Flood makes reference to the disciplinary divisions of Orientalist discourse in South Asia: "the disciplinary divisions written into Orientalist discourses on South Asia at its inception frustrate the assumption of a diachronic approach to the material culture of the region" (95). The material culture of the region found in artifacts such as the Delhi mosque and Qutb Minar predate the construction of the "monster terrorist," which resonates with the American government's "terrorism studies" project and its ties to disciplinary forms of colonial governance in which excluded bodies are produced through categories of Western science, tied to a history of making racially and sexually "pure" colonial subjects (Flood; Rai and Puar). Puar and Rai discuss discourses of terror and the historical relationship between idealized racial and sexual subjects and colonial discourses of civility. They state that

> The forms of power now being deployed in the war on terror-
> ism in fact draw on processes of quarantining a racialized and
> sexualized other, even as Western norms of the civilized subject
> provide the framework through which these very same others
> become subjects to be corrected. (118)

In contemporary India, the quarantining and correction of both the "monster" Muslim and queer body happen within an ongoing genealogy of colonialism. As mentioned in this book, precolonial histories should not be romanticized as free from oppression. However, outside of the disciplinary quarantine of the language of "terror" and the rule of law, the spatial construction of Indian cities is historically impure in ways that turn Modi's modernist discourse of "terrorism" and neoliberal Hindu masculinity, funded by Western multinational corporations, into a bad joke.[5]

The construction of "others" as not being part of "our culture" is not only an act of epistemic violence against those marked as "other" but also misrepresents the polyphonic and culturally chaotic beauty of India itself. Puar and Rai go on to discuss the relationship between sexuality and similar modernist anxieties:

> the uncanny monster-terrorist-fag is both a product of the
> anxieties of heteronormative civilization and a marker of the
> noncivilized—in fact, the anxiety and the monster are born of
> the same modernity...the monster-terrorist-fag is reticulated
> with discourses and practices of heteronormative patriotism

but also in the resistant strategies of feminist groups, queer communities, and communities of color. (139-140)

In the context of the Modi moment in an "India shining," how do anxieties regarding sexuality, gender, and "terror" attach themselves to certain bodies to justify the construction of "non-citizens"? The 2013 decision to uphold Section 377 of the Indian Penal Code, a ruling made shortly before Modi's electoral victory, challenges all rights of "citizenship." The uncanny figures of the "terrorist-monster-fag" also emerge within the Modi moment and a wider context of a neoliberal "Hindustan" through a language of monstrosity, disease, and dysfunction. In considering the "monster terrorist" in relation to the "fag" in India, what unites Modi's language of monstrosity with homophobia and Hindu right-wing ideology is a similar language of mental and physical disease and a discursive making of bodies that have no nation, and can therefore be exiled in both legal and symbolic terms.

The Muslim body within Modi's India, an India that is increasingly politically aligned with Israel and the global "war on terror," can become queer to the nation in ways that resonate with Amit and Puar's reading of the "Muslim terrorist" as a figure associated with sexual perversion in conservative American discourse. What is interesting and may be specific to the Indian context lies in how Puar's homonationalist body, an ostensibly proper queer subject associated with Western capital and whiteness in ways that make such a figure viable for the biopolitical aims of the state, is not wholly applicable to the Indian context given the 2013 decision to criminalize same-sex desire. Puar argues that increasingly idealized queer bodies, namely affluent white gay men, are associated with market vitality and used to pink-wash nations against the imagined anachronistic sexual backwardness of "terrorist" others (Puar). Yet within a neoliberal Hindu nationalist India of Modi and money, both the Muslim and the queer are made deviant to an idealized image of an "India shining."

There is an implicit relationship between Modi as a figure of monied, aggressively chauvinistic, heteronormative success, and new national ideals of Hindu masculinity. As my conversations with many feminists, queers, activists, and everyday people in India attest to, the power of hegemonic masculinity and its attending forms of justified violence move across a range of bodies. Within an "India shining," the scripted patriarch of the day can easily turn from a man commanding a position of economic power to an upper-class and upper-caste woman wielding power over the poor and queer of the nation.

I speak with an activist in India who discusses the election of Modi to PM as a specific threat to religious minorities, both male and female. She makes reference to Muslim women raped in Kashmir and Gujarat by Hindu men and to the bodies of Dalits, male and female, shamed, abused, tortured, and cast out of the bounds of humanity by a religiously driven patriarchy that changes shape and form faster than any shape-shifting figure from Hindu mythology. I speak with a young man from the Northeast of India who tells me of being bullied and abused by female teachers at his college by upper-caste Hindu women whom he says enact worse forms of patriarchal violence than any man.

THE SHAPE OF SCAPEGOATS:
CONSTRUCTIONS OF MIGRANT MEN IN A NEOLIBERAL INDIA

Pierre Bourdieu suggests that "nothing classifies someone more than how she or he classifies" (19). Just as Modi used the language of monstrosity as part of an Islamophobic rhetoric to constitute Muslims as not only antithetical to the figure of the Indian citizen but as inhuman, the "monster" was also invoked in the Delhi gang rape case to pathologize migrant men. Following the 2012 Delhi gang rape case, Prime Minister Manmohan Singh made monsters, not out of hegemonic heteronormative masculinities or rape cultures, but out of migrants. *The Hindustan Times* discusses instructions that Singh gave police following the Delhi gang rape case:

> Police should not lose sight of the human rights of citizens and should be prepared to deal with challenges associated with urbanisation that is assuming "a monstrous shape." ("PM Warns of 'Footloose Migrants'")

The discursive invocation of a "monstrous shape" was tied to the impoverished migrant man, seen to possess an uncontrollable aggression. While those who murdered Jyoti committed monstrous acts of violence, the case was politically used to symbolically redraw national boundaries. The impoverished man was discursively and ideologically produced as the antithesis of the "Indian citizen." The monsters made out of migrant men aligned the 2012 Delhi gang rape case with the interests and ideologies of a neoliberal India in which "citizenship" is synonymous with the urban, Hindu middle class who are the benchmark not only of citizenship but humanity. The pathologization of migrants as inhuman and deviant fails to ask broader questions about how and why migrants are displaced within urban centres, often subject to harsh forms of economic, psychosocial, and political violence (Atluri).

The many interviews and conversations I have been lucky enough to have with feminists, activists, and many others in India suggest that the 2012 Delhi gang rape protests are expressive of a deep level of frustration on the part of many. I speak with Naisha who participated in the Delhi gang rape protests and is involved in contemporary feminist campaigns in Delhi and throughout India. She comments on the underlying emotions and impetus behind the Delhi gang rape protests of 2012:

> What happened was that in 2012 there was a huge aggression within the national community and specifically in Delhi, an aggression on the part of the people against the government. People treated this case as a failure of the government, a failure of law and order.

Efforts to redirect public rage towards the figure of the impoverished migrant man, can be read as an attempt by state power to colonize the emotions and actions of politicized people to serve conservative interests. Omesh, an activist in Delhi, further states,

> It was very easy to say this is a problem because they were poor people and there are not very good jobs for the poor and poor migrants. They were Bihari. And it was easy to blame them. There is often blame placed on Biharis because it is a place where many poor migrants in Delhi are from. And maybe it was also that there was this feeling of "how you dare to do this to our woman," from the Hindu upper class.

Following the 2012 Delhi gang rape protests and the use of water cannons against protestors in Delhi, former Prime Minister Manmohan Singh further stated that India was a "functioning democracy" and suggested that a loss of faith in the Delhi police should be restored to protect "human rights" and "citizenship." The ability for political leaders to construct migrant men as subhuman, not counted as "citizens," is demonstrative of the shaky nature of Indian citizenship and conceptions of humanity within a neoliberal India. Those without a place in a neo-liberal agenda that privileges profit, foreign investment, and aggressive competition hold no place as full citizens within the nation-state. Omesh further comments on political governance in Delhi:

> I don't think in any way, Delhi is able to represent India. Delhi very much looks to Washington, to New York as a model. If you see the road, the hospital, the transport, Delhi is totally different than other Indian cities. So when all work is central-ized in Delhi, when all opportunities are centralized then what will happen? People will try to use any chance to survive. If so many migrants are coming to Delhi for work then this is the government's problem. They have made Delhi the centre and themselves in Delhi the centre and they ignore so much of the country. If you gave people the same opportunity in other states, then why would people come here?

Blaming impoverished migrant men for gender based violence diverts attention away from larger failings within state bureaucracy, gover-nance, and the deeply unequal distribution of wealth. Such a strategy makes the misogyny of migrants into a "monstrosity" in ways that normalize the madness of middle-class, heteronormative, brahmanical patriarchies (Rege).

LIGHTEN UP?
THE COLLECTIVE UNCONSCIOUS OF POSTCOLONIAL LAUGHTER

Journalist Libby Perves shocked the left-leaning sentiments of many when, following the Delhi gang rape case of 2012 and the subsequent global media focus on violence against women in the Indian subcon-tinent, she referred to Indian men as "laughing hyennas." In an article titled "Indian Women Need a Cultural Earthquake," Purves wrote that "hyena-like" contempt towards women in India is the norm. Purves drew on *Jungle Book* imagery of wild, animalistic men who subject women to dehumanizing ridicule and violence (Purves qtd. in O'Neil). As discussed in the introduction of this book, many Western journalists and commentators who have used this case to pathologize Indian masculinities have made little mention of the sickening assault of Awindra, Jyoti's male friend, who was also subject to traumatic violence on the night of the 2012 Delhi gang rape case and who disappeared from many narratives of the case arguably because of efforts to construct the case as one the victimization of brown women by brown men (Roy). Journalists and bloggers throughout the world responded to Purves's writing by pointing out the racist undertones of her comments. Others commented on the clear hypocrisy of her writing by making reference to the commonplace sexism and gender-based violence found in the supposedly "free West;"others wrote in defence of the Indian man, citing examples of loving, non-hegemonic masculinities and pro-feminist male activists and leaders in the subcontinent (Sharma; Roy). Yet I make reference to Purves's article because her racist reading of the Indian man offer evidence of the colonial baggage that discussions regarding gender-based violence in India often carry. Brendan O'Neil discusses Purves's article and the colonial history that drags at the heels of her racist rhetoric:

> Echoing those Victorian ladies who visited faraway continents and were shocked by the sexual depravity of foreign menfolk, Purves claimed that in the subcontinent "sexual harassment and assault" are looked upon as a "male birthright," especially in Delhi, where there are[as Purves argues] "tens of thousands of newly urbanised men, from villages still almost medieval." (O'Neil)

Purves's makes an Orientalist and nonsensical argument that implicitly constructs the West as having developed beyond patriarchy. The irony of this idea of Western "progress," which the author compares to a colonial construction of a "medieval" India lies in how Purves's authority to make sweeping and racist statements about India is haunted by the racist arrogance of all those white Victorian ladies who came before her. The joke that history tells is in the anxious will on the part of benevolent white Westerners to save the "oppressed Indian woman" in ways that mask how contemporary racism is informed by colonial history. The further joke of Western missionary narratives of salvation lies in the ongoing economic profit that Western nations enjoy, through the continued impoverishment of formerly colonized countries such as India. Purves can and does take her role as a benevolent heroine of the universal and universally oppressed Indian woman against the universal oppressor, the Indian man in ways that forego any mention of the obscene privileges that many in the West can access, as opposed to the oppressive conditions that define many people's lives in the Global South. The harsh realities of poverty and politics interrupt a seamless narrative of both global sisterhood and universal patriarchy. Yet Purves's racist rants are also interesting because they use the trope of laughter to discuss Indian masculinity. It is to these jokes—the jokes that colonial history tells and the jokes that masculinity tells—that I turn.[6]

Kavi, a prominent queer activist in Delhi, discusses the use of jokes in India as a common and everyday act in which gendered and sexual norms are reinforced at the level of speech and in the forming of social bonds between men. Kavi tells me that if I am unable to enjoy a sexist joke, I might have a difficult time in Delhi. He states, "Every other sentence in Delhi ends with a sexist joke, so if sexist jokes offend you, you might have a bad time in Delhi." Kavi subsequently says that hearing both sexist and homophobic jokes in India can be used as opportunities to create spaces of dialogue regarding sexual politics in India:

These days, all I do is preach. I try to give more and more examples of how feminism and queer people are part of India and our history. If I'm at a metro station and I hear some sexist and homophobic joke, which happens all the time, I try to give more and more examples. I try to respond and sometimes I just try to say something so crude in Hindi that they don't know what to say. And then I give them examples from the Gita and from the Veda and from Khajuraho temples of how all these different kinds of sexuality, have always been part of this country. So the way of putting these ideas forward changes depending on the audience and context, but at the end of the day, whether in jokes or speeches, you are putting forward the same content. So whatever I have spoken about to you today, this is the same

message I am putting forward in all these every day incidents.
I think that doesn't change.

While Kavi finds space for dialogue in the joke, one can also analyze the psychosocial nature of the comedic.

In his 1929 essay, "Jokes and their Relation to the Unconscious" Sigmund Freud discusses the joke as revealing a deeper anxiety that is both released and contained in its telling. The joke reveals as much as it conceals; not only for those who share in its telling and reception but as an expression of the collective cultural, national, and communal unconscious of jokes taken out of context, which in a different time and place might make little sense. To "get the jokes" of gender and sexuality in India, to "get the jokes" told by left-leaning feminist and queer activists, or the jokes told by patriarchal men, one must in some way share in the collective unconscious of a group and the anxieties that jokes both release and preserve. The joke takes the temperature of the collective anxieties within a place and among a community or group of people who share in similar fears and desires.

IMPOTENT ECONOMIES:

MASCULINITY, CLASS, AND ENGENDERED FEARS

Kalsang, a Delhi-based activist reflects on masculinity following the Delhi gang rape protests of 2012 and argues that the economic realities of a neoliberal India affect the anxieties and aggressions of men and their attitudes and enactment of violence against women:

> One thing is, violence happens because the social norm and the notion of masculinity have not changed. The situation is that now the girls are growing up to have better capability, better capacity than the boys. So there is now a huge opportunity for girls in the economic sector. And in South Asia, there are not jobs for everyone. So the boys have a fear that once the economic opportunities have to be distributed, all these girls in my class will be competing with me and they will be better at securing a job than I will. More and more, I think that is one fear young men have.

Kalsang goes on to discuss the relationship between what he terms an "old patriarchy" and a new structure of labour relations and migration patterns that are also relevant to feminist and queer movements in contemporary India:

> There is an overall fear that men have, that they are not able to control women, not able to be leaders economically, not able to be breadwinners. So this is the one fear of young men. Even if they want an equal partner, they have this anxiety of how they will control their partner. So if they can see girls in their class, girls in the workplace as equals, this might change things. And we are interested in how they can be taught to see these women as equal in every area, through a new imagination. Many men are living in this contemporary scenario where women are in their classes and in the workplace and will compete with them as equals, but they are trying to practice gender relations and form relationships as if they were living fifty years before and it is not possible. The fear is that they have seen this one way of acting when they were growing up, this one system, this one way men and women related to each other and now they want to practice this same system in a scenario that has changed.

From interviews done with feminist and queer activists in contemporary India, the potential generational changes within family and work structure in India are often discussed as a site of both potential backlash and political change. Rape, physical, and emotional violence is often overlooked because of the patriarchal ownership that men claim over women within caste-based organizations of the family. The Supreme Court of India's decision regarding Section 377 and the decision not to criminalize marital rape valorizes the heteronormative bourgeois family structure and legitimizes sexual violence, contrary to the rights enshrined in the Indian Constitution. The fear among many in contemporary India appears to be a potential change to family structures, systems of inheritance, desire, sexual agency, and kinship that may be brought about by queer relationships and by more women entering the workforce. Yet this potential disruption of the space of the conservative family often brought about by globalization and urbanization may have uneven effects in its ability to usher in new ideas of femininity, masculinity, and "family" itself.

CAST(E) ING AGAINST TYPE:
STAGING MASCULINITIES IN "HINDUSTAN"

Uma Chakravarti discusses the historical relationship between gender, caste, and brahmanical patriarchy[7]:

Caste hierarchy and gender hierarchy are the organizing principles of the brahmanical social order and despite their close interconnections neither scholars of the caste system nor feminist scholars have attempted to analyse the relationship between the two. (579)

Moving away from speaking strictly about the oppression that upper-caste men have historically enacted against lower-caste men and women, Chakravarti discusses the overlapping nature of gender and caste. He writes that,

A marked feature of Hindu society is its legal sanction for an extreme expression of social stratification in which women and the lower castes have been subjected to humiliating conditions of existence. (579)

I want to consider how an ideal of brahmanical patriarchy that involves hegemonic masculinist control over property, labour, and female sexualities acts as a model that both women and lower-caste men are violently regulated by but paradoxically taught to mimic. Chanpreet, another activist in India, suggests that within contemporary urban India, women who occupy positions of authority often enact forms of epistemic violence that mimic patriarchal authority:

A successful woman, you will find, is often more patriarchal than a successful man. You see this playing out very much in class-and caste-based terms in India. You see this through the kinds of violence upper-caste women are doing against their own daughters-in-law. And, if they are holding any office you will find that sometimes you see this perverse enjoyment among these women who start shouting at their junior men. I have seen this in the corporate office. Also, you see it in schools. I have witnessed women teachers suppressing women's sexuality and bullying the students.

Scholars writing about oppression argue that those who are excluded from positions of authorial power often commit similar acts of violence as their oppressors (Freire). Women who hold positions of class and caste-based power within urban India, can and often do use masculinist forms of authority that mimic brahmanical patriarchal power. Similarly, men of all classes often use bodily power through sexual and physical violence to regulate women. Chakravarti states that historically, upper-caste women were controlled, disciplined, and violated by the caste system through an obsessive control over their sexuality. Much like other bids to racial superiority, caste miscegenation had to be guarded against to prevent upper-caste women from diluting the imagined purity of upper-caste lineages. Chakravarti argues that,

The central factor for the subordination of the upper-caste women ... lies in the need for effective sexual control over such women to maintain not only patrilineal succession (a requirement of all patriarchal societies) but also caste purity, the institution unique to Hindu society. (579)

Upper-caste women are often valued based on their imagined bodily purity and a focus on caste-based marriage. One can ask how class and gender circulate as forms of power wielded at different times by rich women and poor men. Within a neoliberal India of "new women" whose imagined progress is defined in consumerist and capitalist terms, the "new woman" of India can exercise patriarchal violence against lower-class and lower-caste men and women, while deep anxieties remain concerning her reproductive and sexual control. Both the 2012 Delhi gang rape protests and ongoing contestations regarding the 2013 criminalization of same-sex desire in India should be understood in reference to wider discourses of masculinities and sexual anxieties.

In the similar ways that feminist and queer politics can be easily co-opted by white Western imperialists to suggest that India has not "progressed" and requires missionary salvation, the energies and work of activists and feminists who were part of the 2012 Delhi gang rape protests could be used by conservative forces to support narratives of female purity and protectionism. As Chakravarti states, "The purity of women has a centrality in brahmanical patriarchy... because the purity of caste is contingent upon it" (579). Jagat, an activist and feminist who is part of new and ongoing social movements regarding sexual politics in Delhi, discusses how mainstream media coverage and protests against gender-based violence may implicitly support patriarchal thinking and structures of familial and communal honour:

> There's lots of domestic violence. Lots! There are many dowry deaths, suicides, and emotional violence. And when public rape is going on and there is a big protest I think many times it can be in the name of community and public honour, not in the name of basic human rights. Because when it's in the home, many of these middle-class people say nothing. If you really respect human rights you have to respect everyone--all the time. And a sex worker? The middle classes will not consider this case or protest it, violence against Africans will not be considered or protested against, crimes against Dalits will not be considered as worthy of attention or outrage, the wife of rich man who is raped and beaten will not be talked about, dowry deaths remain silenced. The middle classes often only care if it is public. And if the assailant is from higher caste, they don't say that it's a problem. If it is a lower-caste man, Muslim man, a foreign man like an African or someone from a poorer region in India that commits a crime of rape, then they take issue with it. Then the middle class cares because they see it as that community trying to destroy their honour through the body of the woman who is not a person but just some symbol of their honour.

The concept of "communal honour" among the Hindu middle class was a recurring theme in interviews conducted with feminists and activists throughout the region. Constructions of honour and respectability among the Hindu middle class, often located in the body of the Hindu woman, are connected to debates regarding Section 377 of the Indian Penal Code, used to criminalize same-sex desire. What unites these two political discourses is the linking of sexuality, desire, and agency to caste, class, religious, and racial "purity." Jagat, a queer activist in Delhi, discusses the community and caste-based shame that his parents have faced since he came out of the closet and he began to publically discuss being queer. He talks about the extreme pressures to keep up gendered and sexual appearances within religious and caste-based "communities":

> When you talk about homophobia, I think that homophobia is not affected by class and caste in the sense that it has become completely normal for there to be homophobia among all castes in India. If there are gays, there will be homophobia. And if I'm from an upper-caste, the whole issue of respect and honour comes into play. I come from a Rajput family and my parents have so much shit going on because of the community stigma and gossip. And if you go to another family, it's not as though because these people come from a lower caste they don't have honour and community appearances to uphold either. India is very community bound. Everyone worries about judgment from the community.

Hindu nationalist ideals of masculinity along with a will to maintain and uphold communal constructions of honour that are tied to religion, culture, class, and caste are used to discipline sexuality across caste and religious lines. The regulation of upper-caste female sexuality can be read as corresponding to the disturbingly normalized abuse of lower-caste and lower-class women. Simultaneously, male sexualities across the spectrum also act as sites of shame if they are seen as being unable to fulfil the idealized role of the patriarchal head of household who is able to control women's bodies. Saurabh, a queer activist in Delhi, tells me that his status as an out queer man in India is used to defame his masculinity:

> If I say no, I don't want to have sex with women, I don't want to have this patriarchal power over women, then many people assume that I am no longer a real man because I am a gay man and a progressive and feminist man. So when you talk about masculinity and patriarchy these have always been issues that are connected, and especially in India. That's how we have always thought of things in India. The man is the head of the household and he is married to a woman, and he is in charge of everything and in charge of her.

Seeing the 2012 Delhi gang rape protests as being ideologically and politically tied to the 2013 protests against the Supreme Court's decision to criminalize queer desire allows a revisioning of masculinity. These moments also offer a chance to consider the production of failed masculinities within an India shining in which the successful man is an idealized and heteronormative Hindu middle-class patriarch, set against other images of masculinity often scripted for death.

HANGING FARMERS AND PUBLIC HANGINGS: GRAVEYARDS OF MASCULINITY IN AN "INDIA SHINING"

The mass suicides of farmers throughout India can be considered in relation to broader systems of both neoliberal capitalism and structures of patriarchy in India. Ranjana Padhi discusses the relationship between an inability to fulfil traditional patriarchal roles of archetypal masculinity and farmer suicide throughout India because of farmer indebtedness. Padhi tells the story of Najam Singh who drowned himself in the Mansa district in 2000. Singh was heavily indebted and was unable to receive further loans. She writes that Singh "had got his sister married and his younger brother too and his loans were over Rs 3 lakh [300,000 rupees]" (54). When Singh could not obtain further loans to cover the costs of the martial ceremonies and dowries he committed suicide, a deeply disturbing example of the casualties of both masculine norms and neoliberal capitalism. In the narratives that outline farmer suicide throughout India, an inability to fulfil gendered obligations as a husband, a father, or a brother owing to agrarian crises is what finally pushes farmers to take their own lives. Padhi discusses the suicide of Dhyan Singh, a North Indian farmer who committed suicide because of the outstanding loans that he was unable to pay. The author states that "He had a loan of Rs 60,000 already and was trying to take a fresh loan. The marriage expenses of his sisters were weighing on Dhyan Singh's mind before his suicide" (54). She further comments that Singh and his partner had been married for ten years but were unable to have children because of financial instability. Padhi writes,

Although the couple has been married for more than ten years and was also greatly troubled by their childlessness, the situation was triggered by his sister's wedding, which obliged him to arrange for the dowry money. That was four months before the suicide. (54)

In several cases of farmer indebtedness, financial burdens are magnified by societal mores, customs, traditions, and selective gendered ideologies of religious heteronormative patriarchy. Within the lives and deaths of farmers, "the imperative of safe guarding the honour of the community of Jat Sikhs acts as the biggest debilitating factor" (Padhi 54). The concept of honour prevents many men from taking up other forms of work outside of their caste and class position that would allow them to survive using different financial means. Feminists writing in regards to gender and sexuality in India have for decades politicized the idea of "honour," and how it is used to police and regulate female sexuality. However, research regarding farmer suicide suggests that narrow conceptions of familial and communal honour also structure masculinities and male psyches in India, often in deathly ways. The hypocrisy of an "India shining" in which agriculture industries are offered little governmental support while gendered societal norms value men as patriarchal providers leads to deep psychological stress on the body and mind of the indebted farmer, who is constructed as being unable to fulfil his idealized role as an archetypal man (Padhi).

Praveen, an activist in the Indian subcontinent who works with NGOs in Delhi and throughout urban India, discusses the deep shame and humiliation that exists on the part of indebted farmers, something that cannot be divorced from masculinity:

Farmer suicide is an instance of masculinity being publically defeated. It is a form of extreme bodily humiliation in public. Why do you think, many men and boys commit suicide? You see, boys in India are socialized in a way that makes them unable to deal with defeats or losses. They have been socialized to only deal with success. Women are socialized to deal with loss and defeat, but they are not socialized to deal with success. That is a basic contradiction in gender socialization. When men feel defeated they cannot cope and many will harm themselves or others.

Praveen sees that the systems of work and finance in India have shifted a great deal since the economic liberalization policies of the 1990s.

However, he argues that the ways in which people must live and work to survive in an India of exploding cities and rotting farmland have not led to a consistent and meaningful change in gender roles. Hence, farmers who suffer the losses of neoliberal capitalist globalization experience these losses as personal failings rather than as part of a wider political design. While women are taught to be dependant as wives and daughters, men are taught to retain an illusion of autonomy and self-sufficiency that does not reflect the forced dependency that neoliberal capitalist globalization produces among many Indian men. One can ask how the obscene spectacles of violence that defined the 2012 Delhi gang rape case are tied to the more minute workings of patriarchal ideology in India that contributes to mass farmer suicide. While migrant men were scripted as sexual and physical aggressors in this case, the violence enacted against the body and psyche of the indebted farmer—pushed to his death not only by global capitalism but also by gendered and sexual norms—is often silenced.

WOMEN AS WOMBS, WORDS AS POWER: THE LINGERING GRAMMARS OF PATRIARCHIES

Rather than seeing feudal forms of patriarchal authority as better or worse than capitalist patriarchies, it is important to consider how the two work in tandem and are informed by histories of colonialism and casteism that now comingle with emerging images of "new" Indian masculinities tied to the spread of transnational capital. Ali—a long-time activist who is part of many campaigns regarding violence against women and has worked with several feminist NGOs in India for decades—discusses the lingering ethos of feudal patriarchy that continues to affect the political intelligibility of feminism in the country. Ali states,

> You see, if we look at the constitution of India it says all of these things about equality. But if you look at the character of our institutions and how they are managed, it is a feudal patriarchy at work. And from parliament, this feudal mentality percolates down to every layer of governance.

The relationship between governance and gender has real life effects in the work of activists and in the material realities of gendered and sexual lives in India. After over a decade of experience as an activist working to stop violence against women, to challenge hegemonic masculinity, and to promote feminism in India, Ali discusses how language is used to construct women not as individuals but as those who are only intelligible through their place within a communal and idealized familial system. He states,

> In 1985, we wanted a separate ministry for "Women's Development." The government agreed but they said it had to be "Women *and Child* Development." A woman without a child does not exist in the system of a feudal, communal patriarchy. That kind of formulation and that example teaches you how women are viewed and how for the state, their development matters only in relation to the child.

Ali goes on to discuss a similar experience of advocating for a governmental ministry that would deal with women's reproductive rights. Again, language was used to construct the reproductive "rights" of women as being tied to the maintenance and development of the idealized "family":

> We wanted them [the government] to set up other programs for "reproductive health" ...They [the government] said okay but then it had to be called "The Reproductive Health and Child Survival Program" [laughter].... That is an expression of the feudal, communal patriarchy of the government. We kept on saying why do you want the word child there? Why can't you ever have the word "women" without the word "children"?

Ali further comments on a program that has set up a series of strategic five-year plans regarding feminism in India, in which women are constructed as agents and not subjects of change. He suggests that the idea of women as agents of change rather than as reproducers of conservative notions of tradition and family is a very novel idea for many in contemporary India, particularly those in positions of state power. He further reflects on his experiences of trying to set up a ministry for "Women's Empowerment":

> We called it a "Women's Development Ministry" because we

thought that "empowerment" is a big word and it might not be accepted by the government. So, we said okay, we will call it this. We set this up because we were asking, where will the woman who doesn't have a child or doesn't want to have a child go. I guess they will have to find some child somewhere to get any assistance [laughter].

"Women's Development" is only seen to be valuable when it is imagined to be tied to the maintenance and preservative of conservative familial, religious, and nationalist ideology. Similarly, powerful differences between masculinities are being produced within contemporary neoliberal India, where the bodies of rural farmers, migrants, queers, and all those whose lives and livelihoods do not correspond to biopolitical constructions of heteronormative patriarchies and capitalist models of success are increasingly scripted as "failed men."

ANXIOUS MEN AND UNSETTLED FUTURES: THE UNCONTROLLABLE ETHOS OF GLOBAL CAPITAL

To discuss the horrific ways in which powerless men enact gendered and sexual power against women's bodies does not excuse their culpable and sickening crimes. To try to understand, as Hannah Arendt once remarked, is not to condone or to forgive (219). To try to understand is an effort to place spectacles of violence within a longer and broader historical and political context. In speaking with members of an NGO (non-governmental organization) that works with men to question hegemonic masculinity and its relationship to violence, they argue that men who "fail" to live up to patriarchal expectations often act out violently against others, themselves, or both. The landless, emasculated, and indebted farmer, dependent on moneylenders and the world economy and constructed as a "failure" because of myths of masculinity is subject to the violence of neoliberal capitalism in ways that cause deathly forms of self-immolation. The violence of impoverished migrant men can also express itself in forms of embodied madness such as the enactment of unspeakable violence against women. As Sanjeev, an activist, states,

> Whoever's masculinity is not able to control women and to control female sexuality and to protect women, they lose this

appearance of masculinity, they lose face and "honour" within the society and the family. This is just one way sexism also hurts men and especially poor men.

The inability to control ones increasingly unstable role in a competitive neoliberal India of exploding cities, towering malls, rotting farmland, and burgeoning slums may have deeply violent ramifications. Citing a review of Jasbir Puar's work, Rahul Rao writes that "for every biopolitics, there is a necropolitics" (Rao). For every "new" Indian body invested with market vitality, there are corresponding staged deaths.

HOLY COW BOYS
NARENDRA MODI AND THE "NEW HINDU MAN"

Narendra Modi represents a "new" form of Hindu masculinity within a globalized India. Modi projects a hyper-masculine image of "modernity" through his connections to major transnational corporations, as evinced in his media-driven election campaign and the funding that he receives from major multinational corporations. Tridip Suhrud writes of the relationship between Modi's election in Gujarat and gender-based violence in the state. The author contends that after Modi's election, many boasted that Gujarat was a "safe state" where women could access public spaces at night without fear of harassment and assault. However, he goes on to point out that the so-called safety of Gujarat masks the shockingly high levels of domestic violence in the state:

> We speak with justifiable pride of how women in Gujarat can go out late at night unescorted, free from any fear. This is true, but this narrative does not allow us to look at the alarming slide in our sexratios. This allows us to forget that Gujarat has one of the highest rates of domestic violence and what are termed as "unnatural deaths" of women. (12)

Sanjeev discusses the effect that Modi's election to prime minister could have on gendered citizenship rights in India and suggests that Modi's rise to power will further include women not as citizens or agents of change in the nation but as service providers for patriarchy. He states,

In terms of gender, I think that women will be subject to moral regulations of citizenship. So women will be in the roles of acting as service providers for the patriarchy. So as a mother you will have to provide service. As a daughter you will have to provide certain services. As a daughter-in-law you will have to provide certain services. So we will go back to the era where women were considered as service providers to the patriarchy. We already see an affront to women's basic citizenship rights and with Modi it will be worse.

The concept of women's "moral citizenship" is deeply disturbing as it assumes that certain women who do not follow or are not in a position to occupy the imagined "moral space" of the archetypal Hindu bourgeois home will not be counted as citizens. Furthermore, the valuing of women as service providers within patriarchal homes also affects ideas of political citizenship and civic responsibility.

MODI'S "56 INCH CHEST" AND THE MINEFIELDS OF MASCULINITY: NEOLIBERAL HINDU PATRIARCHIES AND THE GLOBAL "WAR ON TERROR"

Body politics in India have historically been connected to the material, spiritual, gendered, political, and sexual body. As discussed previously in relation to Hijras, the aesthetics and practices of the body within India cannot be divorced from politics. In a subcontinent in which ideas of community, faith, family, and nation weigh heavily on the individual psyche and national political consciousness, the body is a public text. Yet as many feminists, queers, and activists suggest, in an India of gated communities, desire is increasingly privatized. Modi represents this balance between private silence regarding sex and an aggressively public performance of archetypal middle-class Hindu masculinity. Suhrud states that Modi's "references to his `56 inch chest are offered as a measure of his nationalism, his patriotic commitment" (13). What is of interest for my purposes lies in Modi as an example of a "New Hindu man" whose masculinity is entirely tied to public success and national honour, while questions of sexuality and gender identity in the home remain the private and silent business of men. As Suhrud states, nothing of Modi's private world, the world of his emotions, forms part of this public persona. He does not display his familial ties in public. The only emotions that he displays in public are about his commitment to Gujarat and its people and his commitment to RSS [Rashtriya Swayamsevak Sangh]. (13)

As Suhrud and other authors, activists, and feminists in India suggest, within Modi's performance and political rhetoric, femininity and anything associated with the feminine is maligned or made invisible. This is a Hinduism that uses religion as politics and as a tactic when it is convenient. Similar to Zionist Jewish leaders in Israel, faith is always easily negotiated with neoliberal capitalist aims. Modi's political career and his rise to national power can be considered in relation to global politics concerning land, war, and masculinity.

If, as I have suggested in relation to the work of Uma Chakravarti, there is a historical relationship between land and archetypal brahmanical patriarchy in India then the question of masculinity is central to global politics. Modi's masculinity is ideologically, rhetorically, and politically aligned in an "India shining" to warring masculinities, in India and transnationally. Ghosh discusses the investments that Israel has made in the state of Gujarat, particularly into the main chemical industries in the region. The allied relationship between Israel and India can be understood through the lives and deaths of the landless, the rural, the poor, and the Muslim. Muslim men within a global "war on terror" have increasingly been scripted on world stages as failed men, failed citizens, and as being beyond the boundaries of the human. Ghosh suggests that Modi and the BJP have played and continue to play an active role in the global "war on terror," driven both implicitly and explicitly by a racist, Islamophobic rhetoric that scratches old partition itches to construct "the Muslim" as an enemy:

The BJP's hostile rhetoric against Pakistan, and the Islamic world as a whole, has been music to Israel's ears. In 2003, following the Sept. 11 terror attacks, in a speech before the American Jewish Community in Washington, DC, Brajesh Mishra, then India's national security adviser under the BJP government, called for a trilateral alliance comprising India, Israel and the U.S. to "jointly face the same ugly face of modern-day terrorism."

(Ghosh "India's 214 Elections: Narendra Modi, Israel's Best Friend in South Asia")

Those who exist outside of the Hindu patriarchal family, outside of the class and caste-based wealth of the neoliberal economy are classified as not only existing outside the nation as citizens but as existing outside of humanity, defined as "terrors" and "monsters." Hamsa, a feminist who works with a Delhi-based NGO discusses, the rise to power of the BJP in Karnataka and the effects that this had on non-Hindus, and women:

> The BJP has a long history of homophobia and sexism ... Modi appeals to the middle class, the upwardly mobile. I am also worried because I am from Karnataka. I was in Karnataka when the BJP first came into power. And the state got intolerant. It got intolerant to women, it got intolerant to migrants, and it became a very hostile place. It became intolerant to linguistic minorities, to Muslims; they passed the first anti-beef legislation in Karnataka. That's such a typically brahmanical move. Girls were dragged out of pubs by men. I was there then. It was the home minister sanctioning all of it.

As with many of the feminist, queer, and social justice activists I have spoken with, Hamsa is worried about the political power of Narendra Modi. Speaking with her before the election of Modi to the post of Prime Minister of India she states:

> If the BJP comes into power it will become a Hindu country. It already is. But it will be more extreme.... We are concerned with the effect that the BJP will have on queer people. We are also concerned with what will happen to minority women—to Muslim women, to other religious and racial minority women in this country. This is our concern.

Hamsa discusses the relationship between a neoliberal model of an "India shining" in which "progress" is associated with capitalist growth while gender justice is not a political priority:

> The rise of Modi could represent a backlash against the gains

that feminist and queer movements have made. We don't want to think of this, but it could happen. Many of us who work in this sector do think that the country is becoming more and more regressive. Just look at the rise of the Hinduvata and other right-wing groups. And it could actually be a real threat to our work. It's the "India shining" rhetoric where neoliberalism is open for business, but the family values model is more enforced and this could threaten feminists, queers, and activists in the region.

What effect will Modi's election and his aggressive alignment with Israel and implicit and explicit Islamophobia have on marginalized masculinities, such as lower-caste, lower-class, Muslim men? As discussed, following the Iraq war, the world witnessed the almost-unbelievable act of the public shaming of Muslim masculinity through the Abu Ghraib scandal. The complete dehumanizing of Muslim men has been an active and public tool within the "global war on terror." The image of a hooded Iraqi prisoner made to stand on a box and simulate his own electrocution, the images of Iraqi men being made to pose naked in sexualized positions, the images of Iraqi men on leashes being dragged like dogs by G. I. Jane U.S. soldiers, are all chilling and haunting reminders of the sickening crimes that define the "war on terror." These examples are also instructive as they point to the gendered and sexual humiliation of male victims and captives of war. One can ask how the coveting of the new all powerful neoliberal "Hindu man" much like the archetypal "American soldier" happens through and against the body of the Muslim, cast out of the bounds of not only manhood but humanity.

"PENTAGON" SEEDS AND WARRING MASCULINITIES: DESTROYING THE EARTH IN THE NAME OF A NATION

While many authors have discussed Modi's role in the Gujarat riots and his implicit and explicit bigotry towards Muslims and other religious minorities in India, the relationship between the new brand of "Modi masculinity" and land has often gone unanalyzed. "Modi masculinity," much like the construction of masculinist figures of political power in Israel, is reflective of the hypocrisies of those whose manhood is tied to the delusional "purity" of land while they simultaneously invest in capitalist ventures that sell land to the highest bidder, and support irreparable forms of ecological degradation. Joint agricultural ventures have been made between Israel and India. Israel's consul general in Mumbai has made statements regarding the continued growth in agriculture that Israeli investment supposedly supports in India (Ghosh). The rhetoric of agrarian "growth" and "investment" supports a neoliberal brand India in which agricultural growth has indebted farmers whose former subsistence-based agricultural knowledge and livelihoods no longer correspond with market-driven approaches to the agrarian sector. Ecofeminist and physicist Vendana Shiva suggests that when then U.S. President George Bush and British Prime Minister Tony Blair declared a war on the Iraqi people following the attacks on the World Trade Center, they ushered in an era of global political dominance that has subsequently justified the imposition of capitalist models of growth in agriculture. Shiva states that names are given to American-based company Monsanto's seeds which are sold to Indian farmers. Seeds from American multinational corporations are sold to farmers through schemes that often place them in positions of insurmountable debt, leading many to commit suicide. Shiva writes of the naming of these seeds:

> Monsanto's herbicides are called "Round Up,""Machete,""-Lasso." American Home Products, which has merged with Monsanto, calls its herbicides, "Pentagon," "Prowl,""Sceptor,""Squadron,""Cadre,""Lightening,""Assert,""Avenge."This is the language of war, not sustainability. Sustainability is based on peace with the Earth. (37)

The language of war, archetypal masculinity, and bids to control and own land unite the neoliberal Hindu nationalist masculinity triumphed by Modi with the masculinist prowess of other warring states, such as Israel. Those who are left indebted and landless, both Palestinians and Indian farmers, are feminized in ways that gesture to how a monoculture of capitalist masculinity makes monsters and corpses out of those who stand in the way of narratives of capitalist "progress."

E-MOTIONS AND WITNESSES:
GLOBAL SPECTACLES AND POLITICAL (IR)RESPONSIBILITY

A certain political and emotive grammar has been increasingly ushered in as the norm within a neoliberal India, exemplified by Narendra Modi and other aggressively capitalist Hindu nationalists. Suhrud writes of the absence of the figure of the "witness" within contemporary Indian political culture, replaced instead by the "spectator":

> A witness has a duty. A witness is the bearer of truth, while a spectator merely watches something play out before his/her eyes, without any sense of obligation. A witness suffers remorse, does penance, and speaks the truth, while the spectator has no such obligation. (11)

Suhrud suggests that under Modi's reign, Gujarat was turned into a state of spectators in which people were encouraged to watch politics unfold as passive spectators. One can consider this spectatorship in relation to the mass amounts of religious and communal violence that erupted between Muslims and Hindus in 2002 and in relation to the political career of Narendra Modi himself. Modi's career is based on the construction of the Indian citizenry as spectators of his slick public relations campaigns, which include a great deal of Internet-based spectacle, billboards, and images that turn viewers into consumers and consumers into "citizens."

How might this principle of witnessing as opposed to spectatorship pertain to cases such as the tragic Delhi gang rape case of 2012 and the 2013 decision to recriminalize same-sex desire in India through Section 377 of the Indian Penal Code? On the night of the Delhi gang rape of 2012, the young couple that were attacked and maligned beyond all human comprehension are said to have lain in the streets for hours. Naked and bloody, their bodies were left for dead on the busy streets of Delhi as people in suburban suvs and foreign-made cars drove passed. They lay there dying and pleading for mercy, as "good" families, "successful" professionals, tourists, and visiting dignitaries drove past in private taxis and trophy cars, perhaps on their way to hotels, pristine homes, gated "communities," and globalized shopping malls. Where were the witnesses? Many writers suggest that neoliberal India, while advancing a spectacle of supposed freedom in the form of feminist consumerism and branding also ushers in a privatization of gendered and political life worlds. While malls rise, girly drinks are sold, and images of a "new Indian woman" and "new Indian citizen" abound, there is an increased focus on obligations to only private family, friends, and personal financial matters, which become the citizenry's only ethical and political responsibilities.

Indra, a queer activist who has been at the forefront of protests that have arisen since the 2013 Supreme Court decision to criminalize same-sex desire, discusses the call to activism, perhaps as a call to act as a witness after the reinstitution of Section 377:

Section 377 is not just a law we are fighting against. It's part of a whole broader movement and it has so many facets. And there are so many aspects. The societal issues, the psychological issues. It's so wide and vast and that is why I think this movement is so important. This judgment about 377 is bringing together people and making them do something, and you can see it as a beautiful thing to have happened at this moment. Because it has offered a chance to raise awareness and to sensitize people and to really open up a dialogue with the whole society. So for someone like me, who only came out a few months before this judgment, I really didn't know what to do. And suddenly, after this 377 judgment, I knew what to do. Suddenly, I had direction. I met all these people who are part of all these resistance movements and I knew what to do. This 377 judgment made me, and a million other people into activists.

Hegemonic masculinities martyr some and valorize others, criminalizing and pathologizing those bodies that exist outside of the heteronormative Hindu bourgeois family and its attending constructions of archetypal "manliness." Yet brute force produces impassioned resistance. What emerges against the monstrosities of misogyny are the passionate struggles of those who labour for a justice that lies beyond gender itself. Āzādī.

ENDNOTES

[1]Gordan writes, "Haunting is a constituent element of modern social life ... To study social life one must confront the ghostly aspects of it. This confrontation requires (or produces) a fundamental change in the way we know and make knowledge, in our mode of production" (Gordan *Ghostly Matters* 7).

[2]In *Violent Belongings*, Daiya discusses contemporary religious riots in the Indian subcontinent and how these events are haunted by partition. Daiya begins by discussing the murder of Sikhs in Kashmir in 2000 and further comments on the massacre of Muslims and destruction of Islamic sites of worship in India and other instances of religious violence that gained national and global media attention. The author states that,

Like the demolition of the Babri Mosque in Ayodhya (Northern India) which was attacked and vandalized in 1992 by Hindu nationalists who believe it is the birthplace of the Hindu God Ram; like the ensuing Hindu-Muslim ethnic violence, which spread across India in December of 1992; and like the series of riots and state-supported mob violence against Muslims, which occurred in the Indian state of Gujarat in 2002 in the city of Godhra, this attack on Sikhs in Kashmir represents a crisis that refracts the ethnicization of territory and national belonging that marks the checkered history of secularism in the subcontinent. (2)

Given the recent election of Hindu nationalist Narendra Modi, who was implicated in anti-Muslim violence in the 2002 Gujarat riots, the ghostly resonance of partition is important to consider. As Daiya further states,

Partition continues to haunt contemporary life in India. This is true not only for discourses that debate the place of religion in India but also for the historical interpretation of justice and minority belonging, and for the tension-ridden struggle over the production of secular national culture in the subcontinent. (1)

[3]Rega Jha documents some of the uses of humour that emerged over social media in India following Modi's election. Jha writes that "After Narendra Modi secured India's support in a historic landslide election, Indians took to the Internet to express how they *really* felt about their new Prime Minister." Jha cites uses of graphics and design that subtly mocked the BJP's rise to power with quips such as BJP being circulated using the Internet, graphic images of Modi that related his election to the simultaneous release of the film *Godzilla* in India with images of "Modzilla" being used in satirical movie posters, and messages on social media citing the flight prices to other countries. Humour was perhaps used to psychically manage the anxiety, aggression, and loss that defined Modi's election victory for many in the nation. Drawing on comments made over twitter Jha satirically comments that in the recent aftermath

of Modi's victory, "People immediately began booking plane tickets to Pakistan:`Guys Pakistan flight tickets not that bad. Who's coming?'"— gkhamba (@Khamba). (Jha)

[4]Harris further discusses the relationship between neoliberalism, urbanization, and poverty in relation to Muslims in India:

> As a group, Muslims have fallen badly behind Hindus in recent decades in education, employment and economic status, with persistent discrimination being a key reason. Muslims are more likely to live in villages without schools or medical facilities and less likely to qualify for bank loans.

[5]While Modi constructs Muslims as "terrors" to the imagined "purity" of Hindustan and has threatened non-Hindus with deportation, other authors discuss how Western-owned foreign multinational corporations funded his election campaign. Modi has also been accused of allowing Western corporations to have access to India in exchange for campaign funds. Critics suggest that such business deals are a form of political corruption. Modi's espousal of a nationalist rhetoric of a religiously, culturally "pure" Hindustan is a farce when compared to his support of Western multinationals in India. As Menon writes,

> The Delhi High Court indicted both Congress and BJP in March 2014 for accepting foreign funds from Vedanta subsidiaries in violation of provisions of the Foreign Contribution (Regulation) Act. (Vedanta clearly believes in covering all its bases—after all, who knows who will come to power). BJP and Congress in their defence had argued that Vedanta is owned by an Indian citizen, Aggarwal, and its subsidiaries are incorporated here, therefore they are not foreign sources. That's the kind of fine distinction you must learn to make. For instance, there is no cap on parties' expenditure during elections, only on individual candidates' spending. Thus, Narendra Modi's face on the front page of every newspaper and on huge hoardings all over the city did not get counted towards his poll expenditure.

[6]Crooks draws on Freud's essay "Jokes and Their Relation to the Unconcious" to discuss the anxiety of whiteness, which reveals itself in comic moments within colonial discourse. Crooks writes,

> Without being facetious, I suggest that dominant racial identification-or whiteness-is implicated in Freud's theory of jokes, and that when threatened, such identification is susceptible to

uncanny effects…the structure of jokes givesus access to the unconscious manner that usefully lays bare the mechanisms of racial identification and their ability to function in the colonial field. (353)

While Crooks discusses the use of the joke to manage the inherent anxieties of phallic colonial power, one can see a resonance in this anxiety and the use of jokes to maintain dominant masculine egos and psyches within contemporary India. The imagined rhetoric of equality in law and through liberal democratic values of fairness and bureaucratic constructions of citizenship beyond bodies conceals the anxieties of embodiment, in which the unmentioned bodies and sexualities of those who hold power in their skin are anxiously managed through jokes.

7While several authors document the ways in which caste is used to justify and excuse violence, specifically violence against Dalit women, Chakravarti offers a theoretical argument that suggests that gender is a fundamental principle for the organization of caste structure:

> Caste hierarchy and gender hierarchy are the organizing principles of the brahmanical social order and despite their close interconnections neither scholars of the caste system nor feminist scholars have attempted to analyse the relationship between the two (579).

WORKS CITED

Arendt, Hannah. *Hannah Arendt: Key Concepts.* Ed. Patrick Hayden. New York: Routledge, 2014. Print.

Atluri, Tara. "The Young and the Restless: Gender, 'Youth', and The Delhi Gang Rape Case of 2012." *Sikh Formations* 9.3 (2013): 361-379. Print.

Bourdieu, Pierre. "Social Space and Symbolic Power." *Sociological Theory* 7. 1 (1989): 14-25. Print.

Burke, Jason. "Narendra Modi's Landslide Victory Shatters Congress's Grip on India." *The Guardian,* 16 May 2014. Web. 13 Aug. 2015.

Chakravarti, Uma. "Conceptualising Brahmanical Patriarchy in Early India: Gender, Caste, Class, and State." *Economic and Political Weekly* 28.14 (1993): 579-585. Print.

Crooks, Kalpana-Seshadri. "The Comedy of Domination: Psychoanalysis and the Conceit of Whiteness." *The Psychoanalysis of Race.* Ed. Christopher Lane. New York: Columbia University Press, 1998.

353-380. Print.

Flood, Finbarr B. "Pillars, Palimpsests, and Princely Practices: Translating the Past in Sultanate Delhi." *Res: Anthropology and Aesthetics* 43 (2003): 95-116. Print.

Freire, Paulo. *Pedagogy of the Oppressed: 30th Anniversary Edition.* London: Bloomsbury, 2014. Print.

Ghosh, Deepshika. "Come May 16, Bangladeshi immigrants must pack up: Narendra Modi." *n*New Delhi Television Limited, 22 Sept. 2015. Web. 5 Dec. 2015

Ghosh, Palash. "India's 2014 Elections: Narendra Modi, Israel's Best Friend in South Asia." *International Business Times,* 17 March 2014. Web. 5 Dec. 2015

Gordan, Avery. *Ghostly Matters: Haunting and the Sociological Imagination.* Minneapolis: University of Minnesota Press, 1997. Print.

Harris, Gardner. "For India's Persecuted Minority, Caution Follows Hindu Party's Victory." *The New York Times,* 16 May 2014. Web.16 June 2015.

Jha, Rega. "29 Perfect Responses To Modi Being Elected Prime Minister." BuzzFeed, 16 May 2014. Web. 25 June 2015.

Menon, Nividetia. "When Are Foreign Funds Okay? A Guide for the Perplexed." *Kafila,* 13 June 2014. Web. 16 June 2015.

Murshid, Navine. "Bengali Muslims in India: Bangladeshis until proven otherwise?" *BDS News24,* 4 May 2014. Web. 8 Dec. 2015.

O'Neill, Brendan. "The Delhi Rape is Being Used to Demonise Indian Men." *The Telegraph,* 2 Jan. 2013. Web. 5 Dec. 2015.

"PM Warns of `Footloose Migrants' from Rural Areas.'" *The Hindustan,* 27 Dec. 2012. Web. 5 Dec. 2015.

Puar, Jasbir and Amit Rai. "Monster, Terrorist, Fag: The War on Terrorism and the Production of Docile Patriots." *Social Text* 20.3 (Fall 2002): 118-148. Print.

Puar, Jasbir. *Terrorist Assemblages: Homonationalism in Queer Times.* Durham: Duke University Press, 2007. Print.

Rao, Rahul. "On 'Gay Conditionality,' Imperial Power and Queer liberation." *Kafila,* 1 Jan. 2012. Web. 16 June 2015.

Rege, Sharmila. *Against the Madness of Manu: B.R Ambedkar's Writings on Brahmanical Patriarchy.* Delhi: Navayana, 2013. Print.

Ronen, Gil. "India's New PM Touted as 'Israel's Best Friend' in South Asia." *Israel National News.* ArutzSheva, 19 May 2014. Web. 16 June 2015.

Roychowdhury, Poulami. "The Delhi Gang Rape": The Making of International Causes." *Feminist Studies* 39. 1 (2013): 282-292.Print.

Roy, Sandip. "Looking East in Disgust: Delhi Rape through Eyes of the West." *First Post*, 3 Jan. 2013. Web. 25 June 2015.

Sharma, Sadhvi. "India's 'Rape Epidemic': an Ugly Colonial Myth Reborn." *Spiked*, 17 March 2015. Web. 25 June 2015.

Shiva, Vandana. "Monocultures, Monopolies, Myths and the Mascu-linization of Agriculture." *Development* 42.2 (1999): 35-38. Print.

Suhrud, Tridip. "Modi and Gujarati 'Asmita.'" *Economic and Political Weekly* 43.1(2008): 11-13. Print.

Tharoor, Kanishk. "Why Modi's India Aligns More Closely with Israel Than with Palestinians." Aljazeera, 3 Aug. 2014. Web. 6 June 2015.

"We Shall Overcome." *The Indian Express*, 17 Aug. 2006. Web. 16 June 2015.

A CONCLUSION ON THE IDEA
OF CONCLUSIONS

ĀZĀDĪ, BEYOND TRANSLATION:

A CONCLUSION ON THE IDEA OF CONCLUSIONS

SLAVOJ ŽIŽEK makes clear that the spectacle of extreme human suffering often masks deeper foundational questions regarding structures of power that make violence the rule rather than the exception (*Violence*). The phenomenon of staring at single women in Delhi is one that has been well documented and discussed at length in the Indian and international press. A recent media campaign in India challenges the violence of the male gaze. The campaign, which is widely circulated over Internet mediums, features a Hindi song with the chorus "Look how you look when you're looking at me" and an accompanying video, and shows women wearing mirrored sunglasses to return the menacing gaze of patriarchal power (Barry). One activist, who works with a Delhi-based NGO aimed at supporting survivors of sexual violence and creating safe cities for women and queers in the Indian subcontinent, understands staring as being connected to the power to objectify women's bodies, a power justifying sexual violence. She states,

> They feel that they have a right to stare at any moving objects.
> Rape or sexual violence is always about power. They love the
> fact that they can make a person uncomfortable just by staring
> at them. So this always gives them a thrill, a rush. Because the
> woman will squirm and men love this; it gives them a sense
> of power.

While it is often men who stare at women, the disciplinary power of older women against younger women and women who represent elite majorities against those assumed to be "other," often through community gossip and moralistic judgment has also been documented. Shilpa Phadke writes of how many women in India not only fear men in public spaces but also fear the judgment enforced by older conservative women often referred to as "Aunties" within neighbour-hoods and religious and cultural communities. Phadke discusses how within this act of public disciplinary power, people learn they should not only fear lower-class, lower-caste, or "foreign" non-Hindu men but also learn to distance themselves from any association with "bad" women, Hijras, and queers. This creation of objects of fear and anxiety obscures the statistical truth of gender-based violence in India, which is more likely to be experienced in the home rather than in public space. It is within the imagined safety and sanctity of the Hindu middle-class home that many supposedly good wives, mothers, and Aunties often hide the abuse that husbands enact on them, their children, their daughters-in-law, and the domestic workers that they employ (Phadke).

The spectacles of the world's cameras often do not expose the everyday atrocities found in domestic homes and on the streets of India, where minute theatres of cruelty are obscene in their banality. As one woman who works with an NGO, which addresses issues of gender-based violence in Kolkata, tells me, "India is often not sensitive to its women. This is something that is not learned, something rarely taught or encouraged in much of the society. Another woman whom I speak with in Mumbai states,

> Indians are community minded in the best and worst of ways. So you learn that as a woman, you are part of a community and will be judged by a community. I don't think it's better or worse than the West or some other place. I think it's just how we are raised. Even how we are taught to think and speak as women is already made up of knowing that what we do will be judged.

The language of judgment and idea of judgment have been spoken of repeatedly throughout my conversations with many people in India. One woman, a feminist and activist who works with survivors of sexual violence throughout the country, argues that the ideas of "community judgment" and accountability should be questioned:

> Women, even we are part of it. Our social conditioning has been the same as men. We have always been taught that we have to behave as a good woman would behave. Privately and publicly. You are not supposed to smoke. You are not supposed to drink. You are supposed to eat certain things and in a certain way. You only speak about certain topics in public and only in a certain way. You only dress in a certain way. You have to have romantic and sexual relations that are very traditional and with certain men. You have to have friends that look a certain way. And if you defy those norms, you are not a good woman. And this whole concept of someone judging you simply because of the fact that you want to lead your life in a certain way is very problematic. It should not bother me if you are judging me. Because in any way, I do not feel obligated to you, I do not feel accountable towards you.

The idea of judgment is an interesting concept to conclude with, as legal judgments concerning Section 377 of the Indian Penal Code are debated, while The Delhi High Court has ruled to uphold the use of the death penalty in the sentencing of four of the accused assailants in the 2012 Delhi gang rape case.[1] Judgment is also interesting when considering the rise to power of Hindu fundamentalist Narendra Modi, who came to power on a platform of religion and culture coupled with neoliberal capitalism. The judgments of increasingly secularized Indian middle classes towards women and queers, and the judgments of political leaders and judiciaries who use religion and culture as a tool of political power reflect the paradoxes of secular-capitalist narratives of ostensible progress. India shines with the glow of multinational branding. Yet the rise of consumer and corporate labelling as an imagined sign of civility meets the use of secular labels infused with colonial history and used to violently exile "others" from the nationalist imaginary. An iPhone, an iPod, and a MacBook can be purchased by middle-class urban Indian consumers as a testament to "progress" while women, queers, migrants, and the poor are branded with names and labels not of their own design. The power to categorize, order, and defame people whether through law or everyday acts of interpolation by those who hold institutional and societal power, is an expression of the power afforded to supposed majorities to name supposed minorities.

I speak to queer people in Delhi who recount narratives about the collective shaming of sexual minorities throughout the country, particularly by neighbours, teachers, classmates, and family. In smaller cities in the country, I am told chilling stories, rumours of "corrective rapes" of queers by family members,[2] rapes of lesbians, queer men, Hijras, and transgender persons. I am told that the rise of Internet culture, although used by activists to generate new forms of collective action and protest culture, can also act as a way that bodies of "others" are judged, classified, and exposed to violence because of perceived gendered and sexual deviance.

In his essay "Fate and Character," Walter Benjamin suggests that modernity often ushered in a space of judgment in which ideas of fate were divorced from religion and other wordly destinies. Benjamin writes,

> Contemporary ideas do not permit immediate logical access to the idea of fate, and therefore modern men accept the idea of reading character from, for example, the physical feature of a person, finding knowledge of character as such somehow generally present within themselves, whereas the notion of analogously reading a person's fate from the lines in his hand seems unacceptable. (201)

The irony of judgments based on the superficial in contemporary India—on dress, race, skin, gendered, and sexual embodiment—perhaps lie in its modernist ethos that moves at the speed of secular-capitalist temporalities. Drawing on Alan Badiou, Slavoj Žižek suggests that one should not simply state that there are wrong answers to questions but that the questions themselves need rearticulation.[3] While many of my interviewees in India suggest that India has not "progressed" in terms of sexual ideology in comparison to Western secular nations, how can one read the judgments made of bodies marked as "other" as being reflective modernist and colonial ideas of humanity? The constructed physical difference used to ridicule and assault women, queers, Hijras, racialized, and lower-caste and lower-class people is a glaring example of the use of a modernist and colonial understandings of identity to support hegemonic power structures.

Benjamin, citing Goethe, argues that within modernist readings of character through physical features, moral judgment is tied to wealth. While Benjamin was writing in and about a radically different historical and national context, a consideration of how ideas of judgment in contemporary India are increasingly informed by material wealth and aesthetics is of relevance to contemporary sexual politics. A person's fate can be determined by their class and caste, and by their gendered and sexual embodiment, which can cause them to be subject to brutal violence. Benjamin states,

> Fate shows itself, therefore, in the view of life, as condemned, as having essentially first been condemned and then become guilty. Goethe summarizes both phrases in the words "the poor man you let become guilty." (204)

There is a recurring contradiction that emerges from my interviews with activists, feminists, Hijras, and queers across lines of age, gender, race, class and caste. The contradiction is one in which slogans such as "No Going Back" used in campaigns against Section 377 are coupled with a wish to remember and recover histories of precolonial cultures of gender and sexuality. The one whom "you let become guilty" is made guilty within an increasingly urbanized India governed by colonial law, transnational neoliberal capital, and a poverty of Indian history within the popular imaginary. The irony of using culture as a justification for the moral policing of women, queers, Hijras, and the poor lies in how these judgments are rooted in colonial cultures of governance, categorization, and disciplinary power more than any religious, historical, or localized cultural temporalities. While activists quite rightly do not want to "go back" to the period before the reading down of Section 377 by the Delhi high court in 2009, a time in which queer desire was often absent from mainstream political discourse and media, they also make reference to the existence of same-sex desire and alternative feminine temporalities that have existed in India for thousands of years. This ambivalence poses a question regarding time and temporality and its relationship to gender and sexualities in contemporary India.

As I have attempted to illustrate in this text, the cries of Āzādī heard in the streets of India following both the gang rape and murder of Jyoti and the decision to uphold Section 377 of the Indian Penal Code gesture to a messianic temporality in which the language of liberation from colonial norms has never left India. Āzādī now finds renewed articulation in sexual political movements. Both the will to judge the guilt of "the poor man" and the assumed guilt of women and queer bodies is born out of the empty time of capital, one that is not simply a problem of misreading individual desire but of misreading Indian history itself. As I discuss in this book, sex and sexuality are implicitly understood and judged within a system of both class and caste in India, constructing those without access to financial, heteronormative, and patriarchal forms of power as morally suspect. The power to construct some bodies, as not being entitled to belong to nations, cities, and public spaces is an act of power imbued with the unquestioned workings of epistemic violence, which is deeply tied to the workings of ideological violence.

As discussed in the introduction of this book, in reference to the contemporary ethos of fear that often defines neoliberal secular-capitalist life worlds, Žižek suggests that with the rise of neoliberal capitalist privatization and its worlds of gated communities, the only political struggle that emerges is the "right not to be harassed" (Žižek *The Universal Exception*). He suggests that within our contemporary moment of "risk," brought about by the global economy, the rise of contractual labour, and the collapse of the social welfare state globally, people are taught to live in fear and guard against the perceived threat of others (Žižek *The Universal Exception*). Žižek's writings correspond to the increased will in urban India to keep the perceived threats of the poor, the truly marked and wretched of India and of the earth at a distance not only through word and name but through violent policies of exclusion that displace many into slums in the outer regions of city space (Fanon). However, this fear of the other also informs anxieties and aggressions towards gendered and sexual subjects, racialized migrants, and all those marked as "foreign" to the idealized image of the Indian citizen, who is biopolitically constituted to reproduce the nation-state.

This right to not be harassed and to keep others at a distance forecloses an ethical act of witnessing. As discussed in the previous chapter regarding Narendra Modi and the culture of neoliberal spectacle in an "India shining," there is an absence of the ethical witness who is called on, not to simply watch history unfold but to intervene, to question, to think, to speak, and to act.

The fear of the "other" who is kept at a distance through privatized rights and wealth might prevent the possibilities of both intersubjective and ethical relations. Rosi Braidotti refers to the ethics of a nomad that involve an affective relationship to those one encounters, despite the countenance and classifications of the state. Braidotti writes, "Nomadic philosophy mobilizes one's affectivity and enacts the desire for in-depth transformations in the status of the kind of subjects we have become" (204). The will to keep others at a distance, whether through succinct categorizations of difference or neoliberal forms of distancing through privatized property and lives offers no space for political witnessing or affective relationships. The experience of physical, psychosocial, and epistemic violence is often met with discourses of fear. The mainstream political response to the Delhi gang rape case of 2012 and other cases of gender-based and sexual violence is one of protectionism in which women are taught to live in fear. This case has been used to advance a discourse of terror that attaches itself to certain bodies, namely impoverished men and those deemed to be foreign to an upper caste Hindu nationalist vision of India. Similarly, in talking with queer people and queer activists regarding Section 377, what emerges is fear. Queer bodies still haunted by colonial sodomy laws often live in fear of public shaming, judgment, exclusion, and violence.

Yet what has been inspiring has been the incredible courage of those who fight against this trepidation in the spirit of something that might be called Āzādī. Against a petrified phobic rhetoric of fear, many have embraced violent events such as the 2012 Delhi gang rape case and the 2013 Supreme Court decision to criminalize same-sex desire by upholding Section 377 of the Indian Penal Code as opportunities to express personal and political courage, as moments of witnessing, and as opportunities for affective and political transformation. It is the courage of these people that have made it possible for me to write this. I have been inspired by the courage of many of those whom I met in the Indian subcontinent. Many feminists, queers, activists, NGO workers, counsellors who support survivors of gender-based violence, lawyers, academics, and everyday people at political events and in the streets of India took the time to speak with me about deeply personal issues and complex political struggles. It is in their almost incomprehensible ability for affective relations with "strangers," with those whom they work with, support, and advocate for; and with those who have survived countless abuses of power that I have been deeply humbled and inspired. It is in the persistent quest for pleasure, for fun, for revelry and for spaces of desire outside of frigid countenances of colonial law and moralities, subaltern spaces created by so many people in India that I have found pleasure in the city through all the unlikely moments of translation created everywhere, from dancefloors to city parks to market stalls, and, finally, to temple gates where women's singing voices still carry traces of something patient and graceful that can be heard in the streets against the sound of endless traffic and election chanting.

* * *

I want to suggest the "Āzādī" that was heard throughout the streets of India in 2012 and 2013 is reflective of the desire and will of protestors to appear in public space without the constant annoyances, aggressions, and anxieties of sexist, homophobic, and parochial forms of "community" judgment. There was an embodied reclaiming of public space against the Indian state and against extreme threats of violence that define cases such as the 2012 Delhi gang rape. However, these moments were also expressive of a reclaiming of public space from the haunting strangle hold of colonial moralities that govern who has the right to occupy city streets. One feminist and queer activist who took part in both the Delhi gang rape protests and Section 377 protests suggests that there was something different about the Delhi gang rape actions:

It was different. It was different in terms of numbers for sure. It was different in terms of the people that came out on the streets. It was different in terms of the genders that came out on the streets. If it's a typical women's movement protest you have very few men. But at these demonstrations you had many men. And the crowd, a lot of them were young and a lot of them were students who came out on the streets. And it was unprecedented. The sheer number of people was quite unprecedented and they kept at it … even some of the slogans and chants, like Āzādī were not your usual sad feminist ones.

The cries of Āzādī were heard not only in the streets of urban India in 2012 and 2013 but across time, space, and borders. The word was used in anticolonial struggles against British colonial rule, throughout political struggles that defined the partition of India and Pakistan, as a protest chant in Kashmiri revolts against the Indian state, in the Green Revolution protests in Iran, and at Arab Spring protests in Egypt. Within contemporary sexual political movements in India, there is a larger and broader articulation and desire for freedom that is being demanded and created by many people in the streets. There is a greater and deeper hope expressed when they, when we, stand in the streets and cry out Āzādī, a word translated through bodies and borders and all the categorizations and divisions made in the name of both. At a protest following the Supreme Court of India's decision to criminalize same-sex desire in 2013, one protestor tells me:

> I am here to ask for freedom, yes. It's not just about the free-
> dom to love who I want to or about whom I have sex with. It's
> about a wider freedom that threatens people's rights to move in
> public space and that means their whole lives can be changed
> overnight because of some judge.

After he had said these words, we stood in the streets side by side and cried out, Āzādī!

* * *

In a rural sun-soaked village that some once referred to as God's coun-try, we look out onto arid farmland where farmers hang like strange fruit. She pushes glass bangles onto my arms. I notice that her left side is scarred. When she turns to get the chai, I see more scars unfolding across her frame, her skin darker than mine from a life of village heat. A man with degrees and English-language skills—one who knows all the words I know to categorize and classify these scars, to order and name pain inflicted onto a human body—will tell the story. He will finish the unremarkably violent story by saying that the sad part about "these women," is that "they don't even know enough to complain; this is as basic as breathing to them." He will say it in a way that almost makes it seem as though protest against gendered violence is a form of enlightened cultural capital: "These women don't know any better." The language of feminist knowledge as "betterment" meets the truth of entire systems of marriage, property, psychosocial, and political space, of entire histories of colonialism and poverty in the Global South that not only answer questions but allow certain questions to be asked, often on behalf of others. I look at her scars and look then at the bangles that now line my arms, wondering how I will remove them before going through metal detectors in airport security checkpoints, across this border or the next.

* * *

African women. Black women. As a racialized subject, as a feminist, as someone who has identified as a "woman of colour" politically, there is something that haunts the streets of a "Hindustan" bleached out by colonial moralities and Aryan mythologies. African migrants I meet in Delhi share stories of the daily violence they experience in India that ranges from the invisibility of their existence to shocking attacks of physical and sexual brutality. The pulling of Black women's hair and clothes by groups of men, across class and caste lines, the complete objectification and dehumanization of people based on bodily difference, based on skin. As I made reference to earlier in this text, the scandal of Indian racism in 2014—which followed the scandal of India's legalized homophobia in 2013, and the scandal of India's gang rapes in 2012—erupted when the law minister of the Aam Aadmi Party (AAP) party in Delhi was implicated in a raid of African homes in Khirki village.[4] The raid involved forcibly entering the homes of African female students and subsequently subjecting them to invasive medical testing on the suspicion that these African women, these Black women, were involved in sex work and drug trafficking. The sickness of India, the sickness of the gendered and sexual ideology of "Hindustan," was magnified in this moment. Residents in the village reportedly referred to Africans in the neighbourhood as "savages," as subhuman. When interviewed, African migrants tell me of the everyday violence that has become part of the norm for them not only in Delhi but throughout India, with the abuse ranging from slurs to refusals of service to physical and sexual violence and to efforts to force them out of public space. This is violence. This is violence perpetuated by "normal" Indians, by "good" Hindu families, by a delusional ideology of "pure" blood and by those who treat neighbourhoods, cities, and whole nations as their private property, as microcosms for the homes and soil that they are ostensibly entitled to.

She came to study at a university in Delhi in 2009. This was the year that the Delhi High Court made the decision to read down Section 377 of the Indian Penal Code after a lengthy campaign by activists and allies. This was also the year that Dr. Siras, a lecturer at Aligarh Muslim University was found dead following a public scandal regarding his sexuality that led to his dismissal. Dr. Siras's death was reported as a "suicide" within much of the mainstream press; however, there are many who remain unconvinced of this explanation and suggest that he may have been murdered. While I mentioned this case in an earlier chapter in this text, one should perhaps also question how even if Dr. Sira's death was a case of suicide, the death of certain people in India is often brought about by intense community gossip, judgment, acts of exclusion, and the shaming of those who break with heteronormative codes of gendered and sexual morality. The image of the "bad woman," "diseased queer," and "bad man" who is impoverished or deemed as "other" are constructed in the shadows of the idealized figures of ostensibly good women who learn to silently accept and even valorize sexism and other accompanying oppressions for fear of being associated with deviant "others." Years before the 2012 Delhi gang rape case and 2013 Supreme Court decision to criminalize same-sex desire, I stayed in a hostel for international female students in Delhi. I met women from the Democratic Republic of Congo, from Korea, from Iran, from Iraq, from Kashmir, from Palestine, from Tibet, from Afghanistan. These women had all travelled to the Indian subcontinent carrying untranslatable and incredible stories of risk, sacrifice, familial and personal hardship often brought about by genocide, war, displacement, and poverty.

They were all running—all young women from and in the Global South, in the city of Delhi. As part of the sporting events held at the student hostel, young women from around the world were made to compete against one another. The staging of student sporting events, much like the hazing rituals of North American universities, can be seen as expressing the obscene underbelly of cultures of enlightenment education in which schools function as part of state structures and are implicitly and explicitly informed by discourses of nationalism (Žižek *Violence*). Women's bodies were running, playing cricket, playing chess and other old colonial games to compete for trophies and medals, to compete as great men of great nations often do, using their bodies as an appendage of national branding strategies, using their bodies as waving flags for nations. They were all running. Young women in and from the Global South. She was winning: this young African woman who had come from the Democratic Republic of Congo to study social work. She was winning the race against women from the Indian subcontinent. Women, who in Europe, in North America, would be racialized women. This African woman, this Black woman, was winning. And then, the words flew through the hot and arid air of the city, stopping her body in the traffic of the street. "Black Bitch!" An Indian woman screamed these words at her. It was said later that there may have been spit that also flew through the air, just missing the skin of this African woman called Black and a Bitch, because she was winning.

All I could think of in this moment in Delhi, India, when faced with this woman from the Republic of Congo, stopped dead in her tracks by the words "Black Bitch" was the endless cycle of oppression often perpetrated by white women against racialized women, Indian women against Black women, impoverished men against middle-class women, Jews against Muslims, Hindus against Muslims, straight people against Queers, cisgender people against transgender people and Hijras, the old against the young, the rich against the poor, feminists and leftists against each other. People racing against others and implicitly racing against themselves and the shadows of otherness in self that one often keeps at a distance in distorted mirror images of displaced desire and anxious rage. People racing against their own shadows at light speed within cycles of global capitalism and the oppressive and competitive ethos it engenders. People who should find common causes and common courage to form solidarity, who are made to compete for the medals and the attention of "great" men of "great" nations.

I was later asked to give a lecture regarding gender justice at the university. Rather than discussing violence committed by men against women, I discussed this incident of racist violence perpetrated by Indian women. I talked about the racist debasement of the basic dignity and bodily integrity of this African woman by Indian women in relation to the case of Reena Virk, murdered as an adolescent in an incomprehensibly brutal way. Virk was a young South Asian woman who was beaten to death and drowned by a group of white teenagers, the majority of whom were girls, under a bridge in British Columbia, Canada (Bhattacharya and Rajiva).

I have told this story of racist violence in Delhi, a spectacle of spit and hate speech in the city streets to myself and others, differently at different times. I have posed it as a question regarding who can narrate whose pain. A question regarding the ability of empathy and emotion to cross borders of nation, skin, and name. A question regarding the racism of the Hindu middle class and its relationship to caste. A question regarding the insipient hatred that circulates between the bodies of women tied to heteronormative cultures of competition and anxieties based on aesthetic differences. A question regarding how ideas of sexual "respectability" implicitly and explicitly justify the sexual violence enacted against certain women who are "not like us." I have told this story to myself as one of perseverance, human dignity, and grace not only in the face of everyday physical and psychological violence but in the face of politically constituted violence faced by women from war-torn countries in the Global South, those whose bodies become walking "dark continents" in the "fair and lovely" imaginaries of an "India shining." I have been told that this is perhaps a form of feminist over identification, an appropriation of the pain of African women, a narrative that offers little in the way of serious methodology. I have been told that this is not the right story to tell, that this is not the right way to tell it, and that I should not be the one narrating it. Yet I still return to this story. I returned to it in my mind when I stood in the streets of urban India years later and protested the brutal gang rape and murder of Jyoti in 2012. I returned to it when I stood in the streets of Delhi in 2013 after the Supreme Court of India made the decision to uphold Section 377 of the Indian Penal Code, criminalizing same-sex desire through colonial law. I returned to it in my daily life as a woman in India.

After the spit had settled in the streets of some university campus, manicured and trimmed by Dalit and rural village maids riding dilapidated buses to cities to maintain appearances of middle class civility, I asked this woman from the Democratic Republic of Congo, dehumanized in ways that speak to the everyday madness of colonial history erecting and enforcing the borders between us, if she hated India and Indians. I asked her if she hated this nation and its people of deep hypocrisy, a nation of caste-based oppressions that colour Dalits as "untouchable," that has Mahatma Gandhi[5] who once fought against South African apartheid brandished on dollar bills, and treats Black bodies in ways that breach every code of decency. She told me simply, No. She narrated the joys of a life in Delhi, of market walks, of friends, of all of the simple pleasures of urban living. She said that she would remember her time in Delhi fondly. She smiled a smile that reminded me of the incredible survival of a migrant woman, the resilience of those whose tenacity and whose experiences of violence are often never spoken of. I thought of women, people of colour, migrants, workers, transgender and queer people across borders, on other continents, in other cities, family and friends who all carry this stubborn look in their eyes. An undefeatable sense of self-preservation and claim to dignity against all the menacing hands and words of a thoughtless world and the borders and nations erected in the name of chilling human indifference. I thought of the resilient look in the eyes of young women, queer and transgender people in the Indian subcontinent who have been disowned by parents, ostracized by classmates, subjected to physical and sexual violence, isolated to the point of pariah status, and left with the invisible and incalculable marks of exclusion, which brand bodies as out of place, as forever guilty for living in their skin. In contemporary India, following the 2012 Delhi gang rape case and 2013 decision to uphold Section 377 of the Indian Penal Code, meeting and speaking with feminists, Hijras, queers, and leftist activists in India, I see this same look of unshakeable resilience. I see it, perhaps, because there is no other choice but to hope for and believe in better visions of a city, of a nation, of the infinite capacity of the human imagination, when faced with the brutal truths of power.

Ponni Arasu cites the narrative of one woman interviewed in the documentary *Khush* who states, against all usual tragic scripts glorifying the oppression of women and queers in India as objects of pity, that the best part of being a lesbian "is the completely satisfying, exhilarating sex!" What is interesting in making connections regarding sexual politics across narrow categories of identity and name is how Arasu went on to offer a wider critique of normative colonial understandings of sexual pleasure, specifically female sexual pleasure. Rather than isolating "sex" as solely being a "queer issue," Arasu's centring of sex and sensual pleasure as a politically vital issue allows one to problematize the heteronormative bourgeois family, and sexually repressive feminisms. Seeing pleasure as a political issue challenges deeply misogynistic thinking that would see sex as something that men are entitled to and that women provide as a service, outside of their bodily and emotive desires. Furthermore, politicizing sex also allows one to question how an investment in ideas of caste, class, religious, racial, national, and political ideas of "purity" make some sexual, sensual, and romantic bonds criminal or invisible to state interests and within the popular imaginary.

Instead of seeing sexual politics as being tied to neoliberal ideas of "progress" through the corporate branding of bodies, as I have tried to demonstrate throughout this book, sex and the anxieties and rebellion it engenders should be understood as an integral part of the history of India, perhaps well before it was named "India." From narratives of partition in which the bodies of women and abhorrent acts of sexual violence were used as tools to demarcate borders, to the 1857 Criminal Tribes Act through which kinship networks that existed outside of a normative gendered colonial imaginary were made criminal and deviant, and to contemporary feminist and queer movements, sex is and always has been deeply political. Having been involved with legal battles leading up to the reading down of Section 377 by the Delhi High Court in 2009 Arasu argues that discussions of sensual pleasure are often marginalized in a quest for state recognition:

> I don't remember saying or writing anything to do with sex in the past ten years. We have been caught up in making ourselves vulnerable and respectable in our quest for rights. Sex, somewhere, has gotten lost.

The vulnerability of the oppressed often demanded from the state in order to garner attention and political rights, can promote a conservative articulation of "respectability" that allows certain bodies to be counted as deserving of empathy as opposed to others. Poor, lower-class and lower-caste bodies, sex workers, and all those who do not approximate postures of supposed respectability may be ignored and maligned, as they do not appear as "perfect victims" for mainstream audiences. While the supposedly "good woman," and the ostensibly vulnerable and "respectable" queer may be afforded rights, gender-based violence that is often implicitly and explicitly enforced by state power and within familial and societal structures also remains unquestioned. As James Baldwin once remarked, "The victim who can articulate their status as victim ceases to be a victim and becomes a threat" (Baldwin qtd. in Menon 78). Baldwin's assertion can be thought of in relation to the government of India's declaration that the criminalization of "marital rape" would threaten the Indian family. In the wake of the brutal Delhi gang rape case of 2012 and the 2013 decision to criminalize same-sex desire in the Indian subcontinent, one can ask how female sexual agency is itself constructed as a threat to the state and wider societal norms that make women as victims easier to accept than women as agents of political change and as desiring, pleasure-seeking bodies.

I write this after a brutal gang rape and murder case in 2012 led to massive, unprecedented protests throughout the Indian subcontinent. I write this after the 2013 decision by the Supreme Court of India to uphold Section 377 of the Indian Penal Code and following the 2014 NALSA ruling which counted Hijras and transgender people as citizens of India upholding their constitutional rights. In light of these historic moments, broader ideologies and understandings of desire, female sexual agency, masculinity, and the colonial shame that haunts sex within India need to be questioned. In times in which a woman as wife can be legally raped, in which a woman as citizen was gang-raped, tortured, and murdered beyond all explicable language and human comprehension, in which same-sex desire in India makes queers into criminals, the epistemic violence of the language of law itself needs to be questioned. As revolutionary thinker and Dalit leader B.R Ambedkar once stated, "As long as you do not have social equality, the law is of no avail to you" (Ambedkar 246).

* * *

Outside of the bureaucratic language of bill and law and outside the language of state power, I still find this sensual, defiant, pleasure seeking spirit and inquisitive will to pose meaningful philosophical questions in so many of the people whom I encounter in India. I find inspiration in these people who fight the rhetoric and rapid news updates that India is "shining" through the banal glare of globalized mall lighting and satellite television with their enduring will to have a good time, in the largest and smallest acts of public and political subversion. I find this recovered loss of some semblance of bodily and psychosocial justice in those who seek pleasure in grammars of unabashed joy, raucous protest cry, and a silent meditative prose beyond translation.

I finish with this spirit of resilience, a spirit found in so many of the spaces we occupy. Spaces we all somehow find ways to inhabit and find pleasure in— that we occupy and share in spite of ourselves. Spaces that carry haunting traces of the worst and the best parts of humanity, of chilling indifference and poignant intersubjectivity in which people can both remember and forget the "Other" that lurks in the shadows of one's self image. Spaces that haunt humanity with lingering and ghostly reminders of unresolved violence as an inspiration for undetermined political futures.

There is no conclusion to an ongoing struggle for something perhaps beyond translation, a cry of public judgment and collective resilience heard in the streets: "Āzādī."

I remember all those who spoke with me throughout India, often discussing violence that chills to the bone. I remember all those who challenged me to see every injustice as a question to be asked and answered by oneself as much as by others. I remember protestors, every day people in the streets of an "India shining," holding candles that flickered in hues that shone brighter than the glare of mall lighting and MacBooks, people crying out for Āzādī, an untranslatable desire for freedom in a steady hum that I carry with me in memory across borders like the chorus of some old song. I remember that village girl turned woman, her scars beyond translation, her gift of bangles left in airport security bins across this or that border, falling like flowers from the hair of rural women catching city buses in a rush of traffic. As Arundhati Roy once wrote,

> To love. To be loved. To never forget your own insignificance. To never get used to the unspeakable violence and the vulgar disparity of life around you. To seek joy in the saddest places. To pursue beauty to its lair. To never simplify what is complicated or complicate what is simple. To respect strength, never power. Above all, to watch. To try and understand. To never look away. And never, never to forget. (Roy para. 25)

Āzādī.

ENDNOTES

[1]Writing in *The Hindu*, Nirnimesh Kumar reports,
  The Delhi High Court on Thursday upheld the death sentence of all four convicts in the December 16, 2012 gang rape and

murder of a physiotherapy student. Dismissing the appeals of the four convicts —Akshay Kumar Singh, Mukesh, Vinay Sharma and Pawan Gupta—for commuting the death sentence to life imprisonment, a Division Bench of Justices Reva Khetrapal and Pratibha Rani said the "rage of the society would not be satisfied ... and that it is a case of the gravest crime of extreme brutality."

Also writing in *The Hindu* shortly after the decision to enforce the death penalty in the trials of four of those accused of the 2012 Delhi gang rape case, J. Venkatesan discusses the curative petition launched by activists regarding Section 377 of the Indian Penal Code:

Gay activists and the Naz Foundation…moved the Supreme Court with a curative petition, seeking to correct its judgment, which upheld the validity of Section 377 of the IPC [criminalising homosexual relations]. Responding to a plea by senior counsel Anand Grover for an open court hearing, Chief Justice of India P. Sathasivam said he would consider the request. Curative petitions are heard in the judge's chamber and if found fit for admission, will be posted for hearing in open court.

[2]Bhalla discusses the use of "corrective rapes" by families of queers in India and cites the film *Satyavati*, which discusses "corrective rape" in the Indian subcontinent and "is named after the lesbian protagonist who is raped by a family member." As Bhalla writes,

Families in India are using "corrective rape" to convert their gay, lesbian and transgender sons and daughters, the director of the first Indian film on the issue said, urging society to confront the brutal, hidden practice. Corrective rape, which is known to happen in Africa and the Caribbean though largely perpetrated by strangers or acquaintances, in India can involve families and is thus seldom reported.

The director of *Satyavati*, Deepthi Tadanki, states,

People are very afraid to tell anyone that their son is gay or daughter is lesbian, and they think that they can change their orientation if they get them into contact with someone of the opposite sex…. They can't approach outside people to do it as they are worried about the family's name and reputation…so they get a family member to do it. (Bhalla)

[3]As Žižek writes,

There are not only true or false solutions, there are also false questions. The task of philosophy is not to provide answers or solutions, but to submit to critical analysis the questions themselves, to make us see how the very way we perceive a problem is an obstacle to its solution. (Žižek "Philosophy")

[4]A detailed analysis and discussion of the Khirki village raids and the genealogical foundations, psychosocial implications, and political contours of anti-African and anti-Black racism in contemporary India is beyond the scope of this work. I hope to discuss these issues in other forthcoming pieces of writing.

[5]While I make reference to Gandhi, it is important to note that political commentators and writers in India such as Arundhati Roy argue that Gandhi supported the caste system and should therefore be critiqued due to implicit and explicit casteist ideologies (Burke).

WORKS CITED

Ambedkar, Bhimrao Ramji. *The Essential Writings of B.R. Ambedkar*. Ed. Valerian Rodrigues. Oxford: Oxford University Press, 2002.

Arasu, Ponni. "My Favourite Part of Being Lesbian Is the Exhilarating Sex." *DNA India*, 8 May 2011. Web. 13 June 2015.

Barry, Doug. "Leering Men Have Their Leers Turned against Them in New Indian Ad." *Jezebel*, 22 Dec. 2013. Web. 13 June 2015.

Bhalla, Nita. "Film Lifts Lid on 'Corrective Rape' in Families of Gays in India." Reuters India, 11 June 2015. Web. 18 June 2015.

Bhattacharya, Sheila and Mythili Rajiva. *Reena Virk: Critical Perspectives on a Canadian Murder.* Toronto: Canadian Scholars Press, 2010. Print.

Braidotti, Rosi. *Transpositions: On Nomadic Ethics.* Cambridge: Polity Press, 2006. Print.

Benjamin, Walter, *Walter Benjamin: Selected Writings, Volume 1: 1913-1926*. Eds. Marcus Paul Bullock, Michael William Jennings, Howard Eiland. Boston: Harvard College, 1996. Print.

Burke, Jason. "Arundhati Roy Accuses Mahatma Gandhi of Discrimination." *The Guardian*, 18 Jul. 2014. Web. 7 Dec. 2015.

Kumar, Nirnimesh. "High Court Upholds Death Sentence in Delhi Rape Case." *The Hindu*, 14 March 2014. Web. 17 July 2015.

Lorde, Audre. "Eye to Eye: Black Women, Hatred, and Anger." *Sister Outsider: Essays and Speeches*. Berkeley: Crossing Press, 1984. 145-175. Print.

Menon, Nividetia, ed. *Sexualities.* London: Zed Books, 2007. Print.

Phadke, Shilpa. "Dangerous Liasons: Women and Men Risk Reputation in Mumbai." *Economic and Political Weekly* 42.17 (April 28 2007): 1510-1517. Print.

Roy, Arundhati. "The End of Imagination." *Outlook Magazine,* 3 Aug. 1998. Web. 17 Sept. 2015.

Venkateswan, J. "Recriminalisation Betrays Bias against Gays: Curative Petition." *The Hindu,* 4 April 2014. Web. 17 July 2015.

Žižek, Slavoj. "Liberal Multiculturalism Masks an Old Barbarism with a Human Face." *The Guardian,* 3 Oct. 2010. Web. 16 June 2015.

Žižek, Slavoj. "Philosophy, the 'Unknown Knowns,' and the Public Use of Reason." *Topoi* 25.1-2 (2006): 137-142. Web. 17 July 2015.

Žižek, Slavoj. *Violence: Six Sideways Reflections.* London: Picador, 2008.

Žižek, Slavoj. *The Universal Exception.* London: Continuum, 2006.

Tara Atluri has a PhD in Sociology. Between 2012-2014 she held the position of post-doctoral researcher with Oecumene: Citizenship After Orientalism at the Open University in the United Kingdom. She joined Oecumene as part of a project funded by the Social Sciences and Humanities Research Council of Canada. During her time as a post-doctoral researcher, she conducted research in India regarding the 2012 Delhi gang rape protests and the 2013 protests that followed the decision by the Supreme Court of India to uphold Section 377 of the Indian penal code, criminalizing diverse enactments of sexuality in the Indian subcontinent. The protests that emerged were remarkable examples of postcolonial sexual politics that inspired the writing of this book.